DATE DUE

DEMCO 38-296

A PORTRAIT
OF THE
FRASER

Mighty River

Richard C. Bocking

Douglas & McIntyre
VANCOUVER/TORONTO

University of Washington Press
SEATTLE

Copyright © 1997 by Richard C. Bocking

Vancouver, British Columbia
V5L 2H1

CANADIAN CATALOGUING IN PUBLICATION DATA

Bocking, Richard C.
    Mighty River

    ISBN 1-55054-523-X

    1. Fraser River Region (B.C.)—Description and travel. 2. Fraser River (B.C.)—History.
3. Stream ecology—British Columbia—Fraser River. I. Title
FC3845.F73B62 1997   971.1′3   C97-910398-3
FC1089.FB62 1997

Originated by Douglas & McIntyre and published simultaneously in
the United States of America by
The University of Washington Press
P.O. Box 50096
Seattle, Washington 98145-5096

LIBRARY OF CONGRESS CATALOGING-IN-PUBLICATION DATA

Bocking, Richard C.
        Mighty river: a portrait of the Fraser / Richard C. Bocking.
            p.   cm.
        Includes bibliographic references and index.
        ISBN 0-295-97670-5
        1. Fraser River (B.C.)—History. 2. Fraser River (B.C.)—
Description and travel. I. Title
F1089.F7B63   1997
971.1′3—dc21   97-23760 CIP

Editing by Nancy Pollak
Cover design by Peter Cocking
Typesetting by Val Speidel
Maps by Stuart Daniel, Starshell Maps
Printed and bound in Canada
Printed on acid-free paper

The publisher gratefully acknowledges the support of the Canada Council for the Arts and of the
British Columbia Ministry of Tourism, Small Business and Culture.

For Winnifred; and for our sons
Michael, Douglas, James, Christopher, Stephen and Patrick.

Contents

List of Maps

Preface

This book culminates an odyssey that began more than two decades ago. In my 1972 documentary film and book, *Canada's Water: For Sale?*, I examined the issue of water export from Canada to the United States. Several more films dealing with water, energy and the environment followed, and while making them I explored many of the great rivers of North America, from the MacKenzie to the Mississippi, from the St. Lawrence to the Colorado, from the Churchill to the Old-man. I learned how rivers have created the landscapes that support us, how they maintain life in all its complexity and beauty, and how our modern civilization is dependent upon the way in which we treat them. I came to see water and the water-centred landscape as a subtle, mystical, almost magical aspect of the living world. And I saw little of this understanding reflected in the management of rivers and their watersheds.

Throughout these years I was drawn back again and again to the Fraser, fascinated by the magnificence of the river and its territories, by the power and often the ferocity of its massive flow, and by the richness of life within the river and throughout its basin. I recognized that the Fraser is central to the life, personality, history and future of British Columbia. I saw too that in the Fraser Basin are reflected the social, economic, environmental and political forces sweeping across the nation and around the world.

Fifty years ago, journalist and author Bruce Hutchison wrote his fine book *The Fraser*. Reading it today is still a joy, but Hutchison's narrative confirms the fact that momentous changes have transformed many aspects of life along the great river during the intervening half century. It seemed time for a new book that would celebrate the natural history of the Fraser and portray the extraordinary human drama along its spectacular journey from the Rocky Mountains to the Pacific Ocean. Although the basin is currently dominated by rapid exploitation of resources and extreme rates of population and economic growth, a new book could explore values that offer hope for a sustainable future. *Mighty River* is my attempt to fulfill this need.

This book owes much to the remarkable people I met while exploring the Fraser and other North American rivers. Robert Newbury, Canada's leading stream hydrologist, helped me understand not just how a river works, but provided insights into the deeper significance of free-flowing water. Few people know the Fraser like Department of Fisheries and Oceans biologist Otto Langer, who has fought for the river and its fishery for decades in spite of bureaucratic indifference and periodic political hostility. Forester Ray Travers guided me through some of the intricacies of B.C. forestry policy. In fisherman Terry Slack I recognized the devotion and concern the Fraser inpires in those who know it best.

The work of ecologists C. S. Holling and William Rees has been of critical importance to the philosophy of this book, as has that of urban planner Rod Clack and biologists Carl Walters and Craig Orr. Agronomists C. V. (Bert) Brink, David Sands and Graham Strachan shared their knowledge of agriculture in the Fraser Basin. Nathan Matthew helped me understand the significance of the river to the aboriginal people who have depended upon it for 10,000 years. Conservationists like Will Paulik, Rick and Julie Zammuto and Ruth Madsen are among the many people working unceasingly for the preservation of the Fraser's natural values.

In travelling the Fraser River and researching the issues affecting it, I talked to many people. I am deeply grateful to the following for sharing their experiences, thoughts and aspirations for the future of this great river: Mark Angelo, Uli Augustin, Ken Awmack, Bob Bocking, Victor Bopp, Rob Borsato, Clarence Boudreau, Al Brown, Rob Butler, Marvin Charlie and the people of the Cheslatta Carrier Nation, Michael Church, Marilyn Clayton, Chad Day, Anthony Dorcey, Harve and Dian Eggleston, Larry Fidler, Irving Fox, Richard Gook, Lawrence and Judith Guichon, Ron Hammerstedt, Ted Hancock, Gordon Hartman, Michael Healy, William Henwood, Scott Hinch, Wendy Holm, John Hummel, Karen Hurley, Don Ignace, Ray Jones, Martin Keeley, Cecil Kelley, Alice Kidd, Gordon Kosakoski, Jack Leggett,

Colin Levings, Peter Lishman, George Louis, Dan Lousier, David Marshall, Bruce McDonald, Stephen McDonald, Ian McGregor, Anne McMillan, Michael McPhee, Patricia Moss, Ray and Louise Muller, Phil Munier, Margaret North, Thomas Northcote, Richard Overstall, Robert Pasco, Raymond Phillips, Frank Quinn, Douglas Radies, William Rees, Chris Ritchie, Ken Robertson, Mike Robertson, Horst Sander, Mel Sheng, Vic Skaalid, Carson Templeton, Andrew Thompson, Gerald Walter, Dana Wagg and Roger William.

At the end of the book I note in some detail the published sources upon which I have drawn. A few were of particular importance to my research. An essential Fraser River reference is the superb two-volume set published in 1991 by the Westwater Research Centre at the University of British Columbia: *Perspectives on Sustainable Development in Water Management* and *Water in Sustainable Development*. Edited by Anthony H. J. Dorcey with the collaboration of Julian R. Griggs, the books distill the work and ideas of scholars whose research has been intimately associated with the river. Thomas Northcote and the late Peter Larkin are elder statesmen of fisheries research in British Columbia, and throughout the book I have drawn upon their work. *Biodiversity in British Columbia: Our Changing Environment*, edited by Lee E. Harding and Emily McCullum, is particularly valuable for understanding the impacts of economic development on the landscape of the Fraser; in his book *Seeing the Forest among the Trees*, forester Herb Hammond makes a vital contribution to our understanding of the forests of B.C. Books by Terry Glavin and Mark Hume were also inspiring sources for *Mighty River*.

For his enthusiastic embrace of the book's concept and his steadfast support of the project throughout its four years of gestation, I am deeply indebted to publisher Scott McIntyre. Editor Nancy Pollak's contribution to the structure as well as the detail of the manuscript was invaluable; I particularly appreciated her guidance in the difficult task of reducing the much longer original manuscript to its present form. Finally and most importantly, for her encouragement and active participation, I want to thank my wife and colleague Winnifred Bocking. Companion on journeys of discovery throughout the Fraser Basin, valued collaborator through long days of research and writing, her contribution to the book has been enormous.

The Fraser Basin

Introduction

In rush-hour crawl on one of the bridges soaring over the Fraser River at Vancouver, you may have time to glimpse another world below where a different sort of traffic is bustling. Tugboats tow long rafts of fallen forests to sawmills lining the river; others haul away barges piled high with wood chips destined to become pulp and paper. Ships from around the world unload cars or fill their holds with raw logs. The riverbank is lined with industries dependent on the river to bring them cargo or carry it away, to supply water and remove wastes. From a bridge you are unlikely to glimpse much of the incredible diversity of life the river fosters here where fresh and salt water mingle, but you may wonder about the source of all this water and how it made its way to the city that sprawls across it. For what you see below is the final act of a great drama.

The stage on which the Fraser River performs is almost too vast to comprehend. Few will witness its icy origins high in the Rocky Mountains, a place too rugged and isolated for all but the hardiest adventurers. Water drips from a point of ice on the Great Divide in the mountains about 40 kilometres southwest of the town of Jasper and is soon joined by trickles from other alpine glaciers. During a tumultuous 1370-kilometre descent to the sea, thousands of rivulets, hundreds of streams, many large lakes and a dozen major tributaries will merge into one great river. Each delicate tendril drains a tiny watershed into a larger one, joining, blending and combining into a vast web of water, an intricate network of streams destined for the Fraser River and the ocean.

The waters of the Fraser nourish 234 000 square kilometres of forests

and farmlands, mountain slopes and desert valleys, cities and towns—
about a quarter of British Columbia. The river inscribes a gigantic S on
the landscape of the province, carving canyons through hot semi-deserts,
churning violently down rockbound canyons and flowing placidly
through verdant cropland. This incredibly beautiful landscape is the most
varied watershed in North America and includes nine of B.C.'s twelve
biogeoclimatic zones. In the watershed's valleys are the hottest and driest
places in Canada, and very nearly the wettest, too. The river is a temporary or permanent home for millions of birds, from hummingbirds to
eagles, from sandpipers to snow geese. Grizzly bears, caribou, bighorn
sheep and mountain goats are among hundreds of wildlife species sheltered and fed by the river's marvellous web of life. Flowing water unifies
all this land and life into one vast interdependent system: the Fraser
Basin.

After little more than a week, that drip from a mountain glacier is
part of a mighty river flowing through the city of Vancouver into the
Pacific Ocean. In the final 30 kilometres of this epic journey the Fraser
traverses its own greatest creation: an estuary of 680 square kilometres
whose soil, carried here by the river's current, combines with salt and
fresh water in an exuberant explosion of life. Millions of tiny salmon,
many hatched hundreds of kilometres upstream, surge through the
estuary and into the Pacific to feed and grow and then return, bringing
back in their bodies a flood of energy they will carry to the basin's far-
thest reaches. The fish integrate ocean and river, delta and tributary
stream, interior forest and coastal fishing communities. The salmon is
the soul of the Fraser River and has been a fundamental element of the
culture of this territory for thousands of years; it remains so today.

The deep, fertile soil of the Fraser delta was laid down by the river
during ten thousand years of restless wandering back and forth across
the valley floor. Today, the urban agglomeration of Greater Vancouver,
home to almost two million people, bestrides the Fraser at its mouth.
The river is locked in place by dykes, dams, docks, rock and concrete
walls, jetties and piers. Wild and free for 1340 kilometres, the Fraser is
rigidly regimented during its passage through city and delta. Liberated
again, its mighty flow pushes a plume of brown, silt-laden water far out
over the green, salty expanse of the Strait of Georgia. For a while the
river struggles to maintain its identity; then, finally, the Fraser River is
overwhelmed by the Pacific Ocean.

Like the St. Lawrence in Eastern Canada, the Mackenzie in the
North, or the Mississippi in mid-America, the Fraser River is the central fact of life in British Columbia. Ten thousand years of aboriginal
tradition are written in its flow; two centuries of high drama floated

the Fraser's currents as more recent arrivals searched, dug, hunted, hammered, plowed, chopped and built new lives for themselves along its banks. Pulsing through the heart of British Columbia, the Fraser's life-sustaining power has endowed the province with a unique rhythm. There may be no place in the world where so much diversity and beauty is woven into a single tapestry by the flow of a river.

The Fraser River is much more than a stream flowing through valleys to the ocean. It is the organizing element of a vast landscape, a single unit that begins on the heights of land surrounding it, descends to the sea and extends into the atmosphere. The Fraser Basin encompasses an infinite number of smaller watersheds, each nesting within a larger one. The water that falls within them shapes the land and circulates through soil, vegetation and every living creature, including human beings. Some water returns to the atmosphere in vertical rivers funnelled up through trees and other vegetation, more flows to the ocean from where it will be lifted and transported back to the highlands to fall again as rain and snow, renewing the endless cycle through land, sea and air.

The Fraser River has been flowing west to the Pacific Ocean for about 12 million years. During that time it was repeatedly blanketed deep under the ice of glaciers, the last of which withdrew only 13,000 years ago. When the ancestors of today's Fraser River Natives first entered the basin at least 10,000 years ago, there were probably forty species of fish in the watershed. The annual movement of millions of salmon up and down the Fraser in response to an ancient, mysterious impulse infused the river with a powerful spirit. Through millennia, aboriginal peoples were nourished and their cultures shaped by the great river known to the Carrier Nation as *Tacoutche Tesse*—the Mighty One. Six distinct Native language groups developed in the basin, each living within mutually understood boundaries. The Fraser was the centre of life and culture for about 50,000 inhabitants, people who walked lightly on the land and were deeply respectful of the animals and plants that gave them life. A complex of myths and traditions ensured that their lives flowed in rhythm with the natural systems that supported them. Life was bountiful and good here on the banks of one of North America's greatest reservoirs of food.

When in 1808 Simon Fraser and twenty-three companions descended the river that would be named after him, the aboriginal population had already suffered grievously from earlier contacts with European mariners on the West Coast. Smallpox, measles and whooping cough were unknown to the indigenous peoples, and so their bodies had no defence against the diseases. Infections spread inland with ferocious speed, decimating entire villages. The fur trade that followed Fraser's explorations wiped out much of the region's wildlife within a couple of decades, and a few years later hordes of gold miners poured up the Fraser River and into the Cariboo. After thousands of years, aboriginal cultures superbly adapted to the environment collapsed almost overnight. Many of those who survived were reduced to a state of abject dependency.

For many newcomers to the Fraser Basin, however, the story would be very different. For 150 years the river nourished and enriched a growing flood of immigrants. After the fur traders came the miners, then farmers, fishers and loggers. Gold was washed from every sandbar along the river's length, and dug from the beds of its tributaries. The Fraser Basin was one of the world's great cornucopias, its waters producing vast numbers of fish, its fertile valley bottoms growing food, its rangelands fattening cattle, and its woodlands and wetlands teeming with wildlife. Forests that seemed inexhaustible were converted into logs and floated downriver to mills. The river also carried canoes, rafts, steamboats, tugs and barges, and ocean-going cargo ships. During a century of railroad and highway construction, the Fraser's valleys became corridors for transportation and communication, linking British Columbia to the rest of Canada and pouring the wealth of the Interior down to the port at the river's mouth for export around the world.

The Fraser River became the economic spine of the province, linking population centres with the resources that fuelled the economy. Decisions made in the growing city at the river's mouth controlled the industries of the Interior. Much of British Columbia's recent history is an account of the movement of people, goods and money up and down the great river. The economy of the province flows in its current, and its many watersheds provide the settings within which communities are organized. Towns and cities owe their locations and prosperity to the Fraser and its resources.

Almost two-thirds of the people of British Columbia live and work in the Fraser Basin, and two-thirds of the province's income is generated there. The watershed is responsible for almost 50 per cent of B.C.'s long-run, sustainable yield of timber and 60 per cent of the province's metal mine production. Half of the provincial salmon catch originates in the Fraser Basin, along with half of the total sports fishery. Half of B.C.'s agriculture is based in the Fraser watershed, with about 20 per cent of farmland drawing irrigation water from its streams. The dry lands bordering the Thompson River are particularly irrigation-dependent, while in the lower Fraser Valley the possibility of flooding when snow melts in springtime has worried farmers since settlement began. When the next great flood inevitably occurs, it will severely threaten recent urban development on the floodplains of the city of Richmond.

The physical structure of the Fraser Basin and all that inhabits it evolved slowly. The region was carved by ice and shaped by water, its trees and other vegetation becoming genetically attuned to thousands of different microclimates, each species of fish adapting over millennia to a particular stream. But newcomers during the past 150 years have dramatically increased the speed and scale of change in the Fraser Basin. It is probably impossible to predict the ultimate consequence of all this recent change. So far, however, the power and productivity of the Fraser have been so enormous that each generation has assumed that, no matter what is done to the river, the basin will continue to enrich its people. But can the Fraser provide all that is demanded of it? How well has the river been treated in return for its rich rewards?

In short, not very well. For thousands of years, Native peoples lived in balance with the highly productive natural systems of the watershed. How much larger the aboriginal population could have grown without exceeding the "carrying capacity" of the Fraser Basin is difficult to calculate. But today, population in the basin is perhaps fifty times what it was in 1750, and each person lives in a manner that consumes natural resources many times faster than did an aboriginal resident. The impact is obvious throughout the basin. Since Europeans arrived on the scene, over-fishing and habitat destruction have reduced the salmon fishery to about one-seventh of the pre-contact level. The watershed's forests still produce timber, but much of the best has been cut, and logging is so far beyond sustainable levels that forest companies now reach high into mountain watersheds for wood they formerly scorned as uneconomical. Logging in the upper Fraser Basin has created some of the world's biggest clearcuts, and the impact of overcutting on sensitive wildlife ranges and along spawning channels has been severe. There remain no unexploited watersheds larger than 5000 hectares from Prince George to Vancouver except for the Stein River Valley and its much smaller neighbour, Siwhe Creek.

Vast areas of productive wetlands have disappeared as a result of dyking, draining, damming, paving, plowing and logging. Wildlife habitat has been diminished or degraded from the headwaters of the Fraser all the way to its mouth, where in the lower Fraser Valley 70 per cent of the fish and wildlife habitat dependent on wetlands has been eliminated. Of greenspace remaining in the Greater Vancouver Regional District in 1986, 24 per cent was gone by 1991. Thousands of hectares of deep, black soils in the lower Fraser Valley lie beneath freeways,

Principal Tributaries of the Fraser River

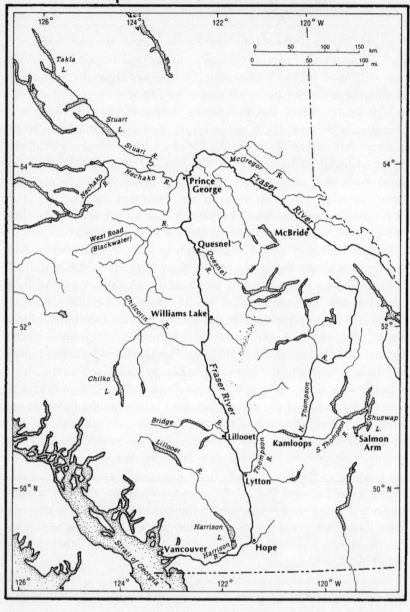

shopping malls and suburbs, while some of the lands still producing food are less fertile as a result of industrial agricultural practices. The enormous migratory flocks of waterfowl, shore and other birds dependent on the Fraser estuary are squeezed into a narrowing band beside the sea.

The natural functions of the river itself have been diminished. Early this century, dykes cut off the lower river from most of the lowland and backwaters that had been an important part of its productivity. On several tributaries, dams decimated some of the greatest salmon runs of the Fraser system. Many runs were wiped out and others reduced to pitiful remnants when railroad builders blasted rock into the Fraser Canyon in 1913. In the 1950s hydro dams on the Bridge River system hit some prolific salmon runs, and since 1954 the Aluminum Company of Canada (Alcan) has reduced the Fraser's flow by diverting 30 per cent of one of its larger tributaries, the Nechako, into generators that power a smelter at Kitimat. The flow of the Fraser has diminished even further in recent years, and its water is warmer, probably in part as a result of clearcut logging throughout the basin.

The ability of the Fraser Basin's water, land and air to absorb waste has been pushed to levels well beyond their absorptive capacity. Industrial effluents pour into the river from six pulp mills, and the city of Vancouver contributes a heavy load of liquid waste, threatening aquatic life in the lower river and the Strait of Georgia. The quality of air in the lower Fraser Valley is below acceptable levels 100 days of the year, with negative impact on human health and crops. Air quality in the pulp mill cities of Prince George, Quesnel and Kamloops often reaches unacceptable levels.

Renowned journalist and author Bruce Hutchison knew and loved the Fraser, and he mourned the changes overwhelming it. In his 1950 book *The Fraser* he wrote, "How fast the time has gone! How little left of the river life we knew in our boyhood, yesterday! All crushed beneath the marching foot of progress, improved beyond recognition, civilized in shape and spirit alien to us . . . We have had the best of it. We have seen the river, naked and virginal, when we were young." But in the spirit of the times, Hutchison did not question the wisdom of doing whatever engineers conceived to be possible. Damming and diverting the Fraser and its tributaries to generate vast amounts of electric power seemed to him inevitable. In those years only a few plaintive voices spoke against diversion of the Nechako River or opposed proposals to reverse the flow of the Chilcotin, divert the McGregor into the Peace and build dams on the mainstem of the Fraser itself. The accomplishment of such projects, many believed, would be a measure of B.C.'s progress.

With an enormous landscape rich in natural resources and a relatively small population, British Columbians have had difficulty abandoning the myth of the frontier, the conviction that over the next hill
there are more resources ripe for exploitation, new land for settlement,
and unfished lakes and rivers. To a small, pioneering population, limits
to any of the Fraser's resources were unimaginable. The vast expanse of
the Fraser Basin and the enormous flow of the river seemed to justify
resource exploitation at ever greater speed and larger scale.

It is now abundantly clear that those resources, though great, are far
from limitless. The huge trees of the ancient forests in the lower Fraser
Valley are almost gone, and logging throughout the basin continues at
levels that will eliminate most remaining high-quality old growth in a
very short time. The salmon runs that are the soul of the Fraser River
are threatened by an armada of technically advanced vessels that could
wipe out every fish in the river were it not for the protection of the
fisheries management system—a system prone to error.

Much of the prosperity of the Fraser Basin has been based on liquidation of its "natural capital." Old-growth forests, fish and wildlife habitats, grasslands, the quantity and quality of fertile soils, the capacity of
water, air and soil to absorb wastes, living species, human cultures and
the flow of the river itself—all have been diminished. Yet the basin's
economic future depends on what remains of that natural capital. The
situation is no different than if we were drawing down a bank account:
less capital remains to earn interest. Ecologist William Rees of the University of British Columbia insists that we have reached a point in the
Fraser Basin where we can make no further trade-offs that sacrifice natural capital to economic development. We must recognize, says Rees,
that the economy depends upon the environment.

Human capacity to transform and to degrade nature is now so formidable, and irreversible changes are taking place so fast, that a considerable price will be paid by future generations for the prosperity of
people in the Fraser Basin today. Even under the best management and
most favourable circumstances there will be fewer, smaller trees of
poorer quality. After a remarkable recovery by some salmon stocks in
the 1980s, the Fraser sockeye fishery was almost cancelled entirely in
1996 following two years of conflict and recriminations. Many salmon
races have been wiped out, and survival of the remaining runs depends
upon more effective fisheries management and a complete reorganization of the fishery itself. The killing power of a technologically sophisticated fishing fleet leaves no room for error, and current federal
fisheries policy seems to leave little room either for small fishers or for
their coastal communities. With no international agreement on rational

sharing of Fraser River salmon stocks, the spectre looms of a no-holds-barred battle with American fishers.

When a growing population exceeds sustainable levels of resource use—as it has in some parts of the Fraser Basin—the result can be a rising level of social strife. In some cases, the heat generated conceals the real nature of the problem. Citizens fight development-minded municipal councils to prevent obliteration of favoured landscapes. People who should be allies—loggers and environmentalists, for example, or commercial, Native and sports fishers—find themselves in conflict over a dwindling resource. But attitudes towards the river, the resources of the basin and the environment in general have also changed to a degree unimaginable half a century ago when Bruce Hutchison wrote *The Fraser*. Massive water developments are now recognized as severe assaults on the natural environment. In the 1970s, with important leverage from the federal Fisheries Act, partisans of salmon and the Fraser River fought B.C. Hydro to a standstill when the utility proposed a dam on the river just upstream of Lillooet at Moran Canyon, and another on its tributary, the McGregor. In 1995 the B.C. government denied Alcan permission to reduce the flow of the Nechako to 12 per cent of normal. In the same year new legislation banned large-scale water export or diversion between basins, terminating the proposal of a Vancouver promoter to divert water from the North Thompson River into the Columbia River for export to the United States. With more stringent regulations, pulp-mill toxins have been greatly reduced in the Fraser in the 1990s, and secondary treatment plants at the mouth of the river will improve the quality of sewage effluents. The Agricultural Land Reserve, introduced in the 1970s, is playing a key role in reducing the rate at which farmland is urbanized. In the 1990s a beginning was made towards rational land-use planning throughout the basin, and the New Democratic Party under Premier Mike Harcourt protected some of the more sensitive regions as parkland. The Fraser was declared a Heritage River in 1996 under the province's new heritage rivers program.

Although the Fraser Basin remains one of the continent's most abundant reservoirs of food and fibre, the question remains: Will its immense productivity be sustained into the future? Will the watershed be as rich and beautiful for new generations as it is for those fortunate enough to inhabit it today? Or will the systems that make the Fraser Basin one of the world's greatest places for human life continue to be wound down by current practices of exploitation?

Sustainability in the Fraser Basin is not just an economic issue. It's a moral question too, a matter of fairness between generations. Some aboriginal cultures require consideration of a decision's implications

seven generations into the future. In the less poetic language of economists, Herman Daly of the World Bank writes, "Each generation
should inherit a stock of natural capital assets no less than the stock of
such assets inherited by the previous generation." And if they don't,
adds economist Paul Ekins, "the sacrifice of sustainability can be
viewed as perhaps the heaviest unpaid bill bequested to this and future
generations by the industrial-economic process."

Conventional measurements of economic progress include no consideration of the need to maintain ecosystems or of the extent to which
our natural capital is being drawn down. Conventional economic measurements and practices actually *discount* the future. The illusion persists
that economies operate independently of the natural systems upon
which they in fact depend. A rising Gross Domestic Product (GDP) in
the Fraser Basin signals profits to corporate shareholders, but gives no
hint that we are approaching the end of the old-growth forests that create those profits. Building shopping malls on the agricultural soils of
the Fraser Valley provides a healthy boost to the GDP today, while compromising food supplies for tomorrow. Financial markets show no
quiver of distress when industrial or domestic effluent pours into the
Fraser or when salmon spawning grounds are ruined with silt flowing
from careless logging operations.

For the aboriginal people who enjoyed the bounty of the basin for
thousands of years, the concepts of individual land ownership and the
management of nature by humans were inconceivable. They considered
themselves part of the natural systems that provided for all their needs,
and their cultures included social and political restraints to protect the
resource base upon which they depended. But with the arrival of
Europeans in the region, decisions about resource use were removed
from local communities to distant centres of government and business.
The impact on Fraser Basin resources was immediate and persists today.
The fur trade, directed from Montréal and London, decimated wildlife
in the basin. The gold rush of 1858 brought a flood of immigrants and,
overnight, a colony was established, British law and customs were
imposed, and Native peoples were crowded into reservations far too
small for their subsistence. Huge blocks of river valleys, of farm and forest lands, and of the new cities of the West were handed over to railway
companies, beginning with the Canadian Pacific Railway in 1871. Most
nineteenth-century logging was in the hands of local operators, but
American companies moved in soon after 1900 as they exhausted their
own forests in the Midwest. Control of the forests narrowed into fewer
and more distant hands as the years progressed, and governments carved
the forests into immense blocks, which were given to corporations for

exploitation. The alienation of the resources of the Fraser is reinforced by modern trade agreements. The North American Free Trade Agreement and the World Trade Organization cement transnational corporate authority and diminish the power of provincial and federal governments to regulate them or to initiate programs for sustaining communities and resources.

A balanced and sustainable economy in the Fraser Basin will require wise use of resources by the people who have a real stake in them. In the forests of the watershed, that means deep change in conditions of tenure, making land available for long-term stewardship by communities, both Native and non-Native, and by smaller, local companies and individuals. Communities must have a key role in management of the Fraser's fish stocks if they are to be sustained. People in the cities, towns and villages of the Fraser must have a strong, clear voice to influence development policies in their communities. After all, asks UBC's Peter Boothroyd, "Who owns the water, trees, and other resources of the Fraser Basin? Who should have the right to use them and the products of their use? Who should have the right to manage them?"

Perhaps a descent of the river from high in the Rocky Mountains to the Pacific Ocean will reveal some answers. This is a journey through centuries as well as kilometres, through astonishing landscapes and a rich tapestry of life. Following the Fraser River is also a search for the human spirit, because much of the drama that has characterized British Columbia's story has been concentrated on the banks of this river.

I invite you to join me in a journey down the mighty Fraser, one of the great rivers of the world.

Upper Fraser River and North Cariboo

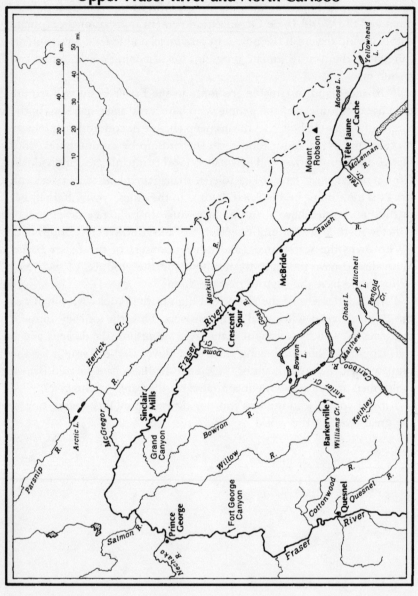

CHAPTER I

In the Beginning

History is a watercourse. A river in the mind.
A precarious pattern we make from the flow of time,
as we try to write our names on the water.

LYALL WATSON, *THE WATER PLANET*

High in the Rocky Mountains, glacial water bubbles from beneath a rock and trickles into a small pond in Fraser Pass. Barely free of snow in midsummer at this elevation of 2100 metres, the pond is known mainly to the mountain goats and sheep, caribou and grizzly bears that pause here as they cross from one alpine slope to another. It is nearly 50 kilometres northwest to Highway 16, the nearest road; the pond soon gives birth to a tiny stream that trickles down a mountain valley in the same direction. Above the stream on both sides of the valley, icy peaks lift 2700 to 3300 metres into the clear, cool air. Their shoulders bear great glaciers, remnants of ice fields that once covered most of British Columbia. The ancient ice surrenders to the warmth of the day. Free at last, drips become trickles, then streams of frigid water tumbling down steep slopes to swell the rivulet. They are the first of thousands of streams and rivers from mountain, forest and wetland that will ultimately drain 234 000 square kilometres of land into a mighty river.

Beside today's highway, just a few metres west of Yellowhead Pass, beavers have built a lodge in a placid pond. Trappers had cleaned out much of the furbearing wildlife of the region during the first half of the nineteenth century, so there were probably no beavers in July 1863 when two British travellers, Dr. Walter B. Cheadle and Viscount Milton, passed the pond and the sparkling brook, now known as Yellowhead Creek, that drains towards the Fraser River. "In the course of our morning's journey we were surprised by coming upon a stream flowing to the westward," Cheadle wrote in his journal. "We had gained . . . the water-shed of the Pacific. The ascent had been so gradual and imperceptible, that, until we had evidence of the water-flow, we had no suspicion that we were even near the dividing ridge. The next afternoon found us encamped at Buffalo-dung Lake."

Cheadle described the setting: "The mountains appeared to rise immediately out of the water on the further or southern shore of the lake, whilst close behind us, on the northern side, commenced verdant and swelling hills, the bases of loftier heights, which rose up farther back in many a naked ragged rock or ice-crowned peak. Two of these on opposite sides of the lake were particularly fine . . . We . . . took the liberty of naming them Mount Fitzwilliam and Mount Bingley." Some-one else renamed the lake, which is now known, somewhat more ele-gantly, as Yellowhead Lake.

Cheadle and Milton were probably the region's first tourists. After their return to London they published *The Northwest Passage by Land* (1865), which became one of the decade's most popular travel books. Historians A. G. Doughty and Gustave Lanctot comment on Cheadle's journal, from which the book was drawn: "This is the journal of the first transCanadian tourist. Before him others either on business, exploration or duty, had crossed overland from Eastern Canada to British Columbia. But Walter Butler Cheadle was the first to traverse the whole country from the St. Lawrence to the Pacific simply 'for pleasure,' for the sheer enjoyment of seeing new lands, hunting the buffalo and visiting the gold regions of Cariboo. He was then twenty-seven years of age, in the prime of his manhood, a sturdy son of Old England and a former Cambridge oarsman." Although he professed to be travelling simply "for pleasure," Cheadle left us a fascinating description of the Fraser River and its peo-ples just as extraordinary developments were changing it forever.

Gold, not pleasure, was the goal of the starving, ragged band of 150 men, 1 pregnant woman and 3 children who had preceded Cheadle and Milton over Yellowhead Pass a year earlier. On August 22, 1862, the "Overlanders" camped on the shore of Yellowhead Lake, known to them as Cow-dung Lake. Mostly Canadians from Ontario and Québec, along with a few Scots and Englishmen, the travellers had set out in early May on what promoters had assured them would be a pleasant sixty-day trip to the Cariboo goldfields.

They travelled by train to St. Paul, Minnesota, then north up the Red River to Fort Garry by paddle wheeler. At the site of today's Win-nipeg, they bought oxen and the remarkable all-wood Red River carts, which they loaded with flour, pemmican and their belongings. A wet summer made the trip across the Prairies slow and painful, but the

Overlanders finally arrived in Edmonton on July 21, convinced that the worst was behind them. Most of the weary travellers were persuaded to exchange their carts for packhorses, but a few insisted on keeping the oxen that had hauled them so far. It was a decision that would save them from starvation. Camping that night in late August at Cow-dung Lake, it is unlikely the trail-weary travellers could appreciate the beauty of the lake, the reflections of slender spruce spires and the magnificent alpine backdrop. With provisions exhausted, they killed an ox and a horse, animals by now little more than skin and bone. But the spirits of the Overlanders were sustained by the conviction that the gold of the Cariboo was nearly within their grasp.

The origins of "Yellowhead"—the pass, the lake, the creek, the mountain, the highway—and its original French version, "Tête Jaune," are uncertain. Drifting down to us from the early nineteenth century is a mélange of vague fact and romantic legend suggesting that this was the nickname of a blond trapper and fur trader of partly Iroquois heritage who had crossed the pass named after him. He is said to have cached his furs and supplies near the community now called Tête Jaune Cache. Some sources suggest that Yellowhead may have been Jasper Hawse, a trader at the Hudson's Bay Company post that became known as Jasper's House. If so, he is also remembered in the name of Jasper National Park. Legend has it that one day Yellowhead set off on a raft down the Fraser River from Tête Jaune Cache with his large family. Like so many who followed in later years, the family apparently perished in one of the river's treacherous rapids.

Yellowhead Lake narrows into a stream that spills down a short stretch to join the Fraser, now a considerable river some 50 kilometres from its modest source. Cheadle reported, "On the 10th [of July] we struck the Fraser River, sweeping round from the south-west in a narrow gorge, to expand some miles lower down into Moose Lake." Like tourists today who travel the Yellowhead Highway in the comfort of cars and tour buses, Cheadle revelled in the mountainous spectacle rising on all sides of the river. Considering the conditions of travel, his appreciation of the landscape is remarkable. "Our route now lay along the north bank of the Fraser . . . the track was completely under water up to the horses' girths, and we spent the greater part of the day in wading and the rest in toiling through swamps beset with fallen timber." At Moose Lake, wrote Cheadle, "accumulations of driftwood barred the passage along the shore in many places, and we were compelled to scale the mountain sides. Horse after horse rolled back in the attempt and we had to cut off their packs in the water and carry up the loads on our backs, to enable the animals to scramble up the steep ascent."

The river is growing quickly now as water thunders down mountain slopes to join it, flows in from relatively sedate streams or trickles from ponds and forests. Spring runoff raises water levels from May to July, occasionally attaining levels catastrophic to human creations. Yet the system is full of natural controls that level out the wildest swings of flow. Thousands of lakes like Moose and Yellowhead combine with wetlands and forests to hold back water and decrease flood peaks throughout the Fraser Basin. The stored water in turn helps maintain river levels when slowly released during periods of lower flow.

In this land of snow-capped giants from which the Fraser River gathers so much water, one mountain dominates all others. At 3954 metres Mount Robson is the highest peak in the Canadian Rockies. But height alone does not explain the awe inspired by its enormous expanse of rock, snow and ice. Working his way along steep rapids churning the glacial, green Fraser into sparkling white foam, Walter Cheadle searched for words:

> . . . immediately behind us, a giant among giants, and immeasurably supreme, rose Robson's peak. This magnificent mountain is of conical form, glacier-clothed, and rugged. When we first caught sight of it, a shroud of mist partially enveloped the summit, but this presently rolled away, and we saw its upper portion dimmed by a necklace of light feathery clouds, beyond which its pointed apex of ice, glittering in the morning sun, shot up far into the blue heaven above, to a height of probably 10,000 or 15,000 feet. It is a glorious sight, and one which the Shuswaps of The Cache assured us had rarely been seen by human eyes, the summit being generally hidden by clouds.

The Shuswaps knew Mount Robson as *Yuh-hai-has-hun*. Although the origins of the mountain's English name are obscure, it was already known as "Robson's Peak" when the Overlanders struggled down the Fraser in 1862. Historians suggest the mountain might have been named for Colin Robertson, a Hudson's Bay Company factor who later became a member of Parliament. Robertson had sent Iroquois fur hunters into the area as early as 1820. Today, Mount Robson's contribution to the Fraser River extends beyond the water that melts from its snow and ice; the peak inspired the creation of a provincial park, whose more important role turns out to be the protection of the Fraser's headwaters. While the mountain dominates the region, it is the river that gives the valley life. Robson seems to stand guard, defying any who would defile its waters. In many places downstream, the river could use such powerful protection.

As he wades carefully into a creek, hydrologist Robert Newbury pauses; soon the stream is revealing many of its secrets to his practised eye and ear. Each swirl and eddy, each watery rise and fall, each curve in the bank, each liquid sound tells a story. After decades studying waterways, Newbury travels Canada and the world explaining how streams work, the role of rivers in nature and in our lives, and how we can begin to heal the waters our industrial society has degraded. At the headwaters of the Fraser he describes the powerful connections of water with land and life. Natural processes function freely here, a benchmark against which we can measure the impact of downstream activities. Here we can recognize what Newbury calls "the innocence of the headwaters," a quality that will gradually be lost as we descend the river. For the descent of a river is a journey through time as well as space, through history and cultures as well as through landscapes. We can imagine the relationship of aboriginal people with this landscape prior to the arrival of Europeans. We will follow the evolution of wilderness into a landscape shaped in part by fur trading, mining, logging, farming, fishing, industry and commerce, and by the growth of towns and cities. Newbury finds in the innocence of the headwaters a way to understand our own origins and actions as well as those of the river.

After gathering the waters of Mount Robson, the Fraser River becomes the heart of a vital wildlife corridor, a predator-prey ecosystem rich in wolves, caribou, moose, elk and deer. This concentration of wildlife has no protection after the Fraser leaves Mount Robson Park to drop 18 tumultuous kilometres to the Rocky Mountain Trench, a great valley extending the length of British Columbia along the west side of the Rocky Mountains. While discussions continue on how best to ensure the survival of natural systems outside the park, logging has already begun along this stretch of the Fraser. There are even interests promoting logging within Mount Robson Park itself, confirming conservationists' apprehension that protection of wilderness is seldom permanently won. Some wildlife officials feel that the obvious tourism value of the region will ensure that any logging will be required to leave "landscape views" and the wildlife corridor unimpaired. Yet experience offers local conservationists no assurances, and they are convinced the area should be protected by extending the park downstream to Tête Jaune Cache.

Less than five kilometres before it pours into the trench at Tête Jaune Cache, the Fraser River tumbles over Rearguard Falls. Here for the first time we meet the living symbol of the Fraser: the salmon. A Fraser River without salmon is unimaginable. Each year this incredible fish returns by millions from distant reaches of the sea, a great pulse of life and energy surging up the river and its tributaries to spawn and then to die, a source of food for humans and the entire web of life in the Fraser Basin. In late August and early September about a thousand giant chinook salmon, the strongest of their race, will try to leap up over Rearguard Falls. They have already mastered 1200 kilometres of Fraser River, fighting their way up nearly 1200 vertical metres over rapids and falls, through foaming white water, swirling whirlpools and endless kilometres of fast current. A few miraculously find the energy to surmount the descending torrent at Rearguard Falls and swim on up the rushing river for another 10 or 12 kilometres to spawn at the mouth of Swiftcurrent Creek. But for most, this is the end of the line and they will retreat downstream to spawn at Tête Jaune Cache Islands.

In August 1862, the Overlanders straggled the last few kilometres down the Fraser towards Tête Jaune Cache. From there, they believed, the river would afford an easy downstream float to the goldfields of the Cariboo. With flour, salt and pemmican long exhausted, even finding a skunk to roast was cause for rejoicing. The pack animals were in desperate condition, their feet badly damaged by sharp rocks. Some passages were so difficult for horses that the travellers had to carry the loads themselves. One Overlander recorded that on the day of their arrival at Tête Jaune Cache, "the horse carrying our cooking utensils and all the dishes and china plates got tired of life and ran over the bank into the Fraser and was drowned, sinking with all his cargo, and was washed up on a sand bar about a mile below with nothing upon him except his saddle."

On the afternoon of August 26, the Rocky Mountain Trench opened before the Overlanders. When the Fraser pours into this mighty gash in the British Columbia landscape, it has already lost most of its original altitude, dropping 1400 tumultuous metres from its source in the Rockies 150 kilometres upstream. Now the river is only 700 metres above sea level, with another 1200 kilometres to travel before meeting the ocean. As it enters the trench, the current slows and the gravel washing down its bed drops and settles into braided bars, creating superb salmon spawning grounds. From the south, McLennan River and Tête (Sand) Creek join the Fraser, adding silt to small islands that continually form, wash away and rebuild as the rivers flood and ebb.

Across this remarkable delta the exhausted Overlanders could see the tepees of a village between the two tributary streams. This was home base for about 250 Shuswaps, who ranged east as far as Jasper and west to Raush River near today's McBride. Through intermarriage the band had absorbed Crees from east of the Rockies and Iroquois from Eastern

Canada who had travelled west earlier in the century with fur traders. The Overlanders found the Shuswaps occupied with some of the year's most important activities. The giant chinook salmon had arrived, berries were ripe and people were gathering and preserving both in preparation for winter. But they were not too busy to trade with the newcomers and soon crossed the river to barter salmon, berries, dried mountain sheep and skunk meat, and tallow in exchange for ammunition and clothing. For the hungry travellers, the fresh 12- to 13-kilogram chinook salmon they bought from the Shuswaps were cause for celebration; they probably didn't notice the toll that 1200 kilometres of upriver struggle had exacted on the fish.

Native people lived at this confluence of three rivers because the Fraser provided all the salmon they could use and an abundance of wildlife. The incredible biological productivity of the delta sometimes triggered conflict when neighbouring tribes of Sekani, Carrier or Cree tried to get in on the bounty. The Shuswaps of today still remember that late in the 1700s their people retaliated against continual Sekani harassment and kidnappings. Shuswap war parties moved down the Fraser towards present-day Prince George, wiping out a couple of large Sekani villages in order to diminish the Sekani threat to their own village at Tête Jaune Cache.

This Shuswap band had benefited by its isolation from Europeans until 1827, when Hudson's Bay Company factor George McDougall travelled east through Yellowhead Pass. For the next few years the HBC sent an annual expedition through the pass, carrying mainly dressed moose and caribou skins, a trade that caused the Yellowhead to be known as "Leather Pass." These annual expeditions didn't much disturb the Shuswaps, and renowned historian Father Adrien Gabriel Morice wrote that the band, "owing to the perfect seclusion of their quarters, were still, at a comparatively late date, destitute of most of the comforts of civilization." But when "civilization" made its presence felt, it was not in the form of "comforts." The Overlanders met the Shuswap just before they were struck with the horror of a smallpox epidemic in 1862. The plague wiped out a third of B.C.'s Native population that year, and the white travellers would soon be confronted with evidence of its savagery.

The Shuswaps who survived the epidemic watched the following summer as the Cheadle and Milton expedition arrived on the bank of the Fraser across from their village. In his journal, Cheadle recorded, "We reached Tête Jaune Cache on the 17th of July, and on the morning of the 18th were ferried across the Fraser by the Indians. The water rolled over the bed of boulders at a great pace, swelling into large waves,

on which the light dug-outs of the Shuswaps tossed like a nutshell."
Cheadle observed only two old men and their wives, and two young
men and their families. "Women clothed in marmot-robes. Men in
capotes and moose-skin breeches. Kids nearly naked. Live on the wild
goats and marmots." One of the elder women drew for the travellers a
map of the route down the North Thompson River to Kamloops.
Cheadle doesn't comment on and probably didn't know if these people
were the only survivors of the 1862 smallpox epidemic, or whether
other members of the band were away on hunting expeditions.

The village did survive another fifty years, however, and comprised
perhaps seventy Shuswap when it was finally overwhelmed by the
arrival of railway construction crews. The Grand Trunk Pacific Railway
crossed Yellowhead Pass heading west in 1911. For three years and 500
kilometres, all the way to Prince George, the Fraser River would play a
vital role in building the new railroad. The tranquillity of the upper
Fraser was broken by the sound of steam whistles echoing from the
mountains and by the 5,000 to 6,000 thousand workers who lived in
big, moveable work camps set up at the end of steel. Most of the camps
virtually disappeared when the work moved on.

A reporter for the Fort George *Herald* seemed shaken by his visit to
one of the construction camps. In September 1913 he wrote, "An 'end
of steel' village is made up of booze, billiards, and belles. It is the home
of the illicit liquor traffic of construction, the location of enough pool
tables to stock a large city, and the residence of women who never elsewhere enjoyed so much freedom. An 'end of steel' village is a disgrace,
but Tête Jaune was indescribable." A photograph of Tête Jaune Cache
in 1912 shows a single street lined on both sides with one-storey log
cabins, each fronted by a door and a single small window. Louis Knutson was a trapper operating nearby at the time of the railway construction. Some years later he described the town: "The big amusement was
drinking. The drink came in from down Prince George way. They got
it in every way they could." More than sixty years later, local historian
Marilyn Wheeler was able to look back on the camps with a bit more
charity. "There is no doubt that they were wild," she writes. "The men
worked long hours in conditions that were sometimes intolerable from
swarms of mosquitoes, while the clay made working with the teams
almost impossible after rain. Much of the roadbed had to be built up
across swamp and slide areas. All things considered, it is hardly surprising if the men wanted to 'live it up' in their time off."

Like many other places in Western Canada where the railroad boom
spawned dreams of glory, Tête Jaune Cache was expected to have a

brilliant future. Railway publicity emphasized a mild climate, vast areas of farmland ready for settlement and unlimited power generation potential on the Fraser River to provide for "a great manufacturing industry." The surrounding mountains were said to be rich in gold, silver, lead and mica. A 1910 railway report stated, "Steamboats are advertised to make regular trips from Soda Creek to Tête Jaune Cache [about 750 kilometres] and as soon as navigation opens next spring it is expected there will be a great rush of people up there—miners and prospectors, land seekers, sportsmen, travellers, railway engineers and contractors, and navvies. Hotels and stores will . . . have to be established and the place will soon become an embryo city of considerable importance . . ."

For those few heady years, Tête Jaune Cache reverberated to the sound of steamship whistles as well as those of locomotives. The raucous railway town was head of navigation for sternwheelers travelling the perilous waters downstream 500 kilometres to Prince George, and on for another 250 kilometres to Soda Creek. Construction camps could conveniently be supplied by ships and scows since the railroad tracks followed the river. The 150-foot-long steamers could only operate at high water, generally from May to September. Two of the ships, the *Conveyor* and the *Operator*, were dismantled in Victoria, transported through Alberta to the end of steel in Yellowhead Pass, then hauled by mules over the tote road to Tête Jaune Cache where they were reassembled. Years later, a Robson Valley pioneer, Sadie Frye, wrote, "They could carry 200 passengers and a 200-ton cargo as well as tow a loaded barge. They burned wood, and settlers along the riverbank had a ready market for cordwood. I recall seeing piles of wood that were left after the river became impassable for these steamers." The death knell for steamboat travel was sounded in 1913, when railway contractors broke their agreement with ship operators and built a bridge near Dome Creek that was too low for sternwheelers to pass under.

Steamboats provided relative comfort for frontier travellers and were the only convenient way to travel upstream, but most of the material and equipment required to build the Grand Trunk Pacific Railway was carried downriver on scows capable of 27-tonne loads. At the height of construction between 1912 and 1914, up to one hundred scows were built in Tête Jaune Cache each week and sent off downriver. Many houses in Prince George were built of wood salvaged from the scows. For many of the men who guided them downstream, it was a spectacular trip that ended their lives.

When the last railroad worker moved on and the last steamboat whistle echoed from the hillside, the Shuswap community at Tête Jaune

Cache was a shattered remnant, decimated by disease, its self-sufficient life on the rich delta only a memory. For a time the federal government intended to set aside a reserve for the remaining Shuswaps, but the people were dying so rapidly the plan was abandoned. Years later, Charles Blackman recalled a childhood image of a sad procession of about seventy Shuswap people burdened by their belongings, led by their chief on horseback, moving south towards the North Thompson Valley. Most of them would become part of the North Thompson Band at Barrière.

Fortunately for the flora and fauna of the region, the dreams of the boomers collapsed soon after railway construction moved on. The rich, biological mother lode at Tête Jaune Cache Islands could not have survived urban development on any appreciable scale. The townsite of railroad construction days was washed away by Fraser River floodwaters, and the settlement moved to higher ground. Today only a general store and a few houses survive. But natural life in the delta prospers. With so many different habitats compressed into a small space, the level of biodiversity here is four times greater than that of surrounding areas. In the 1980s an average of more than 4,250 chinook salmon spawned annually in the gravel beds of channels threading through the islands, achieving a high of 6,500 one year. Young chinooks grow for a year here or in another favourable habitat a few kilometres downstream before undertaking the long trip to the ocean.

The chinooks are the key to this incredibly rich ecosystem. In all stages of their lives, they attract a wide range of predators. During spawning season, bald and golden eagles eat their fill of exhausted adult salmon, and from the surrounding 100 square kilometres come bears and coyotes to join the feast. Rainbow trout grow fat on salmon eggs while young salmon nourish mergansers, loons, herons and kingfishers. Beaver, marten, fishers and otters find good homes and plenty to eat along the river channels, especially when a log falls and traps some fish in a drying pool.

Crossbills, kinglets, woodpeckers, swallows, shorebirds, ruffed grouse and many other bird species feed and nest here in large numbers because the habitat is so diversified and the food web so rich. On the islands and bottomlands, white spruce is dominant. Along with black spruce, cottonwood and aspen, they shelter an understorey of dogwood, willow, alder and many shrubs that provide good browsing for deer, moose and elk. On higher ground, Douglas fir and grasslands provide winter shelter and food for larger animals. Mule deer, white-tailed deer, moose and elk, mountain goats and wolves travel down the Fraser River from

Mount Robson Park each fall to these lower, warmer wetlands. In the spring, trampled trails along the shoreline signal that the return trek from lowland winter shelter to mountain slope has begun.

This concentration of wildlife from such a vast region into less than a thousand hectares in the Tête Jaune Cache Islands is not only a miracle of nature. It is also a death trap for animals with no defence against their greatest predator: a person with a gun. The animals are easy to shoot—an illegal road allows vehicles to drive to gravel bars where hunters can wait to pick off bears as they come to fish. Hunters have nearly wiped out the grizzly bears that fished here until around 1980. The outlook for black bears is also bleak; in the fall of 1992, five black bears were killed in one week along one short stretch of riverbank. As deer and moose travel the narrow corridor, they are easily shot from a nearby hillside. And so the region has become what wildlife scientists call "a man-induced mortality sink," where animals from a vast region are concentrated for a time in a manner that exposes many of them to death at the hands of hunters. Hunting in this small area endangers wildlife populations throughout a much larger part of the Robson Valley. But hunting isn't the only danger.

In 1991–92 clearcut logging was permitted on a block of land overlooking salmon spawning grounds in the delta, causing an unstable clay bank below the cut to erode into the gravel spawning beds. A muddy plume half a kilometre long washed downstream, blanketing the area where baby salmon normally grow during their first few months of life. Strange treatment for the birthplace of 5 to 10 per cent of all the Fraser chinook salmon caught at sea—yet permits were issued that allowed more logging a few years later.

This small but extremely important stretch of the Fraser River has no formal protection. A 1993 study for the Ministry of Environment, Lands and Parks documents the values of the area and recommends protection for the Tête Jaune Cache Islands along with surrounding uplands, a prime salmon rearing and waterfowl nesting area about two kilometres downstream, the migratory corridor from Mount Robson Park to the Tête Jaune Cache Islands, and the Jackman Flats area south of the delta along the McLennan River. Public support for preservation of this extremely sensitive area is growing along with awareness of its unique qualities. Indeed, these connected areas on the Fraser River offer one of the best remaining opportunities for fish and wildlife protection in the entire Rocky Mountain Trench.

Below the delta at Tête Jaune Cache the Fraser flows much more sedately, its wide expanse providing no hint of what awaits the unwary traveller downstream. The Overlanders set to work felling cottonwood trees to build rafts 12 metres long and 6 metres wide. Some had rails to contain live oxen; all had fireplaces of stone and clay so no time would be lost for meal preparation. One group joined two rafts together to create a craft of imposing size. The Shuswaps watched the preparations with foreboding, advising against the trip and refusing repeated pleadings by the white travellers to guide them downriver. Although they didn't explain their reluctance, the Shuswaps had very good reasons. They knew of the tortuous reaches of the Fraser River ready to claim the lives of travellers. And their own territory ended at Raush River, less than 50 kilometres downstream. Memories of skirmishes and outright warfare with adjoining Sekani or Carrier rivals served to encourage respect for boundaries. Some of the Overlanders were persuaded by Native warnings, and set off overland. But the remainder were determined to descend the great river even without guides, risking whatever perils might await them as they floated through this unknown land.

CHAPTER 2

Ancient Forests

A thing is right when it tends to preserve the integrity,
stability, and beauty of the biotic community.
It is wrong when it tends otherwise.

ALDO LEOPOLD, *A SAND COUNTY ALMANAC*

As it flows away from the islands of Tête Jaune Cache, the Fraser seems determined to curb rambunctious habits acquired during the steep descent from alpine heights to the Rocky Mountain Trench. As if to disguise its real nature and destination, the river flows sedately northwest, meandering in great oxbow curves through the pastoral lands of the McBride region, behaving more like a river of the plains than a mountain stream. Soon farmlands yield to remnants of ancient forests of western red cedar and western hemlock, the glory of the Interior cedar-hemlock biogeoclimatic zone created by generous rainfall and warmer temperatures at these lower altitudes. Giant cottonwoods thrive in the lowlands of tributary valleys, Douglas firs seize the drier, warmer ground, while spruce and pine clothe higher slopes.

Only five or six kilometres wide at McBride, the valley floor broadens gradually as the river descends. The Fraser's tranquillity is seriously disturbed only twice: first at Goat River Rapids and then, dramatically and ferociously, at its Grand Canyon. About 350 kilometres from Tête Jaune Cache, the real intentions of the river become evident. Finding a break in the walls of the trench, the Fraser sweeps through the opening and turns sharply south, completing the first arm of the great S it will inscribe on the face of British Columbia before reaching the sea. But even before this southward bend, the "innocence of the headwaters" begins to slip away from the river.

When the railway builders moved on in 1914, they left bands of steel through an upper Fraser River Valley blackened by fire. Surveyors had sometimes burned the forest so they could see the lay of the land, and construction workers often preferred matches to axes. Trapper Louis Knutson recalled that "the railroad burned the slashing and paid no attention, they let the fire go. The valley was just full of smoke, and for two years you couldn't see the mountains." One worker had contracted to clear land for the new town of McBride; the day after his arrival a rising wind swept one of the valley fires across the site, and his job was done. Easiest money he ever earned, he declared. Some of the settlers who straggled into the valley tried to shortcut the land-clearing process by burning the forest covering their land.

The raucous railway construction camps were reclaimed by wilderness. Only a few workers remained in the scarred valley, and they were among the men who lined up at the land office in the new town of McBride in 1914 to claim homesteads along the Fraser. They were joined by newcomers attracted to the valley by government and railway propaganda. A brochure advertised land for sale in McBride: "It lies in the midst of a tract of excellent agricultural land, which will prove especially valuable for mixed farming purposes." The valley was described as "The New Garden of Canada," where "what is now primeval forest will be cleared and converted into an immense garden."

Some of the settlers took up land as a speculative venture and soon moved on; many more could not stand the loneliness and hardships of frontier life. Then there were the problems promoters neglected to mention: the valley was hundreds of kilometres from markets for produce, and production costs were high. Travel within the valley was difficult, a combination of slowly growing stretches of rudimentary road sometimes linked across the Fraser by ferries powered by the river's current. Today, some valley farms show signs of the prosperity that eluded most of the settlers who struggled for decades to make a living in the Robson Valley after the Grand Trunk Pacific Railway provided access in 1914.

Rick and Julie Zammuto live in a comfortable log house on the banks of the Fraser River not far from the small community of Crescent Spur, about 120 kilometres downstream from Tête Jaune Cache. Moose and deer wander through their yard; in winter a black bear usually hibernates in a hollow cottonwood behind the house. Wolves sometimes trail prey across their land. A short walk from their house towards a decaying trapper's cabin reveals a torn-up mound of earth and claw marks on a stump—evidence, to Rick's practised eye, of the recent passage of a grizzly bear.

Had Julie and Rick Zammuto lived here 130 years earlier, they could have watched the strange spectacle of large, rough-hewn rafts drifting down the river, each carrying about twenty-five gaunt travellers: the Overlanders. A few cattle and oxen were penned on some rafts, and some men paddled canoes they had hastily hollowed from cottonwood logs. The weather was cold and wet, but huddling for warmth on the crude rafts was preferable to the tortuous foot-slogging across prairies and through mountains that had been their lot for many weeks. They cheered themselves with tales of the wealth of Barkerville, confident the Fraser's current would carry them to the Cariboo goldfields and their share of riches.

A few years after earning his doctorate in biology, Rick abandoned a university career so that he and Julie could move here in 1986. They were intent on reconnecting with the essentials of life in one of Earth's great landscapes. They have explored many of the tributary streams that race, tumble and flow to the Fraser, carving grooves and valleys deep into the forest and rock of the Rocky Mountains to the northeast and the Cariboo Mountains to the southwest. In this spectacular environment, Zammuto observes, studies and reports on the life forms of a region that is biologically among the richest in the world. Standing in a grove of western red cedars two metres and more in diameter, the emotional attachment the couple feel for the land is undisguised. Yet Zammuto's scientific background is evident as he describes why they chose this place to live.

"We have some of the world's oldest, most productive and most bio-diverse forests right here on the upper Fraser." Zammuto is talking about *big* trees; they reach an astonishing size in old-growth forests of Fraser tributaries such as the Morkill and Goat Rivers, and Dome Creek. The Goat sparkles in the sun against a dark backdrop of green cedar, hemlock and spruce as it descends a deep valley to join the Fraser. One grand old cedar measures four metres in diameter and some Douglas fir trunk diameters approach two metres. Bounding Creek rushes down to the Goat through patches of blueberries, its crystal flow sweet to the tongue in the heat of the day. But viewed from high on a rocky promontory, these fine old-growth forests contrast sharply with giant clearcuts spreading across the mountain slopes.

It takes time for forests to mature. How much time varies with location and climate. In the cedar and hemlock forests of the interior wet belt, trees aren't mature until they have lived 250 or 300 years. Lodgepole pine forests of the dryer Cariboo and Chilcotin may develop attributes of old growth at just 150 to 200 years of age. Here in the Robson Valley, recent research by botanist Trevor Goward has shown that some of the old-growth forests are much older than their oldest trees, quite possibly thousands of years old, and deserve to be called "antique" rainforests. Most forests date from the last fire that swept through them. But antique forests have a biological ancestry that stretches back unbroken for generations. Over that time they have developed characteristics that are richer and more varied than those found in single-generation, old-growth forests, so they are important sources of biotic diversity. Some recently discovered specimens of tree-dwelling lichens have until now been known only in coastal rainforests. "The oldest forests of the Robson Valley doubtless contain some of the most complete records in existence of inland B.C.'s biological past," says Goward. "They may in fact contain one of the longest unbroken biological traditions of any forested inland region [in the world]." These ancient Robson Valley rainforests, so far from the ocean, appear to be unique.

An old-growth forest includes big trees, of course, and in their branches entire plant, animal and insect communities thrive. Many such species live only in these old, mature trees, which may show signs of decadence in their broken, deformed tops. Some of the small animals resident in such trees descend to the ground to eat mushrooms and spread the spores of mycorrhizal soil fungi throughout the forest, organisms that trees require in order to absorb water and nutrients. Some dead trees, or snags, stand among the living, providing habitat for a wide variety of creatures. Birds feed on the insects that infest them, woodpeckers and flickers drill nest cavities that will serve a succession of other birds and animals after they have moved on. When finally the snags fall, they are even more valuable, eventually becoming the soil in which the forests of the future will grow. But while the log decays it is home to myriad insects and other organisms, some of which protect living trees by preying on leaf-eating insects like the spruce budworm. Some trees fall across slopes, reducing erosion and holding soil that encourages new plant growth and provides shelter for small animals. Others topple into streams, slowing the flow, creating pools and riffles, an ideal environment for a variety of fish.

When trees fall in an old-growth forest they open spaces to sunlight. Such openings renew the forest while fostering diversity of habitat for wildlife and other organisms. Small plants colonize the forest floor; shrubs spread through the next level, some producing berries relished by bears, others the browse sought by grazing elk and deer. Higher still, the boughs of new understorey trees reach upward towards the mature canopy. More species of birds live in much greater numbers in a forest with old-growth characteristics than in other kinds of forests. This is also true of fish: the salmon is a forest animal, thriving in the high-quality water of shaded streams in old-growth forests, nourished by plant and animal life flourishing on the stream bank.

"When I was young, I was convinced that I wanted to live where I could drink pure, clean water from streams," says Rick Zammuto. "Here in the headwaters of the Fraser we can do that. The streams feed the Fraser River, and the Fraser is the lifeblood of this area. Just as the sun's energy is essential to growth, the river is flowing energy, its flowing nutrients nourish the surrounding biology, like a battery that keeps this natural productivity happening."

In fact, all this energy really originates in the Pacific Ocean, whose westerly winds sweep across British Columbia, dropping up to 2000 millimetres of rain on the coastal mountains. The wrung-out winds have only 400 to 800 millimetres of moisture available for the dry lands of the Fraser Plateau, but when they are pushed higher by the Cariboo Mountains and then again by the Rocky Mountains, cool air extracts most of the remaining moisture. From 1000 to 2000 millimetres falls annually on the slopes here, enough to sustain the lush interior rainforests.

It wasn't until the 1960s that highways made life easier in the Robson Valley, as this part of the upper Fraser Basin is called. People had fought for a good highway for fifty years, organizing caravans to publicize their plight while government after government promised they'd have it "next year." During those years the road became a sort of Holy Grail that would solve all problems. On August 20, 1970, Premier W. A. C. Bennett officially opened the Yellowhead Highway (Highway 16) in a ceremony at Mount Robson. It was another five years before the highway was entirely built, and the road remained a lonely one for many years after. But it brought changes to the valley of the upper Fraser at a rapid rate. Farm products could be marketed more easily, seasonal tourism grew, easier access to forests rapidly increased the cut. But much of the wood went down the new road to Prince George, along with a large part of the region's administration. Local historian Marilyn Wheeler writes, "To those who came to the area because of its isolation, this apparent 'demotion' is difficult to accept." To many residents, Robson Valley's independent spirit seemed to be slipping away.

The new highways and logging roads of the 1960s dramatized in a tragic way the vast natural richness of the upper Fraser Basin. Highway 16 cut across a caribou migration route. Louise Muller of Sinclair Mills has lived on the banks of the Fraser for more than half a century, and she remembers what happened: "The first two years that the caribou went down from the mountain and across [the highway] for the winter . . . there were hundreds of caribou killed and left laying. Every winter it was just sickening over there." After only two years the annual caribou migration was nothing more than a memory. Across B.C. in the early 1970s, the caribou population plummeted, due in large measure to road construction allowing hunters access to their habitat and to elimination of habitat by logging: caribou depend for winter survival upon the lichens found only in old-growth forests.

Even when not as dramatic as the Robson Valley experience, the fragmentation of forest lands by roads and logging creates barriers to the free movement of plants and animals between remaining islands of suitable habitat. Biologists Lee Harding and Emily McCullum write in *Biodiversity in British Columbia*, "As the size of an intact ecosystem dwindles, species diversity declines [and] . . . the ecosystem becomes unstable, less resilient and less productive." In the forests of British Columbia, 10 000 kilometres of roads are constructed each year, about double the rate at which they are being "decommissioned" in accordance with the recent Forest Renewal B.C. plan. Many new roads are being driven into pristine valleys far beyond current cutblocks, presumably to preempt efforts to protect wilderness and wildlife values.

"The seclusion is another thing that's important to us," says Zammuto. "You can still find lots of untouched wilderness in the region, though it's going fast. We can still go to an uncut valley to find wilderness but some of the animals aren't so fortunate—they find their migration routes cut by logging roads and clearcuts. Streams where salmon spawn and other fish live are silted, their banks are stripped of vegetation." Discovering that the values they treasured in the Robson Valley were not at all secure, Rick and Julie found themselves before long in the thick of battles for the survival of wilderness and wildlife. An important one involves the Morkill River, which flows into the Fraser near their home, about 50 kilometres downstream from McBride.

The Morkill descends some 60 kilometres through Rocky Mountain valleys, sometimes dropping off ledges in breathtaking waterfalls. When the sun is just right, rainbows gleam in the delicate white spray. The river nourishes fine forests, fosters habitat that supports a diversity of animal life, and provides spawning grounds for deep-bodied chinooks in its lower reaches from mid-August to mid-September. Rainbow and dolly varden trout lurk in its deeper pools. Old-growth forests along the Morkill and its tributaries link alpine meadows high in the mountains to the sheltered valley of the Fraser, providing a corridor for grizzly bear and caribou, moose and mountain sheep. "We find here the greatest number of different kinds of animals to be found in B.C. with the exception of parts of the Prince Rupert area," says Zammuto. In fact, these rainforests and the mountains above them support more than one hundred kinds of birds and about sixty species of mammals, eighteen of them large carnivores and ungulates. "To find so many of the animals I've been seeking throughout my life all in one place—caribou, grizzly bears and wolverines as well as all the moose, deer, elk, mountain goats and sheep and so many others—it's a dream come true," Zammuto says.

Not long ago this was untouched wilderness, and conservationists like the Zammutos have fought to keep it that way. They insist that the Morkill Valley provides values far greater than the market price of logs, and the B.C. government's Old Growth Strategy Committee agreed, recommending the preservation of old-growth blocks in the valley. But corporate power prevailed, and now a logging road pushes far up the valley into the Morkill's high mountain origins. In places such as the confluence of the Hellroaring River and the Morkill, clearcuts have stripped the forests to stream banks despite laws prohibiting the destruction of fish habitat. The Morkill's delta was the largest wintering ground for moose in the Robson Valley; in spite of years of community protests dating back to 1986, the B.C. Forest Service allowed clearcutting and chemical spraying of the area, and now the moose are gone.

In the summer of 1993 there were indications that better industrial practices were mitigating the impact of logging in the Morkill Valley. As well as clearcuts there were some small patches where loggers had left prime trees spaced throughout the cut to reforest the land, and snags to provide wildlife habitat; there were places where slash burning had not reduced woody debris to ashes, where no chemicals had been sprayed to eliminate brush. Higher up the valley overlooking a green-mantled mountain slope, careful scrutiny revealed a couple of places where disturbances seemed to have occurred, but their extent or nature could not be discerned. In fact, no fewer than six small blocks had been logged on this particular slope, using methods carefully adapted to the terrain and natural vegetation. Efforts were made to retain the habitat of wildlife and to perpetuate a functioning forest rather than cutting, burning and replanting an even-aged plantation. It was the work of Zeidler Forest Products, directed by its chief forester at the time, Ron Hammerstedt.

Hammerstedt is a direct, determined man whose experience in the woods has led him to a position on clearcutting that is unpopular in some sectors of his industry. "I think basically you're witnessing its demise right now," Hammerstedt says. "There's still a number of people, companies and ministries who will support the system for a while yet, because they're used to it, and you know how hard it is to let go of something that you're comfortable with."

Hammerstedt explains how he tries to leave the natural system still operating, while providing for a strong regrowth of commercially valuable trees for the next harvest. Seed trees and planting of seedling trees both play a role. One problem, though, is that while the Forest

Service says logging and reforestation is to be carried out in a "site specific" manner, in fact clearcutting and slash burning is prescribed for 90 per cent of all B.C. forest harvesting. "Every single prescription is clearcut and slash burn," says Hammerstedt. "This is what foresters have been doing for years and years in this country, and particularly in B.C. and Ontario and other places where they can clearcut. We've been practising one prescription for every forest type at all times, and that to me is a travesty and insult to my professional status." With the introduction of the Forest Practices Code of B.C. (FPC) in 1995, Hammerstedt was hopeful that real change in logging methods might occur; by 1996 he felt that some improvement was evident. But many forestry companies, particularly the larger ones, continued clearcutting to the limits allowed by law, while waging a constant propaganda war against provincial logging regulations and those loggers who would introduce more sustainable practices.

And what does all this mean for the Morkill Valley? The first pass of loggers up the valley will remove a third of the old-growth forest. The second and third passes a few years later will take the rest. All that will remain of the old-growth forest, says Hammerstedt, will be those bits left within cutblocks where more enlightened logging occurs, and along stream banks where the FPC requires a narrow buffer of trees. The annual allowable cut in the entire Robson Valley remains unchanged, though new forest inventories show much less wood actually exists in the forests than the amount upon which the cut is based. Better practices required by the FPC should leave more trees standing, but that's not reflected in the new allowable cut either. Some Forest Service managers welcome the code as a way to improve forest practices; many consider it a nuisance that interferes with their principal job, which they see as the delivery of publicly owned wood to privately owned forest corporations.

At Tête Jaune Cache in the summer of 1862, a few of the Overlanders preparing to float down the Fraser to the Cariboo decided they wanted no part of the cumbersome, 12-metre-long rafts some of the travellers had built out of cottonwoods growing on the riverbank. Instead they hollowed trees into dugout canoes and set off downstream ahead of the rafts. All went well for more than 180 kilometres. Then, as they drifted, a distant sound of turbulent water swelled to thunderous dimensions. Beaching their canoes, the first three men cautiously surveyed the rock and water chaos now known as the Grand Canyon of the Fraser River. They discovered two canyons separated by a basin perhaps half a kilometre in length. The upper canyon is by far the most ferocious, squeezing the full force of the river between narrow walls, tormenting the current with sharp turns and innumerable rocky promontories. The lower canyon forces the water into a gigantic whirlpool that rhythmically fills and empties.

Convinced they could not survive the turbulence, the men tried to lower a craft through the rapids at the end of a rope. It quickly foundered, disappearing in the foaming water with all their equipment. The next three Overlanders attempted to run the rapids in a pair of canoes lashed together. The first rough patch wrenched the canoes apart and capsized them. Two men, Warren and Douglas, were non-swimmers, so the third, Robertson, told them to stay with the wreckage while he tried to swim for shore. Warren and Douglas managed to hold on as they plunged through the maelstrom and eventually washed up on an island in midstream. Robertson was never seen again.

Most of the crew were sleeping as the first of the Overlanders' rafts drifted towards the canyon. As Thomas McMicking, one of their leaders, wrote, "At half-past 5 o'clock in the morning of Saturday, [September] the 6th, we were suddenly startled by an unusual roaring noise that broke the stillness of the morning, the cause and source of which was soon explained by the lookout shouting 'Breakers ahead.' We had reached the big rapids, and we were already so near them and were being swept toward them by the current so rapidly that we had barely time to row ashore and make fast before we were drawn into them."

Without any real alternative, the travellers decided to trust their raft to the current. McMicking continued:

About ten men remained on the raft, and the balance of us stationed ourselves along the shore where we might possibly be able to render some assistance . . . the ropes were untied and the frail bark pushed into the current . . . They seemed to be rushing into the very jaws of death . . . With fearful velocity they were hurried along directly towards the fatal rock. Their ruin seemed inevitable . . . Every one bent manfully to his oar. The raft shot closely past the rock, tearing away the stern row-lock, and glided safely down into the eddy below. The agony was over. The gauntlet had been run, and all survived.

As September wore on, successive parties of Overlanders faced the Fraser's Grand Canyon. The majority made it through, but strange tales surround some who didn't. Three men named Carpenter, Jones and Alexander arrived at the canyon in two dugouts lashed together. They beached the ungainly craft while they explored on foot what lay ahead by water. They decided to run the rapids; just before setting off, Alexander noticed Carpenter writing in a notebook that he then slipped into his coat pocket. They pushed off, leaving the coat hanging on a tree bough.

"We went at a tremendous rate for a while," Alexander later wrote in his diary, "when we got among some big waves and the canoe filled over the stern and went down. When it came to the surface again Carpenter was holding to the stern and I to the bow. Then I let go and swam for it. Carpenter I never saw again, nor yet the canoe." Incredibly, Alexander somehow lived through the boiling waters of the canyon. He remembered and retrieved Carpenter's coat and notebook. In it he read: "Arrived this day at the canyon at 10 A.M. and drowned running the canoe down. God keep my poor wife!"

Half a century passed before the canyon again echoed to the shouts of helmsmen. From 1912 to 1914 hundreds of scows were built in Tête Jaune Cache and floated down the Fraser to supply crews building the Grand Trunk Pacific Railway. At least 10 per cent of the scows didn't survive the trip, and unknown numbers of crewmen died in the tormented waters of the Grand Canyon; records show that the canyon claimed at least fifty scowmen in 1913 alone. Legend in the Robson Valley has it that many helmsmen put aboard the scows for the trip through the canyon were Chinese, inexperienced in the ways of the river, but considered expendable by the railroad contractors.

Sternwheel steamboats were the unchallenged queens of the upper Fraser during those brief glory days of river transport, but the Grand Canyon was a supreme test for even the most experienced river captain. Steaming upstream they had to time their passage through the lower whirlpool precisely, then they would winch their ships up through the upper gorge on a cable placed there for the purpose—a process called "lining."

Descending the canyon by steamboat was quite another story. Willis West tells of running the rapids in the summer of 1913 in the steamer *B.C. Express*, commanded by Capt. J. P. Bucey:

> *The ship arrived at the Grand Canyon the next forenoon where the passengers as usual were disembarked while she ran the upper canyon . . . From the moment the steamer left the landing to head down the canyon, there was a continuous ringing of bells as the captain sent the engine-room the necessary signals for his intricate manoeuvring. The current at times was so strong that although the big sternwheel was reversing at full speed, she was driven downstream at a speed of 10 or 15 miles an hour. The most dangerous point was a sharp left turn in the canyon where the full volume of water in the Upper Fraser was hurled against the perpendicular wall of the abyss. It was here that many of the railway scows were smashed in attempts to run the canyon.*
>
> *To an inexperienced observer watching as the tumultuous waters carried the ship towards this dangerous turn it would appear impossible for Captain*

Bucey to pilot his heavily laden steamer safely past this terrifying spot. When the ship reached the abrupt turn, the captain suddenly spun his steering-wheel as though he were going to fling the side of his ship against the canyon wall. He knew, however, that when the current carried the ship to within 6 or 8 feet of the canyon side, the cushion of water would prevent her from crashing into the wall and she would be headed around the sharp curve. He swiftly signaled for full speed ahead at the turn and shortly afterwards brought the ship out into the calm waters of the basin to the immense relief of the few observers who, with his permission, had stayed on board.

An old beehive burner leans tiredly, trying to legitimize the name Sinclair Mills claimed by this tiny settlement on the banks of the Fraser. Not far downstream from here the river begins the great bend towards its destination far to the south. Ray and Louise Muller live in a well-cared-for home beside the river that has been central to their lives. Ray was sixteen when he came here from Saskatchewan with his family in 1925; he and Louise married in 1938. Like his father, Ray was a logger in the days when sawmills marked each stop along the railway. After somehow surviving the depths of the Depression, the mill at Sinclair Mills finally closed in the early 1960s.

As trapper, guide and, above all, as riverman, Muller has come to know the upper Fraser River Valley as few non-Natives ever have. He carefully brings out a smoothly shaped maul that terminates in a tiny birdlike face. "I was up the creek that day and it started to rain," Muller says, "so I got under a tree and had my dinner there. And then I happened to touch this with my foot, and you know grass had grown over it, and boy I dug a little bit and that's what it was." As the little face stared at us across the centuries, we wondered at the artistry of the Native craftsperson who had carved it, probably a Carrier, and in whose hand cedar would have been shaped to many uses.

Muller shows another treasure, a gigantic woolly mammoth tooth that he found above the Grand Canyon. Woolly mammoths, Grand Canyon, Rocky Mountains, mighty river—everything is vast in this upper Fraser Basin country, but the Grand Canyon has probably impressed, frightened and killed more people than anything else. Once a terrifying hazard for everyone travelling in the region, now it is barely known since there is no easy access and the river here is no longer an important transportation route. But Muller knows it intimately; he has traversed the Grand Canyon hundreds of times in every kind of river craft, he knows every deadly rock and whirlpool, every rush and swirl that must be taken at just the right angle and speed if disaster is to be averted.

For loggers using the Fraser River to transport wood to the mills, the canyon could be a bottleneck. Low water would leave logs entangled on the rocks, where more quickly became snagged, gathering into what would become a major jam. That's when they called on Ray Muller. "The logs would pile up, they'd back up and then they'd hit the other bank, and it was an awful mess," says Muller.

It was a job to be done, nothing particularly dramatic. But as Muller speaks, an image forms: within the cacophony of the canyon a few small men surrounded by a maelstrom of rushing water jump across entangled logs, crosscut saw and peavey in hand, cutting and levering logs off rocks, ready to leap clear when the mass of wood surrenders to the rushing current. "There were no lifejackets at first, but later on we got them," says Muller. "You were on your own entirely, if you fell in, you'd get out the best way you could. The water in the Fraser here is always cold, even when it's a hot day and especially when you're sweating and you fall in, it makes you grunt like when you hear a moose call." Eventually the river was replaced by road and rail, and there were no more logs to drive. But into the 1990s Muller continued his trips up and down the river in his long, narrow riverboat with its powerful outboard motor, often taking parties of hunters and adventurous travellers through the whirlpool, rapids and fierce currents of the Grand Canyon of the Fraser.

The water of the Fraser River assumes many guises in its descent to the ocean. A thousand brooks tumble over rocks as they race down mountain slopes; quiet shaded streams nurture rainbow trout in deep pools, then sparkle over shallow riffles that recharge the water with oxygen; grey-green glacial rivers join slower, darker streams. In places a rocky sill slows the flow, pushes it outward, creates a lake. Often the water is hidden, stored underground in an aquifer or moving down a valley beneath the surface. It may emerge into a stream, then withdraw again into subsurface flow. When summer sun dries the forest floor and streams slow to a trickle, underground water continues to nourish life.

As the river rises and falls with the seasons it erodes some banks and builds others, carves new channels and abandons old ones. A stream speeds up or slows down with changing terrain, its pace helping determine whether the bed will be sand or pebbles or rock, and which plants and insects will thrive there. With less friction from banks and bed to hold it back, a larger stream will flow faster than a smaller one; even the air has a braking effect, and so a stream flows fastest just below the surface.

Near McBride where the land is relatively level, the Fraser River wanders down the valley in great loops or meanders, carving sinuous oxbows that bend first towards one side of the valley and then the other as the current carves sediment from a concave bank and drops material on a convex one. The flow is more complex than it appears; in a shallower, "riffle zone" between the two bends, secondary currents push the main current from one side of the river to the other, positioning it higher or deeper in the water. Currents even cause the main flow to rotate: counterclockwise in a bend to the right and clockwise in a bend to the left. These rotations increase the rate of erosion, hastening the day when the river breaks through the narrowing neck of an oxbow to create a new and shorter course.

Leonardo da Vinci was fascinated by flowing water, and in Florence 500 years ago he passed many hours on the Arno River, studying relationships of land and water, sketching the swirls and turbulence caused by the pilings of the Ponte Vecchio or rocks near the banks. He began to understand the way in which water creates its own universe and described many principles of flowing water that we still use today. Until the late seventeenth century, people thought water came out of the depths of the earth through springs and alpine streams. Then Edmund Halley, discoverer of the comet that bears his name, measured European rainfall and found that it was roughly equal to the amount of water carried to the sea in streams and rivers. He was probably the first to recognize that water evaporates from the surface of the earth, circulates in the air and drops to earth again in an endless hydrological cycle. In this system, rivers are the living link between mountain, sea and sky.

"Once you walk through a watershed and understand it, you will always know where you are in any river system," says hydrologist Robert Newbury. "Every stream is fed by three or four smaller streams—the average throughout the world is three and a half, and that applies to the tiniest brook or the largest river. It also applies to your blood vessels, to lightning strokes, tree branches, everything. That's because this is the form that requires the least amount of structure for the greatest dispersal of energy. So nature builds this form again and again. That means when you do something upstream, everything below it is going to be affected. If by damming and diverting you take the energy of flow of one stream and direct it into another, you can be sure you will damage the natural systems of the area. Upstream damage from logging or mining always extends downstream far from the point of injury."

Hydrologists like Newbury have discovered that the succession of pools, rapids and riffles, wave forms, meanders and other phenomena common to streams can be measured, predicted and sometimes restored when the system has been damaged. But much of the manipulation of water in this century has been guided by principles of "hard" engineering rather than by an understanding of natural aquatic systems. The often catastrophic results can be seen throughout the world. Dams and diversions are obvious examples. Another is channelization: the bulldozing of a natural, curving stream into a straight, sterile ditch, destroying its pools and riffles, the fast currents that alternate with lazy ones, the abundant natural life on its banks and in the water.

Newbury explains how such damaged streams can be restored. "Normally I try first to understand the natural system and how it works. Why do certain insects, plants and fish thrive in this part of a stream and not another? Why do ancient Indian middens reveal that man once lived on this bay or riverbank and not another one? What are the important streamside trees and other vegetation? Then I think about the fish. A fishery is possible only at the upper level of water health, so if you can find a way to restore the fish, most of the requirements of a healthy stream will be met.

"But most important of all, I try to get people to see the stream and its landscape as a very subtle, mystical, magical thing, and their relationship with it as an intimate one. Sometimes I make a model of a watershed and suddenly people understand what is happening right here on their stream, and they recognize the unity and value of that watershed. Sometimes a trout will do it. When people understand what it is that attracts a fish to this place in a stream and not another one, it's a kind of revelation, and they often become keenly aware of their landscape and the place of the stream within it. In ways like these, people become sensitive to their environment and want to ensure that it lasts."

On Wednesday, June 12, 1793, fur trader and explorer Alexander Mackenzie and his crew of nine men were pushing their way southeast up the Parsnip River, a tributary of the Peace in northeastern British Columbia. The Parsnip dwindled, then turned towards its source in the Rocky Mountains. So the travellers branched into a small creek that led them to Arctic Lake on the divide between two great aquatic systems. From here the waters of the Peace River flow north to the Arctic Ocean and those of the Fraser River south to the Pacific. After paddling to the southern end of Arctic Lake, Mackenzie related, "We landed and unloaded, where we found a beaten path leading over a low ridge of land of eight hundred and seventeen paces in length to another small lake." The route was obviously well used by Native travellers, with campsites and various goods stored at points of portage.

Their canoe was more than 7.5 metres long, with a beam of 1.5 metres. The canoe was so light, said Mackenzie, "that two men could carry her on a good road 3 or 4 miles without resting." The voyageurs paddled the length of two more tiny lakes at the summit and then launched the canoe downstream for the first time since the journey had begun a month earlier at Fort Fork, near the confluence of the Smoky and Peace Rivers. But the current wasn't much help. The stream was blocked by fallen trees, gravel bars and rocks. Mackenzie named it "Bad River"; on their second day of travel on the stream, the canoe was swept broadside into rocks that smashed bow and stern and punched holes in the hull. Mackenzie had to use all his powers of persuasion and even threats to convince the men they should continue the trip. Reluctantly they repaired the canoe, dried out their equipment and pushed on, with great relief finally reaching Herrick Creek.

The Herrick carried them into the McGregor River, a major tributary of the Fraser. The McGregor's clear green water sweeps westward through a gap in the McGregor Range where rock lifts steeply into grey clouds. Black trees on upland slopes catch and momentarily hold wisps of passing mist. As Mackenzie paddled westward he could not have imagined the temptation those stony shoulders would represent to engineers of the dam-building trade almost two centuries later.

The valleys of McGregor River and Herrick Creek rise quite slowly over long distances upstream, and a dam at this place would create an enormous reservoir cradled in the mountains. Engineers promoted three benefits of such a dam: generation of electric power, reducing flood possibilities in the lower Fraser Valley and diversion of McGregor water into the Peace River over the low summit travelled by Mackenzie. The additional water could generate more electricity at the W.A.C. Bennett Dam on the Peace River.

The prospect of mingling the waters of the two watersheds terrifies biologists, because each aquatic system has evolved its own biological balance over a very long time. Parasites kept under control by other organisms in one watershed might explode in population when introduced into another watershed where such controls do not exist. Parasites normal to arctic char in the Peace system could be devastating to Fraser River salmon. And there were many other potential problems. A lower flow in the Fraser River would reduce survival rates of young sockeye salmon and raise Fraser water temperature by one degree centigrade, causing more adult sockeye to die before spawning. Downstream spawning grounds of pink salmon would lack sufficient water. And the list goes on. Due to the potential for environmental catastrophe the proposal was dropped, though as recently as 1989 a "McGregor Dam" remained on B.C. Hydro's list of possible power sources for the period 2000 to 2027. The threat of such a structure lurks in the shadows simply because it would be so easy to construct in this location.

Herrick Creek is the principal tributary of the McGregor, and the exuberance of life in its isolated valley makes the stream a jewel by any standards. A dam on the McGregor River would flood most of the valley, but logging is a much more present danger to the Herrick Valley: Northwood Pulp and Paper of Prince George wants to grind its trees to pulp. This is traditional territory of the Carrier people, and in particular of the Lheit-Lit'en Nation whose home settlement for centuries was at the confluence of the Fraser and Nechako Rivers, the site of today's Prince George. Former Lheit-Lit'en Chief Peter Quaw goes into the Herrick Valley every year—the region is an important hunting and fishing territory for his people and it is here, he says, that they find their most precious medicines.

In the Herrick and in all other tributary valleys of the Fraser River, connections between water and life are strong and easily seen. Much of life depends upon this extremely productive and sensitive meeting place of land and water along alpine brooks, valley streams and rivers, around lakes, wetlands and estuaries. These "riparian zones" provide corridors along which animals, large and small, move with the changing seasons. Bears descend from alpine meadow to salmon-rich valley streams; moose, caribou and most other ungulates migrate with the seasons. Even plant species travel these watery trails, their seeds carried by the current or spread by migrating animals.

A riparian zone is home to an extensive menu of insects favoured by a large and varied population of birds, and by fish that feed on morsels dropping into the water from overhanging leaves. Small animals scurry through dense streamside growth while above them in decaying trees woodpeckers drill for insects or hammer out hollows for nesting. The streams of the Fraser Basin shelter more cavity-nesting birds than any other place in Canada; twelve species of woodpecker breed here and the cavities they carve provide nesting sites for twenty-two other bird species. In fact, 20 per cent of all birds here, and about 30 per cent of the mammals, depend on cavities in dead or dying trees. Some biologists suggest that a tree's greatest contribution occurs after death. Where a tree falls across a stream, waterfowl nest and rear their young in the quiet pool. High above in the tallest trees, bald eagles build massive nests not far from the water that provides much of their food, especially when salmon are spawning.

These rich riparian zones link together in networks encompassing entire watersheds, which in turn are connected across highlands between valleys by forest corridors through which migrating animals move. Protecting riparian zones and the forest corridors that link them is essential for the preservation of healthy watersheds. With Northwood wanting to log the Herrick Valley, environmentalists wanting it preserved and the Lheit-Lit'en Nation claiming it as theirs, the Herrick became one of the first testing grounds for new land-use planning processes introduced in British Columbia by the New Democratic Party government in the early 1990s.

The Commission on Resources and Environment (CORE) was set up to design a system whose goal would be an end to the "war in the woods." Bitter battles were being fought throughout the province over dwindling old-growth forests and wilderness landscapes like the Herrick Valley. In the fall of 1991 a group of about twenty people representing most interests in the valley—the logging industry, labour unions, the environmental movement, the Lheit-Lit'en Nation, government departments concerned with forests, parks, wildlife and fisheries—came together to work out a "Local Resource Use Plan," or LRUP, for the Herrick Valley.

Vic Skaalid of the B.C. Forest Service describes his view of the process. "We started essentially from a clean slate. We looked at all of the issues, tried to get a balanced view. There was a point where we knew everybody quite well, we knew their views, we knew the issues, we decided to sit down now at a workshop with the objective to set out resource management units, to try to zone the area a bit. And that was really successful." The group held almost fifty meetings over two years to work out the details.

Rick Zammuto was one of those defending the Herrick's environmental values. "If they do what they say they're going to do, the Herrick is a milestone," he said in 1993. "Sixty per cent of the watershed is proposed as a protected area, 98 per cent of the old growth over 240 years old is fully protected." In many places Herrick Valley soils are very sensitive to disturbance and, under the plan, if Northwood couldn't log in such areas without excessive damage, they would have to stop, and the areas would be set aside for protection. This meant smaller, less damaging machinery and perhaps some horse logging if objectives set for the Herrick were to be achieved.

Victor Bopp was district director for B.C. Parks at Prince George at the time of negotiations. "Once you finally get people together, they come with very strong positions and the first tendency is to fight for those positions," says Bopp. "A sort of an evolution in a group of dynamics develops, and after a few meetings, people learn to understand other interests and then you use the energy, the intelligence and the information from all sides to come up with resolutions. The product is usually better, because at that point you have considered all sides."

Yet a key participant, the Lheit Lit'en Nation, pulled out of the Herrick LRUP discussions about halfway through. Chief Peter Quaw said his people could not be considered one more participant, just a "user group" like many others. These lands belong to his people, and the fate of the Herrick Valley couldn't be discussed, he insisted, until treaty negotiations covering the lands claimed by the Lheit Lit'en are completed. Until then, said Quaw, the valley must be considered sacred and be unconditionally protected.

After all the talk, after "the plan" is agreed to by the remaining participants, it is only, finally, a recommendation. The minister of forests still has the right to make the final decisions. Many of those involved think the advice can't be ignored, that neither bureaucrats nor politicians can easily turn away from recommendations arrived at through consensus by most parties interested in the valley. Victor Bopp said in 1993, "I've never been as optimistic as I am right now, if we continue these processes. Because, as somebody said not too long ago, 'When they let the consensus cat out of the bag, once you get public involvement . . .'" Rick Zammuto hoped Bopp would turn out to be right, but he was skeptical: in another community process, the Robson Valley Round Table, the consensus position had already been overruled by regional Forest Service bureaucrats in Prince George.

Resource consultant Larry Fidler of Tête Jaune Cache was also worried about the lesson of the Robson Valley experience, particularly because of the way Forest Service administrators seemed to dominate B.C. Environment officials and their concerns. No one knows the directions local forestry managers get from head office in Victoria, Fidler says. "There's no clear indication that Victoria is demanding that the views of fisheries and wildlife people be respected and implemented. The Forest Service people kind of go ahead and do what they please." And that, he suggests, basically means serving the interests of the timber companies.

In Prince George, federal Department of Fisheries and Oceans biologist Bruce McDonald looks out for the interests of salmon in a number of these land-use planning processes. "I do see them as being positive," he said in 1993, "because for a long time forests were managed by government and industry, exclusively. And now people have awakened to the fact that forests belong to everybody. And they should have a say, and I think they are getting a say, but I think the other shoe is yet to drop. And the other shoe is when the decisions are made."

Many of the Robson Valley citizens who contributed hundreds of hours to the planning process grew disillusioned as their hopes for change became mired in bureaucratic manoeuvring. They found that essential elements such as tenure (who gets to cut the public forests), allowable annual cut (how fast the trees will be cut), and clearcutting and other forest practices were not allowed on the planning agenda. At the same time, environmentalists had to table their suggestions for protection of old-growth and critical ecosystems; these areas seemed to then become targeted for early logging. The Robson Valley Round Table, conservationists insisted, was overweighted with logging interests participating under a number of different labels but pushing the same agenda: the least possible protection for marketable trees and the maximum possible access to old-growth forests.

"The other shoe" anticipated by Bruce McDonald has dropped in many land-use planning procedures, and in the Robson Valley the worst fears of conservationists were realized. Very little of the ancient forest of the Robson Valley has been set aside for future generations. Less than 5 per cent of this unique region of biological wonder is slated for protection, after years of negotiation and compromise. The Robson Valley Round Table, which started out (perhaps naively, suggests forester Ron Hammerstedt) with great optimism and hope, was largely subverted by Forest Service managers, probably under pressure from logging corporations. Even consensus agreements that would have ensured protection of a minimum of representative landscapes in the valley, about 15 per cent of the area, were vetoed. The provincial government's target of protection of at least 12 per cent of representative B.C. landscapes was nullified by the simple bureaucratic gambit of declaring long-established Mount Robson Park part of the region covered by the round table planning process, leaving very little of the natural heritage of the Robson Valley from Tête Jaune Cache to the McGregor River eligible for protection. Magnificent though it is, Mount Robson is an alpine region having little in common with the ecosystems of the lower elevations of the Rocky Mountain Trench. Yet the park was used as the excuse for turning over almost the entire ancient interior rainforest to logging corporations.

In the Herrick Valley, the resource use plan was eventually signed by all remaining participants, though some conservationists considered its provisions inadequate. Victor Bopp, now retired from B.C. Parks, says Northwood seems to be following the plan. But he stresses the need for periodic public reviews of such plans by those who participated in developing them. He's convinced that the land and resource planning process, along with the Forest Practices Code, mark an enormous advance over practice in B.C. just 5 years earlier. But it's absolutely essential, says Bopp, that the public continue to be involved. "We must make sure that it doesn't slip back," he says.

Environmentalists in particular will have to watch carefully what

happens. The problem, says Bopp, is that there aren't enough of them
with an understanding of the issues, and those who do are stretched to
the point of burn-out. Sometimes, he says, what really happens is
"consensus by exhaustion." At land planning sessions, industry is repre-
sented by salaried officials, the environment largely by volunteers.

Clarence Boudreau strains to lift his dipnet. A magnificent female chinook salmon lies in the web, plump with the eggs she has carried hundreds of kilometres from the Pacific. Here in Dome Creek, more than
100 kilometres downstream from McBride, Boudreau has trapped the
fish in a fence he built across the creek for the Department of Fisheries
and Oceans (DFO). So far in this summer of 1993, about 350 of the big
fish have passed through, and Boudreau counted another 200 before
the end of the run. About the same number showed up the following
year, and in 1995 numbers were running even higher when a flash
flood took out the counting fence at the peak of the run. Since there
were none at all in the creek a few years ago, or at least none that anyone saw, the numbers are remarkable. When Boudreau counts chinooks
here on Dome Creek, he's providing information useful to the DFO's
management of the ocean fishery.

As in many other Fraser River tributaries, Dome Creek's salmon
were wiped out by flash dams built by loggers. The dams stored water
that could be released in a rush, flushing logs down the valley to the
Fraser. The logs ripped out salmon spawning beds as they tumbled
downstream. Boudreau remembers those dams. "I know of three right
in the immediate area here. Never thought about a fish, they never did
in those days. When they had big logjams they got in there with the
Cats and pushed them out, and some of them they blasted. Well, the
salmon were wiped right out according to the old-timers, and then
they slowly came back in again over a period of years." Dome Creek
sawmills ceased to operate when bought out in 1966 by Northwood,
which hauls the logs to Prince George. Boudreau points out that by
paying half the cost of the enhancement operation, Northwood is
helping bring back the chinook runs decimated by earlier loggers.

So far this year the biggest chinook caught in the fence weighed in
at 15 kilograms—34 pounds. The chinooks are the giants of the salmon
family and by this point, about 1100 kilometres up the Fraser River,
they've left all other salmon species behind. Clarence Boudreau's devotion to the big fish is obvious. "Do you know of anything that doesn't
eat off the salmon? Including us? Just stop and think about it. Right
from the start, from the eggs on down through, it seems like half the
planet at least lives on the salmon. The bears come down, they feast on

them. I opened up one Dolly Varden—it had fifty little salmon in it. Fifty! That's only one meal. It's a wonder that any salmon come back!"

Boudreau was born at Penny in the upper Fraser River Valley more than sixty years ago. "My mom and dad came here in 1923, the railroad went through in '14, so they weren't too far behind it. It's a young country you know. My dad worked for the mill and logging, and he worked on the river." Boudreau also operates a hatchery for the DFO, which has helped bring the chinooks back more quickly than natural increase would have achieved. He and fisheries biologist Mel Sheng figure the river could handle about a thousand adult chinooks, so they are planning a rearing channel for little salmon from the hatchery.

Although some Fraser River salmon runs are being restored, Boudreau worries about other fish. "One of the things that's changed over the years is that the trout are disappearing from our streams along the Fraser," he says. "Nobody knows why. Nobody's studying them either because nobody cares about trout." Then he points into the clear, smoothly flowing water. "Did you notice the salmon spawning right here, maybe she's still here. See? In the gravel?" He indicates an extensive mound of gravel and round river rocks, about two metres square. Some of the rocks the spawning female chinook has flipped into place with her tail are up to 12 centimetres across. "That's a salmon redd [a stretch of gravel in which the female spawns]," Boudreau observes. "It's full of eggs now. What happens is, a dominant male will chase everything away from that female, he just works his heart out, and there may be four or five more males around trying to sniff in on him. And when she spurts out some eggs, they all go in and fertilize them, so his work is all for nothing but he doesn't know it, I guess. We've seen five or six of them go in and all give a spurt at the same time, and the water below runs a kind of greyish colour, like somebody dumped flour in it.

"When she's finished spawning, she'll stay here and guard the eggs until she dies. It might be a week, it might be eight days but she'll stay right there and she'll chase away the biggest male or anything that comes along. Until she dies."

On June 18, 1793, the McGregor River carried Alexander Mackenzie's canoe into the Fraser. Since he did not know of the river's existence, he assumed that this big waterway, called *Tacoutche Tesse*—the Mighty One—by members of the Carrier Nation, was in fact the Columbia. His impression seemed confirmed when the river completed its great arc through the Cariboo Mountains and headed south. A new stage in Mackenzie's epic journey, and in the journey of the Fraser River to the Pacific Ocean, had begun.

Nechako River and Stuart River Watersheds

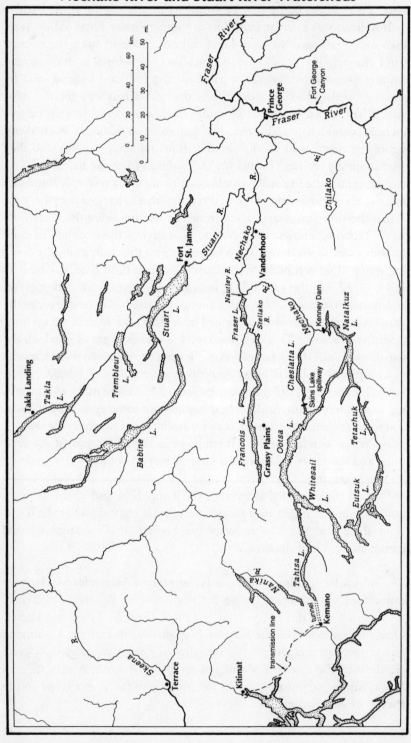

CHAPTER 3

Reversing a River

We are a restless, dissatisfied novice species, clamoring for
rulership of a planet toward which we display not even
a rudimentary form of allegiance.

ROBERT F. HARRINGTON, *THOUGHTS ON AN EARTH ETHIC*

Soon after breaking through the massive walls of the Rocky Mountain Trench and steadying on a southward course, the Fraser River is joined by one of its greatest tributaries. The Nechako River pours in from the west at Prince George, draining a vast and spectacular land of lakes and rivers. Interlaced with Fraser-bound streams in that watery landscape are rivers destined for the Arctic Ocean, and for the Pacific by a more direct route. A minor height of land or an ancient landslide may direct a waterway's flow towards a destination thousands of kilometres from that of a neighbouring stream.

More than 200 years have passed since the foggy Wednesday morning of June 19, 1793, when Alexander Mackenzie and his crew paddled down the Fraser River in their battered birchbark canoe towards the site of today's Prince George. At least, Mackenzie writes that it was foggy at 3 A.M. when the day's travel began, and he adds that fires lit by Natives filled the air with thick smoke. That would not be surprising, because this is the ancestral homeland of the Lheit-Lit'en Nation. Fog and smoke could explain why he drifted past the mouth of the Nechako River without seeing it. Fifteen years later the next European on the scene, Simon Fraser, was less charitable; he suggests Mackenzie was simply dozing as his canoe passed the Nechako. "This River is not mentioned by Sir A. M. K. which surprises me not a little, it being in full sight and a fine large river," wrote Fraser. Had Mackenzie noticed it, the Nechako River would have helped him reach his goal at the Pacific coast by an easier route than the overland trail he eventually followed.

It was July 11, 1806, when Simon Fraser arrived at the confluence of the Nechako and Fraser Rivers with his clerk, John Stuart, and ten voyageurs in three old and leaky birchbark canoes. The previous day he had paddled for the first time on the river that was to bear his name. He had followed the route blazed by Mackenzie up the Peace and Parsnip Rivers, over the divide into streams of the Fraser system and down the McGregor. Now he turned off the Fraser and headed west, struggling up the rapids of the Nechako to Stuart River and on to Stuart Lake. There he met a band of Carrier people who were not too anxious to supply him with food or furs. Their reluctance may have been because Fraser had very few goods to offer in trade, and because the salmon run upon which the Carrier depended was late. In fact, the fish didn't arrive for another six weeks, and both the new arrivals and the Carrier went hungry. It may have been a poor year for the early run of Stuart River salmon, whose numbers can be affected from season to season by water temperature and the water level in the river. Perhaps it was another run, the "late Stuart," that eventually saved them from starvation.

Fraser and his men set to work building a fur trading post he called Fort St. James, a structure that still stands on the shores of Stuart Lake. Although Fraser was born in the United States and had never seen Scotland, family tradition suggests that he named the northern interior of B.C. "New Caledonia" because the country recalled his mother's description of the Highlands of Scotland.

As the weeks advanced without arrival of the salmon, Fraser finally had to abandon for that year his plans for an expedition down the Fraser River, which, like Mackenzie, he assumed to be the Columbia. Instead, he established another trading post on Fraser Lake, which drains into the Nechako River south of Stuart Lake. It was not until a year later, in the fall of 1807, that supplies from east of the Rocky Mountains reached him by canoe, at last enabling him to prepare for a trip down the Fraser. In the meantime he built still another trading post at the confluence of the Nechako River with the Fraser. He called it Fort George; this would be the jumping-off place for Fraser's epic journey to the Pacific Ocean the following year.

A century after Simon Fraser and his companions pushed off from Fort George determined to paddle to the Pacific, a freewheeling promoter named George J. Hammond was advertising the wonders of Fort George around the world. He subdivided and sold off hundreds of lots at inflated prices, encouraging a spurt of settlement that soon inspired construction of a rival community about five kilometres south along the banks of the Fraser. Known as South Fort George, the new community had an important advantage: paddle wheelers plying the Fraser could berth easily at the town, something possible only at high water in the shallow approaches to Fort George itself. Both communities stabilized and grew, reaching about 1,500 each by 1913, when thousands of railway workers flooded in for construction of the Grand Trunk Pacific Railway.

Then a thunderbolt: the railway company spurned both towns and opted to build a new one between them so it could profit from land sales in the new location, called Prince George. There was one temporary inconvenience: 1,366 acres of the land were occupied by the Fort George Indian Reserve, a Carrier community. The "problem" was solved in a manner similar to that used across Canada wherever Native communities stood in the way of entrepreneurial profits. Using the influence of a missionary, government officials forced the Carrier to accept a total of $125,000, or $91.50 per acre. At the time, land surrounding the reserve was selling for $1,625 per acre, with some lots going as high as $10,000 per acre. It seems the federal government had earlier rejected offers of $4,000,000 and $1,300,000 for the reserve lands. Apparently the smaller sum was preferable to a government whose financial interest in the railway was more important than its duty to protect Native interests.

The obvious advantages of Prince George's location helped make credible the extravagant claims of promoters. The confluence of two great rivers had provided aboriginal communities with ready access to the vast region for thousands of years. Fur brigade canoes from Fort George had later hauled their wilderness bounty down the Fraser en route to Kamloops and the Columbia River, while others travelled upstream through the Yellowhead Pass. In 1871 the whistle of the first steamboat to reach Fort George echoed through the little settlement.

The 33-metre sternwheeler *Enterprise* was built of hand-sawn timbers near Fort Alexandria in 1863; she was powered by a steam engine hauled from the coast in pieces on the backs of mules. Gold fever north of Fort George in the Omineca Mountains persuaded her owners to send the *Enterprise* into these uncharted waters. She pushed up the Fraser River, through the white water of Fort George Canyon, turned up the Nechako River at Fort George to struggle another 300 kilometres into distant reaches of the Fraser watershed. The ship threshed up Stuart River, across Stuart Lake and up connecting rivers and lakes to Takla Landing, far up the eastern shore of long and narrow Takla Lake. But the journey was too hard for a successful commercial operation; during the return trip, the *Enterprise* was abandoned on the shores of Trembleur Lake.

Navigators didn't reconsider the dubious rewards of running the Fort George and Cottonwood Canyons of the Fraser River until the speculative excitement of 1908 stirred up by promoters at Fort George. That year, the *Charlotte* managed her way up and down the Quesnel-Fort George stretch of the Fraser, and continued the service until she foundered on rocks and sank in Fort George Canyon in 1910. By then other ships, larger, more powerful and more luxurious, were making the trip. During three years of railway construction they churned their way farther upriver to Tête Jaune Cache, a total of more than 700 kilometres.

But it was never easy, and even the more placid stretches of river concealed perils that could be discerned only by navigators skilled at reading every changing nuance of the water. They learned how to follow the shifting channels, how to handle currents on or below the surface that could thrust a ship onto jagged rocks. With experience they could estimate the depth of water flowing over any underwater obstruction. Even so, every season saw new holes punched in the thin wooden hulls of these shallow-draft ships. One of the most powerful and luxurious steamers, the *B.X.*, on one occasion ripped a hole 19 metres long and 1 metre wide as she sped down through Fort George Canyon. Watertight compartments kept her afloat long enough to allow the captain to beach her before she sank. The *B.X.* was back in service in less than three weeks.

The trip upstream required a lot of power to drive the churning paddle wheels. When steam power wasn't enough, a capstan on the ship's bow could haul in a cable securely attached on shore, lining the boat upstream against the current. But the trip down offered its own challenges, as Willis West described from his own experience on the steamer *B.X.*: "The *B.X.* would enter the head of the canyon at a speed of about 20 miles [33 kilometres] an hour. She would maintain this speed until she had passed a point in the channel where the cross-currents would threaten to throw her on the reefs in the centre of the canyon. As soon as she had passed this dangerous point, Captain Browne would signal to the engine-room for full speed astern and start drifting his ship, manoeuvring her so that she would enter and pass through the narrow low-water channel at the canyon's southern end." A few kilometres below Fort George Canyon, Cottonwood Canyon was an easier passage but a fast one: here the *B.X.* would reach speeds of 48 kilometres an hour.

Although steamboat service continued on the upper Fraser until 1921, it was sporadic in later years; the big ships were queens of the north for only five years, until railway construction ended in 1914. Construction crews moved on from Prince George, businesses serving them declined or disappeared, and national and international attention centred on the conflagration enveloping Europe. Dreams of easy wealth faded, lots that sold for high prices during the years of speculative frenzy grew brush instead of houses, and Prince George began a slide into recession that deepened as the years wore on through World War

One, the 1920s and the depression years of the 1930s. World War Two revived the hopes of the community when Prince George became an important stopover for aircraft flying to Alaska. Sawmills along the river thrived, and as the population grew to 5,500, old-timers recalled the heady days of railway construction.

Today, a vantage point high on the eastern bank of the Fraser River opposite the mouth of the Nechako provides a superb overview of the modern city of Prince George. Below, a massive bridge carries Highway 16 over the Fraser into the city that extends into the distance. Traffic swirls around a fine hilltop park overlooking the city centre. Three pulp mills stream vapour into the summer sky, signalling their importance to the region's prosperity. With a population of 68,000, Prince George is the third largest city in British Columbia. True to the vision of its pioneers, it has become the central administrative, commercial and industrial community for a vast region in central and northern B.C. Here, in the summer of 1994, Queen Elizabeth II formally opened the University of Northern British Columbia, confirming the city's educational and cultural aspirations.

Relatively pristine until now, it is at Prince George that the Fraser River first feels the real impact of industry. The three pulp mills pour their waste into the Fraser; though improved treatment has greatly reduced the toxicity of mill effluent in recent years, the Carrier people who historically depend on resident Fraser River fish have been warned not to eat them. When an atmospheric inversion over Prince George traps fumes exuded by pulp mills, the city in summer can be enveloped in a mustard-coloured pall. Occasionally in winter air quality in the central city worsens sufficiently that people are warned to stay indoors to avoid threats to their health.

Across the Fraser at the mouth of the Nechako, glistening sand and gravel beds break the surface of the water, a telling reminder that 40 per cent of the river's normal flow no longer reaches the Fraser. Those Nechako waters now flow westward to the Pacific Ocean through generators at Kemano operated by the Aluminum Company of Canada (Alcan) to power its smelters at Kitimat. The story of the only significant diversion of water out of the Fraser system illuminates many of the issues involved in charting a sustainable future in the Fraser Basin. The Nechako-Kemano saga illustrates the consequences of large-scale manipulation of rivers and of delivering public resources into the hands of transnational corporations in the name of economic growth. The story underlines the responsibility of scientists and other professionals to society, particularly when efforts are made to silence them. And it demonstrates the influence aboriginal, environmental and community activists can have when they confront with courage and tenacity the power of great corporations backed by federal and provincial governments. The Kemano-Nechako issue is far from settled, and the way in which it is eventually resolved may provide an important indicator of the future of the entire Fraser Basin.

The story begins just after World War Two. In the late 1940s the Canadian hinterland, particularly the North, was considered vast and empty, full of untapped riches that would be of value only when economic development and industrial society were imposed upon the land. Territory occupied and used by aboriginal Canadians posed no problem; the concept of *terra nullius*, a land empty of people, remained as popular in the twentieth century as when it was used by the first European arrivals to justify taking possession of North America. Dreams of mega-projects of all kinds swept across the continent in this postwar period. In the United States concrete was pouring into every feasible canyon to harness free-flowing rivers for irrigation, hydroelectric power and flood control. In British Columbia in 1948, the provincial government invited Alcan to undertake a major industrial project on the central coast of the province.

Aluminum smelting requires vast amounts of electricity, so inexpensive power is an important advantage in global competition. The B.C. government's offer of a deep-water ocean port and the company's very own river high above it was irresistible. The government passed the Industrial Development Act in 1949 especially for Alcan, giving the company wide-ranging power over an immense landscape. Alcan was given mineral rights and timber rights with no stumpage charges on all the land it would flood; the company paid $1.60 per acre for 14,000 acres at Kitimat to be used for industrial and residential development. In 1950 the provincial government gave Alcan a water permit entitling it to all the water in the Nechako and Nanika Rivers. Almost no obligations were placed upon Alcan. In their detailed study of the project, J.C. Day and Frank Quinn noted, "The negative effects [of the Kemano project] on all other interests were largely ignored: erosion, fish, timber, minerals, provincial parks, air and water quality, Indian bands to be displaced from their homelands, and archeological records."

Kemano was the largest corporate undertaking in Canada at the time of its construction. The key to the project was the building of a massive dam in a canyon of the Nechako River that would block water draining towards the Fraser River from a watershed of 14 000 square kilometres. Far to the west of the dam, the reservoir would be tapped and the water of the Nechako drained to a powerhouse on the Pacific coast. As the enormous bulk of the Kenney Dam rose above the Nechako River, it inspired such superlatives as this advertisement by a Canadian bank: "This is among the greatest things to happen to the West since the transcontinental railroads were built—one of the biggest strides yet in Canada's march to greatness."

Below the construction site, the river ebbed and died when the dam was finally closed in October 1952. Above the Kenney Dam, water rose on the banks of the Nechako. It rose on the shores of Natalkuz Lake, the beaches disappeared on Ootsa Lake, the water crept into the branches of trees on Whitesail Lake, Eutsuk Lake and Tetachuk Lake. As the water deepened, the lakes flowed together into one huge circular reservoir of 900 square kilometres, drowning one of the most magnificent recreational waterways in the world. The nine lakes and linking rivers had formed a 400-kilometre "Great Circle" canoe route of incredible beauty in B.C.'s biggest provincial park, Tweedsmuir. Alcan paid ten cents an acre for the flooded land and water, and paid no compensation for its destruction of the park. The provincial government's solution to this loss was stark and simple: it "removed" 400 000 hectares of the flooded northern section of the park, replacing it with a 50 000-hectare block added on the south. The jewel of the B.C. parks system was gone.

The water rose over the streams and portages between lakes, inundated the traplines and cabins and centuries-old trails of the Cheslatta people. Before the water stopped rising it had drowned 48 000 hectares of forests that now stand stark and dead in the water, rendering a pristine waterway ugly and dangerous. A great sports fishing region suffered the greatest single negative impact ever experienced on lake fish habitat in the Fraser Basin. Native people tell of the moose and other animals that died in the tangle of dead trees, unable to reach shore when swimming across a lake. If a boater is caught today in open water by a sudden storm, a margin of dead forest may bar him or her from the safety of shore; fourteen human lives have been lost on the reservoir. In recent years Alcan has been removing some dead trees to improve boating safety.

The rising water pushed westward up the Tahtsa River into Tahtsa Lake, where it was blocked by the coastal mountains. Here, 200 kilometres west of the Kenney Dam, Alcan drilled a tunnel 16 kilometres through the mountains, dropping almost 800 metres (or about sixteen times the height of Niagara Falls) to a powerhouse carved in rock. Here, the force of falling Nechako River water spins dynamos capable of generating 896 megawatts. About 250 people live at Kemano, servicing the powerhouse. High-tension lines carry the electricity across 75 mountainous kilometres to Kitimat, where it powers a huge aluminum smelter employing about 2,200 people. Ocean freighters haul raw bauxite up Douglas Channel to the smelter and carry away aluminum ingots.

Kitimat prospered; a town of about 13,000 people grew up around the smelter. The power and the port attracted a forest products mill and a methanol plant, and other economic development was encouraged by Alcan's hydroelectricity. The goal of government to initiate industrial development in the region had succeeded.

When the last trickles of water dried in the sun below the Kenney Dam in 1952, the riverbed revealed more than 4,000 stony redds where for millennia huge chinook salmon had deposited their eggs. For almost three years as the gigantic reservoir behind the dam filled, no water entered the river; for another two years, until January 1957, only sporadic releases occurred. The chinook salmon of the Nechako River were decimated by lack of water, and many resident freshwater fish species such as rainbow trout and char were hard hit as well. Although provincial water authorities had maintained the project would have only minor impact on fish, federal fisheries experts recognized the threat to salmon and freshwater species. Their minister asked Alcan to build a tunnel through the dam to allow releases of cold water from deep in the reservoir. The hope was that sufficient cool water would aid sockeye salmon migration and provide enough water for winter survival of other species. Alcan refused. The company chose instead a cheaper way to release water from the reservoir: a spillway built at Skins Lake would direct water from the reservoir through Cheslatta River, Cheslatta Lake and Murray Lake into the Nechako, about eight kilometres downstream from the dam.

News that their home on the shore of Cheslatta Lake would soon be flooded was delivered to the Cheslatta people on April 3, 1952. Feet sank in mud and melting snow as the people assembled at their local church to hear officials of Alcan and the federal government's Department of Indian Affairs (DIA) tell them they must leave immediately. Negotiation was out of the question; the officials would return in a few days with documents the Cheslatta would have to sign, officially surrendering their lands to Alcan. Less than a week later, on April 8, Alcan closed a temporary dam downstream and the waters of Cheslatta Lake began to rise.

On April 21, DIA and Alcan officials returned and demanded signatures of the Cheslatta people on the surrender documents. Many band members were far out on traplines, unaware of what was happening or unable to travel home through the mud and rotting ice of spring breakup. Few of the Cheslatta could speak English, but they managed to insist that new land and buildings be supplied before they moved, that pensions be provided and that the loss of flooded traplines be compensated. Their demands were termed by the DIA "fantastic and unreasonable . . . definitely out of the question." The officials said if they wanted any compensation at all they must move immediately; if they did not accept the terms, they would have to move anyway, but would receive no compensation.

When the Cheslatta objected, officials took them aside for individual persuasion, knowing that the people had lived in relative isolation and knew little of current land and other market values. Recognizing the deep concern of the Cheslatta over their several cemeteries in reserves along the lakeshore, Alcan promised that they would move the graves and reestablish the cemeteries on higher ground. The company also promised to pay all moving and resettlement costs of the people, and assured them they could leave knowing their belongings and farm equipment would be safely stored for later retrieval.

Records of the DIA show that band members then voted unanimously to surrender 2,600 acres of their land for $130,000. Yet some did in fact refuse, in spite of the threats, and many did not sign because they were absent, far away on traplines. Most of the signatures or marks on the surrender documents were later shown to be forgeries. Faced with water creeping up over their land, the band members slogged off towards the community of Grassy Plains, where they were expected to pick up the pieces of their lives. To ensure the Cheslatta would not return, Alcan contractors moved in as soon as they were gone, burning the villages to the ground and destroying all the belongings and equipment they had promised to safeguard. Only a church remained standing; when contractors refused to burn it, a DIA official flew to the scene to do the job himself.

This was the scene of devastation that greeted Cheslatta trappers when they returned home after spring breakup. They eventually traced their families to Grassy Plains, where for months the band lived in tents. Gradually over three years they found isolated bits of land, mostly inadequate for family support. Instead of touring the close-knit community of lakeshore reserves, a Cheslatta chief now had to travel 275 kilometres to visit all members of the band. Traplines and cabins, trails and hunting territories that had provided livelihood for the Cheslatta were all flooded, with no compensation paid. Alcan fulfilled none of its promises to pay for relocation and resettlement of the people. Non-Native residents were paid $250 per acre and relocation costs; Native people received $40 per acre and no costs. Jobs were almost nonexistent for Indians whose skills on the land did not suit them for industrial employment. The culture of a proud and independent people all but disintegrated, and the Cheslatta people slid into despondency, poverty, alcoholism and suicide.

Alcan drove the waters of the Nechako down the Cheslatta River, a small stream usually averaging 5 metres in width. The Cheslatta immediately became a great sluiceway 75 to 150 metres wide. Its normal flow of about 5 cubic metres of water per second multiplied more than twenty-five times, sometimes raging through the valley at a hundred times normal flow. The torrent of water scooped out a ragged gorge up to 15 metres deep where once a meandering stream provided important fish and wildlife habitat. Millions of tons of gravel, thirteen times the volume of the huge Kenney Dam itself, were carved from the valley by the rushing water and carried into Cheslatta Lake. All the productive spawning areas where tributaries met the Cheslatta River were destroyed. The lowered stream beds drained three small lakes; this loss was particularly important because the Cheslatta people depended upon freshwater fish—salmon can't get up Cheslatta Falls to the lake. Alcan decided the graveyards could not be moved, so floodwaters pouring down the Cheslatta River ripped through one band cemetery and flooded others. In succeeding years the grieving people retrieved caskets, bodies and bones washed up along the shoreline. Overlooking the lake, an Alcan-erected aluminum plaque reads: "May they rest in peace." The plaque was considerably less costly than a proper outlet in the Kenney Dam.

Tributaries downstream of the Kenney Dam gradually restored part of the flow of the Nechako. When the reservoir was full, about 60 per cent of the Nechako's water was released into the river through the Cheslatta system. Fish stocks began slowly to recover, but other impacts downstream were permanent. The Nechako's rhythm of flow was changed, with the spring freshet much reduced. Shallow water spread over the wide bed of the Nechako, warming in the sun towards temperatures lethal for fish; periodic gushes of water from the new system washed silt into spawning beds. Wetlands dried, and at the wildlife sanctuary near Vanderhoof, migratory birds were deprived of habitat. Dogs and other predators could now cross through shallows to take young birds. The Nautley, an important sockeye-producing tributary of the Nechako, began eroding its bed to the level of the diminished Nechako, forcing Alcan to build a protective weir on it.

Over a couple of decades, some fish populations in the Nechako system gradually rebuilt. Then everything changed again. In 1978 B.C. Hydro extended its power grid out to the central coast. Alcan tied into Hydro's network, providing the company with an instant market for all the power it could produce. Alcan cranked its generators up to full capacity, pouring 67 per cent of the Nechako's flow down the mountain tunnel. Federal fisheries biologists soon realized that Nechako system salmon were facing a crisis and ordered the company to release enough water into the Nechako to maintain water and temperature levels adequate for spawning. Alcan refused. The minister of fisheries took the company to court where Alcan argued that Canada's Fisheries Act was unconstitutional. Among other things, the act says: "No person shall carry on any work or undertaking that results in the harmful alteration, disruption or destruction of fish habitat." Alcan's argument was rejected, and the company was ordered to release more water into the Nechako. But it set to work to disprove the need for the flows demanded by the DFO.

The reason for the company's tenacity was simple enough. Alcan profits handsomely by selling surplus power to B.C. Hydro in addition to smelting aluminum with very cheap electricity. A Simon Fraser University study showed that Alcan paid about 1 per cent of the water rate that should have been charged according to normal opportunity cost principles. Researcher Richard Overstall points out that Alcan's water-rental bill of about one-third of a cent per kilowatt hour to power its smelters is about one-eighth of the world average for producers of aluminum, and less than 10 per cent of the rate paid by other producers of hydroelectricity in the province. Overstall estimates that the B.C. taxpayer subsidized Alcan by about a quarter of a billion dollars during the twenty years ending in 1990. By far the greatest part of that subsidy occurred in the 1980s when water rentals paid by B.C. Hydro rose dramatically while those paid by Alcan remained extremely low.

Economic studies by the School of Resource and Environmental Management at SFU reveal that "the original Kemano Project has not been justified from a social perspective," even if no value at all is placed on the loss of recreational opportunities, wildlife habitat or forests in the Tweedsmuir Park region, and even without considering the loss of salmon or freshwater fish populations downstream. In part, this failure is due to the fact that, though B.C.'s electricity is used to process bauxite ore into raw aluminum at Kitimat, most of the jobs and profits are created after the aluminum ingots leave the province.

The impact of lower flows in the Nechako after 1978 was all too evident in the 1980s. Few chinook salmon were returning to the river, grass and weeds often encroached where once the river flowed sparkling and free, and broad margins of rock and sand lined the banks. Lakes were drying up and streams withering throughout the Nechako watershed, and intake pipes of irrigation systems dangled uselessly far above the river's water level. For many who lived there, the Nechako River and its valley were dying.

But the company wanted still more water; it wanted all but 13 per cent of the Nechako in order to generate more power, mostly for sale to

B.C. Hydro. And Alcan's time was running out. According to the Industrial Development Act of 1949, Alcan could drain the Nechako and the Nanika River, a Skeena River tributary, and retain forever the rights to whatever water it was taking from the two rivers by the year 2000. After that year, rights to unused water reverted to the province. The bonanza had a time limit. So in the early 1980s Alcan pressed ahead with a second phase of its Kemano project, called the Kemano Completion Project (KCP). Another tunnel would be bored through the mountains to the powerhouse. Water pouring down that tunnel would generate an additional 500 megawatts of electricity.

The impact of the original Kemano project on the natural systems of the Fraser Basin were now more clearly understood, and federal scientists were deeply concerned about Alcan's new proposal. A special task force of DFO scientists concluded that the KCP posed grave dangers to a fishery worth hundreds of millions of dollars. With the year 2000 looming, Alcan challenged in court the right of the federal fisheries department to control the flow of the Nechako. As the courtroom confrontation approached in 1987, it seemed likely the strong federal case would win the day.

At this point, events become shrouded in secrecy. But the evidence suggests that just a few days before the federal case was to be made in court, federal fisheries minister Tom Siddon, a member of Brian Mulroney's Progressive Conservative cabinet, convened a meeting with Alcan Vice-President Bill Rich and University of British Columbia President David Strangway. They agreed that a "working group" under Strangway's chairmanship would meet to settle the issue out of court. The Nechako River Working Group comprised representatives from Alcan, the province and a federal delegation that included none of the scientists most knowledgeable about the issues involved.

The group met over a weekend in Vancouver and emerged on September 14, 1987, with a "Settlement Agreement." Alcan would be allowed precisely the water it wanted: 87 per cent of the flow of the Nechako River. The federal government had abandoned its legal responsibility to ensure flows adequate to protect fish. Alcan gave up rights to the water of the Nanika River and agreed, forty years after the DFO requested it, to install a passage through the Kenney Dam for cold water from deep in the reservoir. A computerized system would deliver the water at times and in a manner calculated to limit damage to salmon populations. Alcan would be responsible for maintaining a minimum number of chinook salmon in the river, but would have no responsibility for protecting sockeye salmon runs or freshwater fish. That would be paid for by the taxpayers of B.C. and Canada.

Minister Tom Siddon wrote to the president of Alcan that he had been persuaded that the proposed low flow provided "an acceptable level of certainty" that the fishery would be protected. No evidence has ever been forthcoming as to how he had been convinced of this; the only known defenders of such levels were on the Alcan payroll. In fact, modern ecological science shows that predictions of the impact of disturbances on natural systems will usually be wrong. C. S. Holling, one of the world's great ecologists, puts it this way: "No amount of observation prior to a project will reveal what impacts the project will eventually have . . . the post-project system is a new system, and its nature cannot be deducted simply by looking at the original one."

However, experience in similar systems can provide some guidance as to what might be expected. To gain some indication of possible impacts of lower water levels in the Nechako, DFO scientists D. W. Burt and J. H. Mundie studied eighty-one regulated rivers in the Pacific Northwest. They found that "negative effects outnumbered positive ones, that prediction was usually incorrect, and that, even where flow regulation was implemented with the express intention of increasing numbers of salmonids the results fell short of expectations." The KCP, they concluded, "carries a high risk for the affected salmonid populations." So much for Siddon's "acceptable level of certainty."

In his book *The Run of the River*, author Mark Hume describes the close ties between many members of the Alcan board of directors and the Mulroney cabinet; a later RCMP investigation into the matter suggested that the Settlement Agreement was a purely political decision made in secret. Certainly, no input was allowed from the general public, aboriginal interests, environmental groups, commercial, sports or Native fishers—or anybody (other than Alcan) with economic interests in the matter.

If the benefit for Alcan from the KCP was obvious, the payoff for the people of B.C. was not. After a brief flurry of construction activity, just eight permanent jobs would be added to the Alcan payroll. No new industrial activity was planned at Kitimat or elsewhere in the region, and no employment requirement was attached to the agreement. The project in fact threatened thousands of existing jobs—those of the Fraser River-based fishing industry. Justa Monk, chief of the Carrier-Sekani Tribal Council, of which the Cheslatta band is a member, said of the KCP, "First Nations in this area will be sentenced to a slow death of our way of life." Since the KCP power to be sold by Alcan to B.C. Hydro is not presently needed, it would likely move south of the border into the United States. As Pat Moss of the Rivers Defence Coalition put it, "Once more we are trading a Canadian resource for jobs in the United States."

The Settlement Agreement described a series of steps to be taken if fish populations were found to be in trouble. But fisheries experts insisted that most of the technical measures proposed were unproven or had failed in other jurisdictions. Experience soon confirmed their opinions. At hearings into the KCP held by the B.C. Utilities Commission in 1994, Dr. Cole Shirvell of DFO's Pacific Biological Station testified, "Remedial measures tested in the Nechako River since the Settlement Agreement have largely failed. Remedial measures untested in the Nechako but tried elsewhere have either failed or have had negative side-effects on other important aquatic resources. Of the 27 measures alleged by the Nechako River Working Group as able to maintain fish production in the Nechako River at [Alcan's proposed flows], none is certain to work." The Settlement Agreement was running into strong opposition, and the KCP was anything but settled.

The original Kemano project closed off many opportunities for people of the Nechako Valley, and the KCP would surely foreclose many more. The Great Circle water route in Tweedsmuir Park, for instance, would have become a world recreational destination had it not been flooded in the 1950s. Now it is an oscillating reservoir ringed by dead trees, rising and falling over a range of about four metres. The KCP would increase that range to nine metres, drastically reducing the shoreline productivity so important to birds, fish and other animals. Low water levels would cut fish off from the tributaries in which they spawn. Environment ministry personnel feared the KCP would ruin many trails, boat-launch sites and other recreational facilities they reestablished after the original flooding.

Below the Kenney Dam, the KCP would mean a further deterioration of the spectacular canoeing and kayaking for which the Nechako is renowned. Communities were concerned about water supply and the ability of the lowered river to assimilate wastes. Less water in wetlands throughout the region could have serious consequences for spring and fall migrations of geese, swans and a host of other wildlife species. Although salmon were at centre stage in the debate, many of the resident freshwater fish had also been seriously affected by the existing Kemano project, impacts that could only increase in severity with the lower flows of the KCP. For example, the giant white sturgeon, the oldest freshwater fish in the world, lives only in rivers of the Fraser Basin in B.C., and needs cool, deep-water pools to survive.

Agriculture is already threatened by a freeze on irrigation licences through much of the region; with Alcan taking so much more Nechako water, the remainder would have to be reserved for fish. As local rancher

Janet Romain says, "Our children are going to need to irrigate farmland here in the valley. And we aren't going to be able to take the water from the river if there isn't enough water. Opportunity for the children is being dried up along with the river." Downstream on the Fraser, farmers and ranchers feared losing rights to water they were drawing from other Fraser tributaries if less water would be coming down the Nechako. At Prince George, effluent from pulp mills and the city's domestic sewage would be less diluted and more toxic if Nechako flows diminish.

Under pre-KCP conditions 20 per cent of all Fraser River sockeye salmon—hundreds of thousands of fish—turn up the Nechako on their way to spawning grounds in the Stuart River system and in the Nautley River. Some of those spawning beds are 1200 kilometres from the mouth of the Fraser; the sockeye that make the journey are usually older and bigger than other sockeye, so they are particularly prized. Based on the amount of excellent natural but underutilized spawning territory, fishery experts are confident that the Fraser Basin can produce many more salmon than it does at present. The upper limit for sockeye may be about 30 million fish in one year, or three times current average production. Much of this increase could occur in the upper Fraser Basin, of which the Nechako is a vital part. The International Pacific Salmon Fisheries Commission estimated in 1983 that, based on available rearing area, the Nechako-Stuart-Nautley system has the potential to increase its production to 55 per cent of total Fraser River sockeye. But there is growing concern about factors that may limit production. Fisheries biologist Michael Henderson writes that water volumes and temperatures are marginal in some key areas of the upper Fraser; the Nechako-Stuart system is one of these.

When the early Stuart run of sockeye arrives in Stuart Lake in July after a thirty-day trip of 1100 kilometres from the Fraser's mouth, the fish are reaching the limit of their resources. They have not eaten since beginning the long journey, and the supreme effort of spawning still lies ahead. Their remaining energy provides a narrow window of opportunity, a few days at most, in which they either fulfill their destiny or die from exhaustion. Any factor reducing this narrow margin threatens spawning, and water temperature is chief among those factors. Sockeye swim most efficiently at 14 to 15 degrees centigrade; at 18 degrees their energy is rapidly depleted, and at 21.5 they will usually die.

Water temperatures have always been marginal for salmon in the Nechako-Stuart system. Being a shallow river, the Stuart River draws warm water from the top of Stuart Lake, raising water temperatures all the way to the Fraser River. Before the Kenney Dam was built, colder Nechako water cooled the warmer Stuart River water pouring into it, providing a better environment for migrating salmon during the hot days of summer. Fish migrating up the Fraser sometimes tarry at the mouth of the Nechako to get accustomed to its warmer water, but with only a few days of spare energy, the temperature must not be high enough to deter them for long. Once into warmer water, the metabolism of the fish increases, further reducing their available energy.

In 1994 and 1995, UBC biologist Scott Hinch found temperatures running to 21 degrees in the Nechako and a degree warmer in the Stuart—fatal temperatures for sockeye. Hinch theorizes that since the Stuart's flow is very slow, the salmon can get upriver quickly and into the cool, deep water of Stuart Lake. The crucial requirement is to keep the water of the Nechako between the mouth of the Stuart and the Fraser cool enough. That's why the DFO asked Alcan back in the 1950s to build a passage for cold water into the Kenney Dam, and that's why the installation remains essential today. Warmer water from the Cheslatta system makes the situation worse, as does the lower water level in the Nechako itself: the water spreads out across a channel carved for a much larger river, its shallow depths warming in the summer sun. The KCP would only worsen the situation.

And Stuart River water may get warmer for other reasons too: loggers are moving in force into the Stuart-Takla watershed, to the distress of resort owners and Native people in the region. A recognized impact of logging is the warming of groundwater and streams. Scientists led by the DFO's Stephen Macdonald are carrying out a multiyear research project in the watershed aimed at a better understanding of the ecological and physical processes at work in streams of the Interior; they will try to determine precisely how forest practices affect those processes, particularly water temperatures and flows, the survival of salmon eggs and the food supply for young fish. Another factor that may push temperatures closer to the edge in the Fraser Basin is global warming: very high temperatures in the Fraser River in 1994 suggest to some scientists that this phenomenon may already be affecting the river.

Water temperature is now recognized as a key factor in the wellbeing of the entire Fraser River system, in particular its salmon runs. Yet it is just one of many stresses that include level of flow, pollution, fishing pressure, urbanization, dyking, sedimentation from logging and others. Large rivers like the Nechako and the Fraser are extremely resilient, capable of absorbing and recovering from powerful assaults. But that resilience has limits. With each additional stress, the system becomes more vulnerable. If it is driven beyond its "boundary of stability," if a combination of stresses pushes it over a threshold, the system may be radically transformed.

Alcan proposed to control the temperature of the minuscule flows it would allow into the Nechako after construction of the KCP with a complex computer-based system; technology would replace normal ecosystem functions in the Nechako watershed. According to environment Canada, ecosystems can have integrity only if they are "self-sustaining and self-regulating; they must have a full complement of native species that are capable of maintaining population levels; they must have complete food webs; and they must have naturally functioning ecological processes." Even if everything functioned as Alcan hoped it would—if the company could indeed run the river by computer—the Nechako would no longer meet the criteria of ecosystem integrity: it would be neither self-renewing nor self-regulating. Even the most sophisticated technological fix cannot begin to replicate a naturally functioning ecosystem.

After fisheries minister Siddon accepted the Settlement Agreement of 1987, DFO scientists were forbidden to express their views in public. Eighty-five thousand pages of research documents were sealed to prevent public perusal of them. When several federal scientists who had studied the KCP proposal as members of the DFO's Kemano task force retired, they used their freedom to speak out on the issue. Dr. Don Alderdice, Dr. Gordon Hartman and Dr. William Schouwenburg condemned the KCP and the entire secretive process that led to the Settlement Agreement. Then in yet another effort to prevent public examination of the issues, the federal cabinet tried to exempt the KCP from the Environmental Assessment Review Process (EARP).

With the Settlement Agreement in hand, Alcan began construction of the project in 1988. But the battle wasn't over. Native people, conservationists, scientists, fishers and many others tried to force the federal government to carry out the EARP, and a federal court agreed that the cabinet had acted illegally in exempting the KCP. Alcan shut down construction of the tunnel at about the halfway point while the court ruling was challenged. Although the appeal supported the position of the federal cabinet and Alcan, Parliament later concluded that the cabinet had indeed acted illegally.

Elections in the early 1990s overturned governments in Victoria and Ottawa. The KCP was an issue during election campaigns in which both the NDP in B.C. and the federal Liberals promised an open review of the project. But because their predecessors had signed the 1987 Settlement Agreement giving Alcan a green light to begin construction, both new governments were terrified of being stuck with the bill for work already completed—at a cost, said Alcan, of over $500 million. So the B.C.

government commissioned an analysis of the project by lawyer Murray Rankin. Rankin's report is noteworthy because it became, for a time, the basis of government policy on the KCP, and because it represents the kind of reasoning that has led to the current crisis in the Fraser Basin.

Rankin recommended that the government approve completion of the KCP, from which, he stated, "there are undeniable benefits to be derived by all B.C. residents and B.C. Hydro customers." He went on: "Some well-informed critics strongly believe that there may be significant impacts upon fisheries, aboriginal rights, agriculture, tourism and recreation. Nevertheless, this report concluded that the economic benefits will far outweigh potential costs, even on worst-case projections . . . The Kemano Completion Project may visit detrimental environmental consequences on a small region of the Province while benefiting the provincial population as a whole." In fact, benefits from the KCP would mainly accrue to Alcan and, to a lesser extent, to B.C. Hydro, at the same time exposing the entire Nechako-Stuart-Fraser River system to well-documented environmental and economic risks—risks that extend to fisheries dependent upon Fraser River salmon along the length of the B.C. coast.

Rankin spent pages pondering whether the people who have lived in the Nechako Valley for 10,000 years have any rights to the land, but he had no doubts whatever about the right of a transnational corporation to reverse most of the flow of a great river. He worried about discouraging investment in the province, yet showed little concern for the people of the Fraser Basin who would have to live with the consequences of the KCP. Unable to assess the cost of environmental destruction, in the tradition of such analysis he simply dismissed it. Rankin grossly undervalued the current and future value of the fishery and its essential role in the life of the entire Fraser Basin.

Rankin told the government that it would be unthinkable not to proceed with the KCP because so much money has already been spent on the project. But nature has taken millions of years to create the species and ecosystems upon which life in the Nechako and Fraser watersheds depends, and to which Rankin assigned no value. Simon Fraser University criminologist and avid steelhead fisherman Ehor Boyanowsky suggests that a river should be valued at its replacement cost, in keeping with modern insurance practices. "Ask yourself, 'What is the replacement cost of a river?' " says Boyanowsky. "What would it cost to build such a river with its twists and turns and quality of water, its fish and wildlife habitat, the various species that have evolved there over hundreds of thousands of years, and its importance to the ecology of its valley? No corporation, regardless of how grand, could afford to build even one major river. That is the true value when determining the cost of diversion."

The Rankin report was the sort of conventional economic analysis that, if followed, would degrade the Fraser Basin stream by stream, valley by valley, until its incredible wealth and productivity were reduced to pathetic remnants. But the report and the KCP itself were facing a new social landscape. The Cheslatta people had developed an astonishing capacity for research and public relations; from their band office at Grassy Plains they sent out a constant stream of information to media and everyone interested in their cause. Chief Marvin Charlie, his councillors and staff turned up at meetings, rallies and conferences wherever the issue was to be discussed. The Rivers Defence Coalition, chaired by Pat Moss, coordinated the environmental campaign against the KCP, joined by local groups such as "A River Forever" and most environmental organizations across the province and nationally. Individual citizens like Ben Meisner of Prince George threw themselves into the battle with considerable effect, and the story of the KCP and the Nechako became the focus of many journalists on radio, in TV and newspapers.

The B.C. government accepted Rankin's recommendations for a while. It initiated hearings before the British Columbia Utilities Commission (BCUC) in 1994, at which Alcan justified its proposals, supported by officials of the DFO who had been involved in the Settlement Agreement of 1987. The KCP was roundly condemned by scientists, citizens and organizations whose concerns ranged from Native affairs to fisheries to agriculture to the environment and recreation. The BCUC, instructed by the government to assume the KCP would proceed, found that the proposed flow could not protect the fishery or agriculture and would compromise many other uses of the river.

Just over a month after receiving the BCUC's report, Premier Mike Harcourt announced on January 23, 1995, that the Kemano Completion Project would not be allowed to proceed. "The Fraser River system is the heart and soul of British Columbia," Harcourt said, "and home to the world's richest salmon-producing waters . . . it's important that this river system and its fish are protected today and for our children tomorrow." An enormous threat to the future of the Fraser Basin had been averted, though ahead lay years of negotiation as Alcan tried to exact as much compensation as possible from the people of B.C. And as the report of the Fraser River Sockeye Public Review Board in 1995 emphasized, "cancellation of the Kemano Completion Project does not restore original river conditions. To what degree arrangements can be made at the [Kenney] dam site to restore river conditions for salmon stocks remains to be seen . . ."

A Nechako Basin spared the impact of industrial mega-projects has enormous economic potential. The natural beauty of the lakes region is astounding, and tourism potential throughout the area is endless. Appreciation for a productive freshwater fishery can only increase; growing markets for salmon and farm products are inevitable. A productive agriculture, community-based sustainable forestry and a wide range of wood-based, value-added products could provide a lot of employment. Jobs and entrepreneurial possibilities for British Columbians will abound in the Nechako Valley and the upper Fraser Basin generally if the interests of its people, resources and environment are given pride of place over that of distant corporations.

The Cheslatta people were not waiting for the rehabilitation of their lake to begin the long road back to self-sufficiency and the recovery of their traditions. In the summer of 1993 young people of the band were learning the skills needed to undertake guiding and tourism projects in the beautiful valley of Cheslatta Lake. At a camp on the lakeshore, experienced guide-outfitters Harve and Dian Eggleston provided instruction in horsemanship and all the other skills required to assure the comfort and enjoyment of visitors to the valley. Elders like George Louis and Minnie Peters helped them understand their history and culture, and the meaning to the Cheslatta of each stream, island, hill and historic settlement. As the young people talked around a table, and the mountain slopes turned pink in the evening sun, it was evident that new hope was being kindled in their lives. Although they hadn't been born when the village on this site was burned by Alcan more than forty years ago, they've lived with the consequences of the uprooting and displacement of their people.

This 1993 redevelopment project, which the Cheslatta called "A New Beginning," was to create at least thirty-five new jobs based on the primeval beauty of their valley, its lakes and streams. Yet the program did not follow through in succeeding years because Cheslatta Lake is still the sluiceway used by Alcan to direct water from the reservoir into the Nechako River. Water levels rise and fall suddenly, flooding boat ramps and campsites; the water at such times may be dark with silt and laden with debris. It is not yet an environment into which guests can be invited for a wilderness experience.

Although a moratorium has been placed on logging in the valley of Cheslatta Lake, gigantic clearcuts have advanced to the surrounding heights of land. Logging roads bring outside hunters, and the region's wildlife has been decimated. The people are convinced that a new mine planned for the shores of the Nechako Reservoir, the Huckleberry, threatens water quality and a large block of land they have traditionally used. The basis for hope for the Cheslatta people is the land and the water; if despoilation of these resources by outsiders continues, their future is not bright. Ironically, the short-term hopes of the Cheslatta people in the summer of 1996 depended upon a contract for cutting and removing trees drowned decades earlier in the Nechako Reservoir.

The future of the Nechako remains in doubt. The December 1994 report of the B.C. Utilities Commission emphasized the necessity of installing a cold-water release in the Kenney Dam to improve the environment for salmon in the Nechako and to start the rehabilitation of the Cheslatta Valley. In January 1995, the provincial government announced its intention to begin discussions of the release facility with Alcan and the federal government. By mid-1996, nothing had happened. Alcan's only movement seems to be a successful public relations effort to convince the people of Kitimat and Kemano that somehow they were victimized by the cancellation of the KCP. In fact, Alcan still generates up to 35 per cent more power than required by the industrial facilities of Kitimat. But the company has persuaded some people in Kitimat that aluminum smelting is subsidized by power sales, an unlikely corporate practice.

As a former DFO scientist on the Kemano task force, fisheries biologist Gordon Hartman knows intimately the issues involved in the KCP. He had retired when the federal government silenced its scientists, so he was one of the few DFO experts able to speak out publicly. While compensation negotiations between Alcan and governments proceeded behind closed doors in 1996, Hartman called for a totally new vision for the Nechako system, in which Alcan would be one of a community of users of the river, not its proprietor. Alcan could continue to divert the water required for industrial activity at Kitimat; after that, fish and downstream users would have first call on Nechako water, and every effort would be made to return the Nechako to a state as nearly natural as possible.

The biggest challenge in the Nechako and the upper Fraser, says Hartman, is understanding and dealing with the cumulative effects on the river of all human activities. Lower flows, higher water temperatures, more sediment from logging and higher concentration of pollutants—such changes in a river are complex and difficult to handle in themselves, but together they can create what biologist Henry Regier calls a "multiple stress syndrome," whose impact will be unpredictable, but probably severe. Recognizing and addressing cumulative impacts will be crucial to the sustainability of the Fraser River.

CHAPTER 4

A Province Built on Gold

*It seems clear beyond possibility of argument that any given
generation of men can have only a lease, not ownership, of the earth;
and one essential term of the lease is that the earth be handed on to
the next generation with unimpaired potentialities.*

RODERICK HAIG-BROWN, *MEASURE OF THE YEAR*

The Fraser River flows directly south from Prince George. Broad,
smooth and swift, the river seeks a break in the ramparts of the Coast
Mountains, an opening through which it can finally reach the Pacific
Ocean. That was Alexander Mackenzie's goal too as he drifted south in
1793, but only 25 kilometres below the mouth of the Nechako River he
and his companions faced the white water of Fort George Canyon. The
rapids were impassable for their frail and battered canoe, forcing a difficult portage over a rocky hill. The men were cheered a little by finding
wild onions growing abundantly on the riverbank. The onions made the
dreary and unchanging menu of pemmican more palatable, but even this
became a problem: Mackenzie wrote in his journal that the onion-
sharpened appetites of his men were cutting too deeply into their dwindling provisions.

After Fort George Canyon, Mackenzie was ready to heed warnings
by Native people that much worse awaited anyone foolish enough to
continue downstream. Since his goal lay to the west, the river's south-
erly course didn't seem too helpful anyway. So with his eight companions he abandoned the Fraser and pushed up the West Road River, a
tributary usually known today as the Blackwater. Guided and supplied
by local Natives, Mackenzie crossed the Chilcotin Plateau following a
"grease trail," one of the trade routes over which coastal people transported the highly prized oil rendered from the small, fat-rich oolichan
that annually throng up coastal streams.

The little party made its way through the Coast Mountains and down into the lush forests of the Bella Coola Valley. They were welcomed by local Native people and guided down the salt water of Bentinck Arm to Dean Channel. Here they were confronted by a hostile group from Bella Bella who apparently had not appreciated a recent experience with other white men in their territory. Just forty-nine days earlier, a cutter from Capt. George Vancouver's *Discovery* had made its way into the channel while charting the Pacific coastline. Before retreating hastily to safer terrain, Mackenzie wrote in letters of reddened bear grease on the rock face above his camp: "Alexander Mackenzie, from Canada, by land, the twenty-second of July, one thousand seven hundred and ninety-three." He was the first European to cross the North American continent. Although the Fraser and its tributaries had been crucial to his success, he had no idea that the great river he had abandoned was unknown to white travellers; he still believed it to be the Columbia.

Fifteen years after Mackenzie's epic journey, Simon Fraser and his men set off down the Fraser from Fort George. It was May 28, 1808, and they too believed they were descending the Columbia River. For a while they floated south through limitless fire-born forests rising gently from the river to clothe a vast plateau in green. The landscape was very different from the rainforest upstream in the Robson Valley. Fraser wrote in his journal, "The country all along is charming, and apparently well inhabited; having seen a large number of houses . . . This country, which is interspersed with meadows and hills, dales and high rocks, has upon the whole a romantic but pleasant appearance." Not a bad description of the land today.

Relatively flat and stone-free land extends south from Prince George almost to Quesnel, west to Vanderhoof and east towards McBride. This is one of the few places in British Columbia where mountains are not a dominant feature. When the ice that covered B.C. began to retreat about 13,000 years ago, melt water remained here for a very long time, dammed into a huge lake by glacial barriers. The heavy clay soil of that ancient lake's bottom, more than 400 000 hectares of it, can be farmed if a lot of organic matter is worked in. Like clay-belt lands across mid-Canada, this soil may someday play a more important role in food production, particularly if the trend to a warmer global climate persists.

The ice that once extended over all of B.C. and much of Canada was the greatest force in the creation of the Canadian landscape. Ice and glacial moraines dammed and even diverted the flow of Fraser Basin waters in directions quite different from those we know today. At various times, water from the Fraser drained northward into the Peace River and Arctic Ocean from a divide somewhere in the vicinity of Riske Creek. Much later, after the recent ice age ended 10,000 years ago, a dam of ice some 1050-metres thick near Dog Creek temporarily diverted Fraser water east into Kamloops Lake and south through the Okanagan Valley into the Columbia River. After a warmer climate melted glaciers back to their last holdouts in the mountains, flowing water replaced ice as the most powerful element in the creation of the face of the land.

In early September 1862, a weary band of Overlanders drifted south into the northern fringes of the vast, mythic land just beginning to be known as "the Cariboo." At first, Cariboo referred mainly to the goldfields of the Quesnel River region. Named for the woodland caribou that roamed its hills and valleys, the Cariboo still today has no fixed boundaries: where it begins and ends depends upon whom you ask. Most broadly, the region is considered to span 200 to 300 kilometres of high, rolling plateau between the Coast Mountains to the west and the Cariboo Mountains to the east. It extends about 300 kilometres south from Quesnel to Cache Creek or Ashcroft. West of the river lies the Chilcotin, reaching across the Fraser Plateau to the Coast Mountains. The Chilcotin is a region separate and distinct to some, a section of the Cariboo to others. "Cariboo-Chilcotin" is commonly used to clearly encompass the entire area.

    The Fraser River carried these Overlanders through forests stretching unbroken to the northern horizon. The mantle of green rose to the east over the Quesnel Highlands until broken by the rocky core of the Cariboo Mountains. To the south and west of this vast region, sunbrowned grasslands roll into blue distance, creased by fast-flowing streams. This great interior plateau can be an unforgiving land of summer heat and bitter winter cold, yet it is home to vast wildlife populations: grizzly and black bears, mountain caribou, moose, wolves, mountain sheep and goats, and birds in dazzling variety. From snowy summits flow streams and rivers to fill deep lakes reflecting the clear sky of early fall; then they flow on to nourish the land before merging with the Fraser River slicing south across the great plateau. In return for these waters gathered from east and west, the Fraser offers millions of spawning salmon, whose offspring will grow for a while in the lakes of the Cariboo before descending to the faraway ocean.

    For the Overlanders, Cariboo meant gold—gold in such quantities that reports and rumours had drawn them from distant homes and enabled them to endure extraordinary hardship. Now, as their battered rafts grated on gravel where the Quesnel River sweeps into the Fraser, their excitement was palpable. In 1862, this juncture was the point of departure for the last 100 kilometres of the journey to the fabled goldfields. On September 11, R. B. McMicking wrote in his journal, "Got to the mouth of Quesnel at 2:25 P.M. where there is abundance of provisions, there being two stores and eating houses and other little buildings, Indian huts etc. Flour $50, salt $1 a pound . . . The day was very fine and pleasant. I got my supper off a table, the first time in four months, at Whitehall store for $1.50."

But jubilation faded as the Overlanders watched a steady stream of disillusioned miners struggle through Quesnel, men for whom the dream of Cariboo gold had brought only tribulation and misery. Reality was not easy to face, and all the next day the Overlanders debated their options. Exhausted by months of arduous travel, with winter imminent in the high goldfields, most decided to abandon the dream at least for the winter. They continued down the Fraser and on to Victoria. Some actually did walk to the mining country at Barkerville where they found that for a fortunate few the wealth of the Cariboo was real, even fabulous. But with provisions in short supply they too were forced to travel down to the coast before winter set in.

The Overlanders had descended the Fraser from the north, but they were the exceptions. Almost all other gold seekers had come upriver from the south. Indeed, the gold rush in its initial stages had been mainly confined to sandbars and creeks along the Fraser, sifted and fought over by throngs of men, most of them from the United States. James Douglas, the first governor of the new colony of British Columbia, reported to his London superiors that with a few exceptions they were "the worst of the population of San Francisco; the very dregs, in fact, of society." In the summer of 1858, 30,000 men had struggled up the Fraser; before long most of the gold had been worked out of the sandbars, and the rush was being called a fraud by men disappointed in their dreams of instant wealth. At least 25,000 of them were gone within a year. Most departed defeated and impoverished, but others drowned in the wilder reaches of the Fraser Canyon, succumbed to sickness or died from wounds suffered in skirmishes with Natives who resented this invasion of their lands and the murder and mistreatment of their people. As the white men moved on, many Chinese miners replaced them on the bars; with meticulous work they managed to extract considerable wealth from discarded tailings.

As word of invading hordes coming up the Fraser reached Native people in the Cariboo, concern mounted. When aboriginal nations met in the summer of 1859 at traditional intertribal games at Lac la Hache, Chief Dehtus Anahiem of the Ts'ilhqot'in (Chilcotin) people advocated an alliance with neighbouring Secwepemc (Shuswap) and Carrier to deny these strangers entry into their land. In his Cariboo history, Robin Skelton quotes eyewitness accounts: " 'We must keep these white men out,' Chief Anahiem said. 'We tribes must act together. If we do not act immediately, we will only have to drive them out later. This will result in much bloodshed, for them and also for our own people. We must act now or we are lost.' "

Other chiefs agreed that the menace was real, but they refused to go to war. Chief LooLoo of the Carrier was convinced that the white man's "numbers, his guns, his learning and his craftiness" meant Natives could not win in any confrontation. " 'We will not join forces in this useless war,' " he announced. Chief Williams of the Shuswap at Williams Lake agreed. According to Skelton, "Chief Williams said it would be better to trade with the strangers than kill them, for a massacre would be quite useless. However many were killed, there would be more following. It would be like the salmon run. They would come up the river in their thousands." The nations assembled at Lac la Hache finally agreed with this view, and the 1859 meeting ended most threats of war between Natives and miners. It was an important turning point in B.C.'s history; had Chief Anahiem prevailed, the gold rush may have been a bloody affair. Instead, many aboriginal people traded with the miners and guided them, and some young women married them.

But peacemaking did little for Chief Williams or his people. White men moved into their valley, took their land for farms and established the village that would become the city of Williams Lake. In 1862 two-thirds of the band, including Chief Williams, died of smallpox. The survivors, led by the chief's son, known also as Chief Williams, were forced off their land to wander homeless for decades. In 1879 he wrote to the *Colonist* newspaper in Victoria, "The land on which my people lived for 500 years was taken by a white man; he has piles of wheat and herds of cattle. We have nothing—not an acre." Only in 1884 was a tract of 1640 hectares finally set aside for the Williams Lake Band.

During the summer of the momentous 1859 meeting at Lac la Hache, a group of Americans were led by an aboriginal man to the Horsefly River, a tributary of the Quesnel. His story of gold "like beans in a pan" turned out to be true. It was the first important discovery in the Cariboo, and word of it flashed through that rugged country where not even rudimentary communications existed. By 1860 miners were plodding up other creeks of the Quesnel River system, and at the confluence of the Quesnel and Cariboo Rivers the first gold rush town took shape. From there, Americans "Doc" Keithley and George Weaver pushed farther into the mountains, exploring rivulets cascading from mountain tops through wooded valleys and rocky canyons. They discovered gold in a creek they called Keithley flowing into Cariboo Lake, and though it wasn't a huge producer, this stream turned out to be the gateway to the fabulous riches of the Cariboo. Nearby creeks and lakes yielded enough gold to support a new town at the creek's mouth, and by the fall of 1860 miners were pouring gold into the gambling saloons of Keithley.

But all this wasn't enough for Keithley and Weaver; later that fall they set off up Keithley Creek and worked their way to the mountain-top divide. Unknown streams flowed north, east and west to the Fraser River across a landscape of mountain peaks, deep forested ravines, canyons and rock slides. Pushing along the summit, the miners settled on a creek flowing north down a narrow valley flanked by alluvial deposits on benches and flats. Their very first attempts yielded gold; some lay shining in the sun and much more could be seen in the bedrock not far below the surface. It was the biggest strike in the Cariboo. Attempts to keep the site secret were futile, and when the snow melted, 1,200 miners were digging the creek bed, with thousands more pouring into the country. Here on Antler Creek another instant town sprang up; by midsummer it boasted sixty houses and performances by touring theatrical groups. Champagne was sold in ten saloons, newly rich miners were just as quickly impoverished in casinos, while others imported racehorses from England to run on the town's new track.

And still the action moved on. William "Dutch Bill" Dietz and some companions crossed a mountain ridge from Antler Creek where, one story goes, he slipped in an unknown creek and fell flat on his back. Regaining his feet, he sluiced the stream's gravel in his pan. Gold! His appreciative friends named the creek "Williams," staked their claims and almost immediately the valley was filled with miners loading their sluices with gravel as fast as they could dig. The payoff wasn't as great as expected until a miner named Jourdan dug through the hard, blue clay others supposed to be bedrock. With his partner he dug as much as 18 kilograms of gold a day. Other claims turned out to be even richer, but sadly, Dutch Bill's claim turned out to be one of the poorest on the creek.

Miners swarmed over the Cariboo that summer, abandoning one find in hopes of a richer one, stampeding to the latest strike when rumours raced along the creeks. Towns materialized overnight, but their stores, saloons, houses and hotels were abandoned just as quickly. Merchants, packers, blacksmiths, barbers, bakers, barroom dancers and prostitutes followed the mobile miners from strike to strike.

Among the men who fought their way up the treacherous trails to the Cariboo in the spring of 1862 was an English sailor named Billy Barker. Seeing so much goldfield wealth pouring into Victoria where his vessel was docked, Barker jumped ship and joined the rush. When

the stocky sailor with a greying black beard and bowed legs arrived at
Williams Creek he found the rich land above Stout's Gulch completely
taken. Experienced miners agreed there was no hope of finding gold
below it. But Barker figured the creek had long ago diverted into a
new course; if he could find the old riverbed, he should find gold too.
So he staked a claim and with some partners started digging. Deeper
than any other shafts had gone they found nothing, but still Barker per-
severed until at 15.5 metres he struck gold—lots of it. Miners rushed in
to stake claims all around the Barker shaft, about 3,000 of them along
just 11 kilometres of Williams Creek. In 1863 4,000 miners churned
through the gravel and clay of Williams Creek alone, taking more gold
from it than the California gold rush yielded in its heyday.

The intrepid English travellers, Dr. Walter B. Cheadle and Viscount
Milton, arrived in Barkerville in October 1863 when the town was at
its raucous height. There were probably more than 10,000 people living
and working along Williams Creek that year, and Barkerville was
claimed to be "the biggest city west of Chicago and north of San Francisco." Cheadle described making his way through the town: "Our path
was a difficult one over endless sluices, flumes and ditches, across icy
planks and logs, all getting tumbles, gumboots being very treacherous."
He portrayed with considerable humour and some wonder the extraordinary society of Barkerville—a mix of characters from around the
world thrown together in an ambience where euphoria alternated with
despair.

Since supplies had to be hauled in over the abominable Cariboo
trails on the backs of mules, prices in the goldfields were astronomical,
often a hundred times those paid in Victoria. It was obvious to Governor Douglas that the potential of the Cariboo and the stable settlement
of the new colony could not be realized without better means of travel
and transportation. In 1861 he ordered surveying and construction of a
new wagon road 5.4 metres wide through the Fraser Canyon and north
to the Cariboo. The road was completed by 1863 to Soda Creek, 120
kilometres south of Quesnel, where the Fraser River once again
became navigable. Sternwheelers built on the site hauled miners and
freight upstream to Quesnel, from where the last stretch of road to
Barkerville was completed in 1865. As historian Art Downs notes in
Wagon Road North, "Considering that the permanent population of the
colony was under 7,000, the project was a stupendous undertaking."

The Cariboo Road was pressed into use even before it was finished.
Soon trains of freight wagons pulled by a dozen or more oxen or horses
lumbered along it; stage coaches pulled by half-broken horses dashed
between the roadhouses that sprang up every 15 to 25 kilometres along

the road. Named for their distance from Lillooet or from Ashcroft, several survived to become towns like 100 Mile House, 150 Mile House and 70 Mile House. Tales of the roadhouses range from raves about gargantuan meals of superb food to an entry in Cheadle's diary about his stop with Milton on the trail from Quesnel to Barkerville: "Awful night last night; wind blowing thro' cracks in walls & floor; only one blanket apiece; 20 men in room; one afflicted with cramp in his leg which brought him on his feet swearing every ½ hour. Milton & another talking in their sleep; rest snoring. My nose running; little sleep." Here and there remnants of the old Cariboo Road can still be discerned. Cottonwood House, east of Quesnel, is one of few roadhouses to survive, and is now a historic park.

The remarkably good photographs of the time show Barkerville and other Cariboo gold rush towns to be collections of ramshackle buildings thrown up as close as possible to mine workings. Utter desolation of the landscape is the most striking feature. As far as the eye can see every tree has been chopped down to construct buildings, dams, mine shafts, pit props and flumes, and waterwheels to pump water from the shafts. The gold-bearing creeks appear to be destroyed, and the amount of suffocating sediment that engulfed salmon spawning grounds downstream can only be imagined. Of Williams Creek, a contemporary observer named Byron Johnson wrote:

> The unfortunate little stream had been treated in the most ignominious manner. A little above the town it flowed along silvery and clear as it had been wont to do; but soon inroads were made upon its volume in the shape of ditches cut from it, and continued along the sides of the hills, to feed the huge over-shot water-wheels that appeared in all directions. Then its course became diverted into five or six different channels, which were varied every now and then as the miners sought to work the surface formerly covered by them. At intervals dirty streams were poured forth by the sluices, in which the earth dug from beneath was being washed by the water; and here and there the stream was insulted by being shut up for a few hundred yards in a huge wooden trough called a 'flume.'

Barkerville was the only settlement to survive along the gold creeks of the Cariboo. Burned to the ground in September 1868, the town was immediately rebuilt in a flurry of optimism with finer buildings, better spacing and at least a semblance of planning. But with most accessible gold exhausted, the richest days of Williams Creek were over. Gradually people moved away and the town declined. When author Bruce Hutchison visited in 1921, he described Barkerville as a "desolate jumble of shacks . . . cramped between Williams Creek and a naked hill." The single-minded scrabble for wealth had left it "a sterile valley." But many of the abandoned structures survived the decades that followed and in 1958, to mark the centenary of British Columbia, Barkerville was designated a provincial park. Restoration began and today, in much greater numbers than at the height of the gold rush, people from around the world once again make their way to Barkerville—almost 200,000 each year. Now however, they bring "gold" with them rather than carrying it away.

The gold rush was much more than a long-ago drama of greed and courage, desperation and heroism, incredible hardship and bursts of outrageous celebration played out against a backdrop of rugged Fraser River wilderness. The gold rush was in fact the explosive beginning of modern British Columbia. To head off expansionist American ambitions that might follow the flood of miners from the United States, the colony of British Columbia was proclaimed in 1858, ending the long reign of the Hudson's Bay Company over the vast region known until then as New Caledonia. Not long after, the new colony would become a province of the Dominion of Canada.

The impact of the gold rush on the original inhabitants of the Fraser Basin was instantaneous and disastrous. In a single year a horde of strangers greater than the Fraser's entire aboriginal population swarmed up the river. Within two or three years these foreigners had pushed Native people off much of the land that they had occupied freely for millennia. Aboriginal people were confined to minuscule reservations with none of the rights given newcomers to acquire land; soon they would even be deprived of the right to fish for the Fraser River salmon that were the basis of their life and culture. Disease carried by the invaders wiped out entire villages, and in many surviving communities the culture that had given meaning to their lives collapsed.

The gold rush forced rapid creation of new systems of justice, transportation and communication. Many of the settlements it spawned, from New Westminster to Quesnel, are important centres today; the Cariboo Road that linked them became a highway that remains the "main street" of the Cariboo. The names of lakes, streams, mountains, towns and roads recall participants in the events of that extraordinary epoch. Many who came for gold found quite different reasons to stay, becoming farmers, ranchers, merchants and tradesmen, or simply doing the work that had to be done, from labouring on roads to driving stage coaches, freight wagons and pack trains. Many stayed on in the Cariboo simply because they couldn't afford to leave. In that brief, chaotic period called the Cariboo Gold Rush, bold outlines of the British Columbia we know today were sketched on the province's landscape and society. Along the banks of the Fraser River, its tributaries and its high mountain creeks, legends of those extraordinary days will long survive.

The journey to Barkerville is very different today from that described by Walter Cheadle. East of Quesnel the paved highway rises and falls in growing sweeps as it approaches the Cariboo Mountains and the streams tortured by miners to yield the gold hidden in their beds. A few hand-lettered signs suggest old dreams still linger: "For Sale—Gold Leases," "The Long Shot Gold Prospectors," "The Diggings."

As the rolling, tree-clad hills of the Quesnel Highlands swell higher, signs of a more recent and much larger "gold rush" become evident. Green slopes are replaced by denuded hillsides, clearcut to supply the stream of trucks piled with logs that labour westward to feed the pulp and sawmills of Quesnel. Such traffic is a sight common to roads throughout the Cariboo, where the forest industry dominates the economy, landscape and communities of the region. But instead of a multitude of individuals attracted by gold fever, the rush for timber is dominated by giant transnational corporations, following a tradition established by the fur trade in which the resources of the Fraser Basin were first exploited by corporate outsiders.

Since the arrival of Europeans, logging has been a part of the Cariboo way of life. Creek valleys were stripped of trees by miners needing logs to reinforce mining structures; with whip-sawn lumber they built instant towns as the land was settled; long, slender lodgepole pines enclosed cattle and horses in corrals and fences still typical of the Cariboo landscape. Logs housed and warmed generations of Cariboo residents, and sod roofs on abandoned cabins still grow green after a rain. Some of the Cariboo's finest houses are built of logs even today.

Hundreds of small logging operations and mills sprouted along the Fraser River and its tributaries when lumber markets exploded during World War Two. The Pacific Great Eastern Railway, now B.C. Rail, extended its reach to Prince George soon after the fighting ended, creating access to markets around the world. The forest industry of British Columbia was quickly concentrated in the hands of fewer, larger corporations, which were granted logging rights over vast areas.

The awarding of valuable public resources to corporations at essentially no cost is a highly political process. In B.C., it has seen one minister of forests wind up in jail, and another, Claude Richmond, leave office to chair a forest industry lobby group. Mike Apsey, the deputy minister of forests who decreed extremely favourable terms for corporate exploitation in 1981, moved on to become (and remain to the present day) president of the Council of Forest Industries (COFI). The most powerful corporate timber group in B.C., COFI largely dictated provincial forest policy in the 1980s, with many of its recommendations for reduced regulation implemented by the Social Credit governments of the day. In 1987 the same government was preparing to turn most remaining public forest lands over to large corporations as tree farm licences at no cost—essentially privatizing the public forests—when public protest finally slowed the juggernaut.

As big timber corporations moved into the Interior in the 1970s, they built pulp mills and large, efficient sawmills, taking over and shutting down small operators and many of the smaller communities that depended on them. Six of those pulp mills are in the Fraser Basin; five of them draw wood from the Cariboo-Chilcotin and from Fraser watersheds upstream. Prince George, Quesnel, Williams Lake and 100 Mile House prospered, growing rapidly from frontier towns into attractive modern communities.

The corporations convinced governments that the prosperity of these communities would be dependent on easy access to huge volumes of wood. So the allowable annual cut of B.C. forests, supposedly a permanently sustainable amount, was increased from 25 to 75 million cubic metres to give the companies the wood they needed to feed the new mills. The B.C. Forest Service justified the amounts the companies could harvest by including in their calculations trees of small size, poor quality and in marginal locations. Even more imaginative calculations in the 1980s projected a "sustainable" annual cut of 120 million cubic metres by the year 2020, rising to 160 million a few decades later. Not surprisingly, the committee of the Science Council of B.C. that came up with that report was chaired by the president of COFI. Such blue-sky projections were based on inventories that were scandalously inadequate—in 1991, the Forest Resources Commission reported to the provincial government that "the current state of inventory information is a disgrace, given the importance of all renewable forest resources to the people of British Columbia." The B.C. Forest Service did not, in fact, know how much wood was growing in the Cariboo when it awarded extensive cutting rights to the corporations that now dominate the region.

As Richard Gook cooks supper in a Cariboo Mountain valley, he looks beyond his tent to Ghost Lake, its ripples reflecting the gold of the evening sun. Below him, Matthew River tumbles out of the lake in a sparkling waterfall. Above, Mount Matthew towers more than 2500 metres, leading a ridge of mountains from icefields 20 kilometres to the east. The mountains force vapour-laden air from the Pacific up to heights where clouds can hold water no longer. Rain and snow fall heavily onto these slopes and into these valleys, up to 2000 millimetres of precipitation each year. Snow often accumulates three or four metres deep. Like parts of the Robson Valley, this is B.C.'s interior wet belt where luxuriant forests grow trees exceeded in size only by the giants of the coastal rainforest. West from the mountains across the rolling Quesnel Highlands to the Cariboo Plateau, smaller trees, mainly lodgepole pine and white spruce, grow on drier land. Douglas fir dominates in the more arid landscape of the southern Cariboo and across the Fraser in Chilcotin valleys, with the rich, red bark and long needles of ponderosa pines gracing lower, hotter valleys. This is rangeland as well as timber country, where bluebunch wheatgrass nourishes the cattle of the fabled ranches of the Cariboo.

Here in the mountains, Richard Gook's campsite on Ghost Lake is still hot as the sun drops in the west. There is no shade. Vast clearcuts have stripped the mountain slopes rising from Matthew River right to the shores of the lake. In places, small planted trees of tomorrow's fibre farms march up hills in orderly rows. Some day, perhaps, pines planted on the burned-over landscape will offer some shade to the campsite; many years after that, when they are eighty or one hundred years old but still far too young to reconstitute a mature forest, they will be cut and hauled off to mills in Quesnel or Williams Lake.

This evening, even the clearcuts and lack of shade cannot diminish the contentment Gook feels when he contemplates the beauty of lake, river, mountain and forested slopes that still exist farther down the lake. His weathered features reflect a lifetime in this rugged and spectacular country, which he first explored in 1937, leading a packhorse over a mountain pass and down to Cariboo Lake. Years ago he climbed to the top of Matthew Mountain; from that lofty perch the forests still washed unbroken across the undulating plateau and up the slopes of the Cariboo Mountains. Now, says Gook, loggers are shearing the Cariboo Mountains from this side to feed the mills at Williams Lake and Quesnel, and from the other side to supply mills at Kamloops and Valemount. But he doesn't spend a lot of time on regrets—except, perhaps, when he fondly recalls a long-gone hotel at Keithley Creek where excellent meals were served on china and white linen for sixty-five cents. Self-contained with truck, tent and canoe, Gook still floats the superb rivers of the Cariboo, catches rainbow trout, camps by lakes far from the usual tourist trails, a man at one with the magnificent land in which he has lived most of his life.

The clear, fresh water that means so much to Richard Gook is the

essence of the Cariboo Mountains, and a treasure bestowed upon the
Fraser Basin. The lakes of the Cariboo—there are about 5,000 of
them—are the crown jewels of central British Columbia. A few kilometres east of Barkerville, eleven of the lakes form a rough parallelo-
gram connected by streams, sloughs and portages. This is one of the
world's great wilderness canoe circuits; it has been protected since 1961
as Bowron Lake Provincial Park, named for John Bowron, one of the
Overlanders of 1862.

Yellow canoes are drawn up on a sandy beach at Bowron Lake this
August afternoon. The deep blue water reflects the warm sun, the lake's
surface is uncreased by boats. But there are actually about 400 people
paddling in Bowron Lake Park today, making their way over portages
and down streams that link the lakes into a 116-kilometre circle tour. In
the campground near park headquarters a few canoeists check their
equipment once more; others have found a shady spot to read. They're
awaiting their turn on the lakes; the exhilarating natural glory of the
Bowron lakes draws so many canoeists from around the world that
access must be restricted to preserve the quality of the experience. Park
officials allow no more than fifty to set off each day.

Bowron River flows out of Bowron Lake towards the Fraser River
through 50,000 denuded hectares that constitute one of the world's
largest clearcuts. Part of the cut was considered necessary to control
bark beetle infestations; the procedure was biologically dubious and has
seriously distorted the economy of the Cariboo. The flood of "beetle
wood" encouraged the building of milling capacity far beyond what
Cariboo forests could feed on a sustainable basis. Forester Ray Travers
explains that "insect and wind and fire and disease are not aberrations
in the forest, they are the way the forest renews itself." This perspective
has been well established in leading-edge science during the past
decade or two, but is ignored in B.C. forest practice where efforts to
impose rigid control on beetle populations create conditions ideal for
much greater future infestations: vast plantations of even-aged trees.

Biologist Otto Langer of the Department of Fisheries and Oceans has
decades of experience in protection and enhancement of salmon habitat
in the Fraser Basin. He describes how the huge Bowron Valley clearcuts
actually changed the local climate, making it warmer and drier. When
spruce trees were replanted, sometimes they couldn't survive—pines
grow best in the new environment. Water in unshaded streams warms in
the hot sun, and heat accumulating in soil and rocks warms even unseen
groundwater, whose coolness is essential to salmon as they emerge from
eggs. Nor is it just in gigantic clearcuts like the Bowron that water in
Fraser tributaries is heated by current logging practices. Scientists at

UBC's Westwater Research Centre have found increases in water temperatures from logging reported in streams throughout the Fraser Basin.

The gravel road following the Bowron River dwindles and finally ends after about 12 kilometres. Here, bearded trapper Phil Munier guides us past ferocious Labrador huskies he affectionately regards as family. He pours cups of coffee. Munier talks of miners who still sift gold from creeks in these hills. "Gold does strange things to men," Munier says to explain uncommon things that happen hereabouts: two brothers who killed each other, three hunters killed by a grizzly sow after they had killed her cub. There are other haunting stories, and as Munier talks, his deep attachment to the country is evident. He used to operate a trapline, but after logging, the wildlife dwindled and now he hopes to train his huskies to work as a sled team; he plans to guide hunters and wildlife photographers.

In the green water of the Bowron River three red sockeye salmon fan against the current—the first this year, says Munier. He'll be fishing soon for the rainbow trout that come to fatten on salmon eggs. These sockeye last fed in the Strait of Georgia, almost 1000 kilometres downstream. But they won't stop here. They'll travel another few kilometres up the Bowron River to Bowron Lake and then into one of the lake's tributaries, the one in which they were born and where they will spawn and die. Their young will spend a year in Bowron Lake before heading back down the Bowron and Fraser Rivers to the sea.

Quesnel Lake is the Cariboo's biggest, stretching 100 kilometres from east to west with a spectacular and heavily forested arm reaching 49 kilometres to the north. At 530 metres, this is the deepest lake in B.C. and second only to Great Slave Lake in Canada. Quesnel Lake is the heart of a system that gathers water from many streams in the surrounding mountains and valleys, then drains down the Quesnel River to the Fraser. It has the greatest salmon-producing potential of the entire Fraser Basin—in the 1800s runs of more than 10 million sockeye mounted the Quesnel in dominant years. But in 1898, gold miners entirely blocked the Quesnel with a dam stretching 230 metres across the river; no fish passed for two years. Eventually a small fishway was built into the dam allowing a few fish through. Other miners diverted a Quesnel River tributary, the Horsefly, to permit mining in its bed. Volumes of sediment were washed into both rivers from huge operations like the Bullion mine, downstream of the Quesnel dam. John F. Roos, former director of the International Pacific Salmon Fisheries Commission (IPSFC), writes, "It is astonishing that the Quesnel stock survived the Quesnel Lake Dam and placer mining operations." Even today, some of the old mining operations remain unstable and threaten to release quantities of sediment. And fisheries biologists fear that a rise in gold prices might increase placer mining operations in the Cariboo.

Decimated by rock slides in the Fraser Canyon in 1913–14, hammered by overfishing and placer mining before that, the Quesnel sockeye run had dwindled to just over 1,000 fish in 1941. Some people suggested writing off the salmon and developing the river for hydroelectricity. But the IPSFC built fishways in Hell's Gate far downstream and fostered better regulation of the fishery. Spawning channels were also built on the Horsefly River. Stocks began to recover, slowly at first and then spectacularly. In 1989, of 3.1 million sockeye salmon spawning in the entire Fraser Basin, 1.87 million returned to the streams of the Quesnel system, including the Horsefly. Four years later in 1993, more than half the sockeye of the entire Fraser system, 13 million fish, had been produced by the Horsefly—and 3 million of them escaped nets to head upriver to spawn. The big question being asked in the disastrous Fraser salmon year of 1996 was: What will happen when the dominant Horsefly run returns in 1997? Many fishers were convinced the strength of that run would portend the future of the entire Fraser River salmon fishery.

In addition to huge sockeye runs, the Horsefly River supports populations of chinook, coho and pink salmon. Huge rainbow trout, along with lake trout, bull trout, mountain whitefish and kokanee salmon, draw sports fishers from around the world. The key to the health of this entire aquatic system and the vast panoply of life it supports is the forest. Trees clothing the valley slopes influence the amount and pattern of rainfall, determine the rate at which water percolates through vegetation and soil into streams, hold sparse soils of mountain slopes in place, influence the temperature and quality of water and determine the condition of spawning gravels. Water and forest together foster countless complex ecosystems that support life, from the seldom-seen underground community of insects, fungi and multitudes of small creatures, to spectacular animals like caribou, mountain goats, mule deer, moose, grizzly and black bears, to vast populations of birds that nest or pause while migrating to more northerly breeding grounds.

Since trees are such an integral part of life in the Fraser Basin, the manner in which forestry is practised in each watershed and along each tributary stream is part of a cumulative impact on the entire river. Yet until the Forest Practices Code was introduced in 1995, none of the ecological functions of a forest were considered to have any value whatever. The Forest Act of 1978 provides no legal protection for any non-timber values; only the right of logging companies to cut down trees is enshrined in law. As forester Herb Hammond explains in his

1991 book, *Seeing the Forest among the Trees*, it is assumed that the forests belong to the forest industry, and therefore any alternative use of the forests is considered a threat to the timber supply.

Nearly half the land producing commercially useful timber in B.C. lies in the watersheds of the Fraser River; 21 million hectares in the basin are covered by forests, and almost half of that is considered useful for timber harvesting. Much of the wood is in the Cariboo, Chilcotin and Prince George regions. More than a third of the Cariboo's income depends on logging and wood processing, so its communities depend upon sustainable, ecologically sound forestry. Cariboo forests are also of fundamental importance to cattle ranches that rely on forest rangelands. Forests also yield such products as mushrooms, berries and plant parts for medicinal uses. The magnificence of the forest environment draws people from around the world in a large and growing tourism and recreation industry. Increasing numbers are choosing to stay, and as urban congestion grows at the mouth of the Fraser, more people will escape to the open space and clear air of the Cariboo.

Uli Augustin is handcrafting a chalet in the Austrian alpine style. Intricately carved details already ornament some of the logs, reflecting the artistry he also applies to woodblock printing, a skill he learned in his native Germany. Uli and his wife, Corry Lunn, an accomplished sculptor, came to this beautiful place overlooking the Horsefly River to live their dream of a home in the wilderness. But these days in the summer of 1993, a steady stream of heavily loaded logging trucks rolls past their door, hauling logs west to Williams Lake from the headwaters of the Horsefly River high in the Cariboo Mountains. The pace quickened, says Augustin, when talks began that would eventually result in the Cariboo-Chilcotin Land Use Plan. Throughout the Cariboo, environmentalists claim that the best timber in the most sensitive areas is targeted for quick cutting when it appears that planning processes may judge it too sensitive or too valuable for logging.

Augustin can't see the logging from his front yard, but he gets a good indication of what's going on upstream when he swims in a favourite spot in the Horsefly River. "Three years ago," he says, "the water came up to my neck. This year, at the same place the water comes up to my shins. I figure there's about four feet of silt there, covering the salmon spawning gravels." Since the Horsefly is a major contributor to what is potentially the most productive salmon system in the entire Fraser Basin, the silt in Augustin's swimming hole is no small matter. Nor is the impact restricted to salmon. This stretch of the Horsefly is internationally known among fly fishers as one of the best streams in the world for big rainbow trout, which follow the salmon up from Quesnel Lake to gorge on salmon eggs in spawning season. Augustin wrote the district forest manager about the problem, but received no reply.

Travelling farther up the Horsefly River, the source of the silt becomes evident. Lakes stripped to the water line, steep, fragile slopes denuded, streams logged across. Fisheries biologist Bruce McDonald explains that "when you have logging in a watershed, you get more sediment produced. That's a given. It's just a matter of how much." A lot of research shows that logging road construction and clearcutting can increase sediment running into streams by as much as several hundred times normal flows. And logging sediment in upper Fraser streams has been found to decrease the survival of salmon fry by 30 per cent. The logging companies responsible pay no compensation for these losses to the fishery, though under the Forest Practices Code roads are required to be properly engineered for minimal impact and deactivated when logging is completed.

Salmon returns to the Horsefly River were projected to be even greater in 1997 than the mighty Adams River run. But in the fall of 1996, a DFO report deepened the concerns of fishers over the impact of intensive logging in the Horsefly watershed, and they went to Williams Lake to place their concerns before the Cariboo regional resource board. "Logging is carrying on at the same rate," said gillnetter Edgar Birch. "Our concern is that logging will create warmer water . . . and the salmon will not spawn." Mike Romaine of the DFO explained, "The concern is, can you sustain that rate of cut and still sustain the fisheries? The study shows that in some areas there is a very high risk." But logging spokespersons adamantly opposed any reduction in the cut.

Perhaps Augustin, Lunn and their neighbours are concerned about logging practices because they feel personally affronted as they watch the stripping of landscapes that they love. But a more objective view offers little comfort. After a flight over the Cariboo-Chilcotin, one veteran Alberta forester shakes his head. So much terrain has been clearcut he cannot imagine how it can long continue. He understands now why trucks loaded with Alberta timber flow in such numbers—hundreds every day—across the border to feed B.C. mills that are far too large for the amount of wood available in their own regions. Like many of his colleagues in that province, he resents the losses to the Alberta forest industry and the severe environmental cost of stripping trees from unregulated, privately owned forest lands.

Satellite photo maps of the region provide a more detailed overview. In addition to vast clearcuts, hundreds of cutblocks checkerboard the Cariboo-Chilcotin. Green strips of forest between them are supposed to be cut only when the original cuts have "greened up" with a new growth of free-growing, commercially valuable trees. But as wood becomes more scarce, loggers press for an early return to the same landscape, eliminating those remaining scraps of mature forest and linking the cutblocks into giant clearcuts.

The "natural capital" upon which the future of the Cariboo-Chilcotin depends is rapidly diminishing. No matter how the numbers are juggled, much less wood will be cut in the near future. Some foresters and resource economists suggest that "falldown" in timber available in the Fraser Basin is the inevitable and normal result of a transition from logging old growth to harvesting younger, second-growth trees—sort of a biological fact of life. This is nonsense, of course. Falldown fast approaches in the Cariboo because too many trees have been cut too fast. Instead of living on the "interest," or annual growth of the forest, logging corporations have cut deeply into B.C.'s capital, rapidly eliminating old growth and leaving NSR (not satisfactorily restocked) more than .5 million hectares of good- and medium-quality tree-growing land, as of 1990. But as evidence of this mounted, the pace of cutting accelerated even more. More than half the trees cut in British Columbia have been taken since 1977. In the Cariboo, half the timber ever cut was taken in just the eight years prior to 1994. This is a classic scenario of "overshoot and collapse," common around the world whenever resource stocks accumulated over a long time are exploited faster than they are replaced.

The dwindling supply of old-growth timber is of lower quality and more expensive to cut. When second-growth trees are old enough to harvest their quality will be inferior to that of the original forest. Second-growth wood, say craftspeople, is likely to be knotty, hard, weak and coarse-grained, difficult to work, and mainly useful as fibre for pulp and composition building materials. Wood from old trees is clear, strong, soft and fine-grained, lending itself to fine woodwork ranging from cabinets and furniture to guitars. Wood of the quality produced by old-growth forests in the Fraser Basin is found in few other places in the world; the fibre produced by the plantations that replace them will have to compete with a similar product produced faster and more cheaply in warmer climates. Second-growth wood could be improved by thinning the stands and other silvicultural practices, but this is of little interest to logging corporations unless liberally subsidized. Short-term profits are maximized by going after the last remaining old growth, not by tending new growth. As forest researcher Chris Maser explains, "Industrialists may fear the loss of the greatest profit margin they will ever have in the forests: ancient trees that cost them nothing to grow, quality woodfibre that is essentially free for the taking, which if not taken is seen only as an economic waste."

Since accounting practices discount the value of benefits in the future, corporations see no advantage in conserving fine, old-growth wood. So they have "highgraded" the timber of the Cariboo, logging first the forest blocks containing the highest volume of wood per hectare and the best trees. Each year trees of poorer quality on larger areas of increasingly sensitive land are cut to assure the flow of wood into too many very large mills. Surviving forests are on higher, steeper, more sensitive land where trees grow more slowly and the soil erodes more easily. In the last decade, the amount of wood produced on each hectare of forest land in B.C. has steadily declined; in 1989, for example, it was 22 per cent below the average volume per hectare in the 1970s. To acquire the same volume of wood, logging companies must cut trees from a larger area of land each year. In effect, each tree standing today is worth less and costs more to log than a few years ago, says forester Herb Hammond.

A vivid preview of the consequences these practices will have in the forests of the Cariboo-Chilcotin and the rest of the Fraser Basin was provided on October 17, 1996. At Golden in the Columbia River Basin, Evans Forest Products closed its doors and threw 500 hundred people out of work. By highgrading its timber, the company had removed the best and most accessible trees; remaining stands of lower-quality wood on more difficult terrain could not be profitably logged in the traditional way.

There are many unknowns involved in the removal of the forests of the Fraser Basin; this is in fact an experiment on a gigantic scale carried out at such tremendous speed that it will be completed long before the consequences are fully understood. For instance, how many generations can healthy forests persist when deprived of the normal variety of life found above and below ground in a true forest? Trees depend for nourishment upon the mycorrhizal fungi attached to their roots, but these diminish with each clearcut. How much biodiversity, the "stuff of life," will survive the fragmentation and simplification of the forest that is characteristic of B.C. forestry? Foresters who proudly point to lush second-growth forests planted on clearcuts miss the point: these are plantations that will be cut again long before they acquire old-growth characteristics. Since forests play an important role in transferring moisture across the landscape, will less water fall on the slopes of the Rockies as a consequence of vast clearcuts west of the Cariboo Mountains? How much forest can be removed without disturbing its climate-regulating function, perhaps diminishing rainfall and the growth of new forests in the Cariboo?

Ray Jones was born on the Horsefly River, only about 10 kilometres from the comfortable home in which he and his wife Yvonne now live in retirement on McKinley Lake. The water darkens as the sun sets over the silent beauty of the forest-rimmed lake. After a successful career as a mining engineer—he was president of Steep Rock Iron Mines in Ontario—Jones returned to the Horsefly River country. "Like the salmon," he says with a laugh.

But there's sadness as Jones talks in the summer of 1993 about what's happening to his beloved Cariboo. McKinley Lake is to be logged off, and if treated like nearby lakes, logged to the water line. "Just beyond the timber line over here is one of the biggest clearcuts you'll ever want to see," Jones says, pointing to hills across the lake. "Up at the head of the lake there are three big clearcuts, right on McKinley Creek as it comes in. It's the only spawning stream on the lake and all its tributaries are clearcut, logged right to the bones. Used to be the coldest water coming into the lake, nobody would swim up at the head of the lake. Wade that creek in the summertime and it would make your ankles ache. And nowadays it's the warmest place in the lake in the summer. Used to be, if you wanted a cold drink of water, you could just stop at any of these streams. Now you get swamp water because it comes from these clearcuts. The fish don't spawn. No reproduction."

Jones tells of other nearby lakes where for decades a family could catch its limit of rainbow trout in a couple of hours. Streams running into them are now clearcut, and trout numbers are dwindling. And then there are the moose—used to be lots of them, but awfully hard to find now, Jones says, and they are vastly outnumbered by hunters. "The big swamp over there, the last local place where the moose could build up undisturbed, is now all cut out. The moose are shy creatures, they need some place where they can congregate without people around, and it's all gone."

Now anger is mixed with the sadness. "I think this clearcut logging is an obscenity imposed upon the landscape. Not that we don't have to log. We do. Because it's our heritage. Back in the days when selective logging was the general practice, the small loggers would go in and log an area. You go into one of those areas now, and if it hasn't been re-clearcut, it's hard to find the old stumps even. You can't tell it's ever been logged and it's ready to be logged again. But the clearcutting and then destroying the topsoil by burning just has to be wrong. There are places up the river that were logged fifteen years ago, and there's nothing but rock. They tried to replant some of them, and there's nothing to replant on, the soil's gone."

It may take as long as fifteen years for the worst damage to show up on hillsides, for dead roots of logged trees to rot and release the soil they've held in place. Although this higher, steeper land may be marginal for logging, it is often excellent wildlife habitat. In the Quesnel Highlands, for instance, caribou depend for survival in winter on lichens hanging from old spruce trees. Lichens only begin to grow on trees 100 to 150 years old, and flourish more richly as the centuries pass. Replanted forests will be cut again long before the lichens can reestablish, so logged forests will never again support caribou. Biologists hope that smaller, dispersed clearcuts will preserve some of the lichen for caribou—but it is just a hope.

If the condition of Cariboo-Chilcotin forests looks precarious to people like Ray Jones, do hard numbers offer any comfort? In 1988–89, 90 million cubic metres of wood were cut in B.C., almost all by clearcutting: an area of 2700 square kilometres. That's about 200 trees cut every minute, making almost 3 million logging truckloads—about double the rate estimated by the Forest Service in 1992 to be sustainable. When the Ministry of Forests began reevaluating the annual allowable cut in the 1990s, some communities were shocked at reductions in local cutting levels.

But by the time allocations were made in the middle and upper Fraser Basin in the mid-1990s, no reductions in cut were decreed for the Cariboo or the Robson Valley. Yet Forest Service studies showed inadequate timber to sustain Cariboo cutting levels even before allowances were made to protect land under the terms of the Cariboo-Chilcotin Land Use Plan, or to meet requirements of the Forest Practices Code for improved management in riparian and other sensitive zones, or to reduce logging intensity in Special Resource Development Zones. By the spring of 1996, the Sierra Legal Defence Fund had filed a lawsuit protesting the annual allowable cut in the Williams Lake timber supply area because it did not respect new requirements for sustainability and would have "disastrous ecological consequences for the Cariboo."

It's late July. We climb up through sparse trees and grassy meadows where, we have heard, a mother grizzly wandered with her cubs a few days ago. So with conversation a little forced, some whistling more nervous than tuneful, we push on up through lovely alpine meadows bright with asters, columbines, Indian paint brush and yellow daisies. Breaking through a fringe of Engelmann spruce, we see Mitchell Lake about 10 kilometres to the east, stretching deep blue far up a distant valley of steep forested slopes. High above the lake, clean sharp rock thrusts up through the green mantle, necklaces of summer snow still ringing the summits.

With legs serving notice that we have climbed about seven kilometres, the ground suddenly disappears beneath our feet. A thousand metres below, the tip of the north arm of Quesnel Lake gathers water from shadowed valleys reaching up to sources in high mountains whose peaks fade blue in the distance like a storm-tossed sea. Far below, Penfold Creek, Mitchell River and Cameron Creek curve, coil and oxbow their way through the rich wetlands they have created. It is a work-in-progress, a delta building out into the blue waters of Quesnel Lake. To reach this place more than 200,000 salmon struggle up 800 kilometres of Fraser River and tributaries; this is their home, where they were born four years ago, where they will mate, spawn and die. Grizzly bears will scoop some fish out of the streams before this ultimate act, rainbow trout will fatten on salmon eggs, eagles will feast on carcasses of salmon that expire after exhausting their last reserves of strength. While waterfowl feed and gather strength for the long journey south, a moose's head may explode from the water with a mouthful of succulent water plants. Huge cedars and hemlocks push skyward on dryer land fringing the streams.

This magnificent landscape lies between Bowron Lake Park to the north and the 500 000 hectares of Wells Grey Park 30 kilometres south of Bowron. Conservationists campaigned for years to have the corridor protected, because joining the parks into a single 860 000-hectare block of unbroken wilderness would preserve important Fraser River headwaters. Eight watersheds, several of them feeding the Quesnel system in which about half of Fraser River sockeye salmon spawn, would be protected. And it would greatly improve survival opportunities for large animals like grizzlies and caribou, which require extensive ranges of old-growth habitat to forage. "There's no place in B.C. where so much can be saved by setting aside so little land," says Doug Radies, spokesperson for the Cariboo Mountains Wilderness Coalition.

Until the Cariboo-Chilcotin Land Use Plan was finalized in 1994, all the forests in the headwaters of the Quesnel River system were slated to be logged, and clearcuts were pushing rapidly up streams into the high country. Conservationists were gratified when the new plan did indeed link the two parks with an extensive protected area. But they are convinced that a serious error was made by omitting from protection the valleys of the Penfold and Blue Lead Rivers, valleys of extraordinary beauty, rich in fish and wildlife habitat, whose long-term value as wilderness would greatly exceed short-term returns to logging in this wet, mountainous terrain. The Penfold Valley and most of the western slopes of the mountains are classified in the plan as Special Resource Development Zones, which are to be managed in a manner sensitive to their particular values, including those of fish, wildlife, ecosystems, backcountry tourism and recreation. The more stringent regulations of the Forest Practices Code are meant to protect some of these values too. But logging companies quickly punched roads up the Penfold, and by the spring of 1996, conservationists were charging them with extensive stream damage through slope failures, road erosion and siltation.

Laura and Annie emerge from a narrow skid road with 18-metre trees in tow. Rob Borsato unhooks the load behind his fine black Percherons, pausing for a short rest before returning for more logs. Borsato has been logging with horses for more than fifteen years. It can be a precarious way to make a living because a horse logger—or any logger using small machinery—doesn't have access to very much wood. Most forests are in the hands of transnational corporations, which prefer to deal with large contractors using big machinery. A bit of wood is made available each year under the Small Business Enterprise Program, without which small operators in mills and in the woods would be virtually eliminated. As it is, this only accounts for about 10 per cent of the wood cut in B.C.—not nearly enough to satisfy the demand by local small loggers.

"Then there's the wood lot licence program," says Borsato. "It's something that I've always really argued for. In our neighbourhood there was a wood lot came up for bid this spring, and we submitted an application as did sixteen others . . . [but] there's just not enough. They promise it will be increased 50 per cent over the next four years, so we're hoping that does happen." On the very little forest land to which they have access, independent loggers must pay a stumpage fee (charged by the government for trees cut from public forests) much higher than that charged to the large corporations: two to three times as much, and often more. One small-scale Cariboo logger told a CBC radio program that he pays ten times the stumpage while employing three times as many loggers as a big company cutting the same amount of wood.

With all phases of the industry—from cutting to processing to exporting—largely integrated in the hands of a few giant corporations, any semblance of an open market for logs has been eliminated. Since stumpage is supposedly based on the market value of logs, this corporate integration enables companies to force down the fees, reducing the province's income from its forests. B.C.'s stumpage fees were so low that, until forced up by American lumber industry protests in 1993, the income didn't even pay the operating costs of the Ministry of Forests. Cheap wood helps the industry to compete globally the easy way: by selling high-quality wood at artificially low prices. The Forest Service charges as little as twenty-five cents a cubic metre for wood in some Cariboo Mountain valleys, often in particularly sensitive areas.

Selling off resources cheaply in the Fraser Basin doesn't just rob the public purse of revenue. Low stumpage rates guarantee waste and the export of raw or barely processed wood products in huge quantities, depriving the citizens who own the forests of employment and income. Higher resource prices, on the other hand, would promote the manufacture of finished products from smaller quantities of wood. High prices encourage technologies that use resources efficiently rather than simply processing them in vast quantities, says economist Herman Daly of the World Bank.

Sociologist Patricia Marchak of UBC has published authoritative studies of the forest industry in B.C. and abroad. She observes that "a stable and self-sufficient economy cannot be created by exporting natural resources and importing finished products. This practice leads to a weak domestic economy, extreme vulnerability to fluctuations in world demand for single products, and unstable resource communities." In her book *Green Gold*, Marchak goes on to describe how successive Canadian and B.C. governments "have given away resource harvesting rights to large companies in the completely unfounded faith that sooner or later the giveaways would result in a mature industrial economy."

So it is not surprising that corporate domination of the forests is a prime concern of independent, community-based loggers in the Fraser Basin. "The more I investigate the things that rub me wrong with the present system, it's the tenure arrangements that always comes up," says Borsato. "With horse logging the problem we face is there is just no consistency in the supply of wood. There are lots of people who would like to work. We've had several training programs in the last ten years and we've had very good response from people, but the unfortunate thing is that you train somebody, and then they sit idle because there's just not enough work."

Throughout the world, the tenure of forest lands is proving a key factor in assuring sustainability of forest economies. The B.C. Forest Resources Commission, established by a Social Credit government, reported in 1991 that the tenure system in B.C. has become rigid and highly concentrated. It recommended that a much bigger share of the wood go to "smaller tenure holders who will manage the forests with emphasis on such values as community watersheds, range, wildlife, recreation and community forests." In B.C., however, four interlocked groups of companies control 93 per cent of the wood cut on public land. Seventy per cent of their shareholders live outside the province, about 45 per cent outside Canada. These companies receive 97 per cent of the money paid for timber cut in British Columbia.

This is the realization of a nightmare feared by that giant of the B.C.

forest industry, H. R. MacMillan. MacMillan was B.C.'s first chief forester
and the founder of MacMillan Bloedel. His submission before the Sloan
Royal Commission on Forest Resources in 1956 was prophetic:

> *It will be a sorry day for . . . British Columbia when the forest industry here
> consists chiefly of a very few big companies, holding most of the good
> timber—or pretty near all of it—and good growing sites to the disadvantage
> and early extermination of the most hardworking, virile, versatile and inge-
> nious element of our population, the independent market logger and the small
> mill man . . . A few companies would acquire control of resources and form a
> monopoly. It will be managed by professional bureaucrats, fixers with a pent-
> house viewpoint who, never having had rain in their lunch buckets, would
> abuse the forest . . .*

British Columbia's old-growth forests produce some of the world's
finest wood, but the large forest corporations produce less money per
cubic metre than almost any other country in the world. As forest policy
consultant Ray Travers explains, the forest industry in B.C. adds only
half as much value to the wood it cuts as it does in other Canadian
provinces. In the United States and New Zealand, three times as much
value is added to each cubic metre of wood—more than $170, compared
to about $56 in B.C. Those precious manufacturing jobs go to the coun-
tries that buy B.C.'s nearly raw wood. In the states of Washington and
Oregon, some forty mills work exclusively at converting B.C. wood into
higher-valued commodities, while in the Cariboo entrepreneurs have
difficulty obtaining wood for the manufacture of such products.

The B.C. forest industry has entirely changed in the last decade.
Patricia Marchak explains that as corporations liquidate old-growth
wood in the Fraser Basin, they are preparing for a future in which their
fibre is grown elsewhere—in southern states like Alabama, in Chile and
other warm countries where trees grow fast and wages are low. She
suggests that a restructured tenure and stumpage system would encourage the transnationals to leave sooner rather than later, returning the
forests to B.C. residents while valuable old-growth timber is still standing. Forester Herb Hammond agrees. "Western Canada has much of
the high-quality, long fibre growth timber left in the world," he writes.
"We can liquidate it and sell it cheaply as we are currently doing, or we
can cut it on a sustainable basis, make high-quality wood products, and
name our price . . . this is not the agenda of the major timber companies that control forests in Canada."

As huge machines like the feller-buncher march through the forests
of the Cariboo-Chilcotin, the idea of turning to simpler, smaller

technology like that employed by Rob Borsato and his horses may seem almost aberrant. Faith in gigantism and technological sophistication can freeze out new, innovative and competing ideas. The latest or biggest or most technically sophisticated simply *must* be the best—and of course, the cheapest, according to short-term corporate accounting. Yet when the feller-buncher removes entire trees from the land, it eliminates more than jobs; it also takes the leaves and branches essential to the fertility of the soil. The machine in fact removes from two to four times as much phosphorous, potassium, calcium and nitrogen as conventional clearcutting, which itself is hardly a benign practice.

Borsato sees a direct connection between the health of the Fraser River and the way logging is done. "The horse logging community has argued that in the Cariboo there's a whole bunch of transition forest types," says Borsato; "moving out from the dry belt fir that's right along the Fraser River to the plateau country east and west of the river. These are of species and ages that are really important in terms of hydrological functioning, filtering the water. I think we'll be looking a lot more at how we handle water, like the percentage of tree cover you have to leave intact in order for a forest to keep functioning hydrologically.

"Just to look at it purely from the cost side is pretty much skewing the whole vision. If the bottom line is just who can get the wood out the cheapest, well then it's going to cost more to log with horses. But you can start to be competitive when you have some high standards, when you're expecting to leave behind a forest that is satisfactorily stocked with a young understorey. If you have those kinds of criteria, then you can start to say that horse logging is indeed very cost effective, because it's one of the few systems that can actually work amongst really young sensitive trees. Big machines can't hold a candle to what the horses can do in commercial thinning. With a horse you can leave the forest just as densely stocked as you really want to." And not just the forest benefits, Borsato adds. "The job creation is so significant. We worked side by side with a conventional operation one winter, and we generated three to five times more work from the wood than the conventional operation did."

What Borsato sees in the woods is backed by numbers: while more trees were being cut in the Fraser Basin, fewer people had jobs in the woods and mills. In just seven years, between 1979 and 1986, 22,500 jobs disappeared in B.C.'s forest industry. The annual cut of timber in the Cariboo increased by a third between 1980 and 1993, but employment in the forest industry didn't rise at all. In fact, with bigger, more efficient machines in the woods and in the mills, it took 35 per cent more wood to support each job. In B.C. only one person is employed to cut almost 1000 cubic metres of wood; Ray Travers points out that in the rest of Canada more than twice as many people have jobs cutting and processing the same quantity of wood—wood that isn't as good. In the United States, three-and-a-half jobs are created for every 1000 cubic metres; in New Zealand the number is five, and in Switzerland more than eleven. So the people of the Cariboo-Chilcotin lose jobs, and revenue that belongs in their communities goes to distant places where the wood is processed, where the big logging machinery is made and where the corporate shareholders reside.

Oddly, the principal forest workers' union has never made unemployment due to technology an issue. Long-time International Woodworkers of America President Jack Munro presided over enormous job losses and agreed that tens of thousands more jobs would soon disappear. Munro left the union to become chief spokesperson for the transnational logging corporations as chairman of their public relations organization, the B.C. Forest Alliance. In contrast, another forest industry union, the Pulp, Paper and Woodworkers of Canada, condemns clearcutting, overcutting and waste in the forests, and supports partial and selection logging, the manufacture of value-added wood products, the protection of old-growth forests and "new rules to limit the damage done by corporate greed."

The kind of logging that eliminates forestry jobs also reduces opportunities for other economic activities. Tourism, for instance: old-growth forests and the fish and wildlife they produce are basic elements of the natural landscape that make tourism the fastest growing sector of B.C.'s economy. Herb Hammond points out, "The forest-based tourism industry derives revenue from a given forest area every single year and keeps the profits in the community. The timber industry derives revenue from a given forest area once every 80 to 150 years and sends the profits to stockholders."

Hammond describes how hunting and fishing lodges, guide outfitters and a wide range of tourism enterprises have to fight for survival because large-scale clearcutting simply puts them out of business. "Once the forest is clearcut," he writes, "most non-timber uses and values, such as wilderness, tourism, fisheries, wildlife habitat, soil and slope integrity, or water quality, are usually degraded or destroyed for one human generation." A study by the School of Resource and Environmental Management at SFU concluded that implementation of all the parks and wilderness proposals of B.C. conservationists, protecting 13 per cent of B.C. public lands, could be accomplished with no lost forest jobs.

Michael M'Gonigle of the University of Victoria and journalist Ben

Parfitt describe forest operations in B.C. as a "volume" economy. In their remarkable analysis in *Forestopia*, they propose instead a "value" economy that would generate much more income and many more jobs, sustaining communities like those of the Cariboo–Chilcotin along with a quality forest environment. They describe old-growth trees of the Fraser Basin as a rare treasure that should be used for the most valuable products possible. The harvesting of old-growth forests should be stretched out so that future generations can also benefit from them, so new forests have time to achieve maturity and so sustainable technology such as selection harvesting can be introduced to assure a permanent supply of quality wood. Such community-based logging operations will probably be smaller, more adaptable to site-specific, holistic forest practices. They will be better able to produce wood that local companies can remanufacture into higher-value products and to retain a quality environment that provides many economic opportunities in tourism and recreation.

All timber should be sold through public log markets regardless of who harvests it, say M'Gonigle and Parfitt. This will ensure that British Columbians are properly paid for their resource and that manufacturers of specialized, value-added products will be able to compete for wood on an even footing with larger saw and pulp mills. Experimental log markets at Lumby, near Vernon, and on Vancouver Island have been remarkably successful. Revenue from log markets can help fund the transition to a sustainable forest industry in which local communities can prosper. Credit unions often cannot find enough good investments in their own communities, but with provincial backing they could fund the development of community forest operations, wood remanufacturers and other enterprises adding value to wood cut in the Fraser Basin.

Perhaps no one has laid out the choice more simply and clearly than American forester Aldo Leopold in his celebrated book, *A Sand County Almanac*, first published in 1949. "Quit thinking about decent land-use as solely an economic problem," Leopold wrote. "Examine each question in terms of what is ethically and esthetically right, as well as what is economically expedient."

Leopold's philosophy resonates well in this Fraser River forest where Rob Borsato wheels Laura and Annie around and prepares to return for more wood. Borsato reflects on the choice he's made. "I don't think that I can honestly say that I make as much money as I did logging conventionally. But I can say that you can get somewhat close, close enough if you're willing to accept the fact that there's another element there too. You want to enjoy your work and you want to sleep well at night."

The Chilcotin

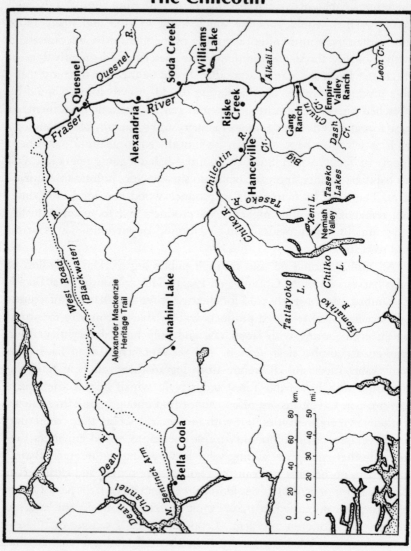

CHAPTER 5

The Vast Dry Land

I do not know much about gods; but I think that the river
Is a strong brown god—sullen, untamed and intractable, . . .
The river is within us, the sea is all about us . . .

T. S. ELIOT, *THE DRY SALVAGES*

South of Quesnel the Fraser River has left behind the lowlands that long ago lay beneath a glacial lake. Downstream, the Fraser Plateau rises to the south, forcing the river into a narrower channel that cuts deeper as it progresses, dividing the Cariboo to the east from the Chilcotin to the west. The banks rise, the current swirls, but for about 90 kilometres to Soda Creek the water remains relatively smooth by Fraser River standards. In gold rush days this stretch of the river was served by sternwheel steamboats, giving travellers a break from the rigours of the Cariboo Road. Art Downs, a fine chronicler of the era, describes sternwheelers as ideal frontier vessels. They could carry 90 or more tonnes in very shallow water because no propeller projected below the hull. Sternwheelers could challenge canyons and rapids, absorb fearful beatings from storms, rocks, ice snags and gravel bars, and were quickly repaired with simple materials when damaged.

At Soda Creek on October 16, 1863, the English travellers Cheadle and Milton awaited the arrival of the *Enterprise* from Quesnel. "Steamer came in about 2 o'clock bringing a host of miners," wrote Cheadle, "two of whom were very drunk and continued to imbibe every 5 minutes . . . the swearing was something fearful . . . After we had been on board a short time, the Captain, finding out who we were, gave us the use of his cabin, a comfortable little room & supplied with cigars and a decanter of cocktail, also books and papers. We were fetched out every few minutes to have a drink with some one, the Captain taking the lead by standing champagne all round." The imposing black-bearded captain, J. W. Doane, cast off his ship's lines at 4 P.M. the next day, and the *Enterprise* headed upstream towards Quesnel. "The boat makes very slow progress against the powerful current," Cheadle wrote, "we had to anchor for the night after doing only 10 miles. At daybreak went on 4 or 5 miles & then delayed by the dense fogs which prevail on the river in the early morning at this season."

Fifty-five years before Cheadle's steamboat passage, Simon Fraser and his companions floated rapidly down this stretch of the river in relative comfort. But they had reason to suspect things might worsen. The afternoon of May 30, 1808, they met some Native men on horseback north of Soda Creek who warned of what lay ahead. "According to the accounts we received here," Fraser wrote in his journal, "the river below was but a succession of falls and cascades, which we should find impossible to pass, not only thro the badness of the channel, but also thro the badness of the surrounding country, which was rugged and mountainous. Their opinion, therefore, was that we should discontinue our voyage and remain with them. I remarked that our determination of going on was fixed."

Next day, the explorers were forced to carry about half their load around the canyon below Soda Creek "for two miles through a very uneven country." Here they met more inhabitants who also told of rough navigation ahead. With eroded canyon walls now rising almost vertically to the plateau far above them, Fraser had little difficulty believing the warning. Seeing the white man wouldn't be dissuaded, the chief of the group near Soda Creek offered to accompany Fraser on his journey, along with another man capable of interpreting languages they would encounter downstream. The two turned out to be indispensable, particularly when the expedition met other Native people not nearly as disposed to welcome strangers to the river. The truth of warnings about the Fraser River became evident the next morning when they had to run rapids near Chimney Creek south of Williams Lake. Far worse was yet to come.

It is just about here that the Chilcotin Highway now gracefully spans the Fraser River over the Sheep Creek bridge at the bottom of a steep drop from the heights of the Fraser Plateau. An endless stream of logging trucks rolls east across the bridge to grind slowly up the canyon slope, hauling the wealth of the Chilcotin to the mills at Williams Lake. Going against this vehicular current, a traveller today climbs the west wall of the Fraser canyon onto the Chilcotin Plateau. The highway bisects the plateau westward all the way to the Coast Mountains, through which it cuts to descend to Alexander Mackenzie's destination at Bella Coola on the Pacific Ocean.

Across this high, dry, rolling landscape some 1200 metres above the sea, grasslands stretch westward in brown expanses, broken by groves of pine on higher land and Douglas fir at lower levels. On this September day, aspen leaves turn golden and tremble in the breeze; here and there a shrub flames red. A drift of rain sifts through a distant spruce-clad hillside. A cluster of buildings and corrals mark an occasional ranch; log houses are common, many of them modern and comfortable. Reminders of the past are frequent; ancient cabins crumble slowly into the ground. Snake-rail fences zigzag up slopes. They last a long time in this climate, and when finally weighed down by years, another wooden fence will replace them; cowboys will tell you neither cattle nor moose in the Chilcotin have much respect for wire. Another common fence, the Russell, looks fragile, but that is a deceptive first impression; the style has long been popular because it requires no posts to be driven into rocky ground, and its slender rails require less wood than most other fences.

A breeze ruffles a small pothole lake. There are endless numbers of them, from fresh to highly alkaline; in spring the little lakes explode with life when ducks and other water birds arrive to nest or to rest on their way to northerly breeding grounds. In just 10 square kilometres near Riske Creek, almost 2,000 breeding male waterfowl of 15 different species can be counted each year. The pulse of life for an entire continent throbs as vast flocks migrate across the plateau. Great flocks of sandhill cranes en route to arctic breeding grounds fly over the deep Fraser River gorge of greening grass and sagebrush. Douglas fir forests echo with the hammering of a dozen kinds of woodpeckers.

The Chilcotin is a vast, sparsely populated land, home to a few huge, almost legendary ranches like the Gang, the Chilko and the Empire Valley, and to many smaller cattlemen whose corrals and barns are often found far up a sheltering valley. About 65 per cent of the region's population is aboriginal, almost all members of the Chilcotin Nation. They speak a distinctive language, one of the six Native languages of the Fraser Basin. Lands of two Chilcotin bands stretch along the Chilcotin River just west of Hanceville. This bright September day haying is in full swing on the river benchlands of the Anaham Reserve. A few kilometres farther west the Chilcotin River pours through a groove of basalt lava called Bull Canyon. A large osprey works the current from a perch on a nearby snag, swooping low over fast water up which hundreds of thousands of sockeye salmon struggle each year on their way to spawning grounds near Chilko Lake. Just over a century ago, Chilcotin people repelled a marauding coastal band from Bella Coola by rolling boulders down on them from red-brown canyon cliffs high above.

This is ranching country, not farmland, which means more than cowboy hats and four-wheel-drive vehicles. The harsh climate, short growing season and low productivity of the high plateau has broken the hearts of many newcomers, and while the land doesn't forgive inexperience, it nourishes devotion from those who persist. The Chilcotin was virtually unknown beyond the Interior until the 1950s and 1960s, when its flavour could at last be savoured across the country in books by authors Richmond Hobson and Paul St. Pierre. Hobson was an American who recounted in best-selling books like *Grass beyond the Mountains* his struggles and adventures as a rancher in remote Chilcotin backcountry. The extraordinary characters bred by this land came to life in St. Pierre's books, adapted from scripts he wrote for the CBC television series *Cariboo Country*, produced by Philip Keatley. With better roads, a new ferry link in 1996 to Bella Coola, campgrounds, wilderness lodges and other accommodation, the wonders of the Chilcotin are now much more accessible.

About 50 kilometres west of the Sheep Creek bridge over the Fraser River, the plateau suddenly breaks and the sheer cliffs of Hanceville Canyon drop to the valley of the Chilcotin River far below. The Chilcotin is another of the Fraser's great tributaries, its grey-green colour signalling origins high in the Coast Mountains. From Hanceville west the river's valley broadens, its alluvial flats producing hay that will carry cattle herds through the winter. Sometimes three or four distinct benchlands step back from the river, a legacy of water-borne clay and silt deposited through the ages, then cut again and again by the Chilcotin's current.

With precipitation so scanty, life on the plateau depends upon water brought from the mountains by rivers and streams cutting across to join the Fraser. Stream-bank ecosystems are rich with vegetation and wildlife; water backs into meadows where native grass can be harvested to carry livestock through the long, cold winters; ranchers divert or pump water onto hayfields. As the Chilcotin River approaches the Fraser, its incision plunges deeper into the plateau, foaming over rapids, undermining banks in steep canyons until great slices of earth plunge into it. Along the way smaller streams cut deeply into valley walls to lose themselves in this larger flow.

The Chilcotin River joins the Fraser in a landscape vast and spectacular, where the mighty river is a small, brown ribbon threading the bottom of a deep crease through dry grasslands. Hot winds, minuscule rainfall and heat-holding canyons characterize this bunchgrass biogeoclimatic zone, where bluebunch wheatgrass predominates, supplemented by fescues and a few other non-grass plants. Grasslands stretch more than 100 kilometres south from the Sheep Creek bridge in golden slopes and benchlands broken by the occasional emerald of an irrigated hayfield. They reach 50 kilometres up the Chilcotin River, almost to Hanceville. A few grace-ful, long-needled ponderosa pines venture down into the valley heat where their shade is welcomed by man and beast. As the land rises and retreats from the river, temperatures moderate a little, moisture increases and more trees join the sparse ponderosas. Still farther back and higher above the river, the Douglas fir with its dramatically corrugated bark dominates, and the grassy forest floor provides excellent grazing for mule deer and elk as well as cattle. Higher still into the mountains, cooler days and nights and more rainfall foster forests of slender lodgepole pines fringing alpine meadows whose brief burst of summer colour is the glory of the mountain slopes.

Under a hot summer sun, the green of irrigated fields stands boldly against the sombre brown of dry bunchgrass. It costs too much to pump water up from the Fraser onto these fields. Instead, the water that makes them lush and productive is diverted out of streams cradled in folds of the hills, draining down towards the river. Many water sys-tems near the Fraser were originally built by Chinese labourers who turned to placer mining when the Canadian Pacific Railway was com-pleted. Needing water to wash sand and gravel from gold and having no pumps to lift it from the Fraser, they constructed small dams on tributary streams to hold the spring runoff. Ditches then carried water as far as several kilometres to their mining operations on the Fraser. Ranchers later took over many of these waterworks to irrigate hay crops on meadows and benchlands. Many a ranch still has its "China Lake" or "China Creek."

The landscape carved through the Cariboo-Chilcotin by the Fraser is relatively new. This array of escarpments rising one above another, separated by steep clay cliffs as they retreat from the river, dates back only 10,000 years or so. As the ice that covered British Columbia began to melt, ice dams remaining in canyons slowed or blocked the flow of the river and its tributaries, allowing sediments to settle. Valleys filled with silt and clay. As the ice dams melted, the freed river cut into these great reservoirs of sediment, sculpting the dramatic landscape. Nowhere is it more obvious that "water shapes the world like a potter's hands shape clay on a wheel."

This process continues today throughout the Fraser Basin. Precipitous slopes await the right moment to collapse into streams; glaciers shrink in the high country exposing moraines to erosion. The Fraser River and its watershed is a very active system. Somebody has described the shaping of landscape very simply: "Water runs downhill and carries soil with it." The Fraser does this on a huge scale, carving, absorbing, carrying, rolling, grinding, picking up and dropping sediment as currents rise and fall, eventually transporting some 12 million cubic metres of material to the Strait of Georgia each year. The process is probably most obvious here in the Cariboo-Chilcotin, where the soil creeps steadily downward to be washed away by the river, assuring its brown, muddy colour. When this happens on a larger scale, the process is called "earthflow," and the rudimentary roads on the west side of the Fraser are often dislocated by earthflows moving down towards the river.

This stretch of the Fraser River is little known, in part because no highway approaches it. Secondary gravel roads serve ranches, Native reserves and loggers along the river. Since the advent of huge inflatable rafts and powerful outboard motors, an occasional river expedition floats through the winding canyons. Travellers experience moments of foam-drenched excitement in rapids where Simon Fraser's voyageurs in fragile birchbark canoes pitted brawn and paddling skill against imminent, watery catastrophe. On the banks they may see an occasional miner's log cabin, long abandoned along with his dreams. They may find evidence on the riverbank of millennia of aboriginal occupation: ancient petro-glyphs carved or painted on rocks, traces of winter pit-houses and salmon storage pits. Eventually the Camelsfoot Range to the west and the Marble Range to the east advance to the Fraser's banks, marking the southern extremity of the Fraser Plateau and replacing silt and clay banks with precipitous rock walls.

Life in the Cariboo-Chilcotin and in the Thompson River water-shed owes much of its character and colour to cattle ranching. Nowhere in Canada are the traditions of the range more palpable. The Hudson's Bay Company brought the first cattle and horses into the region as early as 1846, trailing a few animals to Fort Kamloops and as far as Fort Alexandria, south of Quesnel on the Fraser River. Well before ranching began on the Prairies, the HBC grazed cattle and horses on the rolling grasslands of the Lac du Bois hills across the Thompson River from today's Kamloops. Although the B.C. cattle industry was born here, the company didn't encourage others to follow its lead, believing the land to be exclusively its own.

Like almost everything else in the Fraser Basin, that changed with the gold rush in 1858. Only two months after miners began pouring up the Fraser, the first cattle drive crossed into the Okanagan Valley at Osoyoos from Washington Territory and pushed north as far as the Thompson River. The next year a cattle drive continued all the way to Fort Alexandria. Over the next decade about 22,000 head trailed north from Oregon Territory to feed miners in the goldfields of the Cariboo—about 1,400 animals each year to Barkerville alone. Not all this food on the hoof reached the hungry miners; some of the animals became foundation stock for ranches that spread across the grasslands of the interior drybelt. Many of the great ranches of the Interior were established in the 1860s: Alkali Lake Ranch, the Gang Ranch, 150 Mile Ranch, 100 Mile Ranch, others up the Chilcotin River as far as Alexis Creek, many more along the Thompson River and its tributaries, the Bonaparte and the Nicola.

For almost a century, this grand-scale movement of cattle, horses and even sheep characterized ranching in the Cariboo-Chilcotin. The rangelands were far from markets and from other ranching regions, so moving cattle in to stock the land and moving them out again to market was a drama of epic proportions. In the earliest days, it was mainly Americans who drove the cattle north, bringing with them ranching traditions and practices that endured. Some stayed on in Canada: Joe Greaves, for instance, who drove sheep to the Cariboo in 1859 and returned year after year with big herds of cattle.

By the time the gold rush petered out in the early 1870s much of the land was stocked with cattle. The market for meat evaporated, but the herds continued to grow; soon great movements of cattle began to flow in the opposite direction, south in search of new markets. Incredible stories are told. Thaddeus Harper, who with his brother Jerome founded the Gang Ranch, drove 1,200 head south across the border, intending to ship them to Chicago from the closest railhead at Salt Lake City. But California suffered a drought that year, wiping out entire herds of cattle. Rising beef prices in that state caught Thaddeus Harper's eye, and he switched his destination, driving the cattle to San Francisco instead. Although he made a small fortune, Harper had taken eighteen months to drive his cattle more than 3000 kilometres to market.

In 1880, Joe Greaves also reversed the direction of his cattle drives. He pushed 4,000 cattle south from Kamloops along the Oregon Trail he knew so well, then east to Cheyenne, Wyoming where he could ship them by rail to Chicago. A couple of years later, Greaves established the great Douglas Lake ranch near Merritt in the Nicola Valley.

All this made great stories, yet survival was no easy matter for ranchers far from markets. Some who held on until the 1880s began at last to prosper selling beef to CPR construction crews, but that market only lasted until the railroad was completed in 1885. Chilcotin cattlemen like Norman Lee drove their animals about 300 kilometres south to the new CPR station at Ashcroft, but there wasn't yet much of a market for beef in new settlements at the mouth of the Fraser. So when another gold rush erupted, this time far to the north in the Klondike, Lee decided that at last his cattle would make his fortune. He set off in May

1898 to drive 200 cattle more than 2400 kilometres north to Dawson City across incredibly difficult terrain, a trip of unimaginable hardship that he recounts in a diary peppered with ironic twists and wry humour. It was October when Lee and the skin-and-bone remnants of his herd arrived at Teslin Lake on the B.C.-Yukon border. He slaughtered the cattle, loaded them on scows and headed down the lake towards the Yukon River and his eldorado, Dawson City. When the wind strengthened to a gale, the scows were wrecked on rocky shores and the beef was lost. Lee managed to get to the coast and down to Vancouver by ship where he arrived with his blanket roll, a dog and one dollar—which he spent on a drink so he could make "a fresh start with a clean sheet." And he did, returning to Hanceville to become one of the revered patriarchs of ranching in the Chilcotin. His catastrophic cattle drive is an enduring legend of B.C. ranching.

The arrival of the Pacific Great Eastern Railway at Williams Lake in 1919 provided access to new markets for beef. Chilcotin ranchers switched their cattle drives to this much closer railhead, though by any other standard they still faced a daunting task. Distances were great for remote ranchers, and the Fraser River remained an obstacle between range and market. Cattle drives continued until after World War Two; legendary cowman Pan Phillips drove cattle more than 300 kilometres from the Itcha Mountains to Quesnel every fall until the late 1950s, a month-long expedition he called his "annual picnic." Eventually, better roads and bridges gave trucks an advantage in getting the animals to market.

Since being bypassed by the Cariboo Road back in 1863, Williams Lake had dozed away the years, overshadowed by nearby 150 Mile House. But the PGE railway sparked a decade-long boom in the town. In 1920 construction of stores and other businesses, hotels and houses, continued at a furious pace. Hard work was accompanied by nonstop festivities fueled by bootleg liquor from Alberta. That year the first Williams Lake Stampede drew cowboys to compete from throughout the Cariboo and Chilcotin. It was, in a way, the continuation of a tradition: Williams Lake had long been a place of meeting and games for Native tribes, since it was near the northern extremity of Shuswap territory, the southern border of the Carrier and the eastern reaches of the Chilcotin people.

Most of the good Cariboo-Chilcotin grazing land was occupied well before the end of the nineteenth century. After the early American ranchers came many well-educated British immigrants who brought with them essential items like cricket, polo and afternoon tea. Soon too many cattle were chewing the rich bunchgrass, and each time markets collapsed, more cattle and horses were abandoned on open range.

In drier regions sagebrush began to replace grass, and everywhere the land supported fewer animals. The situation eased in a tragic way when severe winters killed many cattle, but before the end of the 1800s the ranges of the Interior had been devastated by overgrazing.

Grazing regulations were eventually implemented, and in the 1930s a range research station opened at Kamloops. "Over the last twenty, thirty years, there's been a tremendous improvement," says Kamloops agrologist Graham Strachan. "Range is being used sustainably now. That's not to say there aren't isolated pockets where there are specific problems related to livestock use, but over all, with all the work done on range improvement and range management, using systems more attuned to this area, the range is certainly sustainable." Strachan says there is still work to be done in resolving conflicts between wildlife and cattle, particularly where livestock are grazing on key wildlife wintering areas. Current land-use planning processes are supposed to resolve some of these issues. Public rangelands are crucial to ranchers; most of them actually own only a small part of the land they use: where their buildings are located, where they produce hay on irrigated land and where cattle graze in winter. They depend on leases of crown land administered by the B.C. Forest Service for spring, summer and fall grazing; without access to publicly owned land, few ranches could survive.

Ranching along the Fraser River is of a scale almost unimaginable. Many of today's ranches were created by combining smaller properties that had proved impracticable in this dry land. Two ranches, the Empire Valley and the Gang, together occupy about 60 kilometres of the Fraser's west bank. Across the river, Alkali Lake Ranch, the first in B.C. when it was established in 1861, encompasses 15 000 hectares of deeded land alone. Gang Ranch covers some 2330 square kilometres, almost half the size of Prince Edward Island. For more than twenty years, until divided in 1953, the Empire Valley Ranch on the west bank of the river and the B.C. Cattle Company ranch on the east bank were one enormous unit operated by the Koster family.

In the 1930s Henry Koster employed a gruff Englishman named Yates Drake to run the more isolated Empire Valley unit. Drake was an experienced cattleman, particularly proud of the 250 or more horses the ranch kept for herding, haying and travel in this land of rudimentary roads. Drake's grandson, forester Al Brown, remembers arriving as a teenager from Vancouver at the remote ranch in the fall of 1932. His parents hoped the dry climate and outdoor life would help him recover from rheumatic fever, and Brown still remembers his grandfather's greeting: "Well Al, I hear you're all buggered up." But Drake expected the boy to pull his weight on the ranch, and for more than three years he did—forking hay in the heat of summer, up at five o'clock on dark, bitterly cold winter mornings to haul the first of the day's five loads of hay to hungry cattle. There were long days in the saddle, herding cattle in late winter and early spring across Fraser River rangelands. For a few weeks the brown slopes glowed green, especially after a wet spring snowfall. Roundup in spring and fall required days of hard riding; the cowboys from whom young Al Brown learned were mostly Chilcotin men, skilled and hardworking people who usually drifted on after a year or two at the ranch.

Dr. C. V. (Bert) Brink has known this country intimately for sixty years. A soft-spoken man, Brink combined a professorial career at UBC's Faculty of Agriculture with a passion for the landscape of British Columbia that has taken him into the far reaches of the Fraser Basin. As a young man he climbed to the Fraser's source in the Rocky Mountains; as a range specialist he explored the vast Chilcotin grasslands in the 1930s when serious efforts to improve badly deteriorated rangelands were first undertaken. As a historian Brink has documented some extraordinary elements of B.C.'s agriculture, and as a conservationist he has devoted his life to preservation of B.C.'s rich biological heritage.

Brink tells of the sheep that sometimes grazed the high country, of how rancher W. R. Hayward and his sons drove 4,000 ewes and their lambs 200 kilometres west from their Kamloops base into the south Chilcotin mountains every spring for thirty years beginning in 1935. Late each May the sheep set out on the trek, making about 12 kilometres each day. They plodded past Cache Creek and Clinton, then dropped 600 metres to Big Bar on the Fraser. There, a ferry powered by the river's fast flow carried 135 ewes at a time to the west bank. Once assembled on the far side, the animals began climbing almost 2000 metres into the mountains, where they spent the summer grazing the lush alpine meadows. In late September, the long walk back to Kamloops began. Brink was awed by the spectacle of that huge flock moving across the high country; it was, he says, "one of the longest, most dramatic sheep trails in North America."

Both the livestock industry and the wildlife of the Cariboo-Chilcotin depend, of course, on grass—quality grass and lots of it. The vigour of the grass and of the dependent wildlife species can be compromised by two main factors: encroachment of young trees and brush, and overgrazing by livestock. Fires used to sweep naturally across the land every seven to ten years, keeping brush under control. Wild fire seldom gets far these days, and some ranchers now use controlled fires to keep young trees from establishing on grasslands. There is considerable debate about how effective this practice is and how much damage it might inflict on grassland biodiversity.

But there is little argument about overgrazing, which damages or eliminates plants of grassland ecosystems, hurting both cattle ranchers and wildlife. Fraser Basin grasslands have greatly improved over their badly deteriorated state of a century ago, a considerable accomplishment because even when cattle are removed entirely, overgrazed lands in the high, dry Cariboo-Chilcotin take a very long time to recover: from twenty to forty years, researchers have found. Agronomists Michael Pitt and Tracey Hooper write that well-managed grazing may be compatible with some goals of grassland biodiversity, but the effect on wildlife can vary, displacing some birds while improving habitat for others. Cattle can also trample and destroy sensitive streamside vegetation, and wildlife habitat in ponds can be degraded by draining water for irrigation or harvesting native grass for hay.

The extent to which cattle on well-managed range compete with deer, mountain sheep and other ungulates (hoofed animals) during much of the year is not really understood. It is clear, however, that cattle can displace wild animals on low elevation grasslands crucial for winter survival, like those along the Fraser River. Such displacements were happening at the junction of the Chilcotin and Fraser Rivers until the 1970s, when the province's fish and wildlife branch acquired 4800 hectares of this rugged semi-desert of bunchgrass and sagebrush, deep canyons and wind-carved hoodoos. In 1994 the area was permanently protected by terms of the Cariboo-Chilcotin Land Use Plan. Fenced to exclude cattle, the Junction Wildlife Management Area now supports about 500 California bighorn sheep, the world's biggest non-migratory herd of these spectacular animals. They share the land with mule deer, cougars, grouse and bald eagles. Some bighorns from the Junction reserve have been used to repopulate areas from which they had been exterminated in B.C., Oregon and California.

But the reserve is not enough protection for this unique part of the Fraser Basin. These grasslands are of national importance because nowhere else in Canada does so much of the original grassland still exist. Very little remains on the plains of Alberta, Saskatchewan and Manitoba; most have been plowed at some time for crop production, even in very dry regions where bitter experience and shattered homesteader dreams confirm that they should never have been broken. Pitt and Hooper suggest that the ancient grasslands of B.C. are even more endangered than the province's ancient forests.

Recognizing the significance of this interior grassland, the federal government proposed a national park encompassing about 2000 square kilometres. The Churn Creek park proposal includes a stretch of 25 kilometres along the Fraser River, the Churn Creek and Lone Cabin Creek watersheds, and the upper portion of the Big Creek watershed, some 60 kilometres west of the Fraser River. These watersheds include parts of the Camelsfoot and Chilcotin mountain ranges and would be linked by a band about 10 kilometres wide along Dash Creek. The Empire Valley Ranch would be the core of the Churn Creek-Fraser River section of the proposed park, and current owners of the ranch seem willing to sell. The ranch has for many years been a difficult one to operate, largely because it lacks sufficient summer range.

The proposed park would include sweeping bunchgrass benchlands along the Fraser; forests ranging from ponderosa through interior Douglas fir to spruce and pine; rugged canyons and alpine meadows, and unlogged watersheds whose streams originate in dripping glaciers and ultimately lose themselves in the Fraser. The landscape is large and varied enough to provide winter and summer ranges with migration routes between them for large mammals; complete predator-prey relationships could function here, and the area is big enough to absorb attacks of disease, insects and fire. About 1,000 California bighorn sheep already live here, along with about 2,000 mule deer. This is home to mountain goats, black and grizzly bears, cougar, lynx, bobcat and smaller furbearers, about 200 species of birds, 12 species of bats, and various amphibians and reptiles.

The Churn Creek park proposal also includes a unique human heritage reaching back across thousands of years of aboriginal history. Fraser River salmon supported human life through those years, and fishing for migrating salmon remains central to Native life. Beginning in 1858 hordes of miners sifted the sands for gold at every bar along this stretch of the Fraser, and cattle have grazed the bunchgrass since the 1870s. The generations of cowboys and ranchers who herded them evolved a unique tradition that still stamps life here on the grasslands of the Fraser.

Recreational opportunities abound. Churn Creek park could provide some of B.C.'s finest hiking, horseback riding, ski touring, river rafting, wildlife viewing and photography opportunities. The economic contribution of a national park to the region would be substantial. Consider the injection of federal funds alone: existing national parks in B.C. spend about $2.75 million for goods, services and wages each year, along with about $1.2 million on capital projects. But that's just the beginning. A 1995 study found that in B.C., park visitors spend nine dollars for every dollar spent on park operations. Most of those dollars come from outside the province, so parks in B.C. are, in a sense, an export industry. They also create 9,300 jobs and add about $400 million to the provincial gross domestic product.

Objections to the Churn Creek park proposal by the mayor of nearby Williams Lake are therefore mystifying, since the city would gain far more from a park than from logging at an altitude and climate that means, in practical terms, a one-time cut. People living in this vast, sparsely populated landscape treasure their way of life, and many would prefer that it remain unchanged: the prospect of visitors flooding into the region doesn't appeal to all of them. But as the Cariboo-Chilcotin Land Use Plan evolved, it became evident that unless some of this Fraser River landscape was protected as a national park, it would not survive as a unique part of Canada's natural heritage.

The Cariboo-Chilcotin Land Use Plan set aside as separate protected areas parts of the Churn Creek and Big Creek watersheds, about 40 per cent of the land proposed for a national park. But a large and vital block of land between them was left unprotected. So while various interests argued over who should have access to the area and the extent to which the valleys and high country should be logged, timber companies extended roads and built a bridge over Churn Creek. They began hauling trees from the heart of the proposed park in the winter of 1995–96. Corporate logging plans extend from stream valleys to plateaus and up to elevations of 1800 metres; centuries will pass before trees once again grace these alpine slopes, if they ever regenerate at all. This is an area of the south Chilcotin mountains for which protection as parkland has been advocated by conservationists and various government studies since 1937. With logging underway, park proponents hope that at least corridors of wilderness will be preserved between the Churn Creek and Big Creek watersheds, which were designated as a Special Resource Development Zone in which 30 per cent of the merchantable timber is supposed to remain untouched. But in the first year of the Cariboo-Chilcotin Land Use Plan, there was little evidence of changing practices in the SRDZs; indeed, logging companies appear to be targeting such zones for cutting with particular intensity, almost entirely by clearcutting.

Every day 250 trucks loaded with logs roll by Hanceville on the way to Williams Lake. You don't have to drive far off the Chilcotin's main artery, Highway 20, to see where the wood is coming from. The road heads south here, drops down over successive benchlands to cross the glacial waters of the Chilcotin River, then rises out of the valley and onto the Chilcotin plateau. Now, as the kilometres slip by, a vast landscape stretches naked almost as far as the eye can see on both sides, stripped of nearly every tree. It's not surprising that Native people of the Nemiah Valley watched with foreboding as gigantic feller-bunchers marched across the land, cutting trees with a single slice of huge blades, eliminating the forest that supported their way of life. The words of Chateaubriand echo down through more than a century of global exploitation: the pattern of history, he wrote, is for "forests to precede civilization, deserts to follow."

Forester Herb Hammond fears desertification could happen on this dry, cold Chilcotin plateau. The rivers and lakes that give a false impression of a well-watered land are in fact fed by the coastal mountains, and very little moisture is added as they flow across the plateau to the Fraser River. Hammond explains that individual clearcuts link into "openings effectively in excess of 1000 hectares. Dramatic climate alteration occurs with such deforestation. Virtually all of the 50 000 square kilometre area is above 900 metres elevation. Humans do not know how to regenerate such high elevation forests, and Mother Nature regenerates these areas with extreme difficulty. And yet the trees continue to fall, often creating cold desert-like conditions or 'alpine meadows.' " Other researchers expect a large impact from rising global temperatures here on the interior plateau, where conditions will become even drier, making a comeback for trees even more problematical. Large tracts of forest will probably disappear.

The forest of the plateau is the product of fires that until recent decades swept regularly through the Chilcotin. There are still foresters repeating the old myth that huge clearcuts mimic the impact of such fires. But fires don't remove trees from the land. Rather, they always leave patches of living forest to help regenerate the new forest; ashes return nutrients to the soil, and rotting, fire-killed trees provide homes for a vast range of plant, insect and animal life while decaying into the soil, building its fertility and conserving moisture.

About 75 kilometres southwest of Hanceville, the clearcuts end as the plateau drops off into the deep valley of the Taseko River, whose fast-flowing blue-grey water moves urgently towards union first with the Chilko River and then the Chilcotin. The Taseko's incision in the plateau is a long, slim extension into the mountains of the warm interior Douglas fir zone, with landscape and vegetation distinctly different from that of the plateau. Soopolallie and kinnikinnick display their red berries at the base of firs, and bunchgrass carpets the forest floor. The road crosses the Taseko on a bridge built from valley trees by army engineers in 1969, then leads into Nemiah Valley. This landscape, whose beauty and isolation suggests a B.C. Shangri-La, is home to the Xeni gwet'in, a Chilcotin people known also as the Nemiah Valley Indian Band.

Little has changed in this mountain refuge, where warriors who survived the Chilcotin War of 1864 fled with their families. That conflict, which cost the lives of nineteen white men and ten Chilcotin men, was triggered when a speculator named Alfred Waddington attempted to construct a road from the Pacific to the Cariboo goldfields through the Chilcotin homeland. The Chilcotin people had been decimated in the early 1860s by smallpox carried into their territory by gold miners. The disease had flared up again in 1863, when a white trader sold to the Chilcotin infected blankets he had taken from people who had died of the disease. The legendary colonial judge, Matthew Baillie Begbie, believed the Chilcotins had attacked Waddington's work crews because their land was being stolen by the white invaders. Judge Begbie particularly admired their leader, Lhasas?in; nevertheless he sentenced six of them, including Lhasas?in, to hang. In his fascinating book *Nemiah: The Unconquered Country*, Terry Glavin recounts that "even a substantial body of white opinion at the time saw the hangings as a cowardly and deceitful response to peace talks the warriors appeared to have proposed prior to their capture."

During the succeeding 130 years, the Nemiah people lived from hunting, trapping, fishing and gathering the products of the land; they also grazed small herds of cattle on mountain slopes. But in the 1980s another invasion of Chilcotin territory began. The provincial government and logging corporations were determined to clearcut the region, using a mountain pine beetle outbreak as the initial rationale. When the infestation died out, as Nemiah elders and forest entomologists had predicted, the deforestation continued in order to feed the over-built mills in Williams Lake.

Where the road crosses the Taseko River into the Nemiah Valley, the Xeni gwet'in made their stand. A sign welcomes only those who will respect their land. In 1989 they declared their traditional territory would be henceforth known as the Nemiah Aboriginal Wilderness Preserve, in which no commercial logging, mining or dam building would be allowed. Traditional ways of the people would be practised, and non-Natives would be welcome to visit, camp and canoe subject to permits from the Nemiah band. The territory described in the declaration includes the Nemiah homeland on Xeni (Konni) Lake, Chilko Lake, Chilko River and its tributary, the Taseko, which drains Taseko Lake, and Tatlayoko Lake. The preserve is a land of incredible beauty and over it hovers the snowy head of Ts'yl-os (Mount Tatlow), the mountain that once was a man and now watches over and protects the people.

"We are the only Chilcotin band that big industry has not touched," the Nemiah band stated in 1992. "We hear and see the negative effects of development from the other Chilcotin bands. That is why we are protecting our heritage. That is why we issued the Nemiah Declaration on August 23, 1989, and why we sought and won an injunction against logging companies on October 11, 1991 . . . our elders have always said, 'If you take care of and respect the land you live on, the land will take care of you.' That is why we made our declaration—to protect the land."

Not everyone is able to understand the concerns of Native people. In Williams Lake, Ken Robertson works at Weldwood of Canada and speaks for the local SHARE group, an industry-supported body that promotes the interests of logging companies. "The way I see it," says Robertson, "they're asking for us to treat them differently, differently than we treat each other. Take the Nemiah as an example. I assume they want control of the resources, they want to be able to do with it what they please. If that means giving up what we're doing with it now, and giving it to them, *what are they going to do with it?* Are they going to do something for themselves, and that means the rest of society doesn't have access to that? I don't necessarily go along with that, I believe we can share in what's there."

"What are they going to do with it?" Robertson's question encapsulates the chasm between two systems, two ways of thinking, two ways of life. One is derived from living with the land for a very long time, while the other regards the land as a resource to be exploited for immediate gain. If "sharing" means clearcutting traditional Chilcotin lands, a former chief of the Nemiah band, Annie Williams, has no doubt about the consequences: her people will lose their culture and language, their identity and values, everything that matters. "You see in other Chilcotin reserves, where it's clearcut all around them," Williams says. "There's nothing for them to do but go to Williams Lake, Alexis Creek, Lee's Corner. They drink and they drink, they know it's killing them, but there's nothing for them to do. We're lucky. We're so lucky, because that hasn't happened here."

Roger William, a skilled rodeo rider who has been the Xeni gwet'in chief since 1991, agrees. "If you clearcut here, it would be really hard for us to keep the way we live, even to keep our language. We want to be self-sufficient. You cut down all the trees, maybe it won't even come back. The lakes will be drying up and if the land won't hold the rain, the runoff will move a lot of land, destroy the soil. Ranching's been here three generations now. We don't want to lose that, either. We want to preserve the way we live, for our kids. If you don't disturb the nature, you can do it."

Here in the Fraser Basin's Chilcotin country, opposing views of the relationship of people to the land meet head on. Involved are the rights of a people who lived lightly on the land for thousands of years and with whom no treaties have ever been signed. But there is much more. There is the possibility that a people who have survived for so long can provide insights of importance along the path towards a sustainable future. Perhaps there is a way to integrate their traditional understanding with the insights of modern science, to benefit the two societies as well as the land.

You cannot enter the Nemiah Valley casually. When you break out of the trees on a fine September day and comprehend the landscape before you, the heart stops. Ahead and below lies green-fringed Xeni Lake, its blue depths reflecting white puffs of clouds. Bunchgrass slopes lead gently up from the lake, then break steeply to Mount Nemiah on the right. Southern slopes on the left of the lake lift to the noble face of Ts'yl-os. The V formed by the flanks of the two mountains frames a long blue line of white-capped crags: the Coast Mountains. Just beyond that rampart, streams flow west to the Pacific Ocean. But all the water on this side of those mountains belongs to the Fraser River.

The road winds down to Xeni Lake and stretches the length of its north shore. Ts'yl-os has retired behind a veil of clouds. Past the lake a broad valley of bunchgrass and hay meadow is accented by poplar bluffs and bands of brush winding along creek banks. A few rail fences cut across fields, but not many houses are evident; most are secluded in groves of trees or valley creases. A rocky, rudimentary road covers the last few kilometres leading finally to the shore of Chilko Lake.

On a still, warm September afternoon an ethereal calm pervades this place of overwhelming beauty. On the far shore the enormous barrier of the coastal range, a chaotic melange of ragged peaks clothed in snow and glaciers, rises 3000 metres. At their feet Chilko Lake stretches 60 kilometres north and south, its transparent, green-blue water cradled in a basin 1200 metres above the sea. This is just one of thousands of places from which the Fraser River gathers its flow, sources ranging from insignificant springs to spectacular lakes like Chilko.

It is not easy for people to get to Chilko Lake from the mouth of the Fraser; it is a whole lot harder for salmon. To return here, about a third of the Fraser River's sockeye salmon undertake the most difficult journey of the entire Fraser Basin, negotiating horrendous stretches of churning water in the Chilcotin River after mastering hundreds of tortuous kilometres in the Fraser itself. Survivors branch into the Chilko River. Most of them, about half a million fertile sockeye, spawn in a 5.5-kilometre stretch of river bottom gravel just below the outlet of Chilko Lake—a beautiful, broad stream flowing through a majestic mountain valley. These tiny salmon fry swim upstream instead of down after hatching, so they can spend a year growing in Chilko Lake before undertaking the long swim to the sea.

A couple of years after the Nemiah Declaration, the Xeni gwet'in people were included as key participants in the Chilko Lake Study Team, which was assigned the task of reaching consensus on land use in the region. For the Forest Service and the logging corporations, however, it was business as usual; equipment moved in and clearcuts were scheduled in the heart of Nemiah territory in the Elkin Creek watershed. The Nemiah band warded that off with a court injunction in October 1991. The following year, they blockaded a bridge over the Chilko River to keep loggers out of another part of their traditional lands. Finally the message got through; logging in the region was deferred until it could be planned with the participation of the people of Nemiah.

The Chilko Lake Study Team, with Chief Roger William as its co-chair, recommended to the NDP government the protection of Chilko Lake and much of the Xeni gwet'in traditional territory as parkland. In January 1994, the government announced the creation of Ts'yl-os Provincial Park, 230 000 hectares that include Chilko Lake and, of course, Ts'yl-os. The Nemiah band will share in planning the park and participate in its management and employment opportunities. They are also part of the planning process for the Taseko Management Zone bordering the park and other lands traditionally used by the Xeni gwet'in outside the park. Most important of all, says Chief William, his people will pursue their traditional activities throughout the park and special management zones, and other uses will not be allowed to interfere with that right. Although logging will be allowed outside the new park, it must conform to plans that respect traditional and wildlife values. Ultimately, he says, "we want more control over our traditional lands, and that has to do with the treaty process." But right now, protection of the land is of primary importance, and at least in part that is happening.

So far, Ts'yl-os seems still to be watching over his people.

CHAPTER 6

A Tale of Two Rivers

This curious world we inhabit is more wonderful than convenient;
more beautiful than it is useful; it is more to be admired
and enjoyed than to be used.

HENRY DAVID THOREAU, HARVARD ADDRESS, 1837

Throughout the summer of 1970, brightly coloured helicopters fluttered between the black rock walls of Moran Canyon, a new sound competing with the ancient roar of the turbulent Fraser. At this site about 155 kilometres downstream from Williams Lake, engineers bored into the rock, testing its structural strength. Their work proceeded in secret, the flights almost furtive; no proud announcements proclaimed impending mastery of the river. For they were probing the possibility of halting the river and converting its mighty energy to electricity, and the forces opposing this contest of man against nature were gathering strength.

More than a century before, Robert Carson had looked down on the Fraser from a plateau 1000 metres above this site in Moran Canyon. Except for the helicopters and the slender thread of the B.C. Rail line far below, the river and its valley would have looked little different in 1858. Young Carson, a Scottish-born American, had been the sole survivor of an attack by Indians on a wagon train heading for Oregon. Hearing of gold to the north, he worked his way up the Okanagan Valley to the Cariboo. There he gathered up a few horses and became a packer, hauling food and supplies for the miners streaming up the Fraser in their thousands that momentous summer. From Lillooet, Carson led his packhorses about 35 kilometres along a rudimentary trail on the east bank of the Fraser. Then the route climbed to the plateau of Pavilion Mountain, high above Moran Canyon. Instead of a rocky summit normal to this altitude, Carson was astonished to discover a saucer-shaped tableland 15 kilometres across, rich in bunchgrass, watered by an occasional stream and sheltered by fine stands of fir and pine. Determined to make the mountain top his own, he built a log house and barns and set about irrigating the grasslands with Fraser-bound streams.

Beautiful and productive though it was, marketing the produce of his isolated paradise was a problem. When the new Cariboo Road was completed in 1864, he hauled hay and pigs to Clinton to feed horses and travellers. To sell his cattle, he made one of those desperate drives for which B.C. ranching is famous: with two other men, he pushed a herd of 200 animals down the riverbank trail to Lillooet, followed the Harrison Trail across the Coast Mountains to Lillooet Lake, drove the animals along a rough trail to Howe Sound and through the north shore mountains to Burrard Inlet. The few animals that survived the trip were so thin Carson arranged to fatten them up on a Fraser delta farm. While at the coast, he met a daughter of the Magee family, whose farm eventually became the Kerrisdale district of Vancouver. She returned to the ranch as his wife.

Robert Carson and his mountain-top kingdom are woven into the legendry of the Cariboo. The log ranchhouse grew in all directions to accommodate nine children, two of whom became members of the provincial legislature; for decades the ranch was renowned for its hospitality to travellers. Although it no longer belongs to the family, Mount Carson watches the seasons roll by on the beautiful plateau, which has changed little over the years except for the intrusion of high-tension power lines carrying electricity from the Peace River to Vancouver.

Fifty years before Carson looked down into Moran Canyon, Simon Fraser and his companions careened through French Bar Canyon, just above Moran, in four birchbark canoes. On June 9, 1808, he recorded in his journal:

> Here [the] channel contracts to about forty yards, and is enclosed by two precipices of great height, which bending towards each other, make it narrower above than below. The water which rolls down this extraordinary passage in tumultuous waves and with great velocity had a tremendous appearance.
>
> It being absolutely impossible to carry canoes by land, yet sooner than to abandon them, all hands without hesitation embarked . . . upon the mercy of this Stygian tide. Once engaged the die was cast, and the great difficulty consisted in keeping the canoes in . . . [the current] . . . clear of the precipice on one side, and of the gulphs formed by the waves on the other. However, thus skimming along like lightning, the crews cool and determined, followed each other in awful silence. And [when] we arrived at the end we stood gazing on our narrow escape from perdition.

Depressed, and concerned that even worse might lie ahead, Fraser sent two men downstream the next morning to scout out conditions. They returned to confirm that, as Native people had told him, the way through what we now call Moran Canyon was not practicable by canoe. "In consequence we immediately set to work," wrote Fraser, "erected a scaffold for the canoes where we placed them under a shade of branches to screen the gum from the sun, and such other articles as we could not carry along we buried in the Ground."

Loaded with 36-kilogram packs, Fraser and his men struggled down the west side of the river through Moran Canyon, accompanied from time to time by men, probably of the Shuswap Nation, who were generally friendly once they had determined that these strangers were not enemies from other aboriginal nations. The chief who had accompanied them from Soda Creek provided an important assurance of safety. "The old Chief sent couriers to inform the natives ahead that we were not enemies, [and to tell them] not to be alarmed at our appearance, and to meet us without arms," wrote Fraser.

The attributes of Moran Canyon that forced Simon Fraser and his men out of their canoes signalled a great opportunity for engineers. Always on the lookout for squeeze-points in a river where rock canyons provide solid anchorage for their structures, dam builders dreamed for decades of building a hydroelectric dam between the shoulders of Moran Canyon. A concrete plug 230 metres high, taller than Hoover Dam on the Colorado River, would transform the rushing Fraser into a vast reservoir with its tail reaching almost 270 kilometres upstream to Quesnel. The Chilcotin and Cariboo regions would be divided by a lake up to 8 kilometres wide, drowning vast areas of productive rangeland and one of Earth's great landscapes.

Such an engineering dream was actually accomplished on the Columbia River, which flows roughly parallel to the Fraser about 300 kilometres to the east. The Columbia pours almost half again as much water as the Fraser into the Pacific some 350 kilometres south of the Fraser's mouth. A century ago it was an even greater salmon river than the Fraser, with 10 to 16 million fish returning to spawn each year. The Columbia ecosystem was a cornucopia supporting a Native population similar to that of the Fraser—about 50,000 people—until Europeans introduced diseases that decimated their numbers. Almost forty years before drilling and testing reverberated in the Fraser's Moran Canyon, construction began on the Columbia of the greatest dam the world had ever seen. Grand Coulee Dam would rise more that 100 metres above the river, span more than 1500 metres, halt the flow of the Columbia, turn the energy of this great wild river into electricity and divert some of its water onto farm fields. Its reservoir would back 250 kilometres northward almost to Canada. Grand Coulee began a process that would not end until the Columbia and its tributaries were completely under human control with nineteen major and sixty smaller hydroelectric dams. And there are many lesser structures: in the entire Columbia Basin there are more than 500 significant power and irrigation dams.

The Columbia now produces more electricity than any other river in the world, powering a dozen aluminum plants and the Hanford nuclear weapons facility in southern Washington state, and providing power for the entire economy of the American Northwest. Its locks raise and lower tugs, barges and pleasure boats a total of 220 metres so they can travel almost 850 kilometres up this once-wild river to Lewiston in central Idaho. Its waters irrigate 400 000 hectares of farmland. Historian David Wooster's observation about the damming of the Colorado River could be as aptly applied to the Columbia: "the river died and was reborn as money."

Moran Canyon was not the only proposal to dam or divert the flow of the Fraser. Although no dams have ever been built on the mainstem, several were constructed on Fraser River tributaries. Before World War Two, hydroelectric dams were built on Stave River and South Alouette River, and a storage dam on the Coquitlam, all Fraser tributaries near Vancouver. Work began in 1927 to divert the Bridge River near Lillooet through a powerhouse into Seton Lake and on through more generators to the Fraser. By 1954 this was the biggest hydroelectric system in the province.

As the Kemano project was getting underway on the Nechako River in the early 1950s, B.C. government engineers were tempted by the possibility of boring through a few kilometres of Coast Mountains rock to divert Chilcotin River water westward out of the Fraser system, dropping it 900 metres down the Homathko or Southgate Rivers into Bute Inlet on the Pacific. At about the same time a power dam was proposed on the Quesnel River. Later in the decade a proposal to divert water out of the Columbia into the Fraser surfaced during negotiations leading to the Columbia River Treaty. In 1963 a board advising federal and provincial governments recommended a series of nine power and flood control dams in the Fraser Basin. They called it "System E," and it included a dam on the Fraser itself just upstream of its confluence with the McGregor, east of Prince George. Another System E project, a dam on the McGregor, was seriously studied again by B.C. Hydro in the mid-1970s with a view to diverting the river's flow into the Peace River system for power generation at the W.A.C. Bennett Dam near Hudson's Hope. In the 1990s a diversion from the North Thompson River into the Columbia in order to export Fraser system water to the U.S. was proposed. With the important exception of the Kemano diversion of the Nechako River, none of these Fraser Basin projects materialized.

On the totally engineered Columbia, on the other hand, a tide of concrete swept the river from top to bottom during four decades following construction of Grand Coulee Dam, tightly controlling every drop that flows down the river, flooding 2560 square kilometres of rich bottomland and changing forever the natural function of the river. Thirty to 40 per cent of the Columbia's flow originates in Canada, so to complete American control of the river, Keenleyside Dam (1968) and Mica Dam (1973) were built north of the border under terms of the Columbia River Treaty. A hydro dam on the Canadian portion of the Columbia was added near Revelstoke in 1984.

To a traveller familiar with the Columbia River in the U.S., a short stretch of the river just south of the Canadian border is startling. Flowing rapidly towards the sea, its surface boiling and swirling, it looks and sounds rather like a real river. This is the only part of the American Columbia that does, with the exception of a stretch near Hanford that was spared to avoid flooding a huge repository of nuclear waste. The rest of the American section of the river is a sequence of long, still pools behind eleven great dams, the foot of each washed by the upstream tail of the reservoir below. The Columbia lies silent, flat and calm, its energy drained away by generators spinning far below the surface. Only a few decades ago the roar of that awesome power could be heard kilometres away as the river spilled over spectacular waterfalls and cascaded through tumultuous rapids. Now it is an artificial river, completely controlled by people and computers to satisfy the needs of power generation, irrigation and barge traffic. The allure of a free-flowing river is gone, writes William Dietrich in his fine Columbia River book, *Northwest Passage*: "It is not dead but it is confined, as immobile as a beetle thrown on its back."

Any dam creates a reservoir, ranging in size from almost negligible in the case of small, river-run hydro plants, to enormous inundations of hundreds of kilometres of shoreline, as on the Peace, Columbia and Nechako Rivers. Although often called lakes, reservoirs share few of a real lake's characteristics. Water levels rise and fall according to demands for electricity or water in some far-off market. Over a year, the Mica reservoir on the Columbia River in Canada can rise and fall as much as 45 metres. Vegetation, insects and fish, birds and animals, and people too, all thrive where land meets water. And that is precisely where the impact of water projects is most severe. Normal shoreline biology can't reestablish itself when water levels fluctuate so wildly. An initial flush of fish production in a reservoir usually fades a few years after dam construction; those fish remaining in Canadian reservoirs usually contain so much mercury they can't be sold, and they endanger the health of those who continue to eat them. Dams alter water temperatures upstream and downstream, a crucial factor for migrating salmon. Deep in some reservoirs oxygen may be lacking while hydrogen sulfide may be produced. On the Columbia, water plunging from sluice gates in dams captures nitrogen from the air, causing a fatal condition in fish similar to "the bends" in human divers.

So much of British Columbia is rock, ice and snow that most of the small amount of productive and habitable land in the province borders streams, rivers and lakes in low-lying valleys. In B.C. about 330 000 of these valuable hectares now lie under reservoir floodwaters. Productive forests in the biggest reservoirs were simply drowned—enough, in the case of the reservoir behind the sixty-storey-high Mica dam, to feed a pulp mill for thirty years. In the Nechako reservoir, proposals for underwater logging of the dead and dangerous drowned forests are being negotiated, forty years after flooding. For more than a decade masses of trees and other forest debris floated to the surface of Lake Williston behind the W. A. C. Bennett Dam on the Peace River, where it had to be gathered and burned. Clouds of dust blow from clay cliffs bordering the reservoir, and wave action undercuts the slopes until another massive landslide sends great waves surging across the lake. Where once beauty reigned, ugliness dominates; where once recreational potential was unlimited, dam-flooded valleys in B.C. are dangerous and forbidding. In the Arrow Valley behind Keenleyside Dam on the Columbia, where trees were cleared before flooding, the water rose to inundate 16 000 hectares of small farms, white sand beaches and incredible beauty. When water levels drop to meet power and irrigation requirements in the U.S., expanses of mud separate shore from water, marina docks dry uselessly in the sun, recreation opportunities decline and tourism income dwindles.

All reservoirs are temporary creations, eventually filling with sediment and transforming the dams that constrain them into waterfalls. That would be an early fate of any dam on the Fraser River. The arrested river would drop its burden of silt on the reservoir bottom; eroded from below, its clay banks would slump into the water. Downstream, the river would flow clear and blue, capable now of picking up a new load of silt. Erosion of riverbanks, bridge abutments and other riverside structures could be expected, and the river would scoop up material from large existing deposits of sediment downstream.

Few concerns about negative environmental or social impacts were expressed in the 1930s when Grand Coulee Dam was proposed. Possible difficulties for salmon were mentioned, but engineers were soothing in their assurances that they could build structures permitting the passage of the runs. Forty years later in 1975, the utter failure of such promises was noted amid the fanfare of ceremonies marking the completion of the final dam required to bring barges up the Columbia to central Idaho. The state's governor, Cecil Andrus, warned they could be witnessing the doom of Idaho's salmon runs. "I want to point out," he said, "that the cost of this system has been horrendous, both in dollars and in cost to our natural resources." Neither hydro dams nor irrigation facilities have paid for themselves on the Columbia—both have been massively subsidized by the American taxpayer. "Dams are the American pyramids," writes Dietrich, "and the Columbia our Valley of the Kings." Wallace Stegner, one of the wisest observers of the North American West, warned against trying to engineer the land into something it is not: "It will rise up against us in all its wrath some day."

The Columbia River salmon fishery, once one of the world's greatest, now averages about 15 per cent of normal. Many races have been wiped out and others have been declared endangered species. This catastrophe is the culmination of many things: dams that interfered with movement upstream of adults and downstream of their young; spawning streams that vanished under reservoirs or whose spawning gravels disappeared under silt washed from logged-off slopes or farm fields. Water temperatures rise in reservoirs and denuded streams, often to levels lethal to spawning salmon. Desperate efforts to repair the damage have largely failed; from 1980 to 1992, U.S.$1.3 billion was spent on efforts to double remaining Columbia River salmon runs, and more than U.S.$130 million continues to be spent annually on efforts to revive fish populations. Adding the value of power not generated in order to spill water needed by fish, the cost rose to U.S.$350 million in 1994, the year the Columbia salmon fishery virtually collapsed. And as Columbia fish runs disappear, writes Dietrich, "so do the cultures built around them, from tribal reservation economies to Scandinavian gill-netters at the river's mouth."

The Americans didn't set out to destroy a river, explains Chad Day of sfu's School of Resource and Environmental Management. Most developments on the Columbia were preceded by very sophisticated research, and many ways of managing the basin have been tried. But it is unlikely they will develop a satisfactory system at this late stage, says Day. "Whatever you do," he explains, "you've got to foreclose as few options as possible . . . as soon as you build a dam, you've destroyed all other options—it's just like cutting off a person's leg or an arm or his neck. All the options are gone."

Were the Americans able to start over, writes Dietrich, the Columbia complex wouldn't meet today's environmental or economic requirements. The project would be approached very differently, more cautiously, much more slowly, with greater attention to fish and water conservation. A leading authority on the Columbia, Kai N. Lee, suggests that whatever efforts are to be made to improve the situation on the Columbia, they should be regarded as steps towards "adaptive management" of the river, with each change regarded as an experiment from which lessons can be drawn. In this concept pioneered by ecologists C. S. Holling, Carl Walters and their colleagues, all decisions are part of a learning process, rather than the staking of a position to be defended and promoted by those involved. Advocates of holistic resource management take a similar approach: when you've made the best decision of which you are capable, assume that you are wrong; monitor the results and alter course quickly when flaws show up.

Why does the Fraser River still run free, in startling contrast to the imprisoned Columbia? Certainly not because of any greater wisdom north of the border. This story of two rivers spans decades of hard-learned lessons, leaps of scientific knowledge and advances in public understanding of the natural systems that support us. Serious engineering studies at Moran began after the highest tide of faith in engineering mega-projects had swept by and other values were beginning to be recognized. Techno-faith endured a bit longer in some jurisdictions. In Québec the James Bay Project was completed in the 1980s, but further stages of the project have been stalled by public protest in Québec and in client states in the U.S. In the West, right-wing provincial governments in Alberta and Saskatchewan were able to ram through the Oldman River and Rafferty-Alameda dam projects only by subverting environmental law, ignoring scientific studies and scorning public concern.

"When I was a student at engineering school," says hydrologist Robert Newbury, "we knew that the engineer was there to make use of resources for the benefit of people. No one ever said anything about assuring the continuance of ecosystems for the benefit of mankind. It was all about converting raw materials to man's use." That approach has dominated all our relationships with nature, Newbury points out, but the impact of manipulating water is particularly spectacular. "We have preferred not to work *with* water, but rather to force it to do our will. We make sudden, massive changes, unleashing forces and effects we don't understand. From digging small drainage ditches to constructing great hydro dams, we are often surprised at the unforseen impacts of our projects. We often create unstable and unlivable places when we manipulate water and redirect its enormous energy without understanding its role in the landscape. The river, after all, is ancient and indifferent to our society and will still be there when we are not. It can be dangerous to our wellbeing if improperly used."

This has been the hard lesson of massive hydroelectric projects across Canada: the brutal restructuring of the landscape of northern Manitoba when Manitoba Hydro diverted the Churchill River into the Nelson; severe damage to the Athabasca delta, the world's largest freshwater delta, by the Bennett dam 1000 kilometres upstream on the Peace River. Above the Bennett, rising waters flooded more than 360 kilometres of rich valley bottomland, and the reservoir inundated hundreds of square kilometres of productive forests. Across Canada, the first victims of massive water projects have almost always been aboriginal people: the Ingenika people whose land disappeared under Williston Lake behind the Bennett; the Cree, Dene and Métis people who depended on the productivity of the Athabasca delta; the Cree of northern Manitoba whose fishery was destroyed; the Cree of northern Québec whose way of life disappeared beneath the waves of the James Bay Project; the Cheslatta people displaced by Alcan's Kemano scheme. All are people whose lives and traditions revolved around the rhythms of a river; they are, as federal water policy advisor Frank Quinn has shown, "particularly vulnerable to artificial changes in water distribution and quality . . . their lives have been disrupted severely by government-approved corporate resources development."

Along with growing recognition of the negative environmental and social impact of dams, the economics of power generation have weighed heavily against hydroelectric proposals in the Fraser Basin in recent decades. In the 1950s and 1960s utilities extravagantly promoted the use of electricity, then predicted exponential growth in consumption to justify enormous increases in generating capacity. Today, those predictions seem products of a sort of delirium. With each hydro project more costly than the last and with nuclear energy turning out to be an expensive aberration, the price of electricity rose rapidly. Utility customers reacted by reducing consumption, leaving many power companies paying for costly, under-used facilities—even, in the state of Washington, abandoning partially built nuclear plants. American energy expert Amory Lovins showed that a kilowatt saved is cheaper than a new kilowatt generated, so both consumers and power corporations could profit by conserving electricity rather than producing and consuming more. This insight encouraged the development of technology that generated and used electricity more efficiently, and conservation policies like the effective Power Smart program in B.C.

As engineers probed the rock of Moran Canyon on the Fraser, the federal Department of Fisheries and the International Pacific Salmon Fisheries Commission were completing a study of the impacts of such a dam. Their 1971 report stated that a dam at Moran would destroy all salmon populations spawning upstream of it and at least 50 per cent of those downstream. Hatcheries could not compensate for lost natural fish production, said the report, and the cash value of that loss would be so great that Moran Dam power could no longer be considered cheap—in fact, alternative sources of electricity would be less costly.

But there was much more than economics behind the growing opposition to Moran Dam. In the 1970s people were ready to listen to other voices expressing different values. Roderick Haig-Brown, one of the most revered names in B.C. conservation, was particularly eloquent. He strongly endorsed the findings of the 1971 fisheries report, then added:

> To discuss all this factually and dispassionately is in some ways a betrayal of the salmon and their meaning. The Pacific salmons are almost the last of the North American continent's mighty manifestations of abundance . . . Man has responded to the salmon runs, from earliest times, with a sense of wonder and gratitude that adds to his own stature . . . To set against all this power 'needs' that can be better met in other ways is an aberration, an insensate arrogance, that has no place in modern thinking . . . To destroy [the salmon] would be an act of vandalism that British Columbia cannot afford, Canada cannot afford and the world cannot afford. It would leave a burden of guilt that the collective conscience of the nation cannot sustain. To preserve them is an act of faith in the future.

The facts presented in the federal report, the authority of the federal Fisheries Act and the passion of many people as expressed by Roderick Haig-Brown finally forced B.C. Hydro to shelve its plans for a dam at Moran Canyon. In the 1990s the construction of a dam on the Fraser River seems unimaginable. In 1995 Premier Mike Harcourt declared the Fraser "the heart and soul of British Columbia" and introduced the Water Protection Act, which prohibits large-scale river diversions between major watersheds in the province and large-scale export of water from the province. While the legislation does not specifically ban dam construction on the Fraser or its tributaries, in the same year the province established the British Columbia Heritage Rivers Board, which promptly nominated the Fraser as a B.C. Heritage River and recommended its inclusion in the Canadian Heritage River system. "The Fraser is perhaps the most critical river in the province in terms of its cultural, natural and recreational importance," says the board's chairman, Mark Angelo. "Many believe it to be the finest salmon river in the world. Recognizing the Fraser as both a Canadian and provincial heritage river would formally proclaim it as a national treasure and help to ensure that it receives the profile and attention it deserves."

On June 13, 1808, Simon Fraser and his companions camped on the west bank of the Fraser just downstream of Bridge River Rapids. Carrying heavy packs after abandoning their canoes at Leon Creek, they had made their way on foot past the Moran Canyon dam site and struggled along the precipitous slopes of the giant S the river follows to work its way through the Camelsfoot Range. With the thunder of the rapids in his ears, Fraser recounted in his journal, "The country through which we passed this day was the most savage that can be imagined, yet we were always in a beaten path and always in sight of the river, which, however, we could not approach, its iron-bound banks having a very forbidding appearance."

Fraser camped the next night at the site of today's Lillooet, about eight kilometres farther downstream. He was nervous about the intentions of large numbers of people of the Askettih (Lillooet) Nation who met them dressed in "coats of mail" made of strings of hard wood intertwined like basket work. The chief who had accompanied the white men down the Fraser from Soda Creek once again intervened. "Our Chief conveyed our sentiments with great animation," wrote Fraser. "He assured the Askettih Nation that we were good people and had nothing to do with the quarrels of Indian Nations." The concern of the Natives was not unreasonable: they often warred with the Chilcotins to the north, who regularly slipped over mountain passes at night to steal their food, weapons and utensils, and to carry off women.

Their village was on the east side of the river, fortified, Simon Fraser tells us, by pallisades 18 feet high. When the Lillooets had been persuaded of Fraser's peaceful intentions, they crossed the river in considerable numbers in wooden canoes. "I had to shake hands with at least one hundred & thirty seven men, while the Old Chief was haranguing them about our good qualities, wishing to persuade some of them to accompany us on part of the journey to which several did assent." To Fraser's regret, the "old Chief" and the interpreter who had accompanied them such a long way left during the night. Without the old man he felt exposed, as he wrote in his journal of June 15, 1808: "Here we are, in a strange Country, surrounded with dangers, and difficulties, among numberless tribes of savages, who never saw the face of a white man. Our situation is critical and highly unpleasant; however we shall endeavour to make the best of it; what cannot be cured must be endured."

Fraser's fears may have been justified. In 1970 while filming his Fraser River documentary *The Politics of Power*, producer Mike Poole met an elderly Native man named Sam Mitchell at Lillooet. As a young boy, Mitchell had heard his great-grandfather tell of seeing, when *he* was a young boy in 1808, the arrival of Simon Fraser and his men at Bridge River Rapids. He overheard a debate about whether the white strangers should be killed; it was decided that by allowing them to live, more blankets could eventually be acquired than by taking only those that Fraser and his men carried with them.

Plenty of evidence remains to substantiate Simon Fraser's impression that the Lillooet region supported an important aboriginal community. At favourable locations throughout the Chilcotin, round depressions indicate sites of semi-subterranean winter homes known as *kekule* (or *shi-eesh-ti-kin*). These pit-houses provided warm and comfortable accommodation for extended families, usually from fifteen to thirty persons, though some were larger. A framework of poles over the excavation was covered with cedar bark and earth. Smoke from cooking fires escaped and people entered through a hole in the middle of this roof, climbing down a ladder notched into a log. Archeologists have dated some of these structures back 3,500 to 4,000 years, and they were still in use well into the nineteenth century.

Pausing here while rafting down the Fraser in the early 1990s, Bruce Obee writes, "Indians in the Bridge River-Lillooet region thrived in a sophisticated society. Three thousand years ago as many as eight villages were each inhabited by 500 or 1,000 people. But about 1,100 years ago the villages were suddenly abandoned. Archeologists believe the aboriginal culture collapsed when a landslide temporarily dammed the Fraser River, preventing the salmon from reaching spawning grounds. Though the original village sites were never reoccupied to historic levels, large populations nonetheless returned to live along the river." Many *kekule* have also been found around Anderson and Seton Lakes, which drain into the Fraser at Lillooet. A century ago salmon ran so thickly in these lakes and their streams that Native people say it was necessary to go to mountain streams for drinking water. Trout and sturgeon, whitefish and landlocked salmon were plentiful too.

But nature sometimes abandoned the aboriginal population. When

Judge Matthew Baillie Begbie camped at Lillooet in 1859, he reported to Governor James Douglas that "many hundreds of Indians had died of absolute starvation during the winter. The Indians said that the salmon had failed them now for three years altogether." Because they took them only for food, Begbie was not outraged at charges of cattle stealing by Natives. He may have thought they had just cause, because the Natives in turn told him that American miners prevented them from mining gold, stole their food supplies and blamed them unjustly for cattle and horse thievery.

Begbie gave the name "Cayoosh" to this place on the banks of the river where the Harrison trail intersected with the perilous old trail up the Fraser Canyon from the south, both of them joining the new, northbound trail to the Cariboo. Although comprised of no more than a dozen rudimentary buildings, Begbie described it as "decidedly the most favourable position for a town that I have seen above Fort Hope." Two years later Governor Douglas renamed the town Lillooet, after the people who had lived there for so long. By then it was a booming gold rush town of 15,000 people, complete with thirteen saloons and twenty-five "licensed premises" strung out in one long street on a wide benchland overlooking the Fraser River. Throughout the day, the dust of hundreds of horses and mules swirled down the street as trains of animals arrived, repacked and departed from this town known as Mile 0 of the Cariboo trail.

Lillooet declined after 1864 when the new Cariboo wagon road bypassed it. The town flourished briefly again twenty years later when as many as 600 Chinese miners staked Cayoosh Creek to remove gold that had been somehow overlooked in the earlier rush. A decade later the Golden Cache mine exploited a gold discovery on a mountainside above the creek, but that boom soon sputtered out and Lillooet became little more than a ghost town. The arrival of the Pacific Great Eastern Railway in 1915 assured the town's survival, and new gold finds far up the Bridge River Valley breathed economic life into the region again. The Bralorne and Pioneer mines were rich producers for four decades, their convoluted veins of ore perhaps the mother lode of gold particles washed from river sands far downstream by earlier miners. The two mines yielded about four million ounces of gold, worth about $1.5 billion at today's prices, before they were closed in 1971.

In 1912 a surveyor named Geoffrey Downton stood on Mission Mountain near Lillooet and noticed that Bridge River, on one side of the mountain, flowed at a much higher altitude than Seton Lake, on the other side. He imagined the power the river's water could generate if it dropped directly to Seton Lake instead of continuing its more gradual course to the Fraser River. Fifteen years later, construction began on what would be for a time the province's biggest hydroelectric project. Bridge River was dammed in two places, creating Lake Downton and Carpenter Lake. A tunnel was driven 3960 metres through Mission Mountain to drop the lake's water 360 metres to a powerhouse on Seton Lake. By 1960 a second tunnel and powerhouse had been built, and another dam at the exit of Seton Lake diverted water through a power plant close to the Fraser River. All these hydro developments added to the difficulties of local salmon stocks, which had already been hard hit at the turn of the century by canneries at the mouth of the Fraser, by a hatchery on Seton Creek that killed more salmon than it produced, and by rock slides in the Fraser Canyon. Spawning channels built on Seton and Gates Creeks were successful in rebuilding some of the pink salmon runs, and improved management of the dam on Bridge River has helped sockeye to rebuild on that stream. But periodically, poor management of water flows on the river by B.C. Hydro continues to wipe out large numbers of salmon.

The modern town of Lillooet stretches comfortably along the benchlands of the Fraser at its junction with Cayoosh Creek, linked by a bridge to the highway from Lytton, 60 kilometres south, and to Vancouver by a new paved highway southwest through the mountains, via Pemberton, Whistler and Squamish. A backdrop of mountains rises dramatically above the town, reducing it to toy-like proportions. The summer heat lays a blanket of stillness broken frequently by the growl of heavily laden logging trucks. This is a hot country of ponderosa pine scattered across flats and slopes of bunchgrass and sagebrush. Dome-like mountains rear above the brown, fast-moving Fraser River south of Lillooet, sparse pines near the river thickening to greener slopes of fir and spruce at higher altitudes. Where a bench is sufficiently large and level to cultivate, a patch of emerald signals diversion of a mountain stream onto fields to produce winter forage for cattle. Such fields sometimes break so precipitously to the Fraser that one imagines that a rancher working near the edge of his field could easily tumble off. On other large benches, expanses of black plastic fabric shade crops of costly but extremely profitable ginseng.

Fifty kilometres south of Lillooet a rushing blue-green stream escapes through a rocky canyon. Leaving tree-clad mountain slopes behind, the Stein River cuts its way to the Fraser through broad benches of pine and bunchgrass. Round white boulders try vainly to slow its dash towards the great brown river in which all traces of the Stein's transparent water vanish within a few metres. Traces of Native settlements more than 6,500 years old have been uncovered nearby; shelter from wind and an abundance of food and building materials made the mouth of the Stein a favoured wintering place for people of the Nlaka'pamux Nation. About seventy round pits indicating *kekule* houses have been found here, some as large as 18 metres in diameter. Dried foods were stored in smaller pits.

An ancient trail follows the stream up through the canyon into the Stein Valley, an incredibly beautiful watershed of 1060 square kilometres. Streams pour into the Stein River from side valleys leading up to peaks and ridges that surround and define a landscape ranging from hot, dry pine and bunchgrass near the Fraser, to cool, colourful alpine meadows and glacial lakes high on mountain slopes. In the broad central section of the valley, fertile soil supports fine stands of cottonwood, Douglas fir and spruce coveted by logging corporations. Chinook and coho salmon spawn here, sharing the meandering Stein with Dolly Varden char, steelhead, rainbow trout and Rocky Mountain whitefish. This bottomland is key winter habitat for grizzly and black bears, mule deer, moose, cougar and many smaller mammals; mountain goats, grizzlies, marmots and pikas share the high mountain slopes in summer. The trail threads the length of the Stein Valley, climbing out over a mountain pass 50 kilometres from the canyon entrance and continuing on to Lillooet Lake and the coast.

Aboriginal people hunted in the Stein Valley and gathered many kinds of roots, berries and other foods and medicines. But the Stein was much more: it was a secret place of deep spiritual significance to Native people. The river valley provided sheltered isolation in which boys and girls experiencing puberty could live with nature for a period of four months to a year; here they would acquire the strength of character and cultural awareness needed in adulthood. In places of particular power, a solitary boy or girl would light a fire, then sing and dance until overtaken by exhaustion or daybreak; in this state they might receive revelations of a close relationship with a particular animal or bird. "Acquisition of power through a nature helper was the culmination of the puberty experience," write Michael M'Gonigle and Wendy Wickwire in their book, *Stein: The Way of the River.* "After such an encounter, the initiate was able to make both a physical and psychological break from childhood." In the Stein Valley such experiences live on in red pictographs drawn on rock walls. The images originate in dreams and visions of the artists; some are very old, and the most recent appear to have been made just before Native cultures were overwhelmed by the gold rush in 1858.

Faced with the formidable barrier to road-building posed by the

rocky canyon that guards the entrance to the Stein Valley, forest companies delayed cutting the great trees of the middle Stein while logging
almost every other large valley of the Fraser Basin. By the time the corporations were ready to tackle the valley in the 1970s, Native people
and conservationists had begun the campaign to save the Stein that was
to last twenty years and draw thousands of people into active involvement. For many years, "Stein Voices for the Wilderness" festivals celebrated the values of the valley, while books and films carried the Stein
story across Canada.

Still, transnational timber corporations insisted they had to log the
Stein Valley, partly to demonstrate their continuing control over forests
in the province, partly because they had severely overcut the other
forests of the Lillooet Timber Supply Area and wanted the trees of the
Stein to compensate for a dwindling resource. At the Stein festival of
1987, Chief Ruby Dunstan of the Lytton Indian Band demanded,
"What more do these people want? They take our lands. They take our
culture, they take away our traditions. They take our language. They've
anglicized us. They've tried to fit us into a society that we really don't
belong to. Now they're going to go and strip our land. They're going
to take everything that we have. That's the last little bit of dignity we
have, out there in the Stein Valley! . . . And after that what else do they
want—our lives?"

The plea was heard finally by the provincial government. On
November 23, 1995, the NDP declared the entire 110 000 hectares of
the Stein River Valley a Class A provincial park. One of the earth's special places will remain intact to inspire the minds, renew the spirits and
challenge the bodies of future generations of Canadians. After more
than 135 years of boom and bust, an opportunity now exists for the
region to develop a truly sustainable economy.

Near the mouth of the Stein River on June 15, 1808, some Lillooet
men drew a map for Simon Fraser. They showed the tumultuous
downstream course of the river and warned him it was impassable for
canoes. They also indicated another river to the east, flowing parallel to
the Fraser. This was very likely the Columbia, but Fraser still believed
he and his men were following the Columbia River themselves. Actually, it was Fraser's North West Company colleague, the great map-
maker David Thompson, who was exploring the Columbia in
1808—he didn't know what river he was on either. Thompson knew
about the northern arc of the Fraser, the *Tacoutche Tesse* described by
Alexander Mackenzie. And he also knew the location of the mouth of
a large river far to the south, the Columbia, explored by Capt. George

Vancouver's expedition in 1792. Since neither Thompson nor Fraser knew of anything that would suggest the existence of *two* great rivers, it was tempting to draw a line on the nearly blank map linking these two known segments into one river. But when he later drew both rivers on his extraordinary map of 1814, Thompson named the newly recognized river in honour of the colleague whose incredible descent made it known to the world: Simon Fraser.

Today, no traveller would have difficulty distinguishing between these two mighty rivers flowing across the vast western landscape of North America on parallel courses about 300 kilometres apart. One, the Fraser, still runs free, fierce and productive, a fountain of life. The other, the Columbia, is reduced to a string of placid reservoirs where humans rule and the freedom, inspiration and productivity of nature is only a memory. A few pathetic survivors remain to testify that this was once the world's greatest salmon river; billions of dollars have failed to revive it. Circumstances of time and fortune determined the different fates of the two rivers. Today, nothing could excuse the similar destruction of another great river.

Thompson River Watershed and South Cariboo

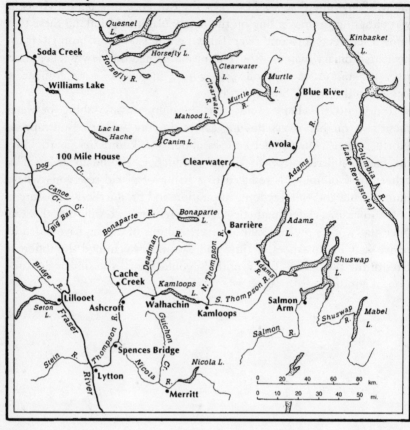

CHAPTER 7

The Great Blue Tributary

It is the salmon that expresses the force of our land. Without the salmon,
the land and the rivers would only survive as a corpse survives the death of
the nervous system and the departure of the spirit.

ALAN HAIG-BROWN, FOREWORD TO *ADAM'S RIVER*

On June 19, 1808, Simon Fraser's little band of explorers rested blistered feet where a clear, fast-flowing river sweeps into the silt-laden Fraser River from the east. Fraser called it the Thompson, after his colleague David Thompson. It is by far the greatest tributary of the Fraser, contributing almost 22 per cent of its total flow, draining an inland empire of 55 000 square kilometres. The power of this warm river enables it to remain aloof of the Fraser for a while; blue and brown currents flow side by side until at last the Thompson surrenders to the might of the Fraser. At their confluence, warm winds blow up the Fraser in summer, and heat builds to torrid levels. This is often the hottest place in Canada. Ponderosa pines space themselves across sweeps of brown dormant grasses awaiting fall rains. Sloping benchlands break and plunge towards the swirling rivers far below, often so steeply that they create precipitous slides of rock and gravel, or cliffs of black rock.

From their ancient village of Kumsheen on the bench above the spectacular meeting of these two rivers, the Nlaka'pamux people must have watched in some amazement the arrival of Simon Fraser's travel-worn group on the opposite riverbank. These were the first white men of their direct experience, though Native people on the Pacific coast had been trading for about twenty-five years with Europeans who sailed around Cape Horn. A few items—kettles, cloth, guns and alcohol—had reached Kumsheen over traditional aboriginal trade routes.

For more than 6,000 years the Nlaka'pamux people had lived here. Known by white settlers as the Thompson Indians, they regarded the land in which they lived and from which they drew all their needs as a house, kept secure in its order and abundance through well-established traditions and ceremonies. The boundaries of the Nlaka'pamux territory were known precisely to the people and their neighbours, and Kumsheen—present-day Lytton—was regarded as the core of their world. As Chief Cixpe'ntlam put it in 1858, "At Lytton is my centre-post. It is the middle of my house and I sit there."

In his journal Fraser recounts the hospitality offered by the people of Kumsheen. "The principal chief invited us over the river. We crossed, and he received us at the water side, where, assisted by several others, he took me by the arms and conducted me in a moment up the hill to the camp where his people were sitting in rows, to the number of twelve hundred; and I had to shake hands with all of them . . . We had every reason to be thankful for our reception at this place; the Indians shewed us every possible attention and supplied our wants as much as they could."

The Thompson combines the flow of two powerful streams, the North and South Thompson Rivers. The North Thompson is born of alpine rivulets in the Cariboo Mountains, only about 80 kilometres west of the glacial trickle high in the Rocky Mountains that gives birth to the Fraser River. As these two streams with a common destiny gather strength, they travel in opposite directions through very different land-scapes. The North Thompson flows south almost 300 kilometres to Kamloops where it is joined by the South Thompson flowing in from the Shuswap Lake region to the east. Together they flow west another 150 kilometres through hot semi-desert to Lytton where their sparkling flow joins the brown torrent of the Fraser River. The Thompson and Fraser Rivers are the southern and northern arcs of a great circle of water enclosing the Cariboo Mountains, Quesnel Highlands and the Cariboo region.

Three years after Simon Fraser's 1808 expedition, David Stuart of the Pacific Fur Company arrived on the banks of the Thompson where its north and south branches unite into one wide river. "Cumloops," the aboriginal people called it, and the site's advantages were obvious to any fur trader. Stuart's company was an American enterprise based at Astoria at the mouth of the Columbia River. In 1812 he built a trading post on the low spit lying between the North and South Thompson. Hot on Stuart's heels came Alexander Ross of the North West Company of Montréal; the Nor'Westers soon took over the Astorians' operation. The fort was moved across the North Thompson and later moved again, this time to the present site of Kamloops on the south bank of the Thompson. In 1821 the North West Company merged with the Hudson's Bay Company.

Until contact with Europeans, aboriginal people used animals, fish and other resources only to the extent required to meet their needs. The relationship between hunter and prey was an intimate one based on deep respect for the being that offered itself to the hunter. Anthropologists Michael Kew and Julian Griggs of UBC explain that this bond was an essential element in the stability of Native culture in the Fraser Basin: ". . . the indigenous cultural systems contained mechanisms of restraint and conservation adequate for long-term protection and maintenance of the resource base." The Native relationship with the salmon in particular depended upon an intricate combination of rights, responsibilities and taboos, and on detailed knowledge of the fish, its habits and relationship with the environment.

The arrival of fur traders drastically changed the relationship of the people with their environment. Commercial hunting, fishing and trapping replaced subsistence use of nature. Native hunters strove to fulfill the expectations of the traders in exchange for seductive goods. It took only fifteen years to strip the region of its furbearing animals; as wildlife populations collapsed, trade fell off so drastically at Fort Kamloops that by 1828 the Hudson's Bay Company post was no longer profitable. This was a repetition of the pattern of exploitation that had propelled the fur trade westward as successive regions were exhausted of animals. British Columbia—known as New Caledonia at the time—had experienced its first bust in a cycle that would recur over and over again.

In the summer of 1862, some of the Overlanders had decided they wanted no part of a perilous raft trip down the Fraser River. Seeking a safer route to the goldfields of the Cariboo, thirty-two of them headed south from Tête Jaune Cache, hoping to reach Fort Kamloops before winter. Driving their remaining livestock and horses, they hacked a trail through the dense forest and over a pass dividing the Columbia and Fraser watersheds. Now travel was downhill, following the Albreda River some 20 kilometres to its junction with the North Thompson. As they struggled south down the heavily forested valley of the North Thompson between the Monashee Mountains on the east and the Cariboo Mountains on the west, they probably had little time or inclination to admire Pyramid Falls bursting in a silver cascade from the flank of a mountain later named for that intrepid English traveller, Walter Cheadle.

Despairing of reaching Kamloops before winter, they decided to entrust themselves to the river. For August Schubert and his family there was additional urgency: Catherine, his wife and the only woman in the expedition, was in the final month of her pregnancy. On hastily built rafts they loaded horses and beef jerky made from their slaughtered cattle. It was tough going; a strong current carried them rapidly between obstructions of tangled driftwood through which they hacked their way. But nothing warned them of the terror to come. In *The Overlanders of '62*, published in 1931, M. S. Wade picks up the story: "Before the travellers realized their danger they ran into the Murchison Rapids and were carried against the shore. Two of the men jumped out and tried to hold the raft, but the force of the current dragged it out of their grasp. It careened down the tumult of waters out of control, finally crashing into a rock in midstream, precipitating the horses into the water. Thompson and Fannin, the only ones left on board, jumped on the rock while the raft, lightened of its load, was borne away in triumph by the raging current. Strachan was drowned in this catastrophe."

This fearsome stretch of the North Thompson River is today the core of Little Hell's Gate Regional Park, about midway between Avola and Blue River. The modern Yellowhead Highway climbs smoothly over Messiter Pass, but for the Overlanders it was a 14-kilometre portage that took three days of struggle in snow and cold rain before finally they assembled at the bottom of the rapids with their meagre possessions. Here they built new rafts and then floated down a stretch of placid, slow-moving river, almost a long and narrrow lake where sandbars reflect the sun when the water runs low in late summer. For good reason, Stillwater Flats was the original name of the village of Avola on the banks of this calm stretch of the Thompson. But the almost idyllic passage didn't last long; after floating 50 kilometres they hit Mad River Rapids. Most of the Overlanders gave up on the river and walked the remaining 165 kilometres to Kamloops. That wasn't an option for the Schuberts; Catherine could not possibly make the trip on foot, so once again the family committed itself by raft to the North Thompson River.

Gaunt with hunger, they ran their raft ashore near a Shuswap village hoping to find food. Seeing no activity, the Schuberts were approaching the houses cautiously when to their horror they saw bodies, dead bodies, lying everywhere—victims of the epidemic of smallpox that swept through B.C. that year. The outbreak had originated in Victoria, brought ashore by a miner from San Francisco; it quickly spread through the city and to Natives camped within and around the town for trade. White people were quickly vaccinated and those infected isolated in hospitals. Native people were driven out of town and their camps burned; with nowhere else to go, they headed back to their home territories, spreading the disease as they went. The *Victoria Colonist* observed, "were it likely that the disease would only spread among the Indians, there might be those among us like our authorities who would rest undisturbed, content that smallpox will rid this community of a moral ulcer that has fostered at our door through the last four years." By June smallpox was in Shuswap territory in the Thompson Basin, where it wiped out thirteen villages. About a third of the B.C. Native population died that year, perhaps 20,000 people.

On October 13, the current carried the Schubert family raft into the mainstem Thompson River at Fort Kamloops. On shore near the trading post a tent was erected for Catherine Schubert, and within hours she gave birth to the first white child born in B.C.'s Interior. Most of the Overlanders soon moved on, eventually returning to their homes in Eastern Canada. Of those who stayed, several became prominent citizens of the province. Very few actually tried to find the gold that had inspired their incredible journey.

A century and a half after the Overlanders' tortuous trip down the North Thompson River, the valley remains sparsely populated. Wending its way southward the river grows steadily with contributions from rivulets and streams, the valley widens, the climate becomes warmer and drier, cedars dwindle and pines are more prevalent. Rushing rapids become fewer, and more frequently the North Thompson is a tranquil, tree-shaded stream winding through picturesque farmland. Countless meanders cut channels, create alluvial fans and sand beaches; they flood across lowlands and undercut benchlands until trees robbed of support tumble into the water. Shifting patterns of land and water reflect the dynamics of flowing water, the complexities of a living stream, the processes through which a river creates and is created by the land through which it flows.

The forests of the North Thompson have been exploited on a massive scale to feed high-capacity sawmills in the region, and a pulp mill at Kamloops. Clearcuts have eliminated forests on entire mountainsides, though new forests are well established on some of the better growing sites. The North Thompson itself is seen by promoters as a commodity marketable in the United States. Multinational Water and Power Inc., a B.C. corporation, is associated with an American dam-building company, KVA Resources Inc., in a scheme that proposes drawing a million acre feet from the river and pumping it through the Monashee Mountains into Kinbasket Lake, a reservoir on the Columbia River in eastern B.C. From here the flow of the Columbia south into the United States is controlled by the Americans under terms of the Columbia River

Treaty. Far downstream in Oregon, the promoters would draw off that million acre feet and pipe it to California, where they expect to sell it for $1000 or more per acre foot.

The project's promoters suggest that a million acre feet is only a tiny fraction of the flow of the waters of the Fraser Basin. True—but irrelevant. It is half or more of the North Thompson's flow where they propose to tap it, only about 30 kilometres from the river's icy origins. Removing a large part of the Thompson River's flow in spring would deprive the watershed of the annual recharge it requires to function, altering the river's hydrology at least as far south as Kamloops. "There's no surplus up there," says resource consultant Larry Fidler. "To propose export for these headwaters areas is just completely ridiculous."

"Surplus" is how promoters describe water they want to export, but of course there is no such thing as surplus water. The entire landscape is a function of the normal flow of a stream, of its floods and low flows. Wetlands, backwaters and other critical land-water margins depend on high water each spring for their annual renewal—and that is precisely what the water promoters want. The North Thompson River and its tributaries support important populations of chinook, sockeye and coho salmon. In Kamloops, fisheries biologist Gordon Kosakoski understands the importance of those backwaters to fish. "Shortly after emerging from the egg, juvenile salmon—particularly coho, but also to some extent chinook—utilize the side channels off the main channel of the river," says Kosakoski. "Many of these areas are inundated only for a very short period during the spring, at a time of very high flow. Yet the fish get into them and use them for that very short period, sheltered from the main current, benefiting from an abundant food supply, then moving out as water drops." Kosakoski adds, "The other thing that high spring river flows do is visibly flush the system: they tend to flush silt from the spawning gravels, maintaining the quality of the spawning gravel in the river."

Any diversion from the North Thompson River or any other tributary of the Fraser would add additional stress to a system already suffering the effects of pollution, logging, overfishing and urbanization. Fisheries biologist Otto Langer points out that the flow of the Fraser River has been declining for more than a decade, whether due to global warming, forest practices or to Alcan's Kemano diversion. Flow through Hell's Gate and other difficult passages of the Fraser Canyon is sometimes low enough already to create problems for migrating salmon, and Langer insists that more diversions would multiply those difficulties. The problems of reduced flow extend beyond the basin: Langer reminds us that the biological productivity of the Strait of Georgia, the Juan de Fuca

Strait and the west coast of Vancouver Island all depend on the strength
and volume of the Fraser's flow. The river carries nutrients downstream
to the sea, and the power of its entry into the Strait of Georgia creates
currents that draw nutrients in from the open ocean and up from its
depths.

Fisheries scientist John Roos, a former director of the International
Pacific Salmon Fisheries Commission, reports a direct relationship
between the discharge of the Fraser and the number of sockeye smolts
surviving the trip to the ocean. More Fraser River water means more
returning adults years later. Michael Healy, director of UBC's Westwater
Research Centre, points out that not only is the character and productivity of a river closely related to its flow, but so is the productivity of
the estuary at its mouth and on the continental shelf hundreds or more
kilometres away.

But what of the plea that new water supplies are urgently needed in
the U.S., particularly California? Every study, report or declaration by
reputable institutions and individuals in the field of American water
resources concludes that there is no shortage of water in the western
U.S. that in any way threatens the life or economy of the region. The
issue is kept alive by those who think that there is much money to be
made if Americans can be convinced that importing Canadian water is
easier than tackling water problems at home, or if Canadians can be
persuaded they have "surpluses" of water that would never be missed.

With the exception of those who envision big profits, massive water
development is generally acknowledged to be an outdated concept. In
parts of the U.S., decommissioning dams is of more interest than building them. Public meetings held in the valley of the North Thompson
River have overwhelmingly rejected any consideration of removal of
water from the river. The project's proponents were resoundingly
rejected when they tried to gain support from unions that might benefit
from construction jobs on such a project. Native people have been particularly vehement in their opposition. Chief Nathan Matthew of the
Shuswap Nation points out that in addition to serious environmental
questions raised by the export issue, the rights of Native people have not
yet been determined by treaty in much of B.C., and he's adamant that
First Nations will not allow their last and most basic resource, water, to
be taken by outside interests. To the Shuswap water is not a commodity;
it cannot be traded nor can anything else substitute for it.

In 1995 the government of B.C. enacted the Water Protection Act,
banning any export of water from the province. Several years earlier the
federal government had stated that Canada does not favour water
export. But serious doubts remain. The Free Trade Agreement with the

U.S. (FTA) and the North American Free Trade Agreement (NAFTA) raise the spectre of international trade agreement dominance over domestic legislation. Neither the FTA nor the NAFTA exempts trade in water from their provisions. Both the Progressive Conservatives under Brian Mulroney and the Liberals under Jean Chrétien have said such a measure is not necessary to protect Canadian water, yet such protection is actually enshrined in the agreements for other products.

Pressure to export water from the North Thompson prompted local NDP MP Nelson Riis to propose in the House of Commons late in 1995 an act that would specifically ban water exports to the U.S. The bill was defeated, though then-environment minister Sheila Copps had long promised such legislation. Riis fears that should water be exported from provinces like Alberta, which has not banned exports, water would then be considered a "good" in international trade, and nothing, including B.C. legislation, could protect it from American corporate interests.

The B.C. government, many trade experts and concerned organizations like the Agricultural Institute of Canada have been joined by tens of thousands of Canadians who signed petitions pressing the federal government to sign a Memorandum of Agreement between Canada and the U.S. confirming that water is explicitly excluded from the terms of the FTA and the NAFTA. Nothing less should satisfy Canadians that their water resources are safe from being categorized as just another marketable commodity.

At the town of Clearwater, about 180 kilometres from the North Thompson's glacial beginnings, the river is joined by one of the most spectacular tributaries of the Fraser system. Clearwater River is the culmination of an incredible concentration of waterfalls, rapids and chutes, probably the greatest in B.C. It is a world of white water and blue lakes protected by one of the province's largest and finest parks, Wells Gray. This wilderness reserve stretches across more than 520 000 hectares of mountains and alpine meadows, recent volcanoes and lava flows, all drained by streams destined for the Clearwater River.

From its source in Clearwater Lake, the river has over eons carved a deep valley through lava and rock to the Thompson. Along the way streams drop into the Clearwater River from a plateau that lifts almost vertically above its east bank. From alpine meadows and tree-bordered lakes, streams tumble down mountain slopes towards the river, bursting suddenly into the valley as dramatic waterfalls, sometimes enfolded by curves of gigantic bowls carved in lava by falling water. Helmcken Falls is the most celebrated; here Murtle River drops 142 metres, creating the fourth highest waterfall in Canada and one of the most spectacular in all of North America. This is just the last leap of the Murtle; trickling from glaciers in the Cariboo Mountains, the river froths its way down a narrrow valley to pause in Murtle Lake, a wilderness canoeing paradise that is one of five large lakes in the park. Setting off again, the water plunges down half a dozen waterfalls before throwing itself off the plateau and thundering into the bowl at Helmcken Falls.

Below the mouth of the Clearwater, the North Thompson is a broad, powerful river. The watersheds of both rivers are traditional territory of the North Thompson Band of the Shuswap Nation. Nathan Matthew is band chief. In the comfortable log house he and his wife Marie and their son Mark have built in a forested area of their reserve near Barrière, Chief Matthew ponders the meaning of river to his people. "It's valuable just for what it is. It's such a large part of our life. You talk to the elders, you know there's a little bend here, that island there, that place there, they all have different names. It's part of our understanding of the world."

Nathan Matthew's ancestors saw the valley of the North Thompson taken away from them almost overnight. He relates that devastating experience to events today and suggests that it is not just aboriginal people who are losing out. "The people in this valley should have control over their destiny," Matthew insists. "And they should connect up with other peoples in other valleys and other watersheds who have a common concern. People with common interests should be banding together in terms of protecting values, not just protecting the bottom line. I'd say that all of B.C. is like a colonial system, with the rest of B.C. supporting Vancouver and Victoria, the large metropolitan areas. All the value of the resources somehow ends up trickling down there, and that's where the big economic benefits are. They're not here in Barrière, or in all the Lillooets and all the Savonas. I know there's real power and there's real value being created from these resources, and it's happening somewhere else."

Chief Matthew is part of a new generation of Native leadership that continues to draw on traditional wisdom while insisting on change. "We sort of beg people to invest in our country, and we say we have to reconstruct our laws so they have free access," says Matthew. "We're crazy! Why should I beg anyone to come in and invest in my resources? We have the trees and the water, which have a way of replenishing themselves. They are living things that continue to grow if we look after them, if we make sure the soil doesn't wash away, if we maintain those things in a long-term, sustainable way. Some politicians are willing to prostitute the resource for a few bucks. And not only for a few bucks, but actually to give the future decision making over those

resources to someone else that really doesn't have our interests at heart.
And I say that's wrong."

When the North Thompson River receives the crystalline contribution
of the Clearwater River, it has already emerged from the dark cedar-
hemlock rainforests of the interior wet belt. Now it's a broad, powerful
river flowing directly south; the valley widens and warms, making room
for graceful, tree-lined meanders. Douglas fir takes pride of place,
bunchgrass openings grow larger as rainfall diminishes, the mountains
withdraw and surrender rocky grandeur in favour of more modest, tree-
clad summits. The heat intensifies, graceful ponderosa pines space themselves across vast gold and brown grassy slopes. Within great loops of the
river and along its banks, irrigated fields grow forage for cattle that range
far back into the grasslands and forests of the surrounding hills. We have
returned to the interior drybelt first encountered south of Williams Lake
on the Fraser River.

In this semi-desert, trees have largely deserted the valleys to cluster on
those hilltops high enough to catch moisture from passing clouds. In
some valleys, abandoned log houses, outbuildings and corrals remain as
witnesses to the shattered dreams of homesteaders who watched crops
sprout and grow, only to shrivel and burn in the July heat. The land has
long since reverted to range, though some of these tiny components of
big ranches are still known today by the names of farm families defeated
by drought.

Dry hills rise behind the city of Kamloops; below, the North
Thompson plays out its final act, pouring broad and strong into the
South Thompson River entering from the east. Together they flow
westward as the Thompson River bound for the Fraser and the Pacific
Ocean. Across the water the brown bulk of Paul Mountain presides
over this union of two great streams. Like most cities Kamloops owes
its location to a river; like a great many, it arose where rivers meet,
offering advantages for travel, trade and productivity of land and water.
For more than thirty centuries before Europeans saw it, this confluence
of rivers was the centre of trade for much of the southern interior of
British Columbia. In summer the Shuswap people hunted and collected herbs and berries in the forests of the plateau. When autumn
came they moved down into the valleys of the Thompson to catch and
dry salmon for their winter food supply. Here they stayed for the winter in round *kekule*, whose depressions can still be found along the
riverbanks.

Although the gold rush had in a sense begun here on the Thompson,
most of the excitement occurred elsewhere, and Kamloops was involved

mainly as a crossroads. Of the many trails that passed through, those of the cattle drives heading for the Cariboo goldfields were of the most lasting importance. A narrow ribbon of buildings clung to the south bank of the Thompson before 1900, growing slowly into a comfortable town of about 10,000 just after World War Two. Today about 65,000 people live here, making it second in size to Prince George in the Fraser Basin upstream of Hope. Residential subdivisions, malls, government buildings and warehouses, fast-food outlets and gas stations spill up the hills behind the narrow riverside bench where town life was originally focused. Developments have spread across the river to the level land of North Kamloops and string out eastward along the South Thompson, sadly similar to suburban sprawl in most North American cities. But in Kamloops even the heavy hand of the real estate developer can't obliterate the awesome beauty of this hot, dry land with its dusty, rolling hills and always, at its centre, the river. Within the city, the parched landscape grows green with gardens, parks and trees blessed by water from the Thompson, its strong, blue current moderating torrid summer days and limiting the bitter edge of cold winter ones.

The desert sky is no longer crystal clear at Kamloops. Thick, sulfurous fumes sometimes hang over the city like a particularly odiferous Los Angeles smog, produced by a pulp mill built in Kamloops in 1972. It's one of the six mills in the Fraser River watershed that contribute 75 per cent of the wastewater poured into the system above Hope; the mills discharge about the same quantity of suspended solids as the three sewage treatment plants serving Greater Vancouver. A range of other chemicals—chlorinated organics, for instance, and highly coloured lignosulfonates—are among the thousands of organic and inorganic substances that pour from mills into the watershed. The use of chlorine for bleaching pulp is related to the production of highly toxic dioxins and furans, which even at very low levels remain and concentrate in living tissue over a long period of time. Downstream of the Kamloops mill, environmentalists have gathered samples from dark, foam-covered pools along the river, and in the widening of the Thompson known as Kamloops Lake, dioxins in trout reach levels making consumption inadvisable.

But the recent focus on pulp-mill pollution—by scientists, citizens, media and politicians in British Columbia, and by markets overseas where consumer demand is growing for chlorine-free paper products—has made an astonishing difference. New provincial regulations governing pulp-mill effluent began the process in 1990, and requirements were greatly stiffened in 1992. By 1993 the pulp industry had spent a billion dollars on improved technology, and the results were dramatic: dioxins discharged into the Fraser River system had been cut by 98 per cent, and furans were down by 85 per cent. By the year 2002 all organic chlorides must be eliminated from pulp-mill effluent in B.C. The eventual goal is a closed-cycle mill, discharging no effluent at all into the river. This has already been achieved at a mechanical pulp mill at Chetwynd in northern B.C., and research continues on technologies that could close the system for bleached kraft mills too.

The pulp mill at Kamloops is downstream of the city's water intake. But Ruth Madsen of the Thompson Institute, a local environmental group, points out that logging activity upstream in the North and South Thompson watersheds compromises drinking water quality in the city. Twenty years ago the Thompson flowed clear even during high water in spring. Now, logging in the Chase Creek watershed is one source of the sediment that pours into the South Thompson each year with spring runoff. The resulting turbidity sometimes requires the trucking of drinking water into the city and may force the expenditure of $30 million or more to filter Thompson River water. As well, free access by cattle to the river upstream of Kamloops can compromise water quality in winter, says the Thompson Institute.

The South Thompson River gathers water from Shuswap and Adams Lakes about 70 kilometres east of Kamloops. The river pauses briefly in Little Shuswap Lake before flowing down a valley that grows hotter and drier as it approaches the city. Native villages dating back at least 5,000 years have been found along these banks, and almost 200 archeological sites are located between Chase and Kamloops, providing ample evidence of a rich, salmon-based culture. Like the North Thompson, the South Thompson owes much of its opulence to heavy rainfall on the slopes of the Monashee Mountains. Shuswap and Adams Lakes reach deep into well-watered cedar-hemlock forests. Shuswap Lake's four arms arrange themselves into a sort of H, and its clear waters and beautiful crescent beaches draw large numbers of summer vacationers. The lake plays a key role in the world's greatest salmon drama: the Adams River run.

Every four years they come, an October celebration of nature's fecundity at its most bountiful, a crimson tide flooding over the shallows at the mouth of Adams River. The sockeye salmon's silvery-blue ocean livery has been transformed to brilliant red, announcing eagerness to mate and readiness to reproduce. The recently developed hump on the male's back may protrude above water, his upper jaw hooks menacingly downward and his large spawning teeth warn off interlopers as he pairs with a female. She is carrying 3,000 to 4,000 eggs; with vigorous flips of her tail she arranges rocks, fans away silt and prepares a nest on the river's bottom. When all is ready, she releases a few hundred eggs that the male instantly clouds in milt containing millions of sperm.

Almost immediately the pair repeats the process just upstream, with rocks displaced from the new nest covering eggs in the earlier one. Along 12 kilometres of the Adams River the drama is repeated, with more than half the spawning concentrated in just 2 kilometres immediately above the river's mouth on Shuswap Lake. Salmon produced in the 60 hectares of good spawning gravel in this river will be worth hundreds of millions of dollars when they return from the ocean in four years. About 2 million of between 6 and 10 million salmon will escape the nets lying in wait for them and make their way back here. Tens of thousands of people will come too, watching in awe from the banks of the Adams. It is fitting that the entire 12 kilometre length of Adams River is protected as a provincial park named for Roderick Haig-Brown, whose superb writing about salmon and passionate efforts to protect its habitat helped British Columbians understand their intimate link with this magnificent animal.

The Adams is, as Mark Hume puts it in his fine book *Adam's River*, a "perfect river" for salmon. Adams Lake lies above it, a steady source of cold, clean water. The gravel bottom of the river and its tributaries provides excellent nesting habitat for the salmon, a place where newly emerged sockeye alevins can survive among the rocks. Below the river, Shuswap Lake provides a productive environment in which salmon fry can live and grow for a year before swimming down to the sea. This combination of clear, cold river and bountiful lake is found throughout the Fraser Basin and is the key to the system's enormous production of sockeye salmon. Lakes like Quesnel, Chilko, Stewart and Bowron team up with a multitude of Fraser tributaries to produce the millions of smolts (year-old salmon) that swim down to the sea each year.

The largest Adams River sockeye run repeats every fourth year (1994, 1998, 2002, etc.) in what is known as a dominant run. In the weakest year of the Adams cycle (1996, 2000, etc.) only a few hundred fish may return. It is not well understood why three years of the cycle produce only a small fraction of the numbers of a dominant year, though theories range from the impact of human interference to natural cycles of plankton abundance. There is no doubt, however, that people have destroyed many runs in the Fraser system and weakened many others.

The Upper Adams River, flowing into Adams Lake, and the Salmon River, emptying into Shuswap Lake at Salmon Arm, are two of many Thompson River tributaries reputed to have seen runs equalling that of Adams River. The Upper Adams sockeye were obliterated by a logging

dam operated on that river from 1907 to 1922. The dam and the logs
sluiced down the river almost destroyed the Lower Adams run too, but
enough survived to enable a recovery to current levels, though it took
more than thirty years. Rock slides at Hell's Gate in the Fraser Canyon
in 1913 and 1914 wiped out a huge summer run on the Salmon River,
among many others throughout the Fraser system. The Adams River
sockeye survived the Hell's Gate slides because it was a late-season run
and by the time the returning salmon entered the Fraser, obstructions
had been partially cleared from the canyon.

Fisheries biologists tried for years to introduce strains of sockeye from
other streams into the Upper Adams with very little success. But in 1996
their efforts finally paid off when about 30,000 sockeye returned to
spawning beds in the Upper Adams that had not seen a salmon for
almost ninety years. For DFO fisheries biologist Ian Williams it was a
dream come true, and if future runs can be protected from overfishing,
he is confident the Upper Adams River can again produce millions of
sockeye salmon. On the Salmon River, a lot of community effort in collaboration with federal and provincial biologists is gradually improving
habitat damaged over the years by elimination of shoreline vegetation,
channellization of the river course, removal of water for irrigation, and
silt from logging and farm operations. Later runs on the Salmon River
may slowly rebuild, but that great summer run is gone forever. Genes
passed from generation to generation for thousands of years in a finely
tuned adaptation to this particular river can never be recovered.

Little is known with certainty of the mysterious process that draws
sockeye salmon thousands of kilometres from the depths of the north
Pacific to the Adams River. For two years they have cruised the ocean,
eating first the plentiful plankton of the continental shelf, then moving
on to squid in the open ocean. Ninety-five per cent of their weight
accumulates at sea; when the call comes, they carry this ocean abundance back to the land and far into the Interior. The timing and direction of the long swim to the mouth of the Fraser seems guided by
some combination of light, magnetic lines of force and electric currents
related to the Earth's magnetic field. Then the smell of the water leads
them home to the particular stream in which they were born.

A sockeye's endowment to its young does not end with exhaustion
and death. Disintegrating sockeye carcasses yield nitrogen and phos-
phorus that nourish blooms of plankton in Shuswap Lake, the plankton
upon which young salmon fry will feed next spring when the current
of Adams River carries them down to the lake. As the tiny fish graze in
large schools along the lakeshore, they in turn are eaten by rainbow
trout, coho salmon, loons and mergansers. This interdependent system

requires good quality water in the lake and lots of undisturbed, natural shoreline. Both are threatened in those sections of Shuswap Lake where development pressures are heavy, for this is an environment extremely attractive to people too. Dredging, filling, replacing natural vegetation with sand, malfunctioning sewage systems—all can be devastating to the Adams River sockeye, to the great chain of life dependent upon it and to an important part of B.C.'s economy and culture.

The Thompson River and its branches seemed obvious transportation routes from the earliest days of European settlement, particularly since Kamloops had to wait many years for even a rudimentary wagon road. The discovery of gold on the Big Bend of the Columbia River at last provided an economic reason for steamship service, and in 1866 the sternwheeler *Marten* was built by the Hudson's Bay Company. The vessel carried freight from Savona's Ferry at the outlet of Kamloops Lake to the northern tip of Shuswap Lake's Seymour Arm, about 70 mountainous kilometres from the goldfields. But the Big Bend boom collapsed within a year and the *Marten* slowly disintegrated at its Fort Kamloops mooring. Through the years about a dozen sternwheelers sporadically plied the waters of the Thompson until the last one, the *C. R. Lamb*, was beached near Kamloops in 1948. The finest ship was probably the *Peerless*, launched in 1880. Forty metres long and capable of making 18 knots, she could sail in water only 45 centimetres deep. The *Peerless* pushed 160 kilometres up the North Thompson in June of 1881, then down the mainstem Thompson to Spences Bridge with supplies for railroad construction crews. Not surprisingly, she was nearly wrecked in the turbulent waters; it took her five days to climb back up through the rocks of Black Canyon.

Today, transportation along the Thompson River owes more to the valleys it carved than to its flowing water. The Canadian Pacific Railway follows the South Thompson to Kamloops, and the Canadian National Railways descends the North Thompson to the city; then they share the valleys of the Thompson and Fraser, often through landscapes with inadequate space for even one railroad. Still to come were highways that somehow squeezed into the canyons along with the railroads, reaching east from Kamloops through the Rockies to the rest of Canada, and west through the Coast Mountains to the Pacific.

Robert Pasco has been searching for stray cattle on the steep sagebrush slopes of his ranch on the banks of the Thompson River. On horseback he opens a corral gate with the easy grace of a life in the saddle that included twenty years on the rodeo circuit. Nearby, the comfortable family home is shaded from the scorching sun by graceful Lombardy poplars. Sprinklers water lush green hay crops just beyond the corrals on one side; on another side the benchland drops precipitously to blue water far below where a miniature train winds its way through the valley along the opposite bank of the river.

Pasco was born in a log cabin just down the road. His ranch here on the Oregon Jack Creek Indian Reserve is a modern operation that reflects his dedication to the land. "I've not done anything to this place that my grandmother or my grandfather would be displeased with," says Pasco. "Only thing is, I haven't built myself a root cellar and I think they would be upset with me over that!" Pasco is chief of the Nlaka'pamux Nation centred at Lytton; his political involvement was triggered by that railway on the riverbank far below.

In anticipation of rapid load growth in the mid-1980s, the federal government authorized the CNR to build a second track along its mainline through British Columbia. That meant wedging yet another transportation corridor into 700 kilometres of Thompson and Fraser River valleys and canyons; in many places there was simply no room for this double-tracking. Sometimes the CNR opted for the cheapest and easiest solution: dump rock into the river to create a bed for the track. This would transform natural riverbanks into walls of stone, sometimes eliminating resting and rearing places for juvenile salmon. The current in the narrowed river would be speeded up, with unpredictable impact on the energy budget of salmon migrating upstream. Fisheries biologist Otto Langer describes how sockeye salmon heading for Adams River hug the shoreline of the Thompson in a 1.2-metre-wide band that is ideal for the dipnetting long practised by Native people. This is exactly where rock would be dumped. Langer points out that fish could perhaps get by one or a few such disturbed areas, "but when you add up many kilometres of increased swimming activity, what does it do to their fat reserves? If you add 1 or 2 per cent more stress they might not make it. And if they get to the spawning grounds, maybe they won't have energy enough to spawn—right now, under natural conditions, some run out of energy."

Between Ashcroft and Spences Bridge, the CNR runs through 13 kilometres of the Oregon Jack Creek Indian Reserve. For almost 3.5 kilometres of that distance, members of the reserve have salmon fishing rights on both sides of the river. They objected to the CNR's intention to double its track by rock dumping, which could interfere with their traditional fishing rights, block access to the river and threaten salmon stocks. The federal government appointed an environmental impact panel to study the matter, but before it could report, the CNR announced it was beginning construction. Outraged, the people of the Oregon Jack Creek reserve threatened to blockade the CNR mainline. The federal government appointed UBC law professor Andrew Thompson, one of Canada's leading authorities on resource law, to facilitate negotiations between the Nlaka'-pamux and the CNR.

On April 1, 1985, Thompson was discussing the issues at a meeting in Pasco's home when the first trainload of rock rumbled across a bridge onto the reserve. Pasco and a friend rushed to the site, scrambled under the railway cars and stood precisely where the rocks were to be placed. They looked up at the men who operated the levers that would spill the rock, friends of many years. If they released the load, Pasco and his companion would die.

Thompson hastened to the scene, as did a DFO helicopter; CNR officials took up position on the opposite bank of the river. Thompson shuttled back and forth across the river in the helicopter, mediating between railway officials on one side and Pasco and his people on the other. Finally, the train backed across the bridge without dumping its load. Charges of trespassing on CNR property were laid against Pasco, but the Oregon Jack Creek Indian Band obtained an interim injunction forbidding the CNR from dumping. It was the only recourse the people had since the railway company ignored their requests to be involved in decisions concerning the project, the DFO took no steps to protect the fishery and the Department of Indian Affairs provided the band with no support. Nor had the people forgotten that this was the railroad whose careless construction practices in the Fraser Canyon in 1913 and 1914 wiped out salmon stocks and shattered Native life through much of the Interior. Eventually the CNR abandoned some of its double-tracking plans because the expected loads did not materialize, but the legal case the project precipitated in this hot, dry stretch of Thompson River Valley will have repercussions throughout the Fraser Basin and across Canada.

Andrew Thompson points out that historically in B.C., "Indian people would be ignored except to the extent that their reserve lands were needed for non-Indian purposes. Then the procedures would be initiated for surrendering Indian lands to the government so that they could be granted to developers." The *Pasco* case may change all that. Already, the decision of the Supreme Court of Canada in the 1990 *Sparrow* case assures aboriginal people the right to fish anywhere in the Fraser Basin where they have historically done so. If the Pasco injunction is made permanent by the Supreme Court, writes Thompson, it will mean that "in addition to aboriginal rights to fish, Indians living along the rivers have rights . . . that may include ownership of the banks and beds of the rivers and of the right to fish, similar to real property rights recognized by the common law . . . this Indian owner-ship of reserve and fishing rights can thwart corridor development such as railways, roads, pipelines and transmission lines unless Indian agree-ment is reached or expropriation procedures are successful."

In 1996, the case of *Pasco v. CNR* was still winding its way through the legal system. The case is a result, says Thompson, of a conflict of values: "the railway's determination to minimize the cost per mile of track as opposed to the Indians' sense of duty to preserve the valley for their children and grandchildren." The final resolution will have extremely important implications for the entire Fraser Basin, since ninety-one Native bands have reserves on the river and its tributaries. Quite apart from aboriginal rights, the case raises again an issue that is crucial to the basin's future: is it to be controlled by corporate interests or by the people who live in it? For Thompson, the involvement of Native peoples as full partners in the management of human activity in the Fraser Basin should be a solid contribution to its sustainability. "Maybe," he suggests, "they can show us a better way."

The branches of gnarled juniper trees are heavy with hard, blue berries. A few paces away the Thompson River flows deep and dark, rushing to join the Fraser. Here at Juniper Beach, about 65 kilometres downstream from Kamloops, not far below the widening of the Thompson River known as Kamloops Lake, the valley bottom slopes away and up, the parched soil supporting mainly sagebrush, bluebunch wheatgrass and prickly-pear cactus. Long needles and red bark mark an occasional ponderosa pine, a grace note in a stern landscape. Black cottonwoods cling to the water's edge; stunted firs scatter down from higher eleva-tions where the hills catch a bit of moisture; they thin and finally vanish in the heat and drought of the valley. This vast and awesome landscape is parched by oven-like temperatures that may exceed 40 degrees centi-grade in summer; during the entire year, rain and snow don't exceed 22 centimetres.

Although this desert land is the hottest and driest place in Canada, it was born of ice and snow. Ten thousand years ago a great horseshoe-shaped glacier curved down the Thompson and up its tributary, the Nicola River. As the ice field melted and withdrew, ice dams trapped sediment-laden torrents in temporarary lakes where the silt dropped and accumulated. As the barriers melted, the currents they released carved terraces and benches that lift in steps from the Thompson River of today. Outcroppings of mineralized rock glow red, yellow and green where they break through eroded soil or rise above the benchlands. In its austere magnificence, the Thompson Valley is unlike any other place in the Fraser Basin. Bruce Hutchison described it as "a wide and empty trench burning in the sun." Many find it desolate, intimidating; it certainly doesn't encourage the intimacy of a softer, greener river valley, perhaps because the cycle of life is not so obvious here.

Yet the Thompson Valley is far from the wasteland it might appear to be to the casual traveller. For Rocky Mountain elk and Rocky Mountain bighorn sheep, the brief sheen of green in March and April is a welcome relief from the rigours of winter. But it is in the river, the Thompson itself, that the life forces of this valley are concentrated. Only the Fraser itself is as rich in salmon and trout. The immense volume of water flowing through the arid valley carries millions of young salmon to the sea each year; four of the five species of Pacific salmon return in response to the primaeval call to spawn in the waters in which they were born. All the way up the food chain to grizzlies and eagles and people, life depends upon this inflow of ocean productivity deep into the mountain-rimmed Interior.

When Charles E. Barnes looked across this awesome landscape in 1907 he didn't see its true wealth; he saw instead what it might be if water could be brought to these parched benchlands along the Thompson. Not far to the southeast, the more hospitable Okanagan Valley was experiencing a boom in orchard development, drawing many wealthy British immigrants. The young American American engineer was convinced that the same could happen here at Walhachin, about 18 kilometres east of Cache Creek. Already, down by the river a farmer named Charles Penny had grown some productive apple trees.

It was a time of great optimism when anything seemed possible in the Canadian West, and Barnes convinced the Marquis of Anglesey to finance his dream. In 1908 their new company, British Columbia Horticultural Estates Ltd., bought Penny's property and about 4,500 acres (1800 hectares) on both sides of the river for a dollar an acre. They tapped nearby Deadman River high in its watershed, conveying its water 32 kilometres along steep hillsides and over deep ravines in what they called the Snohoosh flume. This 1.8-metre-wide structure would be the lifeline of the entire enterprise.

By 1909 steam tractors were breaking the land and Barnes was supervising the planting of orchards. About forty English-style bungalows were built for upper-class English immigrants drawn by effusive advertising to this outpost of empire on the Thompson. A luxurious hotel in whose dining room only formal attire was permitted was officially opened by Prime Minister Sir Wilfred Laurier; a community hall rose complete with spring-loaded dance floor. Soon there was a swimming pool, a skating rink and a polo field. In a grand gesture of faith in the possibility of transplanting English civilization to this stark land, the Marquis of Anglesey built himself an imposing home over-looking the river. The first fruits and vegetables were marketed in 1911, and in 1913 the first carload of apples was shipped. Prosperity seemed imminent.

Instead, catastrophe struck. Twice. And the dream was over.

The first occurred on August 13, 1914, when Britain declared war on Germany. Within a month, half the adult men of Walhachin had left for their homeland; of the 107 eligible men in the community, 97 enlisted. Those left behind could not possibly tend the thousands of irrigated acres or adequately maintain the Snohoosh flume. A cloudburst in 1918 was the *coup de grace*, overwhelming the flume with water and mud. The lifeblood of Walhachin flowed no longer. The Marquis of Anglesey had exhausted his funds and the provincial government refused to help reha-bilitate the project. Not many men of Walhachin survived the war, and fewer came back. The dry ground produced no vegetables and fruit trees withered. The desert reclaimed its own, with only an occasional heat-blasted apple tree hanging on to life amid the sagebrush.

Above Highway 97 today, traces of the Snohoosh flume cling to harsh hillsides, boards preserved by the heat of ninety summers. The sun beats down on the remains of Walhachin. A few houses survive, but the great hotel is long gone and no trace remains of the fabulous home of the marquis. The circumstances of Walhachin's demise were unusual and the flowering of this particular desert was remarkably brief, but the ultimate fate of this dream by the Thompson River was no different from that of many similar efforts around the world.

Bruce Hutchison was sure the demise of Walhachin was temporary. "Another town will rise here some day when the river is pumped and greater orchards will grow in straight lines up the hillside," he wrote. "When cheap power can lift the water of the Thompson upon these benches they will support a hundred miles of cultivation on both sides of the river, from Spences Bridge eastward. This will be another Okanagan fruit valley, a farm area as rich as any in Canada."

But electricity did not become the limitless, cheap commodity envi-sioned in Hutchison's postwar world; instead, conservation is a key ele-ment of modern utility strategy. And half a century of fisheries and other aquatic research has shown that removal of water from the Fraser system can severely reduce the productivity of the river and adjoining ocean. The Snake River in the U.S. is the Thompson's twin—the prin-cipal tributary of the Columbia River, as the Thompson is of the Fraser. But in Idaho, after flowing about a third of its course, the Snake comes to an end behind the Milner Dam. All its water has been diverted for irrigation, its salmon replaced by potatoes. Below the dam the river must begin all over again. The irrigation of vast blocks of the arid American West was undertaken with religious zeal, and during the early stages of development only a few people, like Wallace Stegner, asked "why?" For most, it simply had to be a good idea "to make the desert bloom," particularly when the cost of delivering water to parched landscapes was largely paid for by the American taxpayer. The idea appealed to the giant agribusiness corporations that, along with railroads, insurance companies and others with pools of wealth, bought out the original settlers.

Such could have been the fate of the Thompson if its benches were lower and the idea of public subsidization of irrigation was as powerfully promoted in B.C. as it was south of the border. Kamloops agrologist Graham Strachan describes the quality of the soil as ideal, lacking only the organic material that more moisture and less heat would have fostered. Many fertile benches less than about 60 metres above the Thompson are irrigated with water pumped up from the river, but costs are too great to lift the water much higher. However, all water flowing through the dry lands towards the Thompson River is allocated to human use, mainly irrigation.

Cattle ranching remains by far the most important agricultural enterprise in the Thompson watershed and has shaped the character of much of the Interior. Kamloops is at the heart of B.C.'s ranch country. Cows graze mainly on crown rangelands, producing calves sold in fall to feedlots in Alberta or B.C.; lighter animals are kept through the winter to graze for another summer. In past decades, tomatoes and potatoes of renowned quality were grown along the Thompson, and for many years up to 300 carloads of produce—apples, beans, potatoes, winery grapes, onions, roots, alfalfa seed—were shipped annually from Lytton. But markets for Thompson Valley products were lost to large corporate farms in the western U.S., which could produce more cheaply using heavily subsidized irrigation water. Many American farmers were put out of business by such policies as well. Today, irrigation along the Thompson and Fraser Rivers mostly grows hay to feed cattle during the winter, though increasing amounts are sold to horse owners and dairy farms.

Any vision of miles of fruitlands along the Thompson is a nonstarter according to Strachan, primarily because the climate is too cold in winter. But he predicts new opportunities for vegetable crops, small fruits and dairy farming as urban pressures mount in the lower Fraser Valley and water shortages become more severe in the Okanagan. And there's growing interest in nontraditional crops such as ginseng and other products with specialty markets. "These benchlands have a tremendous capability to produce a range of crops that aren't being grown right now," says Strachan. Although it is not economic today to pump water onto good soil on the higher benchlands, technology or markets may change in future, and Strachan thinks that such possibilities make any thought of exporting water to the U.S. extremely shortsighted.

Fish and wildlife biologists agree that no water should be exported, but they also worry about demands for more irrigation water within the Thompson system itself; the water, they say, is overdrawn already. Most of the streams that run through agricultural regions on their way to the Thompson are completely allocated to farm and ranch use; if everyone used all of his or her allocation, streams would run dry. Miners have been permitted to divert streams since gold rush days, nearly a century and a half ago. Fish, however, have no rights whatsoever to any portion of the flow of a stream under B.C. law, a state of affairs long recognized as ludicrous. When the DFO wanted to install a ladder to help fish over a waterfall on the Bonaparte River near its junction with the Thompson, officials found that the entire flow of the stream was committed to agriculture; the only way to make water available for fish was to construct an upstream dam to catch some of the spring freshet. It is incomprehensible that in 1996, fish still had no legal rights to water in British Columbia.

Here in the Thompson Basin we find a classic confrontation over water known in dry climates around the world. Two vital interests of people in the basin, agriculture and the fishery, must find a way to work together to ensure the optimum use of limited water supplies. With most streams already totally allocated and flows in many of them inadequate for salmon spawning and rearing, new agricultural opportunities must be pursued without drawing more water from the system. Increased efficiency in water use and replacement of low-value crops with more profitable ones are among the ways this can be done. Some of this is already occurring, and Strachan is convinced that better communication can reduce possibilities of conflict. If, for example, ranchers are aware that taking water for irrigation may compromise a run of fish, most will recognize that giving up one cut of one year's hay crop is a loss much less serious than reducing or wiping out a salmon run.

Kamloops fisheries biologist Ian McGregor believes that ranchers are becoming more aware, but says it is still a hard sell. "We aren't protecting riparian habitat as well as we need to, to ensure the integrity of the streams," says McGregor. "There's no legislation to protect riparian zones on agricultural land other than the Fisheries Act, which only

comes into use after the habitat is destroyed. The new Forests Practices
Code allows us to protect habitat on streams, but unfortuntely that legislation does not extend into agricultural areas."

Each fall nature's most magnificent fish, the steelhead, forges up
through the swirling chaos of the Fraser and Thompson Canyons to
calmer water near Spences Bridge, where the Nicola joins the Thompson. There it lurks through the winter in deep water, awaiting a signal
that the moment to spawn is at hand.

The steelhead is an ancient and mysterious fish, and the Thompson
River steelhead is larger and stronger than any other in the world. Even
the steelhead's identity has been endlessly debated. Until a few years ago
it was considered to be a rainbow trout with a sea-going habit; today it is
recognized as a sixth species of salmon. The confusion is not surprising,
for the steelhead combines the habits and appearance of both. It usually
spends its first two years in fresh water, then goes to sea for two years and
returns to its home stream in the fifth. Some survive spawning and
return to the ocean.

The beauty, size and spirit of the steelhead attract the devotion of
anglers from around the world, many of whom return year after year to
wade the Thompson and cast flies in precise arcs over pools they know
the great fish favours. When a steelhead rises to take the hook it
explodes in an awesome display of power, leaping and plunging, "dancing on its tail" across the dark water, battling to exhaustion both participants in this epic contest. And then the barbless hook is released and
the great fish, perhaps 6 to 7 kilograms, occasionally nearing 18 kilograms, glides off into the depths. It has been illegal for anglers to keep a
steelhead since 1987. Long before then, however, many of its devotees
were accustomed to releasing their catch. Communion with this ele-
mental force of nature brought anglers to the river, not a need for food.
They combine their forces in a potent conservation alliance known as
the Steelhead Society of British Columbia.

The steelhead needs such friends. Their numbers are decimated by
nets deployed to catch other species of salmon from the moment they
turn in from the open ocean to swim around Vancouver Island and
mount the Fraser. The gauntlet extends to just below Hell's Gate, and
very few escape it. "The fate of steelhead should be of special concern
to us," writes former Steelhead Society President Ehor Boyanowsky.
"Of all our salmon, it is the best indicator species of whether the decisions we are making regarding it will ultimately prove to be those wisest for our own survival." In the four decades since 1947, when
Vancouver *Sun* writer Lee Straight first publicized the existence of the

steelhead in the Thompson, steelhead numbers dropped by up to 90 per cent. The decline incited sports fishers and Native fishers to cut back drastically on their catches, but the commercial fleet kept taking steelhead along with target fish.

Steelhead numbers were already sharply diminished in the Thompson by 1977 when the B.C. government assigned biologist Ian McGregor to discover what could be done to ensure its survival. His work was handicapped by lack of knowlege; no one even knew where they spawned. So McGregor caught some steelhead and inserted tiny radio transmitters in them. Soon the fish were on the move, and guided by the radio receiver in his truck, he followed them up the Thompson from Spences Bridge, past Ashcroft and on towards Kamloops Lake. Just above Juniper Beach, McGregor was astonished to hear the radio signals turn sharply left into the Deadman River instead of proceeding into nearby Kamloops Lake as he had expected. "It was pretty exciting," says McGregor. "We had no idea where these fish were going. Absolutely no idea."

As Mark Hume recounts in *The Run of the River*, the presence of the great fish in this small river had been a secret "for 10,000 years." McGregor explains that the steelhead slips into the Deadman to spawn during a brief period from mid-April to the end of May when the river is in full flood. No one fishes the stream then, and the torrent carries a load of silt from eroding stream banks that hides the spawners. To ensure unseen passage through shallow water the steelhead travel only at night.

McGregor found that no steelhead in the Thompson system will climb above the Deadman. Some spawn in the Thompson mainstem, along with pink and chinook salmon and rainbow trout; others turn off farther downstream into the Nicola and Bonaparte Rivers. The big problem, of course, is to ensure that enough steelhead return to these streams to maintain the species. "Where the river narrows near Yale a small number of nets can do a lot of damage to a small run of steelhead," says McGregor, describing obstacles the big fish must overcome during the journey back to its place of birth. "The Native people helped us understand the problem, worked with us to gather information, and they're on side with the [steelhead enhancement] program. Then there's large commercial fisheries on the west coast of Vancouver Island, in the Juan de Fuca Strait and in Johnson Strait. They're fishing for chum, pink and sockeye salmon, and along with them capturing steelhead on their way to the Fraser River. Not only that, there's fishing south of the border in Washington state that intercepts Thompson steelhead. So they run a tremendous gauntlet. Just an unbelievable gauntlet. In 1991 only 900 fish came back. But in 1992, with not much fishing in the lower Fraser or in the approach areas at the time steelhead were running, we had the largest run we'd had in seven years—3,000 fish came back." The numbers held at about 3,000 for another two years, then dipped a bit in 1995. Biologists think 4,000 adult fish would make use of most available spawning habitat; 5,000 would provide a margin of safety.

Not far up the Deadman River, a migrating steelhead enters a new domain. The valley widens, carved by the river through ancient lava flows. In places the slopes are gradual enough to support bunchgrass and sagebrush, dotted here and there by groves of pines. Sometimes the valley is rimmed by raw vertical rock, sometimes by steep slopes carved by wind and water into fantastic shapes stained with tones of red and occasionally yellow or green. Deadman River winds its way down the floor of the valley, the natural meadows of its floodplain largely replaced now by hayfields growing green with water pumped from the stream. This hot, dry valley is not an easy place to make a living, and the relationship between ranchers and river is sometimes uneasy. When snow on the Fraser Plateau melts and rushes down the Deadman towards the Thompson, it may carve deep into riverbanks, sweeping away soil from fields and fences; posts stagger and tumble into the water, only strands of barbed wire holding them captive. The sod sags, tears and is gone in the spring torrent. The river may even change its course entirely.

In fact, the entire valley is a watercourse, with the stream itself being just the visible part. Water is also moving below the ground, sometimes emerging to flow with the Deadman, sometimes leaving the stream to flow underground. The groundwater cools the Deadman in the heat of summer and warms it in winter, making it more hospitable for fish year round. Not just steelhead come to the Deadman: coho and chinook salmon also make the journey here to spawn.

On a June day, two men check a winding channel they have built to increase spawning possibilities for cohos. Don Ignace of the Skeetchestn First Nation, whose land this is, manages the project for the DFO as part of the Salmon Enhancement Program; Mel Sheng is the biologist responsible. Ignace says the band is striving once again to pass the salmon tradition along to its young people. He fears, though, that cuts in federal financing of work on the river may seriously set back the patient work of many years.

Sheng and Ignace try to think like fish. They rely less on major technical fixes and more on subtle ways of aiding nature to do what she does best. This 1.5-kilometre channel has been planned to provide a spawning environment for coho by capturing both groundwater and surface stream flow. Cool, clean groundwater percolates up from below, aerating and cleaning the rocky redds in which salmon lay their eggs. Sheng points to watercress proliferating in the water. "Fish are able to hide in the watercress, so it's a refuge habitat for them, and it's an area where they can feed because a tremendous number of aquatic insects live on the watercress." Shrubs and eventually trees will grow, providing shade and protection from predators.

The spawning channel is protected from the periodic floods that sweep away valuable fish habitat in the river. "Look at major river systems like the Deadman, Louis Creek, the Nicola, Salmon River," says Sheng. "What seems unusual is that these river systems are often single channels flowing through the valley. Where are the side channels? Where are the sloughs and the rest of the natural river system? Well, the problem is that they got filled or cut off, so now there's just one single channel. This single channel system scours out the riverbed and further destabilizes the banks. Once that's happened you lose a lot of river complexity—the ripples, glide areas, pool areas, things that happen when the river is doing it's normal meandering." In the Deadman, stream banks are destabilized when ranchers strip vegetation to the water's edge to enlarge their fields, or when cattle are allowed to trample the banks to mud by grazing right into the water, or when the watercourse is straightened to move floodwaters off the land quickly, or its route is changed to go around a field rather than through it. Many of the local ranches are marginal operations, and the fishery they may damage could be far more valuable than the limited farm income eked out of this dry, hot valley.

In recent years, a lot of effort has gone into replacing natural systems that have been degraded. Ian McGregor says ranchers are beginning to understand the problem facing both themselves and the fish. They assumed the stream was stable when they moved onto the land, so they didn't connect the removal of trees and other vegetation with erosion of their land—and they're paying for that mistake now. The province's environment and agriculture ministries are providing help to restabilze the banks of the river, to the benefit of both ranchers and fish. Studies by DFO biologist Gordon Kosakoski show a very high return to the fishery by fencing cattle out of streams, planting trees and allowing vegetation to grow back. Kosakoski is convinced that the farmer benefits from the stream-bank rehabilitation too, because then the land resists erosion. "You drive along any stream and look at where people have removed the vegetation, and you see erosion," says Kosakoski. "Where the vegetation's been left intact, you tend to see a stable stream bank. So I view sound stream-bank management as beneficial to both."

The Nicola River is a beautiful, sparkling stream that descends over gentle, continuous rapids into the dusty heat of the Thompson Valley. At Spences Bridge it joins the Thompson River and welcomes spawning steelhead, chinook, coho and pink salmon. Here and there the Nicola Valley widens into a green oasis of ranch hayfields or an orchard thriving on an irrigated benchland, drawing life from the river. Cottonwoods cling to the stream's edge, while ponderosa pine and sagebrush break the brown slopes rising sharply above. Sometimes life in the emerald fields comes at the price of death in the Nicola River when irrigation ditches divert tiny fish onto the fields along with the water. With increasing frequency, however, landowners are working with biologists to find solutions that will keep fields green and fish in the stream.

The Nicola River waters and drains a vast kingdom of grass centred on the town of Merritt, about 60 kilometres upstream of the Thompson. There the river is joined by another fine salmon stream, the Coldwater, tumbling down the mountains from Coquihalla Pass. Merritt has been a cattle town for more than a century, lying at the bottom of a vast bowl whose slopes of grass wash up mountains to meet trees scattering down from forested summits. A few kilometres from the town along the valley bottom, Nicola Lake reflects fluffy cumulous clouds in its mirror-smooth surface. From the lake a road leads to the headquarters of Douglas Lake Cattle Company, Canada's biggest ranch, founded by legendary cattleman Joe Greaves more than a century ago. Joseph Guichon was hauling freight to the goldfields of the Cariboo in the 1860s when he found this valley of grass—the perfect place to winter his pack animals. Now, four generations later, Lawrence and Judith Guichon operate one of the most progressive ranches in British Columbia from their home at the tip of Nicola Lake.

"Holistic resource management" is the key to the Guichon ranch operation, and maximum beef production is no longer their goal. "Produce at any cost" was putting far too much pressure on their land, water, wildlife, employees and personal lives. It was leading, say Lawrence and Judith, to the degradation of their "biological capital"— the ranch just wouldn't be sustainable over the long haul. The Guichon ranch, its problems and many of their solutions, are a small-scale reflection of those of the entire Fraser Basin. Cattle were being managed efficiently but the soil was being neglected, just as throughout the basin trees are cut, fish caught, farm products grown and urban developments built using capital and technology very efficiently while water, land and air deteriorate. "We've done so much maximizing of production that there's nothing left to maximize," says Lawrence Guichon.

Now the Guichons emphasize quality of life and sustainability of their natural capital. That means, for example, paying particular attention to their grass and the soil in which it grows, mimicking nature as closely as possible. "If the grass is healthy," says Guichon, "the land will be healthy and the cattle will be healthy. Grazing must be carefully managed—grazing too heavily will weaken plants, lead to soil deterioration. Too little, and grazing will be spotty, some grass will grow too big and cattle will return again and again to the places already grazed." In this dry land, the quality of a whole year's grazing depends upon just a month or two in the spring, when care must be taken to let roots grow before turning cattle onto it. "And you can't manage it on the basis of average growth, since years vary so much," says Guichon. "You must manage the land for the worst possible year."

The Guichons see their ranch as part of the larger life of the Nicola Valley and indeed of the Fraser Basin. So they've taken an active role in the Nicola Watershed Community Roundtable, where people interested in the future of the valley are working together to sort out the real goals of the community and how they might be achieved. The keys, say Judith and Laurence Guichon, are trust and community. "There really wasn't much trust between sectors of our local community," says Lawrence Guichon. "Ranchers weren't trustful of the loggers, loggers weren't trustful of the environmentalists, who appeared to trust neither of us." And "community" must be the basis of resource use: decisions imposed from outside by corporations or government agencies might deliver trees efficiently to a mill, but with little concern for the soil or for growing new trees or for sustaining quality of life in the community. The Forest Practices Code might not have been needed, suggests Guichon, if local people had been responsible for the logging.

Below the mouth of the Nicola and downstream of Spences Bridge, the Thompson River flows faster, its surface broken more frequently by protruding rock, the blue water churning white. This is favoured rafting water, all the way to the Fraser River. Inflatable boats provide tourists with a wet, exciting ride through the river turbulence. The mountains rise higher on both sides of the Thompson, squeezing the Trans-Canada Highway and the two transcontinental railways into a narrower, rockbound valley. Soon they are chiselled into the steep slopes of a gorge piercing the inner rank of the Coast Mountains; grey rock stained red is cut by white rock slides; black and brown outcroppings signal geological cataclysms through the millennia. Tunnels and sloping sheds intended to channel rock slides over train tracks and into the river remind the traveller that the mountains still move, crumble and erode. Stand in their way at your peril.

Now the breach is accomplished. To the north and south the great trench carrying the Fraser River opens wide. For a brief moment both rivers flow calmly towards the union of clear blue Thompson with murky brown Fraser. Ahead lies the higher, outer range of the Coast Mountains, which the united power of the two rivers must challenge.

Fraser Canyon and Lower Fraser Valley

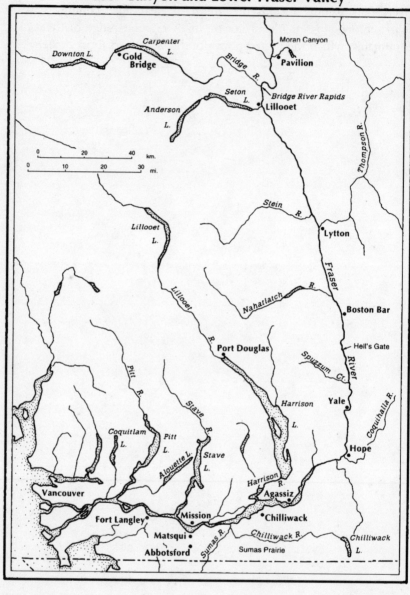

CHAPTER 8

The Wild River

Under heaven nothing is more soft and yielding than water. Yet for attacking the solid and strong, nothing is better; it has no equal.

LAO TSU, *TAO TE CHING*, 500 BCE

Soon after the murky Fraser is joined by the blue Thompson at Lytton, the river becomes a maelstrom of white water and speeding black current, upsurges boiling from the depths, whirlpools imprisoning anything that floats, and powerful backeddies pushing upstream almost as fast as the downward rush of the main current. Water piles deep against broken, sharp-angled rock, then plunges on. Now carrying the flow of the McGregor, the Nechako, the Chilcotin, the Quesnel, the Thompson and hundreds of smaller streams, the Fraser River has accepted far more water than can reasonably expect to pass through the narrow break in the mountains that lie ahead.

Yet pass it must. Angry at this constriction, the river flips on its side, becoming deeper, faster and more menacing as it squeezes between the sheer walls of the Fraser Canyon. This was what confronted Simon Fraser, his twenty-three companions and three Native guides on Monday morning, June 20, 1808, as they pushed off in dugout canoes supplied by the Nlaka'pamux people at Kumsheen. They had warned the white travellers of extraordinary danger if they continued downstream, and the voyageurs manning the canoes were convinced that it would be folly to proceed. But Fraser was adamant. At whatever cost, they would fulfill their assignment to follow the river to the sea. And so the day after arriving at Kumsheen they set off on the wildest part of what had already been a terror-filled expedition.

The borrowed canoes were immediately seized by the tumultuous current, and Fraser quickly realized the accuracy of the warnings. In

the grip of one of the world's most turbulent rivers, he concluded that
the way ahead was impossible for canoes. But escape was almost as
difficult; as the voyageurs tried to land, one of the canoes was caught
by the powerful current and sank, though its crew scrambled safely to
shore. All baggage and the remaining canoes had to be hauled up a
steep slope of rock and gravel that provided no sound footing. One of
Fraser's men was seriously hurt in a fall, and the Nlaka'pamux guides
described injury and death here as frequent occurrences among their
own people.

Almost anything seemed better than hauling everything along these
perilous slopes, so without his approval some of Fraser's voyageurs
decided to try again to run the river. Fraser was writing in his tent
when the Native guides raised the alarm, "running full speed towards
where we were, making signs that our people were lost in the rapids."
Fraser and his lieutenants Stuart and Quesnel worked their way downriver as fast as possible and found the first of the missing men struggling
along the bank, wet and exhausted. His canoe had foundered in the
rapids; he clung to it through wild water that finally threw him ashore.
As Fraser wrote, "we were lost in astonishment not only at his escape
from the waves, but also at his courage and perseverance in effecting a
passage through a place which appeared to us a precipice. Continuing
our course along the bank we found he had drifted three miles among
rapids, cascades, whirlpools etc., all inconceivably dangerous."

Miraculously, all the other men in the three canoes managed to
escape from the maelstrom into which they had cast themselves. By
nightfall the last members of Fraser's party were once more in camp.
"They informed us that the Indians assisted to extricate them from their
difficulties," wrote Fraser. "Indeed the natives showed us every possible
attention in the midst of our misfortunes on this trying occasion."

In the summer of 1993, descendants of the people Fraser met 185 years
earlier make visitors equally welcome in their office at Lytton, as
Kumsheen is now known. Filing cabinets overflow onto desks where
computers glow, fax machines hum, and cellular and radio telephones
help integrate the work of the Nlaka'pamux within their own territory
and with First Nations throughout British Columbia. Led by Chief
Robert Pasco, the people of today's Kumsheen are deeply involved in
the complexities of land claims, fighting politically and in the courts for
their rights to the resources of their ancestral lands.

For ten thousand years Fraser River salmon have been central to the
survival and culture of the aboriginal people of the river. Explorer
Alexander Mackenzie reported seeing fishing weirs and traps in 1793

that clearly could have prevented salmon from reaching their spawning grounds upstream. These barriers were built of stones or brush, or of pilings driven into the stream bed, sometimes of woven latticework; they were broken open when enough fish had been taken. The rich salmon runs and the abundance of resident freshwater fish observed by the first Europeans demonstrated the care taken to allow passage of enough spawning salmon and the free movement of other fish species.

Early in the 1993 season very few fish were making their way up into Nlaka'pamux territory, and many that did were badly marked by the nets from which they had escaped downstream. The band estimates each family needs about 250 fish to see them through the year, but feared that this year they would not catch nearly that many. The early weeks of the fishing season were marked by conflict between commercial and Native fishers, between sports and commercial fishers, and among First Nations. This was not unusual—since the commercial fishery began in the nineteenth century, confrontation between Native and non-Native fisheries has been the rule when catches are poor. For decades federal fisheries officials considered it their primary duty to ensure the canneries at the mouth of the Fraser had enough fish to operate profitably. When runs declined as a result of excessive fishing and waste by that industry, restrictions were usually imposed first on Native fishers.

In 1993 the salmon runs turned out to be late, and when at last they surged up the Fraser there were fish enough for everyone. A bountiful harvest of sockeye salmon quickly evaporated much of the bitterness—for that year. But for a time the anticipated shortage of salmon had brought into the open yet again the potential for deep social divisions when a resource base declines. In the next two seasons, problems facing Fraser River salmon runs deepened, and by 1996 the fishery faced a full-blown crisis. That would normally have been a low year in the salmon cycle anyway, but when predictions of returns to the river were catastrophically low, the Department of Fisheries and Oceans cancelled the Fraser River fishery almost entirely. Once again, conflicting interests surfaced among commercial, sports and Native fisheries, among vessel owners using different types of gear, among coastal communities and the fish processing corporations that were tightening their grip on the industry, and between the United States and Canada over the division of Fraser River salmon.

Native rights to the fishery had achieved some legal recognition in 1990 when the Supreme Court of Canada, in the *Sparrow* decision, confirmed the aboriginal right to fish for food, social and ceremonial purposes, subject to conservation requirements. Following this decision

the federal government began to negotiate separate fishing arrangements with Native communities, including in some cases the right to
sell fish commercially. Aboriginal peoples of the Fraser Basin had fished
commercially following the arrival of the Hudson's Bay Company early
in the nineteenth century, and many bands insist they still have the
right to do so. The Nlaka'pamux people, however, are convinced that
because salmon can be so effectively netted as they fight their way up
through the narrow reaches of the Fraser Canyon, the fish might not
survive a commercial fishery extending the length of the river. So they
refused the arrangement offered by the DFO, proposing instead a
sophisticated fishery management plan that would not compromise
their aboriginal right to unhampered access to fish for food, spiritual
and ceremonial purposes. The federal government grudgingly agreed,
entering into a co-management arrangement with the Nlaka'pamux.
But that lasted only one year; the DFO abandoned the co-management
plan after the 1993 season, and the Fraser Canyon fishery once again
was essentially unregulated.

The Nlaka'pamux traditional territory spans the wildest waters of
the Fraser from Texas Creek, just below Lillooet, to Spuzzum, below
Hell's Gate—a distance of about 120 kilometres. In late August 1993,
on a point of sand between the blue Thompson and the brown Fraser,
Percy Manyberria prepares a powerful jet boat to set off downstream on
the daily fishery patrol. The river is in the blood of Percy and the
members of his crew, John Garcia and Vern Campbell; century-old
photographs show canoes on the Fraser paddled by up to fourteen of
their ancestors. As Manyberria carefully guides the boat through the
least tormented track he can find in the surging water, Garcia and
Campbell scan the riverbanks for fishing rigs wherever a pole and gillnet can be set up and lashed into place among the rocks. Their job is to
know just what is happening on the river: who is fishing and where,
how many fish they are catching. They ensure that only families with
permits are fishing and that they are using authorized gear.

The Nlaka'pamux are the people of the canyon. Fishers tending nets
wave as the boat with "Nlaka'pamux Fishery" emblazoned in large
black letters on its hull forges through the churning waters. They are
not catching many fish today, because a commercial opening downstream means many Sto:lo nets are in the water and few salmon are
escaping them. John Garcia points to his family's traditional fishing spot
near Kanaka Bar. "My father stood on that rock, and so did his father,
and his father before him," he says. Throughout the basin, fishing rights
in favourable locations were owned by extended families whose leaders
were responsible for their orderly use and for conservation of the stock.

Fishing arrangements negotiated by individual Fraser River bands with the federal government may not mesh well with traditional aboriginal organization of the fishery. For instance, hereditary rights are central to the Native fishery, and these can become complicated by intermarriage up and down the river between Native groups with dissimilar views on fishing. The DFO has sometimes negotiated arrangements with individual bands quite different from those made with the nation of which the band is a part. The effect, if not the intent, is one of "divide and conquer," weakening the stand Native people are able to maintain on resource issues. The Nlaka'pamux think agreements such as that signed by the Sto:lo may turn out to be costly, sacrificing what they consider to be the really essential element of the fishery: the right of aboriginal people to a food fishery forever.

An extraordinary account of fishing and other practices of Native people of the Fraser and Thompson Rivers was compiled a century ago by James Teit. Born in Scotland in the 1850s, Teit lived for many years at Spences Bridge on the Thompson River, less than 40 kilometres upstream from its junction with the Fraser. Married to a Shuswap woman, he learned several Fraser Basin languages and became a trusted interpreter and active participant in struggles for Native rights. He collaborated with the great American anthropologist Franz Boas, who edited Teit's definitive study, *The Thompson Indians of British Columbia*, in the 1890s. In his book, Teit described people fishing on the Fraser using "bag-nets" woven from bark twine, with long handles similar to those of dipnets used in the same rushing waters today. "Another favourite method of fishing was by spearing from the shore while the salmon are running," wrote Teit. "The spear, which has a handle fifteen feet or more in length, consists of two long prongs, each of which has a barb pointing inward fastened at the end."

James Teit would find descendants of the people he knew fishing in the same places today, using very nearly the same methods he described. Although modern materials are employed now, the catch is still not easy; very often the family fishing spot is a considerable scramble down steep rocky slopes, and on a good day a heavy catch has to be hauled back up the bank. Upriver past Lillooet at rapids near the confluence of the Bridge River with the Fraser, members of the Fountain band may lead their horses an hour or more down a tortuous trail before arriving at their fishing places. The river roars in their ears day and night; sometimes children frolic in backeddies as their parents repair the drying racks for a new season. The young people absorb the lore of centuries as the fish are pulled from the water and carefully prepared for drying.

In his journal Simon Fraser referred often to the dried salmon pro-
cured from Native people; his expedition down the river would have
been impossible without it. Hot winds blowing up the Fraser quickly
dried the salmon hung on racks, preserving them so perfectly that, in
the words of a member of the Fountain band, "if you put them back in
the water they'll swim again." After drying, the fish were pounded to
pulp with stones, then packed tightly into woven baskets lined with
salmon skins. In these waterproof bales weighing from 30 to 45 kilograms, salmon could be preserved for years; they were an important
trade commodity as well as a principal part of the fishers' own diet.

Today, drying may be done on racks at home rather than down by
the river, where strangers are tempted to help themselves to the fish;
newspapers may replace birchbark lining for storage. But the traditional
food fishery has changed little with the years and the salmon is still
central to life along the river—though with fewer fish in the river, fishers have to work harder and longer. Vern Campbell checks the catch of
one of them, a fisher working his pole net from the rocks. Above them
a freight train emerges briefly into daylight before disappearing into
another tunnel. Farther along the train trusts its ponderous weight to a
wall of stones cut and placed more than a century ago by Chinese
labourers. At the base of a nearby canyon wall, a crumpled heap of
rusty steel marks the calamitous end of the line for one of the many
trains that have left the tracks in this unforgiving terrain.

Campbell grips the handrail as the boat bucks through rapids, plunging into brown depths while white crests sweep over the rails. The bow
surges free, rivulets run down the yellow waterproof suits of the crew.
From the rolling deck they see the canyon as few are privileged to do.
On the highway far above, miniature trucks slowly climb to the road's
summit on Jackass Mountain. Until just over a century ago, this was a
narrow, rocky ledge traversed by trains of heavily laden wagons pulled
by teams of twelve or more oxen. It was part of the Cariboo Road,
whose route through the Fraser Canyon had been outlined by Governor James Douglas himself after travelling the existing mule trail on
horseback during the summer of 1861. Tales of the wealth of the Cariboo had convinced him that a road must be built immediately, so without waiting for approval from faraway London, Douglas commissioned
the Royal Engineers to begin work in the snow and ice of the winter
of 1861–62. Beginning at Yale, about 80 kilometres south of Lytton, the
project required hacking the road into precipitous cliffs, and engaging
contractors to build bridges, trestles and connecting sections of the
route to the goldfields. The Cariboo Road was an extraordinary
accomplishment, pressed into use after just two years of construction.

The modern Trans-Canada Highway remains more or less faithful to the trace of the original gold rush road. It still clings to the side of the canyon, but more powerful machinery has carved deeper into rock ledges and bored more spacious tunnels through granite cliffs. Steel bridges fly over deep tributary canyons that in gold rush days forced mule and ox teams to detour away from the river; many of these spectacular streams are hardly noticed by today's travellers. From Jackass Mountain, the Nlaka'pamux patrol boat is barely visible, a silvery speck on the long, brown ribbon that slices south through the final and greatest obstacle in its long journey to the sea. The Fraser River has followed this course for 12 million years, cutting deeper into hard granite as the coastal mountains and central plateau lifted towards present elevations.

Two-thirds of British Columbia's people live downstream of the Fraser Canyon, and they are extraordinarily if unknowingly dependent upon this breach in the mountains scarcely a kilometre wide. Along with the river, the canyon confines the Trans-Canada Highway, two national railroads, oil and gas pipelines, and pylons carrying electricity from distant power dams. All are destined for Vancouver, the metropolis on the Pacific Coast at the mouth of the Fraser River.

As guides led Simon Fraser and his companions south in the summer of 1808, the canyon became narrower, the roar of the torrent more menacing. In his journal for Sunday, June 26, Fraser wrote:

> We had to pass over huge rocks, in which we were assisted by the Indians . . . I have been for a long period among the Rocky Mountains, but have never seen anything equal to this country, for I cannot find words to describe our situation at times. We had to pass where no human being should venture. Yet in those places there is a regular footpath impressed, or rather indented, by frequent travelling upon the very rocks. And besides this, steps which are formed like a ladder, or the shrouds of a ship, by poles hanging to one another and crossed at certain distances with twigs and withes [tree boughs], suspended from the top to the foot of precipices, and fastened at both ends to stones and trees, furnished a safe and convenient passage to the Natives—but we, who had not the advantages of their experience, were often in imminent danger when obliged to follow their example.

Each voyageur carrying a 40-kilogram load along this fragile web high above the thunder of the river would undoubtedly have muttered a fervent "amen" had he know this place would some day be known as "Hell's Gate."

The canyon walls are only 34 metres apart at Hell's Gate. Through that narrow gap in the mountains must pass all the water drained from a vast interior empire of 234 000 square kilometres, one quarter of the province. In a single year, this amounts to about 2720 cubic metres of water per second (cms), almost 100 000 cubic feet per second. But the flow varies wildly throughout the year, averaging only about 850 cms in the low-flow month of March and eight times as much, over 7000 cms, in June when flows are at their greatest. This translates into a surge of water through Hell's Gate that is about 18 metres deeper in June than it is in March. One more figure: below the boiling surface at Hell's Gate, the water can be up to about 28 metres deep, though in the great flood year of 1894, it is thought to have reached a depth of 38 metres. To visualize what all these numbers mean, a stream flowing at the rate of 145 cms would look like a good-sized river. Looked at another way, just 1 cms is a flow sufficient to supply an average Canadian community of 130,000 people.

The thundering gorge is the critical point in a living system extending over 1000 kilometres upstream, 250 kilometres downstream and far out into the Pacific Ocean. With the exception of those spawning in the lower valley, all Fraser River salmon must fight their way up through the torrents of Hell's Gate, then fan out into hundreds of streams to spawn. Up the Thompson they go, climbing long kilometres of white water to the Adams and the Salmon Rivers; up the Chilcotin and the Chilko they swim, the Quesnel and the Horsefly, the Nechako and the Stuart, up the Bowron, the McGregor, the Dome, the McLennan, the Swift. Then down the same turbulent waters will come their progeny in their hundreds of millions, and they too must safely pass through the boiling gorge of Hell's Gate before arriving at the salt water of the Strait of Georgia. Those surviving two or three years in the open ocean return as a mighty flood of energy surging upstream through Hell's Gate.

The incredible numbers of salmon—tens of millions—that move up the Fraser River each year make it one of the greatest sources of food in North America. Hell's Gate itself was one of the most productive fishing places; upward-bound salmon gathered in tens of thousands just below the gorge, pressing close to black rock walls to avoid the river's central torrent. In such concentration they were easily dipped from the water.

Archeologists digging at what is known as the Milliken site, a few kilometres upstream from Yale, have found evidence that as early as 9,000 years ago large numbers of people gathered here when the biggest runs of chinook and sockeye salmon were mounting the river. They came from as far away as the Saanich Peninsula on Vancouver Island; villages in the lower Fraser Valley, the river's estuary and Burrard Inlet were practically deserted during the canyon fishing season. The ancient fishery continued for many years after Europeans first landed at the mouth of the Fraser. Salmon dipped from the river were dried on racks, then loaded in canoes for the trip back to winter villages. In the last two weeks of September 1828, the chief trader at the Hudson's Bay trading post at Fort Langley counted 750 canoes drifting downstream towards the mouth of the Fraser carrying enormous loads of dried salmon, often on platforms laid across two canoes. By late September most people had returned home, weighed down by the wealth of the river.

Safe passage of salmon through the rockbound chasm of boiling water at Hell's Gate remains essential to subsistence, culture and commercial income for First Nations people of the Fraser River; for fleets of seiners, gillnetters and trollers with all the shore facilities that support them; and for the sport fishery that provides enjoyment, food, employment and profits for thousands of British Columbians. Yet even under normal conditions a fine margin separates success from failure as the adult salmon battles currents, rapids and natural obstructions to reach its destination. Once entering the fresh water of the river, it will never eat again. The fish has stored precisely enough energy to propel itself upriver to the stream of its birth. It may arrive on the spawning grounds with only days or hours of life and strength remaining within which to deposit and fertilize eggs. Some years, natural occurrences may push the fish beyond its programmed endurance; when below-normal snowpack or rainfall in the mountains reduces the Fraser's flow, difficult waterfalls may become impossible and traditional channels may be reduced to trickles.

There remains much that is not known about what happens to fish in the waters of the Fraser. So in the summer of 1993, the rocky walls of the Fraser Canyon and the fishways at Hell's Gate sprouted an array of antennas directed down towards the tumultuous brown water. Downstream below Yale, biologists Scott Hinch of UBC's Westwater Research Centre and Ron Diewart of the DFO had caught sockeye bound for Stuart Lake, installed tiny radio transmitters in their bellies and released them to continue the 1200-kilometre, three-week journey. Now, signals from deep below the surface enabled the listening scientists to swim with the fish, vicariously experiencing their world. They could track the salmon, determine how fast and deep they were swimming, how much energy they were using and the temperature of the water through which they swam.

Water temperature is crucial for salmon. It is a cold-water fish, and in warmer water the salmon's metabolism speeds up, burning its stores of energy more rapidly. This leaves less "fuel" for the journey upstream, but since warmer water is usually flowing lower and slower, the fish can ascend more easily and requires less energy. On the other hand, lower water may also make passage around obstacles in the river more difficult. Higher water makes passage easier. However, when water flows higher and stronger, a salmon's progress is slower; then again, high water is usually cool water, so the fish's metabolism is slower and it retains more energy for the trip. Overall, says Hinch, energy use seems to be the dominating factor; in high water years fewer sockeye arrive on the spawning grounds, and they take longer to get there.

"There are areas in the Fraser Canyon which may appear difficult to us, but actually aren't all that difficult for the fish, and vice versa," says Hinch. "Where the river seems to be quite turbulent and fast flowing doesn't seem to be a problem provided the river is fairly straight, the canyon walls are steep and there are no constrictions. Salmon seem to like the backeddies where the water slows along the canyon walls, and they go deeper sometimes to take advantage of slower water near the bottom." Problems arise wherever there is a constriction in the river, whether caused by an island, a peninsula or an outcropping. Hell's Gate is the ultimate constriction of course, but Hinch explains that there are many other areas where the water is so turbulent that its direction of flow is not clear to the fish, which may not be able to determine the correct way to go. It could be a gravel bar in a relatively shallow place, creating backeddies that confuse the fish. Even after it has struggled though such difficult places, the current may overpower the fish and wash it downstream; often the exhausted salmon can't make it back for another try. With the lower than normal flow in 1993, Hinch and his colleagues found that sockeye took longer to get through Hell's Gate, and many were held up by gravel bars revealed by low water.

Since 1852 according to some accounts, and certainly by 1856, Native people along the Thompson River had been bringing gold nuggets to Fort Kamloops where chief trader Donald McLean was only too happy to provide them with gold pans and shovels. The first discovery occurred in a Thompson River tributary, the Nicoamen, which enters the Thompson about 15 kilometres above its junction with the Fraser. Here, wrote Governor Douglas in his diary, a Native man paused to drink, and "having no vessel, he was quaffing from the stream when he perceived a shining pebble which he picked up, and it proved to be gold. The whole tribe forthwith began to collect the glittering metal."

Rumours of gold drew a few American miners across the border in 1856. The aboriginal people of the Thompson River and Fraser Canyon insisted that their territorial rights included any gold found there, and they expelled the first Americans. Governor Douglas reported that Native people had "openly expressed a determination to resist all attempts at working gold in any of the streams flowing into Thompson's River, both from a desire to monopolize the precious metal for their own benefit, and from a well-founded impression that the shoals of salmon which annually ascend those rivers and furnish the principal food of the inhabitants will be driven off, and prevented from making their annual migrations from the sea."

Native dominance of the gold trade was short-lived. James Douglas and the HBC tried to keep the discovery secret, but by late 1857 the Kamloops trading post had accumulated 800 ounces of gold. Now Douglas made a decision that brought about the realization of his worst fears. He shipped the gold to a mint in San Francisco. No secrets were possible there; the California gold rush was petering out and the city was full of idle miners. Rumours of the riches of "The Fraser" flashed through streets and bars; soon every available ship headed north overloaded with miners and their equipment. By the summer of 1858, exactly fifty years after Simon Fraser's epic journey, as many as 30,000 men poured through Victoria and up the Fraser River in search of gold. Where Fraser's canoes had touched ashore at Yale, paddle-wheeled steamers now disgorged hordes of gold-hungry miners from around the world. Along with them were entrepreneurs ready to mine the miners, and Yale soon became a disorderly collection of wooden buildings scattered along the riverbank, stocked to provision the gold seekers and to relieve them of their new-found wealth in gambling dens, bars and brothels.

Fearing the influx of Americans would stoke annexationist aspirations south of the border, Governor Douglas moved quickly to have the mainland united with Vancouver Island into one British colony. To enforce the majesty of British law, Colonial Secretary Sir Edward Bulwer Lytton sent a London lawyer, Matthew Baillie Begbie.

Begbie turned out to be an extraordinary presence on this chaotic stage, administering justice fairly and quickly over the vast Interior with the help of only a few constables. The tall, arrogant judge with carefully waxed moustache and pointed beard often heard evidence and pronounced sentences from the back of his horse, and his imposing presence was soon known and respected throughout the region. Begbie arrived on the scene in the late fall of 1858, too late to protect aboriginal people from the predations of miners, many of whom considered Native people a minor hindrance to be easily dispossessed of their land, and Native women as a convenience for men far from female companionship of their own race. Within months the aboriginal culture that

had assured the sustainability of the Fraser Basin for thousands of years
was overwhelmed by an invading force prepared to eliminate anyone or
anything that would slow its pursuit of wealth.

When Native people gathered below Hell's Gate for the fishery in the
summer of 1858, they found their traditional sites overrun by gold miners, mostly Americans, who were diverting streams, cutting trees and
digging trenches through spawning beds. Ignorant of the customs of the
river and scornful of its aboriginal inhabitants, the miners considered the
annual convergence of Natives in the canyon threatening, and the
Victoria *Gazette* reported they were there "evidently for no friendly
purpose."

In August people of the Nlaka'pamux Nation gathered near Boston
Bar intending retaliation for the murder and rape of a Native woman
and the killing of her husband by a miner. In the resulting clash, two
whites and ten Nlaka'pamux were killed. Although the Nlaka'pamux
had clearly been losers in the affair, at Yale there was outrage and calls
from miners for vengeance. Hundreds of men formed vigilante groups,
took up guns and headed upriver, vowing to kill all the aboriginal people they could find. Thirty years later James Teit recorded, "This affair
was known as the 'Fraser River War.' "

As the vigilantes pushed up the Fraser, it became evident even to
their leaders that miners had been outrageously brutal in their dealings
with Native people. At Lytton, a settlement was negotiated with
Nlaka'pamux chiefs, who may have been aware of the extermination of
tribes in Washington and Oregon and hoped to avoid a similar fate.
Meanwhile, in the pages of the colony's newspapers, correspondents
debated whether the Natives should be confined to concentration
camps or simply exterminated.

Through the Fraser Canyon a railroad is glued to each rocky wall:
Canadian Pacific Railway on one side, Canadian National Railways on
the other. One of those slender steel bands, the CPR, was the instrument
that brought British Columbia into the Canadian Confederation. The
other, the CNR, nearly destroyed the salmon runs of the Fraser River.

The CPR was the cornerstone of an agreement completed in 1871
unifying the tiny population of about 10,000 white British Columbians
and 30,000 aboriginal residents with the new nation of Canada.
Although Canada was only four years old with a population of about
3.5 million people, the Conservative government, led by Sir John A.
Macdonald, agreed to build a railroad across thousands of kilometres of
rock, plain, muskeg and mountain in order to bring the West Coast
colony into the nation. Ottawa promised to begin work within two

years and complete the entire project in ten. But by 1873 unsuccessful efforts to finance the railway had led Macdonald's government into what became known as the "Pacific Scandal," the discovery that the entrepreneurs who hoped to build the CPR were making large contributions to the Conservative election fund. Disgraced, Macdonald and his party were thrown out of office.

The leader of the Liberal party and new prime minister, Alexander Mackenzie, was a stolid, unimaginative man. Convinced that a transcontinental railroad would bankrupt the new country, he called the plan "a piece of madness," an "insane act," "a piece of deliberate treachery." This kind of language was considered betrayal in B.C., where Amor De Cosmos, the colourful premier, had been a key supporter of the railroad as the price of the province's entry into Confederation. As months and then years passed without the laying of a single kilometre of track, the B.C. economy stagnated and De Cosmos himself became a target of the wrath of West Coast citizens. As a member of Parliament he carried B.C.'s protests to Ottawa, warning the new government that without the railroad the settlement on the Pacific would have no alternative but to seek annexation to the United States. This was no small threat from a man long known to despise the Americans. But while Mackenzie remained in office, De Cosmos's words did little more than echo and die within the walls of the House of Commons.

Sir John A. Macdonald's Conservatives were re-elected in 1878, riding back into power on the strength of Macdonald's National Policy, of which immediate construction of the railway was a major element. After two months of exhausting parliamentary debate that ruined Macdonald's health, the CPR was at last established by Parliament on February 15, 1881. It was a momentous act. In *The Last Spike*, Pierre Berton writes, "no other private company, with the single exception of the Hudson's Bay, has had such an influence on the destinies of the nation."

But before the CPR was organized and its financing assured in Britain, before its contract was approved by Parliament and even before the route the railway would follow across Canada was finalized, Macdonald saw to it that construction began in B.C. To make the western end of the railroad a reality, Macdonald and his cabinet would count on Andrew Onderdonk.

Andrew Onderdonk was an aristocratic New Yorker, reserved in manner, with a solid reputation as a reliable contractor on large construction projects in the U.S. The Canadian government manipulated railroad tenders in order to ensure that his bids were successful, and in 1880 Onderdonk contracted to build 203 kilometres of railroad east from Emory's Bar, just downstream of Yale, to Savona, near Kamloops. Later he was also awarded the contract west from Emory's Bar to the railway's ocean terminal at Port Moody near Vancouver.

Onderdonk began work in the Fraser Canyon the spring of 1880, and after a year of round-the-clock blasting still had laid no track. In the first 27 kilometres upstream from Yale he had to drive thirteen tunnels through solid granite. Just as difficult to build were "galleries"—notches cut just deep enough into the rock overhanging the river to contain track and train. Hundreds of trestles and bridges spanned canyons where creeks and streams joined the Fraser River. This was the toughest terrain for railroad building in all of North America, and Simon Fraser could have warned Onderdonk that the worst section of all would be Hell's Gate.

Pierre Berton describes the construction through Hell's Gate: "It seemed impossible that a road could be carved out of those dripping black rocks. Here men could be seen suspended at dizzy heights against the rock walls, let down the cliffs on ladders secured by ropes attached to trees on the summit so that they could drill blasting holes into the face of the escarpment. Each time a shot was fired, the men had to clamber up the ladders as swiftly as possible to escape the effect of the explosion." They often worked in bare feet, which they believed ensured better footing. A break or a slip in the rope, a rock toppling from above or a premature blast meant certain death. "The Indians were the most fearless," writes Berton, ". . . fortunately, they turned out to be first-class rock workers. Their task was to go down first and blast out the footholds in which other men could stand and work."

It is hardly credible that anyone would consider the tormented waters of the gorge navigable, but Onderdonk wanted to haul construction supplies by ship between Lytton and Boston Bar, just above Hell's Gate. He had a 225-tonne paddle-wheel steamboat built in 1882 at Spuzzum just *below* Hell's Gate, then looked for a captain willing to take her upriver. The first to try pushed the little ship against the raging current time after time, but finally had to admit defeat. Onderdonk found another skilled riverman willing to take on the Fraser, a veteran of the wild waters of the Snake and Columbia Rivers. This time, ringbolts were fixed to the canyon wall. Ropes were passed through them to be hauled in by the ship's capstans at one end and by 150 Chinese labourers at the other. In late September when water levels were low, a final mighty effort was made: the *Skuzzy* steamed, the capstans and winches hauled, 150 workers pulled and the little ship scraped through Hell's Gate. She served her tortuous route between Boston Bar and Lytton for only a year. On each trip, rocks clawed at her hull and crunched holes through it, and splintered her wooden planks and beams. Thoroughly battered, the *Skuzzy* was removed from the world's toughest steam-boat run.

With only 32 kilometres of rail laid in the Fraser Canyon after two years of work, Onderdonk needed more workers. About 10,000 men were required on the job, but not many white labourers or skilled workers were available; the railway construction boom in Canada and the U.S. had absorbed large numbers of them, and dangerous work in the faraway B.C. wilderness at low rates of pay couldn't attract suffi-cient numbers of men. So Onderdonk turned to Chinese labour, and it is unlikely the railway could have been completed without them. More than 10,000 Chinese labourers arrived in B.C. from China between 1881 and 1884; Onderdonk himself brought in ten shiploads, about 6,000 men, in 1882.

Chinese "coolies" were good workers, they were paid less than white workers, and they provided their own subsistence rather than requiring the camp facilities that white labourers expected. The low wages Onderdonk paid Chinese workers saved him millions of dollars and probably spared him from bankruptcy. This exerted downward pressure on the wages paid to white men, which was one of the reasons Chinese employment was so bitterly opposed. Normally accommodating, Chinese workers reacted with fury if they felt they were being unfairly treated by their white overseers. Once assured that their grievances would be adequately addressed, they could be counted on to continue work. Although highly regarded on the job, the Chinese had little reason to feel welcome elsewhere in Canada, where they were widely viewed with suspicion, distaste and even loathing. Editors almost univer-sally accompanied their condemnation of these people with demands that none be allowed to immigrate into Canada. As Berton points out in *The Last Spike*, any people other than white Anglo-Saxons fared poorly in Canadian newspapers in those days; blacks, Jews and members of other less privileged groups could count on regular editorial vilification.

The perils of railroad work in the Fraser Canyon claimed many lives. Explosions, cave-ins, rock and timber falls from precipitous cliffs, bolt-ing horses frightened by blasts, and hazardous trails all exacted their toll. Chinese workers died in particularly large numbers. Scurvy killed many because they preferred a diet of rice and ground dried salmon to the fresh meat and vegetables eaten by white labourers. The deaths of "coolies" were not considered worthy of reporting by local papers. No coroners' inquests followed Chinese deaths and no medical attention was provided by the contractor or the government. The bones of an unknown but very large number of Chinese workers who came to

Canada to make their fortunes line the route of the CPR through the
Fraser Canyon.

With construction costs mounting, the federal government progressively relaxed the standards to which the line had to be built. Slopes
became steeper and curves sharper to reduce tunnelling and filling;
second-rate work was approved by government inspectors. Imperfect
though it was, that railway clinging precariously to the wall of the
Fraser Canyon fulfilled Sir John A. MacDonald's dream of a Canadian
nation stretching from Atlantic to Pacific. But economic concessions to
the railroad company by which the government financed much of its
construction have had enormous impact on the nation's economy ever
since. Huge land blocks granted to the CPR shaped Canadian cities,
dominated rural settlement in many regions, and controlled forest and
other resource development throughout the country. When land
granted along the railway line did not appear profitable to the CPR, the
company had the right to select equivalent land elsewhere. Since the
Fraser Canyon could not by any stretch of the imagination be considered agricultural, the railway selected instead a very large section of the
best farmland in the Peace River Block. In exchange for building a
small and now neglected railway line, the CPR received a huge block of
the most productive land on Vancouver Island.

While the CPR and land speculators prospered, a total collapse of
Native culture throughout the Fraser Basin seemed imminent. James
Teit observed in his study of the Thompson Indians that Native communities of the Fraser Basin had sunk into despondency. Gone were
the days of abundance; wildlife had been wiped out by the fur trade,
and the aboriginal population had been decimated by successive waves
of disease brought by white men. Teit wrote, "The belief that they are
doomed to extinction seems to have a depressing effect on some of the
Indians. At almost any gathering where chiefs or leading men speak,
this sad, haunting belief is sure to be referred to."

Descending smoothly and comfortably by cable car where Simon
Fraser inched his way along the cliff face, today's tourist can hardly
imagine the high-stakes drama playing out beneath the surface of boiling brown water as salmon battle their way upstream. Nor will a visitor
fascinated by the watery maelstrom surging past restaurant windows
easily summon images of mighty blasts, entire walls of rock collapsing
into the water, ruined bodies of railway construction workers floating
downstream, and one of the greatest catastrophes to natural systems
ever known in Canada.

It happened almost thirty years after the completion of the CPR.

Fortunes had been made by the salmon canneries that crowded the mouth of the Fraser River, and this year, 1913, was their greatest yet. A booming provincial economy was enriching land and railway speculators too. Among them were promoters William Mackenzie and Donald Mann, who had enlisted B.C.'s Conservative premier, Sir Richard McBride, in support of a new railway to the West Coast. There was no evidence of a need for more track, but railroad building was the new gold rush and McBride was sure the subsidies he poured into the pockets of Mackenzie and Mann would pay off at election time.

And so the Canadian Northern Railway (CNOR), later to become the Canadian National Railways, hacked its way along the more difficult east side of the Fraser Canyon. Costs mounted as crews blasted their way through the granite walls. Mackenzie and Mann cut expenses and rushed construction schedules by allowing vast amounts of rock to collapse into the river, though laws forbidding such practices existed even then. Workers were exploited and expendable, and many men died in the rocky rubble. A Department of Marine and Fisheries agent described construction through the Fraser Canyon that winter of 1912–13: "In a number of places they have literally shot the whole side of the mountain into the river, filling up numerous bays where fish used to rest and as at Skuzzi [Scuzzy Rapids] new points projecting far out into the stream have been formed so congesting the waterway as to make it next to impossible for the fish to get through."

It was not until August 1913 that the horrifying consequences of the profiteering construction methods were revealed. Geoff Meggs vividly describes the tragedy in *Salmon: The Decline of the British Columbia Fishery*. On August 5, J. P. Babcock, B.C.'s deputy commissioner of fisheries, discovered masses of sockeye salmon milling below Hell's Gate. The congestion extended 16 kilometres downstream; soon he was hearing disturbing reports of very small catches by Natives upstream.

But at the mouth of the Fraser huge catches were swamping the canneries. This was the biggest run of sockeye salmon in history, with peak years coinciding for the Adams, Stuart, Chilko and Quesnel runs, a phenomenon not yet repeated. Thirty-one million sockeye salmon were caught in 1913, canning company profits soared while prices paid to fishermen were driven to record lows and waste reached incredible levels. With catches surpassing canning capacity, salmon rotted in barges at the wharves and were dumped in the sea.

About six million sockeye salmon evaded the curtain of nets at the river's mouth that record year, congregating below Hell's Gate in the masses that so astonished Babcock. By mid-August Babcock had ample evidence of the disaster, yet it was a month before he was sufficiently convinced of its scale to raise the alarm. By then the river for many kilometres downstream had turned black and putrid with tightly packed dead and dying salmon.

Provincial officials warned the federal fisheries ministry that 90 per cent of the sockeye had been cut off from the upper four-fifths of the river for the entire season. They requested federal help in clearing a channel through the rocky debris at Hell's Gate, but it was late September before officials in Ottawa authorized action. Sufficient rock was dynamited away to permit a trickle of salmon to fight their way through. But as the water dropped to normal autumn levels, the newly cleared channel was left high and dry, and again the way was blocked to migrating salmon. A few early migrants had mounted the river in June and July when the freshet raised water levels high enough to cover some of the blocked channels, but just over 1 per cent of the Quesnel River run returned to spawning gravels in 1913, the Shuswap and Adams runs were almost wiped out and the huge summer run of sockeye to the Salmon River was extinguished.

Throughout the Interior, Natives waited in vain at their traditional fishing places. Meggs writes, "At Adams Lake, where hundreds of thousands of spawners were anticipated, only 2,000 appeared. A frantic harvest of fresh-water fish began. As autumn turned to winter, Fraser River bands normally well stocked with fish tried to migrate to lakes in the Nicola region for supplies; women and children died in the attempt as their pack trains struggled over the treacherous trails in freezing rain and snow."

The situation worsened in the winter of 1914. In February, just upstream of Hell's Gate, CNOR construction workers blasted half a mountainside into the river while trying to bore a tunnel through the canyon's granite walls. Some runs were saved from extinction that year when Natives lifted fish across the debris in dipnets. But railroad builders, canneries at the Fraser's mouth and fisheries officials denied the existence of a problem at Hell's Gate. Federal fisheries officers blatantly lied to their Ottawa superiors, insisting that all was well on the Fraser so they could avoid closing down the fishing operations of their friends in the canning industry. When investigation proved that irresponsible construction had caused the problem, the CNOR was first asked, then ordered, to remove the rocky obstructions they had blasted into the river. The CNOR refused to pay, blaming its contractors and subcontractors—most of whom, it turned out, were also owned by CNOR proprietors Mackenzie and Mann.

Fraser River salmon catches declined precipitously following the Hell's Gate disaster, in some years amounting to only one-seventh of former levels. Some races were obliterated, leaving their streams destitute of salmon. Other races were saved from oblivion by the very few fish that managed somehow to struggle through the rocky strictures of Hell's Gate or were manually helped across them. Apart from the enormity of the biological loss of irreplaceable salmon strains, the cost to the commercial fishery was immense. Estimates vary widely, but an indication can be obtained from a 1980 report by the International Pacific Salmon Fisheries Commission, which estimated losses to the sockeye and pink salmon fishery at more than $2.8 billion (in 1978 dollars) during the period 1951 to 1978.

When it became evident that disastrously small numbers of salmon were returning after the blockades of 1913–14, the search was on for scapegoats. As they have been throughout the history of the B.C. salmon fishery, Natives were targeted first. In 1914 government officials banned Native dipnets and sidenets throughout the Fraser Canyon, and tried to prohibit all Native fishing, even for food, between Hope and Lytton. Ten natives were arrested and fined for continuing to fish at their traditional sites.

Famine stalked Native populations throughout the Fraser Basin. In 1914 the Stuart Lake fishery provided only 800 fish for thirty families; two years later only 20 sockeye arrived at the lake. Pink salmon were completely eradicated above Hell's Gate. When J. P. Babcock travelled the Interior two years later, he discovered devastation everywhere. The fabulous sockeye wealth of the Shuswap, the Quesnel, the Chilko and Stuart systems were among those that had almost vanished. Vigorously pursuing their policy of penalizing the principal victims of industrial development in the Fraser Canyon, federal officials patrolled the basin to ensure that Native people took no fish. The total catch of sockeye in the dominant year, 1921, was just over 1.6 million fish, compared to as many as 50 million before the 1913 catastrophe.

Fraser River sockeye journey through American waters too, so the near collapse of the fishery affected both countries. In 1937 the International Pacific Salmon Fisheries Commission was established by treaty between Canada and the U.S. "For the protection, preservation and extension of the sockeye salmon fisheries of the Fraser River." Costs of the IPSFC were to be shared equally, as was the Fraser River sockeye catch. The commission eventually designed and built fishways on both sides of the canyon at Hell's Gate. After the fishways' completion in 1946, the number of sockeye salmon reaching spawning grounds climbed steadily, with catches of Fraser River sockeye averaging 11 million in the 1990–93 period.

The fishways certainly helped, yet they were by no means a total

answer to the problems facing salmon in their upriver migration. As
Scott Hinch and his colleagues tracked radio-equipped sockeye towards
Hell's Gate in 1993, they could sense the difficulty the fish encountered
approaching the entrance to the fishway. Here the river is narrowest
and the current strongest, and a rock outcropping near the opening
creates turbulence that confuses many fish. If they turn left instead of
right at a crucial moment, they are seized by the current and catapulted
far downstream. For some the ordeal is too much, and they never
return to try again.

Although the Hell's Gate disaster of 1913–14 devastated the dominant runs of some of the Fraser's most important sockeye stocks, it was
only one cause of the decline of Fraser River salmon. In his fine analysis of the contemporary Pacific fishery crisis, *Dead Reckoning*, Terry
Glavin quotes eminent fisheries biologist W. E. Ricker as concluding
that the principal reason for the decline of the Fraser fishery, particularly the non-dominant runs of the sockeye cycle, is simply too large a
rate of harvest. Overfishing. Since 1900 at least 85 per cent of returning
sockeye salmon have been taken by fishers, and there were years when
the catch may have reached 94 per cent. Today the killing power of the
fishing fleet is so great that a review board investigating what happened
to "missing salmon" in the 1994 season declared that "one more 12-
hour opening [of the fishery] could have virtually eliminated the late
run of sockeye in the Adams River." The Fraser River Sockeye Public
Review Board, headed by John Fraser, a former Conservative fisheries
minister, had been appointed by Ottawa "to solve a disturbing and puz-
zling mystery which surrounded the dramatic apparent disappearance
of several million sockeye salmon which normally would have migrated
to spawning areas in the Fraser River watershed in 1994."

The sockeye run of 1994 was expected to be one of the largest in
the recent history of the Fraser River. That summer Hinch and his colleagues were again implanting salmon of the early Stuart run with tiny
transmitters and tracking them through Hell's Gate and on up the
Fraser. Salmon behaviour was unremarkable for a week or so while the
river temperature was a normal 14 or 15 degrees centigrade. Suddenly
the temperature began to rise; within about a week it rose 5 or 6
degrees, even approaching the lethal temperature of 21.5 at one point.
"It was one of fastest temperature increases and one of hottest months,
mid-July to mid-August, that we've seen in a long while," Hinch notes.
"When this happened, the fishes' behaviour totally changed. They
stopped moving upriver and in some cases took off downriver when
we put them back in the water. Two or three weeks later we realized
that half of the Stuart run that was thought to have entered the river

did not get to the spawning grounds." Although few dead fish were seen floating downstream, later in the summer the scientists found many carcasses stuck in river mud or buried between rocks. "We think fish were stressed out," says Hinch, "and that a large number of them died naturally." The river flow was fairly high in 1994, which is not usually the case when water temperatures are high; these factors imposed a double whammy on the migrating salmon in 1994.

The 1994 snowpack had melted early, so when heavy rain fell in the upper Fraser Basin there was nothing to cool it as it entered the river. For Hinch, the implications of these climatic events are very significant. "The temperature issue is going to be a big one, it's going to get even worse in the future as the climate warms. When temperatures got above a particular level, [about 18 degrees centigrade] the fish just stopped moving. Climate warming has really serious implications for salmon."

While Hinch and his colleagues were following fish, temperatures were also rising in the entire fishing industry over the "disappearing fish" of the 1994 salmon season. Far fewer fish returned from the ocean or escaped the nets and arrived on the spawning grounds than the DFO had predicted. As the Fraser Commission notes, "By season's end a myriad of claims and counter claims erupted, blaming illegal fishing [particularly charges of poaching by Native fishers], bad management [by DFO], out-dated technology [non-selective, overwhelming killing power in the fishing fleet] and environmental disaster" [high water temperatures in the Fraser River].

John Fraser and his fellow review board members concluded that "if something like the 1994 situation happens again, the door to disaster will be wide open . . . Unless all parties work together and manage much more competently, the tragedy that befell the Atlantic cod fishery will repeat itself on the west coast." The board found that recent cutbacks and re-organization of the DFO had left the management of the fishery "dysfunctional." An atmosphere of uncertainty and total lack of confidence pervaded the federal department, with no clear lines of authority or accountability, and even a denial by some DFO officials of the existence of a problem—an echo from the catastrophe of 1913. Fraser made thirty-five recommendations whose fundamental thrust was that the conservation of the salmon must take precedence over all other interests. To ensure this priority was observed, he recommended the establishment of an independent Pacific Fisheries Conservation Council to act as public watchdog for the fishery, "with no vested interest except the health of the fish and their habitats."

By the summer of 1996, the federal government had not moved to establish the conservation council, nor had it taken action on most of the other recommendations that the Fraser Commission had pronounced essential for the survival of the Fraser River salmon fishery.

On June 27, 1808, Simon Fraser and all twenty-three of his men reached Spuzzum, the southern outpost of the Nlaka'pamux. The river continued threading through spectacular mountain landscapes, but they had safely traversed its worst obstacles. Near Yale the following day, Fraser described an encounter with people of a different nation: ". . . we arrived at the first village of the Ackinroe nation [the Sto:lo, a Coast Salish people] where we were received with as much kindness as if we had been their lost relations. Neat mats were spread for our reception, and plenty of Salmon served in wooden dishes was placed before us. The number of people at this place was about 140." Throughout Fraser's journal his total dependence upon Native goodwill, guidance and food is obvious; nor was he ever in doubt about whose territory he was traversing. Yet in contrast to David Thompson and Alexander Mackenzie, he expressed little admiration for the aboriginal people to whom he owed his life and his success, and seemed to seek control rather than trust in his relationships with them.

As they neared Hope, Fraser was told by the Sto:lo that other white men had been there before them. He didn't believe their stories, though he later wrote that the Natives "evinced no kind of surprise or curiosity at seeing us, nor were they afraid of our arms, so that they must have been in the habit of seeing white people." Apparently Thompson believed the Native accounts, for he noted at this location on the map he produced in 1813–14, "To this place the white man comes from the sea." The aboriginal experience with Europeans from sailing ships might explain the increasingly hostile reception the Fraser expedition encountered as it descended from Yale towards the ocean.

The steep slopes of a mountain landscape reflect the rosy hues of late afternoon sun. The brown river still moves urgently, swirling impatiently around each rocky barrier that would slow its progress. The Fraser continues to grow as silvery streams rush to lose their crystal water in the silt-burdened current. Where a ragged rock or a curve in the river slows the water, sediment settles into sandbars like those that yielded riches in the gold rush of 1858. The mighty Fraser has defeated the last obstacle; now it can cast off its violent nature and assume a mantle of dignity appropriate to the concluding act of a great drama.

CHAPTER 9

A Green and Pleasant Land

*The world was not created for people only, but for purposes that transcend
the human race with its limited foresight and imagination; therefore it
behooves all conscious inhabitants of this superb planet to nurture it
as a garden, maintaining it in health, beauty and diversity for
whatever glorious future its denizens may together share.*

STAN ROWE, *BIODIVERSITY IN BRITISH COLUMBIA*

At Hope, the Fraser River abandons the last remnants of its wild past,
swings westward in a great 90 degree arc and assumes a tranquil face
as it flows majestically, unhurriedly, towards the Pacific Ocean. Still
140 kilometres from the sea, the river at Hope is only about five metres
above salt water. For a while mountains loom darkly overhead, reluc-
tant to let the river go; gradually, discreetly, they withdraw to a respectful distance. Now, at last, the Fraser has space enough to assume a
width appropriate to its grandeur. The valley widens, fertile with soil
carried by the river from eroding slopes hundreds of kilometres
upstream. Caressed by a gentle oceanic climate, this green and pleasant
land is a widening cornucopia pouring its wealth towards the sea.

The river below Hope must have seemed a placid stream to Simon
Fraser after his terrifying descent through the canyon in 1808. Other
changes were almost as dramatic; huge cedars now dominated the
forested riverbanks for the first time since the Fraser turned south out of
the Rocky Mountain Trench more than 750 kilometres upstream.
Before long the explorer detected a rise and fall in water levels, induced
by distant tides. In his journal Fraser noted differences in appearance and
customs among the people the expedition encountered. They fished
with large gillnets, erected totem poles and lived in large, multifamily
dwellings usually built of cedar planks. At the upper end of the valley
Fraser and his men were welcomed, feted and entertained, but the
warmth of greetings diminished as they approached the ocean.

Long before Europeans set foot in this hospitable valley, it was home to the Fraser Basin's largest populations, biggest settlements, most elaborate buildings and richest cultures. The distribution of aboriginal population in the Fraser Basin is mirrored by today's population, multiplied fifty times: more than 80 per cent of basin residents still live below Hope in the lower Fraser Valley. The Sto:lo, or "People of the River," have dominated the valley for a very long time; recent archeological finds on the Harrison River and near Mission confirm the existence of stable communities along the river for thousands of years. Longhouse remains dating back 5,000 and 7,000 years were found in 1991 near Hatzic Rock, about 70 kilometres east of Hope. This one of the oldest Native villages discovered in North America. Archeologist Gordon Mohs and local Sto:lo people like Linnea Battel found the ancient buildings and thousands of artifacts associated with them just as a developer's bulldozer was about to demolish the site.

The wet green winters, moderate summers and wealth of food and other resources available from land, river and sea provided relative ease of living for aboriginal people. There was ample time, particularly in winter, for the evolution of cultural and ceremonial life. Spirit dances celebrated the close relationship of humans with nature; throughout the Fraser Basin aboriginal people believed that humans and animals could change from one form of existence to the other. People were participants in the drama of life, not dominant over it. This respect for other creatures, an "ethic of reciprocity" as UBC anthropologists Michael Kew and Julien Griggs term it, ensured careful and conservative use of the resources that supported the people. In potlach ceremonies chiefs would give away all their possessions in grand and extravagant gestures that confirmed the social and political hierarchy and ensured the circulation of wealth in their communities.

After Fraser's 1808 expedition, aboriginal life in the Fraser Valley continued almost unchanged for a time. The occasional vessel anchored offshore seeking trade, but two decades passed before Europeans established a permanent presence. Then George Simpson, governor of the Hudson's Bay Company, directed James McMillan to establish a trading post at the mouth of the Fraser. In July 1827, McMillan arrived in the vessel *Cadboro* and made his way upstream past the estuary to the mouth of the Salmon River, about 25 kilometres east of today's New Westminster. There he built Fort Langley.

Not all Sto:lo appreciated the presence of strangers, but trade in beaver and other furs began. Observing the huge quantities of salmon caught and preserved by the Sto:lo and other Coast Salish people, chief trader Archibald McDonald saw an opportunity for profit. Experimenting until he found a satisfactory way to cure fish fillets in salt, he bought 7,500 salmon from the Sto:lo in 1829 for packing in barrels. The next year twice as many were salted and packed for the company by Native women and shipped in 300 barrels to Hawaii and California. The trade continued to grow and prosper for almost three decades. By the 1850s fish were more profitable than furs at Fort Langley, and chief trader James Murray Yale had added timber, farm products and cranberries to the list of exports.

The HBC had no wish to disturb Native life as long as furs and fish were brought to the fort for trade; in fact, the company discouraged white settlement throughout its territory, knowing the fur trade and farming could not easily coexist. The company and the Sto:lo shared the lower Fraser Valley fairly comfortably for thirty years. Many of the company's men, including chief trader Yale, married Sto:lo women; the company's guns effectively reduced raids by marauding Natives of other nations, and some key Native leaders valued the HBC's presence.

The gold rush of 1858 changed everything. Overnight aboriginal people were dispossessed of their lands and forced onto reserves. New waves of smallpox swept through the basin, killing off entire populations in some villages. The HBC and the British colony on Vancouver Island feared an American takeover of the territory, and so in quick order the mainland was united with the island to form a new colony, British Columbia. A company of Royal Engineers arrived to assure a uniformed British presence and to lay out townsites and build roads; a European-style economy with an Ontario flavour replaced the indigenous Native economy.

It was raining on November 19, 1858, when the new crown colony of British Columbia was proclaimed in the Big House at Fort Langley. In a last burst of glory for the trading post on the Fraser, Douglas and Begbie solemnly installed each other in office. The HBC immediately lost its exclusive trading rights in the territory and was no longer "the only game in town" for Native people. Miners found alternate sources of supplies, often buying fish and food from Native people, who sometimes joined in the search for gold or guided the newcomers. The last of the fur brigades had arrived a few months earlier, and after the ceremonies of 1858 the fort on the Fraser began a rapid slide into insignificance.

Unlike most newly arrived Europeans or officials of the British Colonial Office, Governor Douglas treated the aboriginal people with relative compassion and understanding, insisting their rights be equal to those of non-Natives. Although he was convinced that assimilation into white society was in their best interests, he instructed Col. Richard Moody of the Royal Engineers to ensure that in surveying Native reserves he include sites required by the people to continue their way of life. Unfortunately, Douglas left office before reserve boundaries were confirmed. A few years later, lands commissioner Joseph Trutch, whose racist views seem to have coincided with those of many early settlers, drastically reduced the size of reserves, and the long history of unjust seizure of aboriginal lands in B.C. had begun. While white settlers could preempt 160 acres and buy 480 more, a Native family was allowed a maximum of 10 acres.

For new arrivals, the Fraser River was the key to dreams of wealth and progress. It provided a gateway to the Interior, transportation for resources, rich alluvial soil and a long growing season in the lower valley, more fish than they could possibly catch and more trees than they could imagine cutting. It fell to Colonel Moody to select a site for the capital of the new colony, and he chose "the first high ground on the north side after entering the [Fraser] river." He thought it could be "defended against any foreign aggression," while providing communication by water with Vancouver Island and the Interior. Queen Victoria named the new capital New Westminster, but the town didn't have long to develop pretensions—in 1868, the capital was moved to Victoria.

On a fine October day at Hope, the Fraser River flows low in its channel, revealing expanses of sandbar and riverbank. The rains of fall have not yet begun. An occasional wisp of cloud lightly veils the dark, rocky face of Hope Mountain, hovering high above the town. This is the divide between two very different aspects of the Fraser Basin: the rugged, spectacular, extremely varied, lightly populated and resource-dependent upper basin, and the gentler, productive and highly urbanized Fraser Valley. The Trans-Canada Highway races nearby, squeezed at first between rock and river, trying to flatten and ignore exuberant Nature, hiding silver streams beneath its bland expanse of asphalt. But not even a freeway can reduce this landscape to monotony. In places, sheer black slabs rise too steeply to hold soil or trees. Shafts of sunlight brighten the green of fir, cedar and hemlock; mountain slopes are splashed with orange and gold and crimson accents. Hunter Creek bursts from deep green slopes in a shower of white foam, but most rivulets are tumbling in trickles rather than the torrents they will soon become. Stream-bottom rocks, white, round and dry, reflect low rays of fall sunlight before clouds gather, rains begin, water rises and the stones disappear beneath cascades during the wet months.

The Fraser River is wide and tranquil as it winds between the Coast Mountains to the north and the Cascade Mountains to the south on this golden afternoon. Almost 140 years ago, steam whistles echoed from these slopes as sternwheelers breasted the current, carrying miners and their supplies, merchants, booze, soldiers, politicians—and descended carrying fortunes in Fraser River and Cariboo gold. The ships linked Victoria and New Westminster to Hope and then pushed on against the turbulent current to Yale, the boisterous town that became head of navigation on the lower Fraser. Fiercely competitive captains pushed steamboats beyond their limits, often tying down boiler safety valves to trim trip time below that of their rivals. Capt. Smith Jamieson in the *Fort Yale* was first to force his way up to Yale, but his triumph was soon cut short: just upstream of Hope, the ship exploded as he pushed her hard while rushing to New Westminster where an American actress awaited him at the altar. Captain Jamieson and the dozen men who died with him were only a few of the casualties of boiler blasts, accidents ruled "acts of God" in the total absence of safety regulations in those tumultuous times. Although sternwheelers churned the upper Fraser until World War One, here below the barrier of the Fraser Canyon they lasted little more than a decade; traffic faltered and failed along with the gold rush.

Across the Fraser, the Harrison River flows in from the north, draining coastal mountains on which Pacific air currents drop enormous quantities of rain. Although its watershed is the smallest of any of the Fraser's major tributaries, the Harrison's contribution is enormous, exceeded only by that of the Thompson River. For a few brief years, the Harrison River and the lake it drains were part of B.C.'s most important transportation network. In August 1858, sternwheel steamboats churned up the Harrison carrying hundreds of men to work on the colony's first major construction project. It had been conceived by Governor Douglas as he contemplated the approaching winter with deepening concern. Thousands of men were clawing their way up the Fraser Canyon, and many were hungry, since the only supplies available were carried by pack train with great difficulty and at great cost up the treacherous canyon trail. When the snow flew, Douglas knew many the miners would be without food and unable to make their way back down the canyon. Without action, mass starvation was likely.

Douglas decided that a new route to the upper Fraser River avoiding the fearsome canyon was the only way to prevent a winter catastrophe. In Victoria he assembled hundreds of miners on their way to the goldfields. He told them of his plan and called for volunteers to build a trail from Harrison Lake to Lillooet and the upper Fraser. He offered no pay at all, even demanding of each man a $25 bond to assure good behaviour on the job. In return they could use the road before it was officially open, giving them a headstart in filing claims on the upper Fraser. The eager miners bought into the idea; 250 men sailed for the Fraser River and Harrison Lake on August 5, followed soon by as many more.

At the top end of Harrison Lake they built a steamship terminus they called Port Douglas. Divided into twenty-five-man crews, the men hacked their way through the bush along Lillooet River and Lillooet Lake, built sixty-two wooden bridges, and climbed to Anderson and Seton Lakes where they built docks for ferry boats that would be hauled in pieces over this new 160-kilometre trail to Lillooet. After three exhausting, perilous months, a triumphant Douglas wrote on November 9, 1858, to the Colonial Office in England, "I have the satisfaction of announcing that the great work is now completed." Supplies got through to the destitute miners that winter and freight costs dropped from $1 a pound to about eighteen cents. The trail was upgraded to a wagon road a year later by a company of Royal Engineers; it would be the principal route to the goldfields of the Cariboo and upper Fraser until the Cariboo Road was completed through the canyon in 1864. The Harrison-Lillooet route was used long enough for legends to accumulate—like that of the astonished miner who, while beaching a canoe on the south shore of Harrison Lake in the fall of 1859, stumbled into water warmed by the hot springs for which the lake and its resorts are now famous.

Although the flow of miners and supplies up the Harrison River dwindled and died after five busy years, a much more important traffic continued in the river just as it had for centuries. Every fall, from 100,000 to 200,000 chinook salmon turn left out of the Fraser to swim up the Harrison; in 1993 an estimated 119,000 made the trip, making the Harrison by far the greatest producer of the mighty chinook in Canada. In this stream scarcely a dozen kilometres long, females build rocky redds and lay eggs. Several million eggs hatch in April and within a couple of weeks the little fish are in the Fraser, slowly making their way downstream. Fisheries biologist Colin Levings has found that they stop and feed in marshes along the way and in the Fraser's estuary, growing quickly and becoming accustomed to salt water until, by June or July, they reach Steveston at the mouth of the river and head out to sea. By this time they are 70 to 80 millimetres long. Levings explains that because they move so quickly to the ocean where food, temperature and other conditions are favourable, the Harrison salmon may survive better than chinooks from farther up the Fraser, which spend up to a year in less productive fresh water before going to sea.

The lower Fraser Valley provides the most favourable climate and growing conditions of the entire coast of British Columbia. Before European contact, its forests of Douglas fir, hemlock and cedar were unmatched, and plant and animal life throughout the valley was diverse and exuberant. The cedar was pivotal to the life and culture of Native peoples of the Fraser Valley and Pacific coast. From the giant trees they cut boards for homes, carved cooking utensils, shaped boxes for storage and travel, hollowed logs for canoes, wove bark into clothing, mats and fishing nets. They created baskets and cradles from cedar roots and withes, and honoured family and beliefs in sculpted totems.

But to settlers moving into the valley after the gold rush, the cedar was an enemy that had to be defeated before a plow could furrow the fertile soil. Even when the great trees were cut and hauled away by loggers, massive stumps had to be dug, blasted and burned. Nor could the settler sell logs to defray costs. If he tried to sell wood from his own land he was heavily taxed, for by the 1880s B.C. governments had already entrenched the system of giving large companies exclusive logging rights in exchange for minuscule royalties. Working from mobile camps, loggers moved up the valley, falling trees, skidding logs to the riverbank and floating them to downstream mills. Soon the great trees that had left Simon Fraser awestruck were gone. Today they are gone from far up tributary valleys too, and only fragments remain of the great coastal forest.

While settlers fought the trees, mosquitoes mounted ferocious attacks from the wetlands, making life in summer a misery for the new farmers and their livestock. Even an 1850s survey party of Royal Engineers had been forced by the insects to retreat to high ground until autumn. Early settlers often considered the Fraser an enemy even though the river had created the soil they worked, provided fish for their tables and transportation for their produce. For the placid face the Fraser shows on a golden autumn day can become contorted and angry. Each spring settlers watched with foreboding as mountain snows melted, driving the river higher and higher, inundating lowlands most years and regularly washing out dykes, roads and bridges.

The high water of spring was a normal part of the river's year and made an essential contribution to the valley's extraordinary productivity. Flooding across the lowlands, the Fraser deposited layer upon layer of fertile silt carried from far upstream. The annual flood filled backwaters, marshes and wetlands in which fish, birds and animals (as well as mosquitoes) thrived. Marshes filtered the water as it moved slowly back into the river or sank into the soil, recharging groundwater supplies. As the floodwaters receded from their annual excursion beyond the river's banks, they carried organic nourishment from the land to the river channel and on to tidal flats and open sea, feeding a vast range of living species along the way. As biologist Henry Regier and his colleagues explain, a large river is part of the ecological processes of the land, each powerfully influencing the other. When land and river are separated by a dyke, there is a price to pay. Denying the river normal access to its floodplain impoverishes both land and water; the river is "decoupled" from the land and some deterioration of both is inevitable.

In the 1870s settlers began building dykes to hold the annual flood-waters off the land. Those early dykes were regularly overwhelmed when the river rose with the spring freshet. Some of the best land lay below high-tide levels, so draining it required considerable ingenuity. John Oliver was a delta farmer who eventually became premier of the province (1918–27). Author Bruce Hutchison knew him well. "[Oliver] told me once when he was an old man and full of public honours," Hutchison writes, "that his most satisfactory achievement was the defeat of the river and the purging of salt from his fields. In a dream, he said, he perceived a simple mechanism, a sluice gate which would open as the ditchwater ran outward but would close against the incoming flow. Probably this device had been used in many places long before but Oliver seemed to regard his discovery as a religious experience, a direct revelation from God."

The Fraser is broad and smooth below the mouth of the Harrison River. On the south bank the mountains have retreated, framing fertile farms where the last of the year's corn crop is being cut, chopped and blown into high-walled wagons. This is the Fraser Valley's oldest and largest agricultural settlement, and Chilliwack is its centre. Sto:lo families once cultivated potatoes here; in 1870 some 130 settlers began the struggle to replace forest with farms. Four thousand people lived in the town in 1950 when Hutchison described it as "the ideal farm community . . . No visitor with a taste for pastoral scenery and fruit will pass by the farmwife's little stand at the edge of the road outside Chilliwack." Today's traveller would have some difficulty following his recommendation—along the highway local produce stands have been replaced by fast-food outlets, malls, car dealerships and golf courses.

Paddling downstream of today's Chilliwack on June 30, 1808, Simon Fraser noted that the river widened into a shallow lake. Later known as Sumas Lake, it provided a perfect place for young salmon to feed and grow and hide from predators before going to sea, and was home to vast flocks of waterfowl. "We were in a second Eden!" wrote naturalist John Lord in the summer of 1858 when he camped beside the lake with a party of Royal Engineers. In photographs of a few decades later, ladies in elegant summer finery enjoy picnics on the beach of Sumas Lake. But when pioneer farmer Edward Barrow looked across the lake, he imagined the crops he could grow on the rich, black soil of its bed—if only he could remove the water. He worked out a plan that would capture the Chilliwack and Sumas Rivers in canals, diverting their natural flow away from the lake. He would dyke the Fraser itself from Sumas to Chilliwack, eliminating openings through which the river backed into the lake when tides were high at the Fraser's mouth, 100 kilometres downstream. With its water supply cut off, he could pump the lake dry.

Barrow's scheme was considered hare-brained, and he was ignored for years. But when he managed to get elected to the legislature, his friend Premier John Oliver made him minister of agriculture. Now Barrow was well placed to turn dreams to reality. Construction began in 1921 with a grossly inadequate budget of $1.8 million. When the pumps were shut off in the fall of 1922, more than 12 000 hectares of rich lake-bottom soil were exposed to the sun, and everywhere fish, even mighty sturgeon, flopped and gasped. Today, Sumas Lake is Sumas Prairie, the richest farmland in British Columbia. But drainage can still be a problem, since the land lies about a metre below sea level.

The Trans-Canada heads east and soon crosses the Vedder Canal, which carries the Chilliwack River towards the Fraser high above the farmland that extends out from the canal banks. Agrologist Dave Sands never tires of the view from his favourite place on the dyke. "I just stand out there and think, 'This is the ultimate—just pure agriculture, cattle everywhere, not too much urban intrusion, the mountains all around . . .' " It is no surprise to hear Sands rhapsodize about the wonders of Fraser Valley farming—after all, agriculture is his profession and this is one of Earth's most productive agricultural landscapes. Valley farmlands produce fresh, high-quality food, provide habitat for fish and wildlife, and generate clean air. Urban residents of the Fraser Valley and Greater Vancouver place a high value on farmland as scenic green space complementing the natural environment.

But the future of agriculture in the Fraser Valley is precarious, its existence threatened as cities and towns sprawl across the land, smothering soil under asphalt and suburban lawn. To speculators who have bought vast acreages, Fraser Valley and delta farmland is merely space awaiting a change of zoning that will permit profitable development. It is a process of private enrichment at enormous and permanent cost to the rest of society, and to the plant and animal species essential to life in the valley. The B.C. Agricultural Land Commission has described this expectation of farmland rezoning as "a fundamental threat to the preservation of the resource and the agricultural industry upon which it is based."

The problems facing agriculture in the Fraser Valley are similar to those facing agriculture everywhere, except that here the stakes are higher because the climate is benign and the soil so fertile. But there is very little of it: only 3 per cent of the Fraser Basin is productive agricultural land, and by far the most valuable part of that lies along the banks of the Fraser River between Hope and the sea. So little of B.C. is useful for farming that this tiny corner produces half of the province's entire farm income—about $600 million. In the Greater Vancouver Regional District alone, farm cash receipts exceed $300 million each year, with another $3 billion earned by services such as transportation and food processing. (The GVRD is a region of 3292 square kilometres including Greater Vancouver and extending south to White Rock, north to Lion's Bay and east to Langley and Maple Ridge.) Because land in the lower Fraser Valley is so productive, farms are smaller and labour intensive, employing almost three-quarters of the basin's agricultural workers.

It doesn't much matter how well we use the land if little of it remains in production. In the landmark 1984 report *Soil at Risk: Canada's Eroding Future*, a senate committee headed by Herb Sparrow made the point clearly: "We must come to the point where we think that the highest use for agricultural land is agriculture." Yet this approach is derided by the mainstream economists whose views dominate much public policy. They recognize no limits to resources, manipulate the economy as if it were totally detached from nature and rely on the free play of markets to solve all problems. So farmlands become shopping centres, parking lots and suburbs in Canada's richest agricultural areas: the Fraser Valley and delta, the Okanagan Valley, the Niagara Peninsula and the region of Toronto.

At the University of British Columbia, William Rees is a voice for the growing discipline of "ecological economics," which recognizes soil and arable land as unique, irreplaceable and essential to the global life-support system. Rees insists land must be protected from market forces that would take it out of productive use in order to turn a quick profit. Useful as markets are, the prices they establish reflect only the marginal value of a product—what it is worth today. Markets don't recognize how much of the resource remains, how necessary it might be for our own future and that of succeeding generations, and whether it is replaceable. Many things don't get counted by markets at all: the absolute need for biodiversity, an intact ozone layer or even photosynthesis, the process upon which all life depends. There's not much photosynthesis happening in a parking lot.

In short, says Rees, "a range of considerations and values beyond short-term economic efficiency bear on critical land-use decisions." Taking farmland out of competition from non-farm uses is essential "to ensure food security in a world of rapid ecological change and political uncertainty. As a bonus, we may succeed in preserving important elements of rural life and landscape, a significant part of our national heritage." This was undoubtedly the philosophy underlying the introduction in 1972 of the Agricultural Land Reserve (ALR) by the NDP government of Dave Barrett. Although it was the product of many years of concern and debate about disappearing farmland, the ALR was the target of rage by those convinced of the absolute rights of every property owner. As author John Cherrington recounts, "The Fraser Valley exploded. Fiery meetings were held in every district. 'Dictatorship' and 'Communism' epithets were hurled from the lips of speculators and community leaders alike . . . The Vancouver *Province* railed: 'The government's farm plan reads like George Orwell's *Animal Farm*. As democracy, it's a scandal. It must be fought. By everyone. With all the strength society can muster.' "

But the ALR became law and ever since has played an extremely important role in protecting farmland in the Fraser Basin. Even so, between 1985 and 1990, 368 hectares of agricultural land were still being lost each year to urbanization in the lower Fraser Valley. This is a slower rate than in the 1960s and 1970s, but still significant, and if continued, will ultimately be fatal to agriculture and the quality of the valley environment.

Much depends upon who owns the land, and on the rights that ownership implies. In the GVRD, more than a quarter of agricultural land is not owned by farmers. In Delta at the mouth of the Fraser, only 35 per cent of the land is owned by the people who farm it. Private speculators have driven land prices far above agricultural values because they are confident that sooner or later a change in political climate will enable them to reap enormous profits by rezoning it to urban uses. The people to whom they lease the land in the meanwhile often "mine" the fertility out of it because their tenure is short and insecure; good farming requires a long-term vision and investment. Mining or simply neglecting the soil plays into the speculator's hands, strengthening the case for removing the land from the ALR.

Control of land speculation and foreign ownership is essential to prevent removal of land from food production in the Fraser Valley. In many countries and some Canadian provinces, foreign ownership of farmland is restricted. And new patterns of land ownership are emerging. The "land trust" concept, which ensures the right to farm the land but not to sell it for other purposes, has been used in the eastern U.S. to protect land from urban development, and there is interest in the concept in the Fraser delta and on Vancouver Island. Resource economist Wendy Holm suggests tax policies that could provide incentives to keep land in food production—for instance, lower taxes could be levied on land covered by a covenant that guarantees the land will remain in agriculture. Leases must be of terms sufficiently long to encourage sound farm practices, and farmers must be adequately compensated for improvements to land and buildings. Speculators holding farmland should be denied agricultural tax exemptions if they can't show that their land is leased under terms providing the farmer with the security needed to properly manage that land.

When the Social Credit party returned to power in 1975, it reduced the usefulness of the ALR by introducing appeals of the land commission's decisions to the provincial cabinet—a process by which well-connected developers could remove land from ALR protection. The Socreds also decided that golf courses constituted an appropriate use of agricultural land, and an explosion of this recreational takeover of farmland and natural landscapes occurred. Social Credit governments also eliminated most regional land-use planning.

When they returned to government under Mike Harcourt in 1991, the NDP eliminated ALR appeals to cabinet and once again prohibited the use of farmland for golf courses. The ALR is again the keystone element in protection of farmland from destruction by urban development, though it is still attacked by landowners determined to gain speculative profits. (In the provincial election campaign of 1996, the Liberal party platform included dismantlement of the ALR in favour of local land zoning, a return to the past that would be disastrous for any modern concept of sound land use.) And there are older farmers who have never been reconciled to the ALR, perhaps because suburban development on their land could offer a comfortable retirement income. Of course, destruction of land that should feed a growing population for centuries to come is not a rational way to resolve current farm problems. But it's urgent that those problems be addressed, by measures ranging from farm income insurance to fair trade policy to marketing programs to education programs that build understanding between rural and urban populations.

Farming has to make economic sense if the Fraser Valley is to continue producing food. So everyone, including a person living in the heart of Vancouver, has a stake in the commercial success of agriculture. More is involved than fair prices for farm products—for example, when speculators buy up farmland, generations of farming expertise is lost. As the process continues, machinery dealers, processing plants and other farm services have fewer clients, so they close or move elsewhere.

Rod Clack, one of Canada's must respected urban planners, points out that city people tend to think of open, green agricultural lands almost as parkland, but private landowners can't be expected to carry the entire cost of sustaining an amenity so important to everyone.

Regional planning emphasizing compact cities, inviolable urban containment boundaries and efficient mass transit systems is also essential to the survival of food-producing land in the Fraser Valley.

Dave Sands can't resist superlatives when he talks about agriculture in the Fraser Valley. "Abbotsford is the raspberry capital of North America, with just the right soils and climate, and lots of fertilizer supplied by intensive chicken operations in the area. We have the highest strawberry yields in Canada here in the Fraser Valley. Vegetables—Cloverdale is great for them: onions, lettuce, celery, carrots." And the list goes on: high-value vegetables right beside the Fraser River on the Burnaby "Big Bend," the fine dairy farms of Sumas, hectares of flowers sold all over the world early each morning through the flower auction in South Burnaby.

But interests of town and country often clash. As housing developments and malls spread across the fertile lands of the Fraser Valley, newcomers are sometimes shocked to find tractors growling across neighbouring fields early in the morning, the air redolent of composting cattle manure, a breeze hinting of a nearby pig manure reservoir, cannons sometimes crashing in blueberry fields to ward off crop-destroying starlings. The dream of idyllic country living can turn a bit sour for a transplanted city dweller, who may forget that the farm was there first, or that milk and pork chops and blueberry pies are not produced by some sort of immaculate conception. If residents of a few dozen new houses built adjacent to a farm object to noise or odours, they can politically overwhelm the farmer. The municipal council may be pressured to enact measures that will seriously impact on normal farm practices. And with time, councillors lacking rapport with agriculture will dominate local governments.

An important step in maintaining viable agriculture on the banks of the Fraser River is the provincial "Right to Farm" legislation passed in 1995. The Farm Practices Protection Act ensures that farmers can work their land without harassment as long as they operate according to norms established for the industry. Without that protection, farm families are less likely to stay on the land, particularly when speculators with very deep pockets hover nearby.

While emphasizing the importance of a close relationship between farm and town, Dave Sands explains that, paradoxically, keeping the two communities apart can be helpful. Buffers between farm and residential land can take the form of highways or natural landscapes like streams and ravines. Problems are more likely to arise if an urban development directly adjoins active farmland, which is why land considered less than ideal for farming should often be left in the ALR. Without its buffering effect, pressure will grow to take good farmland close to urban developments out of the reserve. Town and country relations can also be improved by "clean" farm operations, which is why the B.C. government has developed codes governing storage and disposal of animal wastes and effluent from silage, paddocks, greenhouses and stored shavings. Unless they are grazing on open range—and there's not much of that along the lower Fraser River—cattle must be kept out of streams.

Even when suburbs and malls don't actually eliminate farmland, they can complicate life for a farmer—it isn't easy to move farm machinery along roads congested with commuters. Housing developments may be steered onto high land to preserve fertile bottomland, but rainwater runs off buildings, roads and lawns much faster than from the original wooded slopes, carrying chemicals, oil and sediment from destabilized slopes and construction sites. The fast runoff may flood and pollute farmlands, the sediment may clog farm drainage ditches. A paved urban landscape doesn't allow rainwater to sink into the underground aquifers upon which the majority of Fraser Valley residents depend. The slopes onto which urban development is diverted in order to spare valley farmland may be the last natural or semi-natural landscape in the region, their woodlands and small streams the last precious scraps of wildlife habitat. Green hills above Abbotsford, 40 kilometres east of Chilliwack, have been scraped to bare rock and soil as houses push to higher and higher elevations. Throughout the Fraser Valley it is becoming obvious that while diverting urban development off farmland may be a positive step, it poses a whole new set of problems. No matter how well managed, excessive growth will degrade the environment and quality of life in the Fraser Valley.

Dave Sands finds irritation replaced by understanding when people realize they too are part of agriculture when they shop for fresh food, when they see the powerful connection between eating well, good health and a strong, local agriculture. A variety of approaches show promise in linking consumers more closely to food producers. Farmers' markets are enjoying renewed and growing popularity. A few super-markets feature local produce. Near Aldergrove in the Fraser Valley, John Switzer and Grant Watson grow a wide variety of vegetables, herbs and fruits. About 150 city dwellers are shareholders in their crop, each putting up $600 in advance for a portion of the food they grow. This fee translates into about 13.5 kilograms of produce delivered to their doors weekly for twenty weeks, beginning in mid-June. In this model, known as "Community Shared Agriculture," consumers share the farmer's risk, know where their food is coming from, and are assured of its quality and freshness—the use of chemicals normally declines and organic production flourishes. This secure market encourages the farmer to grow an assortment of produce rather than concentrating on a crop yielding the highest market returns.

Although Switzer and Watson's venture is the first example in the Fraser Valley, the concept (known also as "Community Supported Agriculture") has been spreading for some years in other parts of North America, Europe and Japan. In Switzerland CSAs have been common for more than twenty-five years. They're not limited to fruits and vegetables—a grower in Virginia takes orders each spring from about 400 customers for the chickens, rabbits, beef and pork he will produce organically on his 40 hectares, most of which is seeded to grass. An Okanagan fruit grower has had great response to his offer to city dwellers to "adopt a tree." Everything the tree produces is theirs, and they can follow the progress of their crop through the growing season if they wish. The farmer does all the care and maintenance of the tree right up until harvest, when the "adopter" comes to pick the fruit. A one-year adoption costs $25 to $200, depending on variety and productivity, and the grower expected to have 15 per cent of his 8,000 trees adopted in his first year, 1995.

As productive Fraser Valley ecosystems are crushed by development, reliance on distant places for the essentials of life increases. This has enormous political, social and economic implications, even jeopardizing national security and stability. Gary Runka, former head of B.C.'s Agricultural Land Commission, which administers the ALR, writes, "Without the ability to grow our own food, we leave our children and grandchildren held to ransom to buy food on the world market from whatever source, of whatever quality, at whatever price."

When supermarket shelves are piled high with inexpensive imported fruit and vegetables, there may be little incentive for Vancouverites to support measures required to protect Fraser River farmland. The risk to food supply implicit in the paving of productive land is not readily apparent, and it may seem rational to use land for purposes that, in the short run, yield a higher return. But there is no guarantee that foreign food supplies will always be available, even at higher prices. In the summer of 1996, Canadians were warned not to eat strawberries grown in the U.S. because some were found to be carrying disease-causing parasites. Rapidly growing populations and sharply declining food production per capita are global phenomena. A meeting of leading agricultural scientists from around the world in July 1996 concluded that "The world is headed for an unprecedented food shortage which neither science nor current farming practices will be able to meet." Urbanization and declining fertility are not restricted to the Fraser Valley. If each region of the world depends on the productivity of a distant place while diminishing its own food-growing capacity, the future is dim indeed.

Unfair trade can jeopardize Fraser Valley farmland. American fruits and vegetables are highly subsidized by the U.S. taxpayer, who pays most of the cost of irrigation water. Mexico insisted on the right to levy tariffs on subsidized American produce when they signed the North American Free Trade Agreement, but the Canadian government didn't bother to obtain similar protection for Canadian farmers. And the importation of farm products from poorer countries at prices below B.C. production costs can be damaging to the country of origin as well as to Fraser Basin producers, says William Rees. He points out that such export products are often grown by large operators who have displaced the people who used to grow food for local consumption. Cheap imports may make Fraser Valley farm production uneconomic, adding weight to existing pressures for urbanization of the land. Unregulated trade in food eventually reduces the capacity of the world to support its growing population, says Rees, and increases long-term risks to both exporters and importers.

Rees doesn't suggest that the Fraser Valley and delta can be completely self-sufficient in food, but he does advise as much self-reliance as possible in a world of growing ecological uncertainty and unpredictable geopolitics. Availability of fresh, flavourful, in-season, locally grown produce can only be assured if Fraser Basin farmland is protected, and if urban British Columbians understand their links to agriculture. Recent B.C. government promotion of local food is a step in that direction, as is the new "Agriculture in the Classroom" program that educates students about food sources and community issues.

Protecting the agricultural land of the Fraser Valley is just a first step in assuring its sustainability. How it is farmed is also of crucial importance. As he so often did, E. B. White probably said it best: "The question is not whether the land will support us, but whether we will support the land." If we concentrate on meeting the needs of the land first, fulfilling the needs of the farm family and the community will follow. Economist E. F. Schumacher wrote that the real concern of agriculture must be the health, beauty and permanence of the land; productivity and sustainability will be the inevitable outcomes.

But the goal of industrial agriculture, and the preoccupation of many agricultural experts, is productivity. Highest possible production takes pride of place over the real goals of the farm family, which are usually related to quality of family and community life. High, short-term production goals may be very costly—not just in cash expenditures on chemicals, technology and energy, but in reduction of the biodiversity that supports the entire enterprise. Excessive production goals have been achieved by drawing down the "natural capital" that produces food, a depletion of fertility the Fraser River took millennia to create.

Periodic deposits of silt by floodwaters no longer renew the fertility of the Fraser Valley, and heavy machinery compacts its wet soils. Many farms rely on chemicals for fertility, along with manure from a dense population of farm animals. Yet soil fertility is declining in the Fraser Valley even as chemical fertilizers are applied beside the Fraser River at rates far exceeding those recommended. In fact, chemical fertilizers are applied here at a rate higher than anywhere else in Canada: about 625 kilograms per hectare each year. Soil acidity rises after excessive use of nitrogen fertilizers; nitrates from fertilizers and chemicals from pesticides percolate through the soil into underground aquifers. They wash off the land into streams where they have caused many fish kills, particularly in the Fraser's smaller tributary streams. Chemicals like Dinoseb, used in insecticides and herbicides, are highly toxic to fish, yet are used in large quantities along the lower Fraser River. Pesticides often kill the subsurface life upon which fertility depends, simplifying or eliminating natural ecosystems.

The symbiotic raspberry-chicken relationship that is so productive in the Abbotsford area can have a downside. When excessive manure and chemicals are applied to the raspberry crop, nitrates seep down to contaminate the vast Abbotsford aquifer that extends beneath 200 square kilometres of the Fraser Valley and northwestern Washington state. This is the water supply for up to 100,000 people, for fish hatcheries, farms and industries. Nitrate contamination in drinking water is of particular concern for infants because it reduces the ability of the blood to carry oxygen. Recent research shows, fortunately, that raspberry yields can be pushed just as high using much less manure, thereby reducing pollution in the aquifer.

Intensive livestock production means a lot of manure and, like any good thing, manure is a problem when there's too much of it. In several European countries, laws restrict stock populations to about two animals per hectare, which produce the maximum amount of manure the land can absorb without damaging water quality in streams and aquifers. In the lower Fraser Valley, cattle numbers per hectare are considerably greater than this and, in addition, almost 18 million chickens and 175,000 pigs are raised here each year. Amendments in 1992 to the province's Waste Management Act provided new standards for storage and use of farm waste, and farmers themselves are involved in ensuring compliance. The Fraser River is the ultimate recipient of chemicals from excess fertilizer, pesticides or manure that wash off or seep into the land. This is known as "non-point pollution," because it comes from a great many difficult-to-identify sources.

The sustainability of farming in the Fraser Basin is profoundly affected by changes in agriculture throughout the world. Agribusinesses have expanded into giant agro-chemical conglomerates whose developments in seeds, chemicals, livestock hormones and antibiotics are designed to increase farmers' dependency upon them. Plant ecologist Stan Rowe is sure that biotechnology will accelerate the deterioration of soil, water, air and organisms. It is, he says, part of a system of industrial agriculture that is fundamentally unstable since it is based on high-input farming that enriches the agro-corporations at the expense of soil fertility, the quality of food and the social structure of rural communities.

The industrial model of agriculture is probably unsustainable in the long term and, like some forestry and fishery practices, diminishes the resource base of the Fraser Basin. It doesn't have to be that way, and a growing number of farmers are showing that sustainable agriculture is possible—agriculture that will endure, improving the soil rather than degrading it, while supplying uncontaminated high quality, fresh food for consumption in the huge urban market of the Lower Mainland. Usually this means using less land more intensively while applying fewer costly inputs from off the farm. Many organic farmers are proving that lower costs realized by working with nature can produce net profit for a farm family comparable to high throughput, high-cost industrial agriculture.

"A sustainable society can flourish only if it is founded on a sustainable agriculture." So writes Lester Milbrath in his remarkable book *Envisioning a Sustainable Society*. This view carries little weight with mainstream economists, but is pretty persuasive to ordinary mortals who like to eat. Since eating ties all of us to the land, the more intimate that connection can be, the healthier will be both society and land. So agricultural policies in the Fraser Valley and throughout the basin must reward good stewardship of the land, and sustainable agriculture must be sufficiently profitable that good farmers can survive and pass on their skills. Then we will be assured that the mighty river will continue to flow broad, brown and tranquil through a landscape as productive as it is beautiful. Cattle will continue to graze green pastures, golden corn will greet each new autumn, fruits and flowers will nourish body and soul.

Now, in the last few kilometres of its long journey from the distant Rocky Mountains, the Fraser will encounter its greatest test: the river must make its way through the vibrant, growing city at its mouth. Life throughout the basin will depend upon the state of the Fraser River when it finally flows into the Strait of Georgia.

CHAPTER 10

At the River's Mouth

The care of the earth is our most ancient and most worthy and, after all,
our most pleasing responsibility. To cherish what remains of it, and
to foster its renewal, is our only legitimate hope.

WENDELL BERRY, *THE UNSETTLING OF AMERICA*

Lying comfortably among the peaks forming Vancouver's spectacular
mountain backdrop, the Lions watch the Fraser River advance
towards the sea. Thirteen thousand years ago their round, rocky heads
emerged from the ice and snow that lay 1500 metres deep where steel
and glass towers now dominate a modern city. The massive, frigid blanket melted into tongues of ice that slowly receded along the Strait of
Georgia, retreated up the Fraser Valley and retracted into shadowed valleys of the Coast and Cascade Mountains. Granite shoulders emerged
from ice; meltwater dripped, trickled and poured water into the lowlands, covering today's Surrey with seas 200 metres deep. But not for
long; relieved of the enormous icy burden, the land rose again into the
sunlight.

As the ice age was ending about 10,000 years ago, the Fraser River
flowed into the Pacific at today's New Westminster. Each year its brown
torrent carried 18 million tonnes of gravel, sand and silt, which
dropped to the bottom when the current slowed as river met ocean.
The accumulation of this material between the Surrey Uplands and
Burrard Peninsula moved the river's mouth steadily westward as it still
does today, building about 2.3 metres farther out into the Strait of
Georgia each year. The river built and abandoned its bed over and over
again, always seeking the shortest, easiest route to the sea. Through the
millennia the Fraser wandered restlessly back and forth, building and
eroding, flooding and shifting, dissipating the enormous energy gathered during its descent from the Rocky Mountains, distributing the

sediment carried in its powerful flow from far upstream. Each year 12 million cubic metres of sediment were added to the alluvial plain and its islands, to the peatlands and tidal flats.

Eventually the Fraser River delta encompassed 680 square kilometres of sediment 100 to 200 metres deep stretching along 50 kilometres of the Strait of Georgia. Today the Fraser River divides at New Westminster. The South or Main Arm carries 80 per cent of the flow and at least as much of the sediment load. The smaller North Arm divides again as it nears the ocean, sending the river's Middle Arm around the southern shore of Sea Island, on which Vancouver International Airport is located. The delta's union of water, land and life is one of the biological wonders of the world, a great river's magnificent explosion of generosity just before losing itself in the waters of the Pacific Ocean. This is the richest region of the Fraser Basin and among the most bountiful places in all of Canada.

The wet part of the delta—the meeting and mingling of fresh river water with the salty sea—is the Fraser River estuary. As the delta grew, flood-resistant grasses and shrubs moved in from the south, and clumps of willow scrub, hardhack and crabapple colonized the higher land along riverbanks and on ancient beach ridges. Above the delta, jack-pines flourished and then gave way to fir, cedar and hemlock trees as today's moist, cool climate replaced a warmer, dryer one. Trees crept up mountainsides, and in fertile valleys the giants of the coastal rainforest flourished.

Aboriginal people living along the banks of the river expanded their territory as the delta grew westward, living abundantly from the plentiful fish and wildlife. Archeologists have found evidence of settlements up to 7,000 years old in the delta, particularly on the high ground of Tsawwassen, White Rock and North Delta. The rest of the estuary was regularly flooded, and the flooding helped feed the aboriginal people by discouraging tree growth and favouring grasses and shrubs that attracted large numbers of elk and deer. Blueberries and cranberries flourished in low-lying bogs, marshes supported myriad waterfowl, and mud flats supplied endless shellfish harvests. Natives of the resident Musqueam, Kwantlen and Tsawwassen bands were joined in summer for fishing and berry-picking by other Halkomelem-speaking bands from Vancouver Island.

In the late eighteenth century, Spain was determined to extend its California possessions to the north. Two Spanish vessels commanded from Nootka Sound on Vancouver Island's west coast were already in the Juan de Fuca Strait in the summer of 1792 when Capt. George Vancouver arrived from Britain to chart the coast. On June 13, Captain Vancouver landed at Point Grey, beside the North Arm of the Fraser, without recognizing that he was in the presence of a great river. The river was undoubtedly flowing high and a combination of spring floods and high tides could have backed water over the land now known as Richmond and Delta, creating a vast expanse of shallow water obscuring the river's mouth. It is likely the Spaniards knew of the Fraser, however, and tantalizing tales of eighteenth-century Spanish gold mining in the Harrison Springs area persist to the present day.

Familiarity with white men who had come by sea may have been a cause of Simon Fraser's deteriorating relations with the Natives of the Fraser Valley as he paddled towards the mouth of the river. When the explorer and his companions arrived at the site of New Westminster on July 2, 1808, they were pursued by people brandishing bows, arrows and spears, their paddles beating war-song rhythms on wooden canoe hulls. The river divided; Fraser chose the right branch and headed down the North Arm, his voyageurs straining at their paddles.

The sound of hostile chants faded, and before long the travellers sighted the Strait of Georgia and the distant mountains of Vancouver Island. They headed towards the Musqueam village on the right bank of the mouth of the river. Fraser wrote in his journal:

Here we landed, and found but a few old men and women; the others fled into the woods upon our approach. The fort is 1500 feet in length and 90 feet in breadth . . . One of the natives conducted us through all the apartments, and then desired us to go away, as otherwise the Indians would attack us . . . we went to embark, [when] we found the tide had ebbed, and left our canoe on dry land. We had, therefore, to drag it out to the water some distance. The natives no doubt seeing our difficulty, assumed courage, and began to make their appearance from every direction, in their coats of mail, howling like so many wolves, and brandishing their war clubs. At last we got into deep water, and embarked.

Fraser and his men paddled upstream as fast as possible until making camp on the riverbank late that night. The explorer was deeply disappointed on two counts: he had not seen the open ocean, and his sextant proved that he was far to the north of the mouth of the Columbia River. His mission had been to find a navigable route to the Columbia's mouth, and since this was neither the Columbia nor was it navigable, he counted the trip a failure. Facing an incredibly difficult upstream journey, he took no comfort in having led the first expedition of Europeans to the mouth of a great river previously unknown to them.

Fraser and his band of exhausted men pushed back up the river as quickly as they could. Warriors sometimes gave chase in canoes, and in the lower canyon the voyageurs dodged showers of arrows and rocks. Fraser staved off mutiny when some of his men proposed to avoid Hell's Gate by taking an overland route east; he persuaded them that their only chance of survival lay upstream. When they regained Nlaka'-pamux territory farther up the canyon, they were welcomed and helped along the way as they had been while descending. In an incredible feat of endurance, the half-starved men reached Fort George in thirty-four days—one day faster than the downstream trip!

The floods normal to the Fraser River are produced by astonishing seasonal fluctuations in its flow. Some years, the spring freshet can be almost forty-five times greater than the year's lowest winter discharge: 20 000 cubic metres per second (cms) as compared with 450 cms. Usually, though, when the spring freshet is at its height from May to mid-July, melting snow from the mountains of the Interior will pour an average of 11 500 cms into the Strait of Georgia, fifteen times the average low flow in winter of 750 cms. More variation is added by tides, which rise and fall as much as three metres at the river's mouth, influencing conditions for life throughout the delta and far up the river. Even at New Westminster tides may rise and fall by a metre, and they can affect the flow of the Fraser all the way to Chilliwack, 100 kilometres upstream. When the river runs low, a wedge of salt water will creep upstream along the river bottom as far sometimes as Annacis Island near New Westminster. But when the Fraser is in full flood, its mighty torrent prevents salt water from rising above its mouth.

The sheer volume of water pouring into the Strait of Georgia from the Fraser River draws ocean water from deep in the strait towards the surface at the mouth of the river. This upwelling carries nutrients that support a fountain of biological productivity, from plankton to shrimp to cod to killer whales, waterfowl and bald eagles. The mingling of fresh and salt waters integrates the Strait of Georgia with the Fraser delta as river and ocean together wash over and around the fertile silt of the delta. Nourishment from hundreds of square kilometres of river, delta and ocean combine to create the largest estuary on the west coast of North America and one of the most productive regions on earth.

In late winter and early spring, millions of young salmon from the vast expanse of interior British Columbia descend hundreds of streams into the Fraser and swim down to the great estuary. In tidal channels winding through the wetlands they adapt to salt water while growing and gaining the strength they need for survival at sea. The salmon are not alone; about eighty species of fish spend at least part of their lives in the estuary. At almost any time of year one or more species are moving through the wetlands, usually to spawn. In spring, vast schools of herring lay their eggs in eel grass beds, creating a feeding bonanza for ducks and gulls and a fishing frenzy by fishers keen to profit from high-priced herring roe. Little oolichan or "candlefish" swarm up the river in spring, where Native people traditionally caught them in huge numbers for rendering into oil and grease. Deep in the murky Fraser waters the huge and ancient sturgeon makes its mysterious way, sometimes growing to more than four metres in length and 150 years of age. Sea lions and seals follow the oolichan to the river's mouth in April, and killer whales are enticed by the vast runs of salmon converging here in late summer.

With its extraordinary diversity of climate, terrain and vegetation, the Fraser Basin is temporary or permanent home to vast and diverse bird populations. The most species and the largest numbers are found in the estuary. Two million birds of 230 different species will spend at least part of their lives here each year, for this is a key staging and feeding ground on four great flyways linking three continents. The wetlands, tidal marshes, mud flats and farmlands of the Fraser estuary provide an essential place to rest, feed and regain strength for birds migrating between winter homes in South and Central America and nesting sites in the Yukon, Alaska and Siberia. The food web of the estuary is based on humble aquatic plants: sedges and rushes whose roots nourish successive waves of water birds. In winter, plumes of silt drift seaward as ducks and geese tear up marshes to feed on succulent rhizomes.

The Fraser delta is a biological treasure of international significance. As birds flow in and out of the estuary they provide some of nature's great spectacles. Tens of thousands of snow geese wheel, soar and land in vast flocks when they arrive in October and November from their breeding grounds on Wrangel Island off the coast of Siberia. They have travelled more than 600 kilometres each day to arrive here; scientists have traced the journey by attaching tiny radio collars to their necks. When an incoming flock spots a promising place to land, the birds flip on their backs for a precipitous descent. At dusk snow geese lift in animated clouds of 10,000 or more from farm fields where they've been feeding; they will spend the night on tidal flats, safe from coyotes and other predators. Some of the birds may be fifteen years of age, and they have learned to avoid places where hunters lie in wait.

More than a million shorebirds from forty-five species and up to three-quarters of a million waterfowl stop here to rest, feed and gather strength for their annual migrations. Some remain to nest and raise their young. Most of the Fraser Basin's thirty or so colonies of great blue herons are found in or near the delta; some colonies include hundreds of nests. About one hundred species of woodland birds—songbirds, hummingbirds, woodpeckers and other passerines arrive and depart in waves from early spring to late fall. Forty per cent of them will breed here and about 20 per cent will stay all year round. For a large population of predator birds this is a fruitful year-round hunting ground. In winter there are more hawks, owls and other raptors in the Fraser estuary than anywhere else in the basin. Soaring, gliding and diving, they prey on small rodents like Townsend's voles scurrying through pastures and farm fields, or on starlings and shorebirds isolated from their flocks.

For 10,000 years the Fraser estuary was a work in progress, a landscape being created by a river wandering freely, carving new courses, flooding land and then withdrawing. When European settlement began in the mid-1800s, the restless river interfered with the establishment of permanent towns and farms and with shipping. A war with the river began that has endured for more than a century. The Europeans who replaced Native people on the land brought with them the ideals of the Industrial Revolution, and they set about changing the landscape to accommodate their values. An economy based on markets replaced one based on resource use according to need. The system changed from consumption at levels well below nature's productivity to consumption with no real limits. It was a huge shift—from collaboration with natural forces to mastery of them.

At the river's mouth this meant gaining control of the Fraser as it wended its way through the estuary. Settlers moved onto the rich, tree-free land and began dyking it to ward off spring floods and high tides. By 1900 three-quarters of the marshes and seasonally flooded grasslands of the delta had been converted to farmland. Early in the twentieth century, major dyke reconstruction was undertaken and over the years the network was extended and upgraded; today the river is locked permanently in place by more than 620 kilometres of dykes. Almost all of Richmond and Delta are protected by dykes and drained by deep, pumped ditches.

Behind the dykes more than 70 000 hectares of marsh and floodplain have been converted to agriculture, eliminating from 70 to 80 per cent of the natural wetlands of the delta. Fish and ducks gave way to corn and potatoes; native plants were replaced by grains and forage; pigs and cows took over from deer and elk. A permanently sustainable ecosystem had been replaced by a new one that, though extremely productive in its own right, uses large inputs of chemicals and energy to sustain itself.

Confining the river means that sediment continues to settle in the same bed long after the Fraser would normally have abandoned it, so artificial means must be used to maintain the channel's depth. The first structures to lock the river permanently in place while keeping channels deep enough for navigation were built in the 1870s and 1880s while dykes were being constructed to protect new farmlands from flooding. Wing dams and training walls now line about 20 kilometres of the Fraser to speed water through its principal channels, sweeping sediment along with the current, controlling where it should drop and reducing the need for dredging.

Other projects have also changed the pattern of sediment erosion and deposition. At Roberts Bank near Tsawwassen, the B.C. Ferry's terminal and the "superport" block the Fraser's sediment deposits, causing salt marshes to erode farther back each year. River training walls diminish deposits of new sand on the beaches of Point Grey in Vancouver, contributing to the erosion of seaside cliffs. New islands such as Green, Rose and Keith have risen out of the water near the river's mouth where human structures have steered silt for many years.

Training walls don't maintain as much depth in the river as shippers prefer, so large dredging operations continue to dig the riverbed deeper to allow passage of still larger ships—the bed is a metre deeper in the 1990s than it was in the 1960s. The dredges remove 25 per cent of the sediment deposited on the river bottom each year, about 5.5 million cubic metres. This can be a damaging operation: the dredges churn up young salmon and other marine life along with the silt, and stir up industrial contaminants accumulated in the riverbed. Dredging is restricted during the annual downstream migration of salmon to spare them the worst of this. The dredged material has to be put somewhere, but whether on land or at sea the disposal can lead to serious environmental problems.

Will Paulik has long been one of the most passionate defenders of the Fraser River and its environment, and he is particularly disturbed by the dumping of dredged sand and mud on Steveston Island near the mouth of the South Arm, a place proposed as parkland. Paulik points out that dredged sediment has been dumped on hundreds of hectares of estuary wetlands, destroying in one case a large area of snow geese habitat near the airport. Out in the Strait of Georgia, he says, scows dump dredged material in sensitive areas, far from the zones where dumping is officially permitted.

Imprisoning the Fraser River in corsets of stone and wood has been expensive. With time it will become more difficult and more costly to maintain that control, and the potential for economic loss will mount as urbanization continues behind protective dykes. As the Fraser's bed rises and lengthens, the energy potential of the river increases and the search for a more direct, steeper channel to the sea becomes increasingly urgent. The urge could become irresistible if the right combination of high tides and high spring flows allows the Fraser to break into a new, faster route to the Pacific. The most likely new channel, says UBC hydrologist Michael Church, would be Canoe Pass, which flows out of the South Arm past the town of Ladner. Once breached, Canoe Pass would in short order carry most of the flow of the South Arm of the Fraser. The floodwaters would be unstoppable and devastating.

A flood is usually understood to be a catastrophe. Yet floods are a normal part of the seasonal cycle of a large river like the Fraser. Lands that are periodically inundated, and those that would be if not protected by dykes, are called floodplains. Much of the Fraser Valley from Hope to the sea is naturally a floodplain. The richest agriculture of the Fraser Valley and delta lies behind the protective armour of hundreds of kilometres of dykes, as does billions of dollars worth of urban development, particularly in Richmond.

Although a big flood can't be predicted very far in advance, the causes are well known. Deep, exceptionally wet winter snows in the mountains, a late, cool spring followed by warm days and heavy spring rains can be a recipe for disaster. When such a high flow encounters the damming effect of high tides in the estuary, the danger is compounded. Twice since European settlement began, in 1894 and 1948, these elements have combined to overwhelm the Fraser Valley and estuary.

"Mary Ann McLellan fled upstairs when a wall of water crashed into the main floor of her home," writes historian John Cherrington. "A few minutes later, she went into labour and was delivered of a baby boy by neighbour Agnes Towle, who had to tie Mary Ann's other son to his bed to prevent him from drowning downstairs." Not far from the McLellan home in Fort Langley, embankments near the fort were disintegrating, and water rose above the windows of a hotel. It was late May 1894; a great flood was sweeping down the Fraser, tearing out bridges and railway tracks, inundating 708 square kilometres of the valley. The plank buildings of raw new towns along the river stood naked and vulnerable as instant lakes rose around them. Men and boys in boats, canoes and makeshift rafts evacuated people from buildings along Chilliwack's main street. Telegraph lines collapsed and there was no radio to warn, advise or console; isolated and fearful, people in each community worked without respite to save property and care for neighbours driven from their homes by the relentless water.

In his Fraser Valley history, Cherrington captures the anguish and heroism of people whose lives were convulsed by the force of the Fraser, but an accountant totalling the damage in emotionless arithmetic would say the 1894 losses weren't extreme since so few people lived in the Fraser Valley. And, writes Cherrington, "There was a silver lining to the tragedy. The rich river mud proved bountiful for farmers who replanted crops, and for years thereafter, almost freakishly large vegetables were grown, such as the monster turnips from Silverdale."

Rebuilding began as the floodwaters receded. Mission City, north of Abbotsford, abandoned the riverbank and relocated to higher ground. The provincial government recognized that public assistance was needed to help rebuild and strengthen dykes, but the money was slow in coming and most of the work and cost fell to local residents. Many had been through this before—though 1894 was the biggest, earlier floods had often broken through the dykes.

As years passed, farms prospered and towns grew behind the protecting dykes. From time to time the river threatened to reclaim its floodplain. In June 1925 it broke through the dyke protecting thousands of fertile hectares of Matsqui Prairie. This time, better communications enabled men and equipment to rush from nearby farms, towns and logging camps; frantic effort through the night sealed the breach, and again the dykes were strengthened. But with more development, the stakes were higher with each spring freshet. When deep mountain snows of the winter of 1947–48 were suddenly released by hot days in late spring, river watchers knew trouble lay ahead.

In the early morning hours of May 25, 1948, angry brown Fraser River water swept across Agassiz, east of Chilliwack, creating a vast lake where town, Indian reserve and farms had sweltered in the sun the day before. The crest moved downstream, seemingly intent on removing all traces of human incursion on the land. Just before the dykes protecting the prosperous farms of Nicomen Island collapsed with tremendous roars, the pressure shot an entire tree into the air with a thunderous explosion. At Matsqui, crews feverishly piled sandbags higher and higher, but the base of the dyke, built on river silt, couldn't be reinforced. Pressure mounted until it blew, leaving a 60-metre crater. As the dark waters swirled across thousands of hectares of land on May 30, barns and animal carcasses floated to the surface while small boats carried marooned families to higher ground.

And so the flood crest rolled down the valley. All was not lost; the dykes had held at Chilliwack and Sumas and a few other places. But ten people died, 16,000 others were forced to leave their homes, 22 000 hectares of superb farmland lay under water and eighty-two bridges were washed away. When at last the evacuees straggled back to their homes they faced an ugly mess: ruined homes and furnishings, dead animals, a thick coating of mud and debris, pools of stagnant water and rotting fish everywhere.

The massive effort to help people back on their feet, to return land to productivity, and above all to rebuild and strengthen the dykes, began almost immediately. Hardly had the flood passed its peak when B.C.'s Premier Bjorn "Boss" Johnson flew to Ottawa to seek federal assistance for the massive job that lay ahead. He made his case to Prime Minister William Lyon Mackenzie King—and King flatly refused to contribute a cent.

Carson Templeton picks up the story. One of Canada's pre-eminent engineers, Templeton was assistant chief engineer responsible for rebuilding the dykes. "A furious Boss Johnson boarded a Trans-Canada Airlines Northstar aircraft for the long overnight flight back to British Columbia," says Templeton. "Among the passengers was J. B. Carswell, chairman of the Fraser Valley Dyking Board. He went over to talk with the fuming Johnson, who told him, 'That SOB wouldn't give me a nickel to help with flood damage.' Carswell told Johnson he had made a serious tactical error. 'Mackenzie King just looks after politics,' he said. 'C. D. Howe runs everything else. You should have talked to him.' Carswell knew Howe from their wartime collaboration when Carswell was Canada's purchasing agent in Washington. He offered to help Johnson get to Howe.

"They talked through the night as the Northstar droned across the country. In Vancouver, reporters were waiting on the tarmac to hear from Johnson the outcome of his Ottawa meetings. The premier descended the ramp and announced, 'The federal government is with us 100 per cent! Mackenzie King is a fine, understanding man.' He had forced on King any negative announcement that would have to be made. In the meantime, Carswell telephoned C. D. Howe, telling him of the need for federal assistance. Howe growled back, 'If you think I'm going to pay 100 per cent, you're crazy.' Carswell responded, 'How about 75 per cent?' " Howe agreed, and that became the formula for federal contributions to disaster assistance in the Fraser Valley and across the entire country. MacKenzie King never had to refute Johnson's effusive announcement.

Templeton insisted that rebuilt Fraser Valley dykes be wide enough to bear a truck. This would permit fast, massive action when necessary, a precaution that proved its worth when floodwaters again threatened the Fraser Valley in 1972. By 1994 the two governments had spent almost $300 million on structures and programs designed to reduce future flood damage to 55 000 hectares of floodplain in the lower Fraser Valley. A good investment, said a 1994 report by the Fraser Basin Management Program (FBMP), since without the dykes a recurrence of a flood similar to that of 1894 could cause almost $2 billion damage. The FBMP, established in 1992 and jointly funded by Ottawa, B.C. and local governments, considers environmental, economic and social issues related to sustainability in the Fraser Basin.

Existing dykes are intended to provide flood protection to the 1894 flood level—an event that is calculated to occur about every 140 years. Raising dykes any higher would be extremely costly and would provide a false sense of security. No matter how high they are built, dykes are never impregnable, particularly in a region subject to earthquakes. When, inevitably, water levels exceed the capacity of dykes, the damage from flooding will be greater than if the barriers had never been built. This is because higher and stronger dykes, like dams, stimulate large investments in the regions they appear to protect.

A young American geographer named Gilbert White observed and wrote about this phenomenon in the 1930s, but it took forty years for his ideas to become commonly accepted. Basically, White proposed that people learn to live in harmony with rivers rather than insisting on their total control. He explained that the way we use a river's floodplain is the key to reducing flood losses, and that reliance on structural solutions such as dams and dykes will make flood losses greater over the long haul. White listed other measures that can achieve similar goals at less cost. The most important is floodplain zoning: restricting urban development on lands subject to flooding, while dedicating them to parkland, farming and recreation. When floodwaters retreat, such lands can return to normal use at minimal cost. This approach is far less expensive than herculean efforts to hold back floodwaters, it lessens the pressure a rigidly channellized river imposes downstream, and it retains more fertile floodplain land in food production.

Environment Canada estimates there is a one-in-three chance that a flood of the severity at least equal to that of 1948 will occur sometime in the next sixty years. When the FBMP released its 1994 report on Fraser flood control, board chair Tony Dorcey said, "The Fraser River is due for a major flood. It's not a question of if, but rather when, how big, and are we ready?" American engineers responsible for flood-proofing the Mississippi Valley were sure they were ready for anything. But in 1993, swollen by unrelenting rain, the great river overwhelmed levee (dyke) after levee. Residents fled to higher ground, yet 70 people died, 70,000 were left homeless and property damage amounted to more than U.S.$12 billion.

The agency responsible for Mississippi flood control, the U.S. Army
Corps of Engineers, is gung-ho to rebuild and strengthen all the former structures, but many voices are saying enough is enough; some
Mississippi Valley farm families are moving buildings to higher ground,
some towns plan to relocate entirely. In many areas people want to
allow former wetlands to once again perform their natural function,
while in others normal floods will be permitted to expand across the
floodplain to which the river has long been denied access. As one
floodplain manager told the *New York Times*, "For too long we've been
trying to adjust rivers to human needs, and then we wonder why our
rivers are messed up and why we continue to get flooded. It's not a
mystery. We need to adjust human behaviour to river systems."

To make zoning work, floodplains have to be mapped. Provincial and
federal governments are presently doing this in the Fraser Valley; with this
information, there can be no excuse for building in vulnerable locations
and no right to claim compensation from governments when damage
occurs to developments built on floodplain land. As early as 1966, the
need for restricting floodplain development was recognized in the Lower
Mainland's official regional plan, and the Agricultural Land Reserve
introduced in 1972 helps reduce urban development on flood-plain lands.
But many municipal politicians seem unwilling to understand the rudi-
ments of modern floodplain planning, and some local governments are
slow to adopt floodplain regulations. Urban development continues
apace on Fraser Valley floodplains, where the FBMP values home, farm,
business and other urban development at about $13 billion. Because
developers can make so much money building on level, stone-free floodplains, they put a lot of effort into persuading local politicians to allow
floodplain urbanization—and they're often successful. Allowing development of the Terra Nova lands in Richmond is a recent large-scale example. In 1996 Richmond municipal politicians were still vehemently
objecting to restrictions to major urban development on the municipal-
ity's earthquake-prone floodplains.

Where buildings already exist on a floodplain or must be constructed
there, floodproofing can reduce damage; this usually means elevating the
main part of the building above levels likely to be hit by floodwaters. In
a watershed like the lower Fraser where so much flood-plain development has already occurred, options for management are diminished.
More reliance must be placed on monitoring conditions that lead to
flooding, along with effective warning and evacuation systems. Some
agricultural areas in the Fraser Valley are so low in elevation that farming
is impossible without protective dykes. But it is sometimes possible to
build dykes in a manner sensitive to the natural environment. In Delta, a

dyke built in 1986 provides flood protection while allowing the large
and important Tsawwassen salt marsh to flourish behind it.

For more than ten years, biologist Rob Butler has been studying and
documenting the birds of the Fraser delta for the Canadian Wildlife
Service. Butler is at home on the mud flats with sandpipers or in the
woodlands nearby where herons raise their young. There is no other
place as bountiful as this delta along the entire Pacific coast between
California and Alaska, says Butler, and deterioration of these ecosystems
would affect birds in more than twenty countries and three continents.
Canada's responsibility for the maintenance of quality wildlife habitat in
the delta and throughout the Fraser Basin is an international one, formally recognized by treaty. An essential part of that estuarine habitat is
Boundary Bay, yet until 1995, it was the only key tidal staging area on
this international flyway that had no legal protection.

Boundary Bay stretches about 15 kilometres along the southern edge
of the delta. At one time the Fraser River flowed into the bay; now
most of its fresh water is supplied by the Serpentine and Nicomekl,
two small rivers draining the Surrey Uplands. To the east of Boundary
Bay rises the distant bulk of volcanic, snow-covered Mount Baker. To
the west, Point Roberts peninsula is a mirage of trees and shrubs floating over shallow, shimmering water in the haze of the late afternoon
sun. At low tide on this warm day in May, the rippled mud flats extend
more than a kilometre offshore from the broad dykes that protect farm
fields from inundation by high tides. Here and there a shallow pool
mirrors a passing cloud. Beyond the mud banks, open water hides vast
beds of eel grass that nourish millions of herring. The tide turns, and
incoming fingers of cold water absorb the warmth of the sun-soaked
mud as they advance across it at surprising speed.

In the water beyond the mud flats, reefs reach out into the mouth of
Boundary Bay from Point Roberts. For centuries aboriginal people of
southern British Columbia and northern Washington gathered here to
harvest the great schools of salmon that surged through openings in the
reefs. With ropes of cedar bark they anchored nets of woven willow in
the channels; American canners at Point Roberts soon recognized a
potential bonanza and drove the Native people away. The canners
installed immense salmon traps in the reef openings. Frances Herring
counted forty-seven in 1905 and wrote, "it seemed impossible that any
salmon could make its way to the Fraser, so thickly were the traps set."
When the traps caught more fish than could be canned, the surplus was
dumped. Traps had long been illegal in Canada, and they were banned
in Washington after salmon runs were nearly wiped out. Only pilings

remain at the foot of the steep cliffs of Lily Point to mark the site of the largest of the canneries. In the distance across Boundary Bay a long-abandoned cannery is gradually losing its struggle to remain perched on piles driven into the mud. A coloured buoy swings in the gentle breeze; a heron possesses one of the taller pilings, a forlorn fishing boat sags off its keel in the grassy flats above the mud.

As waves of birds replace one another throughout the year, each finds its special diet on the mud flats of Boundary Bay, in adjacent salt marshes and on abandoned or cultivated fields. Butler and his colleagues have shown that these great flocks can't survive on the mud flats and beaches alone. Most of the shorebirds, ducks and geese, and large birds of prey depend on the farm fields that have replaced native grasslands, particularly those within two kilometres of Boundary Bay. The Fraser River, the Strait of Georgia, the intertidal flats, the beaches, the marshes and the farmlands form one great, interdependent ecosystem. More than 400 studies have documented the natural values of Boundary Bay and the farmlands that border it; dozens of citizens' groups, and in particular the Friends of Boundary Bay, have promoted protection for the wildlife values of the area. Declarations of the extraordinary value of the entire estuary and of Boundary Bay have been made by every level of government, from local councils to the United Nations.

All this effort paid off in 1995 when Boundary Bay was included in the Lower Mainland Nature Legacy program of the NDP government, which conferred park or protected status on several important blocks of natural landscape throughout the estuary and beyond. Permanent protection was given to 4500 hectares of Boundary Bay foreshore lying between the dyke and open water of the Strait of Georgia, as part of an 11 000 hectare wildlife management area. Additions to Boundary Bay Regional Park were linked by a 16-kilometre linear park along the dyke bordering the bay. The Greater Vancouver Regional District was a partner in much of this, since these lands form part of the projected green zone that is a basic element of the GVRD's plans for a "Livable Region."

Scientists like Butler are very encouraged by the progress being made in protecting wildlife habitat at Boundary Bay and throughout the delta. It's a fine beginning, agrees Martin Keeley of the Friends of Boundary Bay. But Keeley points out that by mid-1996 the province had yet to put any money towards management of Boundary Bay, and no area management plan had been agreed upon. This seemed largely due to polarization between those favouring continued hunting in Boundary Bay and those who see no place for hunting in a protected area.

A critical problem remains the ownership by speculators of much of the wildlife habitat remaining in the Fraser River delta, including 70 per cent of the land bordering Boundary Bay. Foreign investors in particular continue to buy the land, and developers continue chipping away at wildlands and farmlands. When local councils try to prevent destruction of natural terrain and farmlands, developers use a wide array of weapons to fight them, including the menace of costly lawsuits. Housing developments and shopping malls aren't the only threats. Expansion of the Roberts Bank superport in the early 1980s and mid-1990s, and of the Tsawwassen ferry terminal in the early 1990s, crushed large areas of intertidal habitat required by shorebirds like western sandpipers, which stop here in vast numbers on their way to northern breeding grounds. Seagrass beds appear to be doing well, however, harbouring the fish upon which herons thrive. The productive intertidal zones are in constant danger of massive oil pollution from the heavy ship traffic at the ports and at Cherry Point just south of the American border. The traffic brings other dangers too: ballast water pumped from foreign ships can introduce exotic species, and coal dust from superport operations spreads across the water and mud flats.

Scientists are concerned that so much is happening so quickly to ecosystems about which they know so little. For Keeley, the real threat is the combination of many impacts. "If you start adding it all together," says Keeley, "you're eventually going to see the entire ecosystem in the area collapse because of cumulative effects." The protection of Boundary Bay and other remaining natural areas is extremely important: 70 per cent of fish and wildlife habitat of the lower Fraser River no longer exists, and much of what remains is degraded or threatened by sewage, toxic industrial effluents and chemical residues from agriculture. After years studying the flora and fauna of the estuary, UBC geographer Margaret North writes, "We no longer have a natural system functioning in the delta; instead we have a number of subsystems collapsing, others have already disappeared, and others are making constant adjustments to man's parasitic and non-contributive use of them." Those adjustments by fish and wildlife have been truly remarkable, and the wonder of the estuary is that it still functions so well, supporting so much natural life in spite of massive urbanization—more than 300 species of birds, 45 species of mammals and 16 species of reptiles and amphibians remain in the estuary.

Biologists Rob Butler and Wayne Campbell are not sanguine about the future of all these creatures, however. As they point out in their study of delta birds, "The single largest threat to birds in the Fraser River delta is the loss of a place to live. Most birds can cope with many human activities if provided with suitable resting and feeding areas." In 1992 the Federation of B.C. Naturalists identified 143 sites in the GVRD requiring protection in order to "maintain the biological and physical life support systems of the Lower Mainland." In addition to these specific sites, the federation stressed the need to protect all streams and rivers as fish habitat and wildlife corridors. Wetlands—marshes, sloughs, ponds—provide essential wildlife habitat, but they are commonly filled in or drained. Keeley says, "We need a really good wetlands law. We need a wetlands law that says 'No, you cannot fill in that wetland; we don't care that you think you can mitigate it, you cannot touch it.' "

Only a small part of the land needed to maintain healthy ecosystems that support fish and wildlife can be set aside in public parks and protected areas; a sound environment also depends upon appropriate management of privately owned land. The Federation of B.C. Naturalists suggests several ways to encourage this, including taxation incentives, conservation covenants, land trusts and voluntary stewardship programs. Wildlife can be a problem for farmers; for example, snow geese have fed for thousands of years where crops are now grown, and farmers may be less than enchanted when thousands of feathered visitors land on their fields to eat and trample crops. Many farmers leave crop remnants unploughed to nourish the birds through the winter, and others plant crops such as fall rye with assistance from the Greenfields program of the Delta Farmland and Wildlife Trust. The trust is a cooperative approach to preserving both farmland and wildlife habitat threatened by urbanization. Boundary hedgerows, grass margins between hedge and field, cover crops for soil building and winter feed for waterfowl, protection and building of ponds and wetlands, and good drainage techniques around farm fields: these are practices that benefit both agriculture and nature.

It is only a kilometre from Boundary Bay to the southern perimeter of Burns Bog, the largest domed bog in western North America and the largest greenspace left in the Fraser delta. Bogs formed in the Fraser River estuary where water could not drain away, creating an acidic environment in which moss flourishes and doesn't rot after it dies. Cranberries also flourish here, along with other plants unknown elsewhere in the estuary. In an increasingly polluted Lower Mainland, Burns Bog is large enough to absorb significant amounts of carbon dioxide while releasing oxygen in cooling, moisture-laden air. As part of the Boundary Bay ecosystem, the 4000 hectares of Burns Bog provide a home or resting and feeding place for 150 species of animals and birds, ranging from black bears to the very large greater sandhill crane, which is on the verge of being eliminated from the Fraser estuary due to lack of habitat. Seven species of owls live here, as does the largest population of bald eagles in the Lower Mainland.

Forty per cent of Burns Bog has been disturbed by commercial peat removal, which leaves open tracts of water 100 or more metres wide. The bog's forests have been diminished by road and bridge construction, and part of it is used as a regional garbage dump, from which polluted water leaches into the bog and surrounding water table. The bog has been and remains the target of many developments, from highways to housing to a superport and a racetrack. With most remaining wildlife habitat in the Fraser River estuary badly fragmented, the continuing existence of this scarred but still functioning ecosystem is of crucial importance. Burns Bog was the obvious missing piece in the parklands program announced for the region in 1995, and negotiations with developers, who hold large tracts of the bog and are demanding vast sums to resell the land to government, continued in 1996.

Below the tree-crowned cliffs of Point Grey at the western extremity of Vancouver, Terry Slack steers his gillnet fishing boat *Aquatic Star* into the brown waters of the Fraser. It is mid-August, 1993. As he passes the Musqueam Indian Reserve at the mouth of the river, the rich green of marshland stands against the brown of the river. No log booms grind the foreshore here; no golf course has replaced the fruitful habitat with sterile fairways. It is not surprising that the Musqueam people won't allow industry to encroach on their marshlands: Musqueam means "people of the grass." The riverbank here is much as Simon Fraser described it when he came ashore July 2, 1808. Buildings have changed, though. The longhouse nestling in a grove of trees is equipped with the facilities of any modern community hall, and fine homes rise on land the band has leased to non-Natives.

The Fraser River, especially its North Arm, is Terry Slack's world—his family has fished the river for sixty years. Slack knows how every change of tide will combine with wind and weather to cause salmon to run up the river or hold at its mouth, how bends in the river and undulations in its bed will steer the migrating fish. He knows when salmon, destined to spawn in a particular stream hundreds of kilometres upstream, will pass a certain bar near the mouth of the river. Even the smell of the river tells him a story. So close is he to the Fraser River and its moods that when Slack is not fishing, he is usually working to protect it. He participates in efforts to improve fish and wildlife habitat, even providing places for herring to spawn right in the heart of the city, in False Creek. He is trying to determine if green sturgeon, almost extinct in the river, can return in sufficient numbers to survive. He has organized volunteers to remove invading purple loosestrife that chokes out other life in wetlands, he joins in battles against contamination of the Fraser from sewage plants and waterfront industries—cement and asphalt plants, paint and chemical industries, ship builders, and steel and machinery fabricators.

As the *Aquatic Star* moves upstream, it enters a different world, becoming part of a watery empire distinct from the landbound one that swirls above the river. Traffic-laden bridges, roads and a tunnel lace the land across the water so efficiently that commuters can traverse the delta from suburbia to downtown without really noticing the great river. Here on the water, diesel power throbs beneath his feet and the deck lists as Slack alters course to evade a tug towing a huge barge of wood chips downstream. "That load is worth maybe $80,000 or $100,000," he says. The barge is on its way to a coastal pulp mill with residue from one of forty sawmills that line this stretch of the Fraser, employing almost 9,500 workers. On the riverbank to the right, a bulldozer moves through waves of smoke like an unholy apparition, piling masses of wood for burning. This is waste from the mills, collected by the North Fraser Harbour Commission for disposal—more than 21 000 cubic metres each year. The smoke rises into the acrid haze that hangs thicker and darker over the river valley each summer.

Slack's gillnetter works past another powerful tug labouring against the current, towing a long raft of big logs, a fallen forest from somewhere along the West Coast. A smaller tug nurses the raft around bends in the river or nudges the floating trees clear of bridge pylons. Soon the two tugs will moor the raft to wooden pilings near the shore to await the appointment with the saw. Mills prefer to have a three-month supply of logs anchored in the fresh water of the river where they are free from attack by the marine wood borers. As the *Aquatic Star* moves upriver, the riverbanks often seem composed entirely of wood. Great Douglas firs, hemlocks, cedars and spruces produced by centuries of Pacific rain in deep coastal valleys now heave gently in the undulations of river traffic. Logs are stored on almost 1500 hectares of the estuary's foreshore, shading marine plants and other organisms in shallow water along the Fraser's banks. Sometimes riverine life is crushed when logs are grounded by the rise and fall of ocean tide and river flow. Bark and other wood debris falls to the bottom, smothering life and depleting oxygen as it decomposes. Near the mouth of the river, however, rafts provide shelter for young salmon. Marinas and docks fill most backwaters in the lower Fraser; 4,500 fishing and pleasure boats find moorage in the estuary.

The North Arm of the Fraser has been almost completely industrialized, leaving only tiny scraps of marsh and other habitat for fish and wildlife. Where land and water meet, life is most abundant; but at precisely this juncture throughout the estuary, economic opportunities also abound. There has seldom been doubt as to the outcome of the contest. Where Native people once harvested fruit and other food on Annacis Island, huge ships from Japan and Korea now disgorge 5,000 cars at a time onto vast parking lots. Ships from around the world navigate as far as 30 kilometres upstream, carrying more than five million tonnes of cargo in and out of the river's main arm each year.

The Fraser River was the centre of life for aboriginal people, and their homes faced onto it. New settlers followed suit for a few years until the ugliness and pollution of Fraser River industrial development during most of this century led Vancouverites to turn their backs on their river. But throughout history, people have preferred to live by water if they could, and a growing awareness of the Fraser has encouraged the recycling of old riverside industrial sites into high density housing, particularly in New Westminster and Burnaby. There is growing pressure too for more public access to the river, with riverbank parkland a favoured way of providing it. Developers still seek to cash in on growing appreciation of the river by building on the Fraser's few remaining pristine sites, often reducing public access to the river and compromising its natural values. Near the mouth of the North Arm, Deering Island was a superb candidate for riverside parkland until it was scalped of natural growth and covered with houses distinguished only by their size and cost. Sometimes, though, developers have improved riverbanks that had deteriorated over previous decades.

Carefully checking the movement of other boats on the river, Slack prepares to set his net at the junction of the Fraser's North and Middle Arms. Overhead, traffic on the Oak Street bridge builds towards rush hour. Slack jokes about the life of an urban fisherman. He throws a large orange buoy, a "dutchman," into the water; to the buoy is secured the end of the net that rolls off the big drum prominent on every gillnetter. Using the duplicate helm and throttle at the stern of the boat, Slack manoeuvres it through a series of delicate curves that weaves the net in deep bights across the river to the other bank. This permits him to pay out twice as much net as a less experienced fisherman would dare to do. His intimate knowledge of the river has ensured that the net will not catch on any rock, log or other obstruction, but he watches river traffic carefully to ensure the net does not cross the course of a tug or ship. Sometimes he reaches for the radio microphone to ask a vessel's intentions. Boat and net drift downstream with the current, passing a large commercial development on the Richmond side of the river known as Bridgepoint. Constructed on a particularly productive wetland, Bridgepoint proved a financial failure and now the buildings stand bleak and empty on the ruined riverbank.

Under the federal government's "no net loss" policy adopted in 1986, riverbank development should be located away from sites of high habitat value; however, if a project considered to be in the public interest will result in unavoidable impacts, developers must compensate for destroyed wetland by creating twice as much new fish habitat. Double the amount is required because it is very difficult to mimic nature; even when successful, replacement marshes require at least a decade to mature. Compensation projects may fail completely, and they will probably be less productive than natural wetlands. Bridgepoint developers replanted aquatic plants taken from their construction site a few kilometres upstream on Mitchell Island. The site looks green from Slack's boat, but it will be years before the project's success is known.

The wetlands upon which so little value was placed for so long are recognized now as a precious and irreplaceable resource; artificial replacement is the last resort. So in 1988 the Department of Fisheries and Oceans collaborated with the North Fraser Harbour Commission in a management plan that would steer development away from sensitive fish and wildlife areas along the river—a sort of "traffic light" system. In a detailed inventory of all fish and wildlife habitat along riverbanks and intertidal zones of the estuary, the foreshore was coded in red, yellow and green. Red means no development because these are productive marsh habitats; yellow may permit development, but any habitat loss must be replaced with twice as much new habitat; and in green areas, development may proceed because habitat values are low.

The plan, many hope, will begin to reverse a century of habitat loss in the Fraser River estuary. In general the approach has proven successful, with problems often the result of political interference. One corporation used political connections with the Mulroney government to cancel red protected status and gain approval for filling in one of the most precious remaining wetlands along the South Arm of the river. The high purpose of the proposed facility: shipment of scrap metal. After destroying the riverine habitat, the entrepreneur changed his mind and offered the property for sale. When the B.C. Ferry Corporation enlarged its Tsawwassen terminal in 1991, it began dredging with no environmental approval and soon 70 000 square metres of eel grass habitat had been lost. In an attempt to compensate, material for replacement habitat was dumped on top of one of the most biologically sensitive sites in the estuary.

Early May 1996. Terry Slack is finding it difficult to sleep these nights. He has a big decision to make, one that will determine the course of the rest of his life. By May 24, he must decide whether to sell his licence to fish with the *Aquatic Star* or to buy an additional licence in order to fish B.C.'s middle coast—and yet a third licence if he finds it necessary to travel to the north coast when fishing is poor elsewhere. A new policy announced by federal fisheries minister Fred Mifflin is forcing the issue. Until now, with one licence Slack could go wherever the fishing was best and use gear appropriate to that time and place. To continue to have that right will now cost him more than $160,000 in licences and gear—an enormous investment in a year in which there may be no fishing at all for Fraser River salmon. But this is more than an economic decision. For Slack, fishing is a way of life in which the mystique of the sea, the beauty of the coast, the wonder of the salmon and his family's long history in the fishery all play a role.

Slack was not alone. Up and down the West Coast that spring, thousands of fishers agonized over the same decision. Anger and despair grew in coastal communities as some of the consequences of Mifflin's plan became evident. The few major corporations that control a large sector of the industry were pleased: Mifflin's plan to cut the fishing fleet and force fishers to purchase multiple licences would mean more fish at less cost for them.

How had the fishery of the Fraser River and the B.C. coast come to this? The story has roots in the nineteenth century. When the gold rush subsided in the 1860s, some people drawn to B.C. in search of mining wealth turned to another abundant resource. They had watched millions of migrating salmon surge into the Fraser and its tributaries every summer and fall; they knew of miners in California who made fortunes canning salmon on the Sacramento River for shipment to England. In Britain, salmon streams were dying as the Industrial Revolution converted them to canals, sewers and power sources. Before long the California fishery too was destroyed by rapacious exploitation and destruction of spawning beds by mining and logging. The British salmon market was wide open.

In 1871 Alexander Ewing canned 300 cases of one-pound tins of Fraser River salmon, and a new B.C. industry was underway. Even after being transported by square-rigged sailing ships around Cape Horn, tinned salmon could be sold to workers in English factory towns at half the price of fresh meat. Canneries sprang up all along the lower Fraser, and by 1896 there were thirty-four plants shipping hundreds of thousands of cases of salmon, mostly to Britain. The canning companies employed local Native people who had been driven off estuary lands, and others from far up the coast. Two men fished from each flat-bottomed skiff, while their wives and children worked in the canneries alongside Chinese labourers. Working and living conditions for both groups were appalling. In *Salmon*, Geoff Meggs writes that cannery workers "differed from slaves only in the fact that they were laid off at ' the end of the season."

Fisheries biologist W. E. Ricker estimates that runs of up to 100 million mature sockeye returned to the Fraser River in the early years of this century. At the mouth of the river this incredible natural wealth was plundered by a fishery that took up to 94 per cent of the fish, leaving a tiny portion of the run for aboriginal subsistence fishing along the river and for spawning. The only check on this orgy of greed and waste was the capacity of the canneries. At the height of the salmon runs, bargeloads of fish awaited processing, and those that couldn't be canned within forty-eight hours were simply dumped in the river. The canneries were built on stilts over the Fraser or on salt flats so that fish offal and salmon species other than sockeye could be easily dumped. Most of the sockeye itself was discarded: it was easiest just to slice and can fillets from the fish's sides. Accounts of the time describe bands of rotten fish and offal more than half a metre thick and six metres wide lining the banks of the river for miles; farmers pitchforked fish out of the river onto fields as fertilizer. The Fraser's current carried rotting fish around Point Grey into English Bay to the annoyance of residents of West End mansions. But the cannery owners made fortunes, and their political influence ensured that no significant conservation measures would impinge upon their profits.

In 1913, 2.4 million cases of sockeye containing about 25 million canned fish were shipped from the Fraser River. It was the last big harvest on the river for decades. Ricker is convinced that the decline in Fraser River salmon caused by massive overfishing had begun well before that year's record run was decimated by the catastrophic rockfalls at Hell's Gate. The road back has been long and difficult, marked by some extraordinary successes, many disappointments and continued brushes with disaster. Decades of study by fisheries scientists revealed many of the secrets of the salmon, resulting in fish ladders to help fish up the river, and spawning channels and hatcheries to build populations. Although it remains a very inexact and error-prone field, fisheries managers learned to regulate the fishery in a way that usually allows sufficient numbers of returning salmon to escape the gauntlet of nets and hooks and reach their spawning grounds far up the Fraser. Many runs were obliterated, but others gradually rebuilt, and in 1993 about 24 million sockeye salmon returned to the Fraser River, the largest run since 1913. Yet three years later, in 1996, salmon returns to the Fraser River were predicted to be so low that DFO managers were preparing to close down the fishery altogether.

What went wrong? There are no easy answers, partly due to the extraordinary complexity of the Fraser River salmon fishery. It begins with the salmon itself, of which there are five species—six with the inclusion of the steelhead. Each species has a distinct life cycle. Within each species there are many runs, each bound for a different spawning stream; some are few in number and others are enormous. There are three types of fisheries seeking a share of the catch: commercial, sports and aboriginal, with deep divisions and sometimes animosity among them. The commercial fishery has always been dominant, catching more than 90 per cent of the fish. Sports fishers claim a higher economic return than the commercial fishery while taking fewer salmon, about 5 per cent of the catch. The aboriginal fishery is by law accorded first priority in the salmon fishery after conservation concerns, but it is actually last in line since commercial and sports fishers have their turn before the salmon arrive in the Fraser River where the Native fishery occurs. Although aboriginal fisheries account for less than 5 per cent of all salmon caught, one organization of commercial fishers—the Fisheries Survival Coalition—often seems solely concerned with attacking aboriginal fishing rights.

The commercial fishery is managed according to gear type, of which there are three: seiners, gillnetters and trollers. Not only do the concerns of fishers vary according to their gear type, but their interests also depend on whether the boats are controlled by large fishing corporations or owned and operated by individuals. Sports fishers participate as individuals or as clients of commercial operations based at resorts or on ships located in the best fishing areas. Aboriginal groups also have interests that differ according to location. Under the federal government's Aboriginal Fisheries Strategy, each First Nation is supposed to have a separate agreement with DFO. As a result, a band on the Fraser River can be seriously affected by a Native fishery downstream; some such disagreements have existed for a very long time.

Then there are the complications of a salmon fishery involving two nations, three American states and a Canadian province. Within Canada there are distinct differences in fishing priorities between the federal and B.C. governments, while one American state can—and does—veto policies approved by the other states and the U.S. government. Many salmon runs heading for the Fraser River pass through U.S. waters and some American runs traverse Canadian territory. The two nations have no choice but to collaborate on fisheries management, and the 1984 Canada-United States Pacific Salmon Treaty was designed to facilitate this process. But in 1994, no agreement for sharing the catch was reached largely because Alaska would not agree to restraints agreed to by all other participants. This led to "aggressive fishing" on both sides of the watery border, a ridiculous situation that could easily lead to decimation of salmon stocks. As the season opened in the summer of 1996, there was still no agreement between the two nations.

While the industry has become more complex, the fish populations that support it are simplifying. Fisheries biologist Carl Walters of UBC finds that most of the fish caught in the 1990s come from about half as many salmon populations as in the 1950s. This dramatic drop in salmon biodiversity has two causes, says Walters. A few populations have been dramatically increased through enhancement measures like hatcheries and spawning channels, and these now make up about half the salmon caught each year. And many smaller populations have declined dramatically or are extinct due to heavy fishing or spawning stream damage by logging and urban development.

Since most fish are caught offshore where many salmon stocks are swimming together, small populations are hit as hard as big ones. This, says Walters, does not bode well for long-term sustainability of Fraser River salmon. The number of fish the Strait of Georgia and the open ocean can support is probably limited, and fish production cannot be increased beyond that point. Even as wild strains are replaced by those from hatcheries and spawning channels, the survival of these "enhanced" stocks in the open ocean seems to be declining. So the total fish population is becoming less resilient, depending upon weaker stocks from fewer sources.

With all its problems, the Fraser River salmon fishery is still the greatest in the world. But biologist Otto Langer cautions realism when predicting its future. For one thing, there remains less habitat for fish throughout the Fraser Basin—logging, farming, urbanization and other human uses have taken their toll. In the Fraser's estuary, only 30 per cent of the original habitat remains; on the Bridge and Nechako Rivers, much habitat has been lost to dams and diversions. So, says Langer, while we can rebuild many damaged runs, there are limits to what should be expected, and the huge runs of the nineteenth century are clearly impossible. Trying to achieve them through artificial means could be disastrous.

With each sector of the fishing industry pursuing its own interests, a very large fleet of 4,500 boats has evolved, many of them technological marvels of fish killing power. Walters describes how "current harvests could be taken by a small fraction of the existing fishing fleet. We now see insane situations, like seine boats lining up at fishing points in the Johnstone Straits [on the east coast of Vancouver Island] to wait turns at setting nets in these favoured locations." In 1994 in a single twelve-hour opening in Johnstone Strait, the seine fleet caught a million sockeye salmon bound for the Fraser River. Only 1.3 million fish of this run eventually headed up the Fraser to the Adams River, so if the seiners had been allowed just another twelve hours of fishing, they would have wiped out the greatest of the Fraser River sockeye runs. Catherine Stewart of Greenpeace Canada told a commission of inquiry, "The current rate of commercial harvest leaves absolutely no room for any margin of error. Combined harvest rates [in 1994] are reported to be around 80 to 90 per cent of the run size. If the estimates of the PSC [Pacific Salmon Commission] are even slightly inaccurate . . . then the salmon are extremely vulnerable to overharvesting."

In 1994 salmon returned to the Fraser River in numbers much smaller than predicted, and only half as many as the DFO intended were able to escape the nets and head upriver to spawn. It was the lowest escapement of Adams River sockeye since 1938 and a major setback to years of rebuilding. A flurry of charges from poaching to incompetent management raged around the Fraser River fishery. The Fraser River Sockeye Public Review Board (the Fraser Commission) stressed the need for a "risk aversion management strategy" that would never endanger the arrival of enough fish on the spawning grounds. This means standing firm in the face of pressure to allow larger fish catches—an essential strategy but not a new one. As far back as 1946, writes Mark Hume in *Adam's River*, W. E. Ricker was insisting that reducing the catch and allowing a higher proportion of salmon to make their way to spawning grounds would be by far the best way of enhancing fish populations.

The following year, 1995, was also disastrous for salmon fishing, with 70 per cent fewer sockeye returning to the Fraser River than had been predicted by the DFO. Fear that the Pacific salmon fishery was destined for the same fate as the Atlantic cod fishery was widespread. In 1996, normally the low year of the four-year Fraser River salmon cycle, only 1.3 million sockeye were forecast to return, barely enough for spawning requirements. The DFO blamed low returns in 1995 and 1996 at least in part on the large numbers of mackerel that swam north with warm El Niño waters in 1991 and 1992. The mackerel ate vast numbers of little salmon heading out to sea, fish that would have returned to the Fraser in 1995 and 1996.

The fish that do return are smaller than they were twenty years ago. Many scientists are convinced changes are occurring in the open ocean that they don't understand, perhaps related to global warming, which is raising water temperatures and could alter ocean currents, or to ozone depletion, which could affect phytoplankton production.

On one thing there is no disagreement: there is far too much killing capacity in the fishing fleet. At the end of March 1996, fisheries minister Fred Mifflin sat down behind microphones in Vancouver, faced a room crowded with fishers, fish company executives, union spokespersons and a battery of reporters. He announced the federal government's intention to cut the fishing fleet of 4,500 boats in half, using a fund of $80 million to buy up licences. Fishers would have to decide by May 24, 1996, whether to give up their licences or to buy more licences for other sectors of the coast or types of fishing gear.

This was the source of Terry Slack's sleepless nights and of the anger that spread through fishing communities up and down the coast. It soon became evident that while fewer boats would be easier for the DFO to manage, no fewer fish would be caught under the plan. Few of the poorly financed independent fishers operating from coastal communities would be able to buy extra licences and would be forced to sell out, while the transnational fishing corporations would easily finance additional licences to be "stacked" on their big boats. "The really large winners will be the processing companies," said fisheries economist Don Pepper. "They will get the same amount of fish at a lower cost."

The future was beginning to resemble that of Canada's East Coast, whose fishery endured for centuries until it became dominated by corporations operating large, technologically sophisticated boats. Because they were so efficient, and the science that was supposed to track the fish populations so badly done, the illusion persisted that the Atlantic cod were still there in large numbers. Although small-scale, inshore fishers warned that cod numbers were dropping rapidly, governments allowed corporate fishing to continue until it had hunted down almost the last fish—then the foreign fleet finished the job. When the Atlantic cod stocks collapsed, tens of thousands of people were left jobless and hundreds of communities impoverished. But the companies responsible for the collapse are doing well, processing fish from foreign waters where stocks have not yet been wiped out. Around the world, corporate fishing is progressively eliminating stocks of fish and moving on to repeat the process, often leaving behind communities deprived of a fishery that supported them for centuries. The worldwide fishery took its greatest harvest, 91 million tonnes, in 1989; the figures have diminished since, and marine biologists at the UN's Food and Agriculture Organization report that all seventeen of the world's major fishing regions are being harvested at or beyond capacity, with nine of them in a state of decline.

The Mifflin Plan appeared to be encouraging a model of highly capitalized industrial fishing that has proven unsustainable for fisheries around the world, and for the people and communities that depend upon them. There is no doubt that the number of fish boats must be drastically reduced, but the federal plan does not provide a way to do that selectively so that conservation and community interests are served. By midsummer of 1996, protests by Premier Glen Clark and most participants in the fishing industry (with the notable exception of large corporations) finally persuaded the federal government to consider greater provincial involvement in the management of the fishery, including a review of the Mifflin Plan. By fall, the plan had cost almost 3,000 jobs, and another 5,000 fishing industry jobs were lost because catches were so poor. Coastal fishing communities were staggering and many were approaching collapse, their citizens certain they were victims of a concerted federal attack. "They are treating us as if we are some enemy country, not a part of Canada," Alert Bay Mayor Gilbert Popovich told the *Vancouver Sun* in November. His town, like most other coastal communities, had been hit not only by the Mifflin Plan, but by Coast Guard and DFO cutbacks, closure of fish hatcheries, closure or downsizing of RCMP and military establishments, abandonment of federal responsibility for harbours and automation of lighthouses.

Faced with the rising tide of protest, Mifflin announced in November 1996 that the federal government would spend $30 million or "whatever it takes" to provide immediate short-term aid to people thrown out of work by his fleet reduction plan. But as the year ended a solution to the salmon fishing crisis was still far off.

Many fishers, scientists and other participants in the fishery are calling for deep changes in the organization and technology of fishing. "I think that what they're doing is fine-tuning a failed system," says Craig Orr of the Steelhead Society of B.C. "They really should be implementing a resource-friendly and taxpayer-friendly selective, live-capture terminal fishery."

"Our current fishery is not sustainable in either ecological or economic terms," says UBC's Carl Walters, "and it will very likely go the same way as Atlantic Canada within the next few decades if profound steps are not taken to restructure and protect it." One of Canada's most respected fisheries biologists, Walters considers the future of Pacific fisheries in his study *Fish on the Line.* He emphasizes that "conservation of all remaining natural populations, no matter how small, should be made an absolute requirement and first priority in all fisheries management planning and administration." Existing legislation allows the DFO to ignore conservation when balancing demands on the resource, says Walters, and that may include hammering wild stocks into extinction by allowing heavy fishing of hatchery fish. Solving the technical problem of taking only the fish targeted when several different stocks of fish swim together is absolutely crucial for survival of Fraser River salmon. As well as dwindling wild stocks of sockeye, hundreds of thousands of chinook, coho and steelhead are caught each year in nets and on hooks intended for more plentiful species. Avoiding this waste requires a reconsideration of how fish are caught—it means using technology that allows precise selection of the desired fish and of the number that can safely be taken.

To do this, the Steelhead Society suggests "going backward—to go forward." Several fishing methods that once were common in West Coast rivers could again be useful in limiting catches to target species. Fishwheels, fish traps, seine nets on boats or on beaches, and reef nets are all methods by which fish can easily be kept alive until non-target fish are freed back into open water. Even the large seine boat operations common in B.C. waters can achieve this when they are operated very carefully and slowly. Unfortunately, there is no way that gillnets can be operated selectively, and most experts see no place for gillnetting in a sustainable fishery. Some Fraser River gillnet fishers are already looking for alternatives. In *Dead Reckoning*, Terry Glavin describes how a few gillnetters are teaming up with Native fishers of the Katzie First Nation at Pitt Meadows to develop a beach seine operation on the Fraser that targets chum salmon in a totally selective live fishery. Farther up the Fraser at its confluence with the Vedder River, Sto:lo fishers are experimenting with a fish trap, and on the Nass River in northern B.C., the Nisga'a people are successfully using a fishwheel patterned on those used decades ago on the Columbia River.

A selective, terminal (in the river instead of at sea), live-capture fishery would undoubtedly cause considerable upheaval in the commercial fishery. But there would be plenty of jobs in an industry that includes producing and protecting fish as well as catching them, with local processing and value-added products replacing the NAFTA-induced foreign processing of B.C. fish by large fish corporations. Instead of pouring money into technically advanced boats to beat the competition in the mad scramble that fishing has become, a much less costly, selective fishery could free up money to employ people no longer required on boats for work at other aspects of the fishery: stream rehabilitation, pollution control, research projects and many other activities necessary to a sustainable fishery.

Involvement in this kind of a fishery is an exciting prospect for fishers like Terry Slack. After a lifetime on the Fraser River, he decided to retire his fishing licence under the terms of the Mifflin Plan. He and the *Aquatic Star* won't be working the North Arm of the Fraser anymore. "We've got to find a different way of fishing," says Slack. "I just can't grasp it yet, but I'm not going to go fishing again." Slack hopes to participate in the fishery in a new capacity, and he's already taken a streamkeeper's course. "I'd love to be involved in a weir fishery or beach fishery," he says. There's no doubt that his intimate understanding of salmon and the river is what's needed in a new Fraser River salmon fishery. Ideas for renewal of the fishery are spreading quickly, and people like Terry Slack will make it happen.

A sustainable fishery supporting as many people and communities as possible requires fundamental change in the structure of its management. Carl Walters stresses the importance of developing "local, community-based management authorities." In their document *Fisheries That Work*, Evelyn Pinkerton and Martin Weinstein report that community-based fisheries management—usually a co-management arrangement involving communities and government—is most likely to achieve a fishery in which both resource and community are sustainable. As conservationist Will Paulik puts it, "We have to look after it ourselves. We can't trust the agencies, we must protect and enhance the fish stocks ourselves." This is the possibility offered by a fishery anchored in the communities of the Fraser River and coastal B.C., instead of one managed from Ottawa mainly for the benefit of corporate fishing enterprises.

Throughout the Fraser Basin, fishing and farming began with a hunger for gold. Among the hordes of miners swarming up the river in 1858 were men who later settled on the land and gave their names to places throughout the Fraser Valley and delta. After ten years of mining and running pack trains through the Fraser Canyon, William and Thomas Ladner turned to raising livestock where the town named for them now spreads along the Fraser near the sea; they were soon to be prominent salmon canners. Manoah Steves farmed the land that became the fishing town of Steveston on the large island still known today as Lulu. Lulu Sweet's acting and dancing were the sensation of New Westminster in 1861; her charms were not lost on Col. Richard Moody of the Royal Engineers, who impulsively bestowed her name on the island as the two of them cruised by en route to Victoria in the sternwheeler *Otter*. Hugh McRoberts failed as a miner, but made enough money working on the Cariboo Road to buy part of Lulu Island and half of Sea Island, where aircraft from around the world now touch down. He called his farm "Richmond View" after his earlier home in Australia; the name persists today in the city built on his fields.

At the mouth of the South Arm of the Fraser, Steveston has been the Fraser River's most important fishing community for a hundred years; at the turn of the century, it claimed to be salmon capital of the world. Modern fish boats are berthed snugly along the fishermen's wharves, a forest of masts, radars and fishing gear rising above them. On the docks, men mend nets stretched out in the afternoon sun. Will Paulik has been a fisherman, and he can't hide his disdain for the "yuppification" that has overtaken his beloved Steveston, where cappuccino and style have marginalized the net lofts, rubber aprons and canneries of his youth. But he also welcomes the influx of visitors seeking the ambience and lore of the river, recognizing that their interest will help preserve its past and contribute to its future.

Marilyn Clayton explains this goal to visitors to the Britannia Shipyard heritage site, built as a cannery in 1889. It was barely completed when the fast, sleek tea clipper *Titania* docked to load canned salmon for delivery in London, a voyage of 104 days. Already there were thirty canneries on the Fraser, and fortunes would be made before the collapse of the industry led to the cannery's conversion to a shipyard in 1918. Now it is the centre of an ambitious heritage maritime centre and waterfront park that Paulik thinks should be expanded to include Steveston Island.

Vancouver has long since exceeded its capacity to dispose of its waste within its own boundaries. The city sends partially treated sewage down the Fraser River into the Strait of Georgia, while westerly winds push its polluted air up the Fraser Valley to Abbotsford and Chilliwack. Some of the metropolis's garbage is trucked all the way to Cache Creek.

As it nears the sea, the Fraser River seems to flow a grubby yellow under a mustard-coloured pall on a warm June afternoon. Vancouver's mountain backdrop is stained and blurred, screening out some of the joy of life in one of the world's most beautiful urban environments. The cost is not aesthetic alone; air pollution costs the people of the Lower Mainland about $430 million each year. Vancouver's air quality is approaching that of Los Angeles, exceeding acceptable levels during 100 days in 1992. Nor is the impact limited to the place and people who cause it. On some summer days the air is warmer a few hundred metres above the earth's surface. This inversion puts a lid on the region, preventing the escape of polluted air. On such a day, a jogger in Port Coquitlam can harm her lungs running in ozone created by Vancouver traffic and concentrated in her community by westerly winds. Sixty kilometres up the Fraser Valley, berry pickers near Abbotsford breathe faster on such an afternoon because their lungs function less effectively in smog and ozone. The berries they're picking are affected too: crop losses due to ozone in the Fraser Valley approach $9 million each year, and the health of dairy cows and other farm animals is a concern. On a slope with a spectacular valley view near Abbotsford, "For Sale" marks a home where asthma dictates a move to a less polluted environment. A local councillor blames Vancouver for reduced quality of life in his community, and pleads for transit planning that will get people out of cars. As the afternoon commute winds down in Greater Vancouver, the pall of polluted air has rolled past Chilliwack, 100 kilometres up the Fraser Valley where converging mountains and temperature inversion allow it no escape. During the summer of 1996, ground-level ozone pollution in the eastern Fraser Valley was so elevated on some hot days that people with heart or lung weaknesses were urged to remain indoors.

Most air pollution in the lower Fraser Valley—82 per cent—is generated in the Greater Vancouver region, mainly by cars—about a million of them. The GVRD aims to reduce air polluting emissions in the region by 50 per cent by the year 2000, but implementation of necessary measures is proceeding very slowly. The provincial government's AirCare program is expected to help, but with vehicle numbers still rising, sweeping changes are needed in the way people and materials move around the Lower Mainland. The GVRD proposes a redesigned transportation network that favours pedestrians and cyclists, followed by public transit facilities and movement of goods, and only lastly by cars.

Fortunately, the same transportation policies that attack air pollution also foster land preservation and the development of compact, self-contained cities. They affect water quality too. Chad Day of the School of Resource and Environmental Management at SFU emphasizes that water quality is inseparable from land and resource use in a river valley. That's why, says Day, it is essential to plan and manage for the quality of water on the basis of an entire watershed. More than 800 million young salmon come down the Fraser on their way to the ocean between February and June each year. This is the time of lowest river flow and highest sewage effluent output into the river by Greater Vancouver's sewage treatment plants. It is also a time when tidal reversals can hold the effluent in the Fraser for almost two days, building concentrations to very toxic levels. Biologist I. K. Birtwell and his colleagues calculate that at least 44 million little salmon must get through this toxic stew when it is at its worst, along with millions of oolichan and other migrating fish. The impact? Nobody knows for sure, but laboratory tests have shown that even low levels of such contaminants have serious effects on young salmon. Fortunately, young sockeye move quickly out into the Strait of Georgia, but other species linger in the estuary for up to a year.

Sewage in the Greater Vancouver region wasn't treated at all before

1961. Now almost all of it passes through treatment plants: two (Annacis Island and Lulu Island) on the main South Arm of the Fraser, and one on Iona Island at the mouth of the North Arm. Until 1996 these had been only primary treatment plants doing little more than screening the sewage. Organic wastes, metals and chemicals poured through the system virtually unchanged. Now the Annacis Island plant has been upgraded to secondary treatment at a cost of about $300 million (it required a lawsuit by environmentalists to get the project underway). Federal fisheries law is forcing the GVRD to upgrade the Lulu Island plant to secondary treatment as well.

Where rainwater is channelled into sanitary sewers, a storm may overwhelm sewage plants and push the overflow directly into the Fraser River. An obvious solution is to separate storm and sanitary sewers, and this is being done in Vancouver and New Westminster; the work will take about seventy years to complete. But separation is not the whole answer. Recent research shows that stormwater runoff is often severely contaminated, and separating it from treated sewage may not be so desirable. An alternative used in some cities is storage: large underground tanks collect the overflow during rainstorms, which is then gradually fed through the sewage treatment plant after the storm has passed.

Dozens of riverside industries dump their effluent directly into the Fraser. This is especially serious in the North Arm, which carries only 15 per cent of the Fraser's flow but receives almost half of all industrial effluent discharged into the river. When flows are low and tides are high, it can take three days for some of this material to travel the short distance to the sea. Chemicals drain into the river from wood treatment processes; pollutants from the Roberts Bank superport, the Tsawwassen ferry terminal, and Vancouver International Airport add to the mix. Dioxins and furans from pulp mills hundreds of kilometres upstream can be found in crabs, shrimps, fish and seabirds in the estuary, and even in sediments on the bottom of the Strait of Georgia. Although industrial discharges throughout the Fraser Basin are improving in quality, their cumulative impact remains serious and persistent.

Hydrologist Michael Church considers the impact of chemicals and metals on the Fraser estuary to be very serious indeed. Changes in the delta's chemistry are, he says, invisible, mysterious and dangerous. Interactions between chemicals from various sources, and between chemicals and the sediments to which they become attached, often are unpredictable. Heavy metals and other pollutants bond with the fine sediment carried by the Fraser's current and settle out when the flow slows in sloughs, tidal marshes and in the deep waters of the strait. The pollutants are then taken up by bottom feeders and by small creatures at the beginning of the food chain, becoming concentrated in the bodies of fish, birds and mammals further up the line.

Organic wastes in the water necessitate "No Swimming" notices and closures of fisheries. Boundary Bay was the single most important oyster bed in B.C. until pollution by coliform bacteria forced its closure in the 1960s. A report by the Westwater Research Centre (WRC) states, "In the fall of 1993, more than 90 per cent of [fish] specimens examined [in the lower Fraser] showed some form of pathological abnormality, with liver damage being the most common observation."

Many chemicals and metals aren't removed by sewage treatment and the only solution is to keep them out of the system. This is called "source control." Although the GVRD imposes such controls on industrial discharge, a large part of the problem remains: 60 per cent of toxic contaminants in sewage originates in private homes and small businesses. Home owners flush old oil, drug prescriptions and pesticides down their drains, and it is essential that widely publicized depots for disposing of such wastes be made available.

Better water quality measures have been retarded by decade after decade of political delays, more studies, shelved reports and inaction. Michael Healy, director of the WRC, points out that "the price tag goes up every time we debate building more effective sewage treatment for the region, always concluding we can't afford it. My view is we can't *not* afford it—the alternatives are just too unattractive." One reason action on water-quality issues in the Fraser estuary has been so slow is a lack of clarity about who is responsible for it. Federal, provincial and municipal governments all have some responsibility for water quality, so there are overlaps and gaps. There is often little communication between agencies within the same government ministry, as well as turf wars. Although representatives of various levels of government do meet to discuss the issues, they aren't required by law to collaborate—and frequently they don't.

The result is very slow progress towards understanding the state of our waters and even slower action in doing anything about it. With all the agencies involved in water quality, none has gotten around to describing the quality of water needed to sustain the Fraser River and its ecosystems. No standards or goals have been legislated by either federal or provincial governments. Existing legislation is based on permissible pollution from particular sources and doesn't account for accumulation from many sources, which individually may not be considered harmful. Nor does legislation deal with the serious problem of non-point pollution.

Yet there has been progress in the 1990s. In addition to upgrading sewage plants, the GVRD's Liquid Waste Management Plan coordinates sewage disposal, storm sewers, runoff from urban areas, and industrial waste. Provincial and municipal standards for water quality are rising, enforcement is more effective and monitoring of wastewater discharge is more vigilant. But federal and provincial frontline officials are too few in number to adequately enforce existing environmental protection laws, and their budgets are being cut while excessive growth imposes more pressure on the natural processes of the Fraser River.

Chad Day says the system is still "secretive, arbitrary, discretionary" and fails to spell out the rights of citizens to a quality environment. It is imperative, says Day, that water quality standards be established that ensure the health of the aquatic ecosystems of the Fraser River and of the marine environment of the Strait of Georgia. These standards must be worked out in a transparent, public manner so that they have the full support of the community. It can be done. The State of Washington, B.C.'s southern neighbour, has clear federal standards and goals for water quality that must be met or exceeded by state and local governments.

A century ago, about fifty salmon- and trout-rich streams trickled and flowed through some 120 kilometres of the site of modern-day Vancouver. Only about 20 kilometres were spared the ignominy of disappearing into the city's sewer and drainage system. In all Vancouver, only Musqueam Creek and its tributary, Cutthroat Creek, still support small populations of trout and salmon.

When a stream is healthy enough to produce fish, it will also be a corridor of life and freedom, fostering a wide range of animals, birds and plants. This is because fish require clean, unpolluted water, shaded and cooled by trees and shrubs from which fall nourishing insects. Alders fix nitrogen in the soil, providing energy for the biological system. Roots hold the soil in place, keeping silt out of the gravelly stream beds in which salmon lay their eggs; vegetation filters out sediment and pollutants from water before they reach the stream. Larger trees drop branches and may eventually fall into the stream, providing shelter and habitat for young fish that some day will contribute to commercial, Native and sports fisheries.

The streams of the heavily populated lower Fraser Valley are very important fish producers. But overfishing, dykes, channels, stripped vegetation, chemical pollution, sediments running off industrial and agricultural lands, urbanization and highway construction are combining to rob the Lower Mainland of the last of this precious resource. The entire coho salmon population of southern B.C. is in serious trouble because of degradation of the small streams they inhabit. Otto Langer estimates that half of all the Fraser River tributaries that produce coho salmon lie between Hope and the Pacific. And, says Langer, the young salmon living in those streams for a whole year before going to sea are exposed to the whole range of urban, industrial and agricultural abuse.

Living fish in a healthy stream signal an environment of quality for people as well, one that provides a refuge from urban pressures, the satisfaction and joy of renewed connections with nature, cleaner air and water, and a moderated local climate. Natural streams are treasured by the people fortunate enough to live nearby, and proximity to a stream increases property values from 5 to 30 per cent. But it is often difficult to persuade developers that a margin of natural vegetation along streams is in their interests as well as that of their clients. With more than 40,000 housing starts in B.C. each year, land zoned for urban development in Lower Mainland is so valuable that few entrepreneurs are willing to regard it as anything but a platform for housing. Federal fisheries guidelines require a "leave strip" of at least 15 metres along each side of a stream, an absolute minimum for stream protection. But developers are often able to negotiate a narrower riparian band through political channels, since many municipal councils are dominated by development interests. These benefits to developers end up being costly for citizens, because nature manages water and streams in a way that evens flow, filters pollutants and limits erosion. When the land is covered with buildings and pavement, these functions must by provided by engineers and paid for by taxpayers. Then there is the cumulative impact on the Fraser as stream afhter stream is degraded. As hydrologist Robert Newbury asks, "How many branches can you cut from a tree before it is no longer a tree?"

The only real protection in law that streams have is the federal Fisheries Act, which prohibits the damaging of fish habitat. The effectiveness of the act is constrained by a very limited DFO enforcement staff, a legal system in which many judges seem to have little understanding of or interest in the issues, and by frequent political interference. One example: in the 1950s more than 10,000 pink salmon spawned in a Lower Mainland tributary of the Fraser, the Coquitlam River. Gravel yards opened up nearby and began scooping rock from the riverbed. In spawning season the gravel ran red with salmon eggs; builders complained the eggs were weakening their concrete. By the 1960s the pink salmon were gone from the Coquitlam. When the Fisheries Act was changed to provide legal protection for fish habitat, DFO officials tried for years to save the remaining coho, chum and steelhead still using the river. They charged the offenders, but the political connections of the gravel companies were impeccable, and DFO officials were ordered to settle out of court. In the 1990s the Coquitlam River is still heavily polluted by sediment from gravel operations, and fish stock devastation continues.

But there is also reason for optimism as support spreads for the idea of "stream stewardship." In Burnaby, many streams have long since disappeared under concrete and asphalt, but efforts are underway to clean up some remaining streams and rebuild salmon stocks in the Brunette River and in tributaries of Burnaby Lake, in Byrne Creek, Stoney Creek and others. Fewer streams survive in Vancouver, but here too tentative efforts are being made to bring some back to life—"daylighting sewers," the process is called. Trout Lake, on Vancouver's east side, has been shrinking over the years because its tributary streams were directed into storm sewers. Now some of these underground streams are being dug out and some storm sewers are being routed back into the lake. They will never be thriving salmon streams again, but at a cost hundreds of times greater than protecting them in the first place, the city is trying to regain at least some aspects of natural streams. Ironically, only a few kilometres away pristine streams are being destroyed almost daily by new developments. Reclaiming what we have destroyed is difficult and costly. Consider the intricacies of designing a normal stream, with meanders efficiently dissipating energy, riffles restoring oxygen, still pools where trout lurk, hundreds of kinds of vegetation and thousands of species of insects, fungi, worms, bacteria—all freely provided by nature and taken for granted until we are faced with the task of replacing them.

Urban streams are beginning to be recognized as treasures, deserving meticulous care and protection. In the lower Fraser Valley and the estuary, schools, community and conservation organizations, farm groups and others are rehabilitating damaged streams and trying to protect them from further abuse. Mark Angelo, chair of the B.C. Heritage Rivers Board, has called for an initiative requiring local governments to protect urban streams and associated riparian habitat. "The Forest Practices Code does a better job of protecting rivers and streams in remote forested areas than we do in urban situations in our own backyard," Angelo says.

One program, Partners in Protecting Aquatic and Riparian Resources, is bringing together all three levels of government and others interested in developing new approaches to protecting streams in the Lower Mainland. Local municipalities control land use, and they are being urged to take a more prominent role by including in their official community plans the goal of protecting fish and wildlife habitats in balance with urban development. Using their official plan and zoning bylaws, municipalities can map and identify environmentally sensitive areas, and ensure that any development is set well back from them. There are many zoning tools —density bonuses, for example—that can make this palatable and even profitable to developers. There is a rich tradition of "designing with nature" upon which developers can draw to their own profit while contributing to the goal of a sustainable, beautiful region. Developers who work with local and senior governments to incorporate stream steward-ship in development plans will avoid the costs, delays and community dis-approval that increasingly accompanies abuse of the landscape.

For the city dweller isolated from nature, one of the greatest opportu-nities for reconnecting with the real world lies in the many streams, large and small, that wind through the Lower Mainland landscape to join the Fraser River. There is deep satisfaction in discovering a shaded stream just beyond suburban pavement, and joy in glimpsing the shadowy form of a trout or salmon moving through clear water. There is delight in bird song echoing through trees and bushes bordering a creek. Watch the eyes of a twelve-year-old girl who sees a few coho salmon tentatively returning to spawn after years of absence. Working with her school class to clean up a stream, creating shade for small fish where bulldozers have ripped away natural shelter, she is becoming part of a miracle that will touch her life. She knows something now of the art and science of stream stewardship, and when there are enough like her, there will be hope for the streams of the Fraser Valley and estuary.

The mighty river has reached its destination. The Fraser's powerful flow drives a clearly defined plume of silt-laden fresh water far out over the salt water of the Strait of Georgia, extending up to 30 kilometres before surrendering to the blue Pacific Ocean. Nourishment from the estuary and from far upstream is borne out to sea where the mix of fresh and salt waters promotes growth of life-giving plankton. The river's oxy-gen-laden flow enriches these deep waters, and its enormous surge draws nutrient-rich water from the ocean depths in through the Juan de Fuca Strait.

Most of the Fraser's water eventually makes its way to the open ocean around the southern tip of Vancouver Island, where it constitutes up to 60 per cent of the flow. The river contributes to marine produc-tivity along the entire length of the west coast of Vancouver Island. The buoyancy of its water drives a current north along the inner shelf of the island while farther out, another, wind-driven current flows south. Between the two currents an upwelling of deeper ocean water brings nutrients to the surface. For fishers, this is one of the most productive sections of the coast of British Columbia. Bird life abounds too. On Triangle Island off the northern tip of Vancouver Island, the world's greatest concentration of Cassin's Auklet depends for nourishment upon movements of the sea triggered by the Fraser River, 600 kilome-tres away—one more reminder of the enormous power and influence of this mighty river.

Fraser River Delta

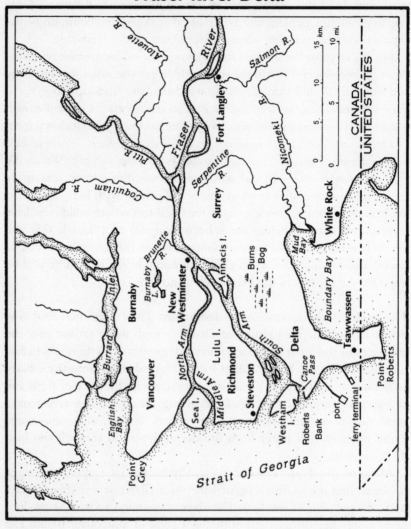

CHAPTER II

A River, a City and the World

*By becoming the first urban region in the world to combine economic vitality
with the highest standards of livability and environmental quality, Greater
Vancouver can represent in history what Athens is to democracy
or Vienna is to music.*

GREATER VANCOUVER REGIONAL DISTRICT, *CREATING OUR FUTURE*

After more than 1300 turbulent kilometres, the Fraser meets the
ocean in a rich union of land, river and sea. The river's vast estuary,
developed in less than 10,000 years, is one of the great biological
wellsprings of the world. Superimposed directly upon the estuary is
Vancouver, which together with its suburbs and adjoining municipalities comprise the Lower Mainland. Almost 1.8 million people now live
in this urban complex at the mouth of the Fraser River, drawn by a
gentle oceanic climate and year-round green opulence in a spectacular
setting of mountain and sea. The region's population is well educated,
its economy vibrant, its possibilities unlimited.

In spite of explosive growth in recent decades, the region enjoys a
powerful and reassuring sense of nature nearby, thriving and accessible.
The north shore mountains rising from the sea enhance this sense of a
natural world only minutes away from a stimulating urban environment. But people of the Lower Mainland compete directly with the
region's remaining plant and animal life for land and water, and sheer
human numbers are obliterating the elements that support life and
assure its quality. The sustainability of the Fraser River and its entire
basin may ultimately depend on whether the river and the city can coexist; whether this community of almost two million people can summon sufficient wisdom to live in harmony with the magnificent natural
heritage upon which it is built.

Greater Vancouver dominates the entire Fraser Basin and is by far the
basin's biggest city, containing almost 70 per cent of its population. It is

the economic nerve centre of the basin; in Vancouver's high-rise office towers decisions are made that determine the futures of people, industries, resources and environment throughout the watershed. With each passing year, however, more of those decisions are made in Tokyo, Hong Kong, New York and Toronto as transnational corporations take control of large blocks of the basin's economy, and executives in Vancouver offices simply carry out orders. As UBC geographer David Ley and his colleagues write, "The province's resource sector is increasingly controlled by distant absentee landlords." This shift in power will profoundly affect the future of the Fraser Basin.

Products from the length of the river and its tributaries descend to the Fraser's mouth for shipment to buyers throughout the world. This pattern is profitable for administrators, financiers, shippers and their employees in Vancouver, but concentration on the export of raw and nearly raw resources imposes deep distortions on the development of many upriver communities. As urban philosopher Jane Jacobs writes, "cities shape stunted and bizarre economies in distant regions. The most important among such economic grotesques are supply regions." The Jacobs thesis is vividly illustrated in the forests of the Cariboo and in the diversion of the Nechako River. Possibilities for development of balanced economies based on the region's natural assets and its resourceful people are largely foreclosed by the current model of economic development driven by distant governments and corporations. In this sense, the destiny of the entire Fraser Basin is too tightly interwoven with that of the urban giant at the mouth of the river.

Greater Vancouver is also an ecological "nerve centre." Because the city bestrides the Fraser River's estuary, the most important and sensitive section of the entire watershed, what happens here will echo throughout the basin. Urban development on the land, sewage and industrial effluent dumped into the river, chemicals washed in from farm and city, fishing practices at the river's mouth—all will influence the river far upstream and out into the Strait of Georgia. Here on the coastal estuary and fertile lands of the valley, human impacts on the Fraser River and its watershed are most significant, and controlling them is the most difficult.

The overwhelming feature of the transformation of the Fraser estuary is the speed with which it has occurred. In 1871 there were fewer than 1,300 non-Native settlers in the lower Fraser region; just 120 years later, in 1991, the population of what became the Greater Vancouver Regional District had multiplied more than 1,000 times. Even more significantly, the population of half a million at the end of World War Two tripled in just forty-five years, then reached 1.8 million by 1994.

By 2024, three million people are expected to be living in the GVRD. Although British Columbia appears to be a vast, sparsely populated region, in fact the lower Fraser Valley's population of about 425 people per square kilometre is comparable to that of the Netherlands, and almost twice that of the United Kingdom.

In the early 1990s more than 40,000 new arrivals each year spurred expansion of the urban agglomeration of Greater Vancouver. The vulnerability of the estuary to this creeping sprawl is best appreciated from the air: blocked by the American border and Cascade Mountains to the south, the Coast Mountains to the north and the Strait of Georgia to the west, urban development advances across the Fraser delta and lower valley from all directions, squeezing remaining farmlands and natural landscapes into smaller spaces year by year. New Westminster and the North Arm of the Fraser are heavily industrialized, and suburbs obliterate farmlands in Richmond and Delta. The process began before World War One, when bridges across the Fraser's North Arm brought streetcar and railway lines into Richmond. The combination of easy building on the flat land of the delta, the enthusiasm of municipal councils for development they thought would solve all their financial problems, and an almost complete lack of planning and zoning restrictions led to the worst excesses of urban sprawl.

Tony Hiss writes in *The Experience of Place*, "overdevelopment and urban sprawl can damage our own lives as much as they damage our cities and countryside." He describes how our surroundings have an immediate and continuing effect on the way we feel and act, and on our health and intelligence. Decades ago, the eminent psychologist Abraham Maslow demonstrated in a series of experiments how powerfully the quality and beauty of surroundings affect the functioning of the human mind. For many people, the loss of treasured or well-known elements of their natural or built environment can be traumatic. A grove of ancient trees chopped down and paved over, a fine heritage house replaced by a shopping mall, a green and shaded riverbank crushed beneath clay fill to accommodate scrap metal shipments, a yellow haze hanging over the Fraser River on warm summer days, smudging the sharp brilliance of Vancouver's spectacular mountain backdrop—all these can cause a sense of individual loss. Changes of "place" over which we have no control can be deeply personal, as well as environmental, issues that have direct impact upon our wellbeing.

Suburban residents may flee the urban core to escape congestion, enjoy the illusion of country life and find cheaper housing. They are attracted by single-family houses on large lots. Yet this is a recipe for consumption of vast amounts of land by relatively small numbers of people who often find that in pursuing dreams of country living, they help destroy the source of those dreams. The greenspace that attracted them disappears under more subdivisions, and the biodiversity of the land crumbles before the onslaught of pavement, lawns and malls. Suburbanites often find they live too far from the cultural, social and economic amenities of the city centre to use them frequently, while the formless suburb is unable to provide similar amenities close to home. Travelling through the urban sprawl that each day blights more of the Fraser Valley and estuary, one is reminded of Gertrude Stein's famed description of Oakland, California: "When you get there, there isn't any 'there' there."

In 1989, Vancouver architect Arthur Erickson challenged his fellow citizens to prepare for a population of 10 million at the mouth of the Fraser River. His view of Vancouver as a major metropolis on the world stage strikes a chord with those who believe economic growth should be the prime goal of a community. But it is a view vehemently opposed by those who recognize that ecology and economy are interwoven, and for whom it is inconceivable that the Lower Mainland would exchange its attributes as one of the world's finest human environments for the values that have created Hong Kong, Los Angeles and other "world cities."

How big should a city be? Plato's ideal city size of 5,000 is neither feasible nor desirable for all communities; nor is the 20 million of Mexico City, in which systems crumble under sheer force of numbers. To a certain point, urban growth enhances the cultural, economic and social life of an entire region; but too much growth creates problems ranging from pollution and urban sprawl to crises in public health, transportation, neighbourhood quality and crime. David Orr sums it up neatly: "Growing cities support symphony orchestras, but when they continue to grow people are mugged leaving the symphony and acid rain dissolves the exterior marble of the civic auditorium."

Growth—economic growth and population growth—is the crucial element in any consideration of sustainability in the Fraser River estuary and in the lower Fraser Valley. There are two basic and very different approaches to the problem. The usual approach, and the one prevailing in the Fraser Basin today, is to continue promoting growth while searching for more efficient ways of using land and resources, and employing better environmental controls to reduce pollution. Politically, this is the easier path, since a growing economy creates a larger pie to share, postponing debate and conflict over the fairness of its distribution among sectors of society.

The problem with this approach is that even with greater technological efficiency, a growing population exudes more waste into air, water and garbage dumps. More Fraser Valley land will be paved for homes, businesses and roads. More fish and wildlife habitat, farmland and forests will disappear. There will be a general loss of biodiversity as plant and animal species diminish and in some cases vanish, and the resilience of ecosystems will be weakened. A larger population will have less land and fewer resources to support each person, and many of the amenities that attracted people to the Fraser Valley will cease to exist.

To a certain point, though, *how* more people are accommodated may be more important than *how many*. This is the essence of another approach to urban development. The quest for cities that incorporate higher human values along with economic opportunity within environments that are harmonious with nature goes back at least to Hippocrates. In this century it has been pursued by visionaries like Ebenezer Howard, Patrick Geddes, Lewis Mumford and Ian McHarg. More recently, the rising urgency of urban problems ranging from sprawl to inner city disintegration has led to an explosion of interest in better ways of designing and living in cities. The quest continues in the Fraser Valley and estuary in proposals by various bodies: the Livable Region Strategy of the GVRD; the recommendations of the Georgia Basin Initiative, organized in 1993 by the B.C. Round Table on the Environment and the Economy; and the round table's 1994 report, *State of Sustainability: Urban Sustainability and Containment.*

Urban planning in the Fraser Valley became much more difficult when the Social Credit government eliminated regional planning in 1983. In spite of this, in the late 1980s the eighteen municipalities that make up the GVRD organized an extensive program of consultations, seminars, community meetings and surveys involving thousands of people in a search for consensus on goals for the future of the region. This effort resulted in the remarkable 1990 document *Creating Our Future: Steps to a More Livable Region.* After another three years of conferences and consultations, the GVRD published proposals for a Livable Region Strategy. It incorporated many of the principles developed earlier, but events were moving fast; one GVRD director pointed out that "creating our future" was quickly becoming a matter of "managing our present." During those three years, the population had grown by 100,000 people and 53,000 vehicles, construction of 38,600 housing units had started, and another 15 square kilometres of land had been converted to single-family residential use.

The GVRD's Livable Region Strategy aims to prevent the endless spread of bedroom suburbs up the Fraser Valley from Vancouver. The plan calls instead for compact communities, each with its own identity, downtown centre and work opportunities—complete cities within which people can live, learn, work and shop, where they can enjoy arts and culture, recreation and leisure. The cities will be set in an inviolate "green zone" of farmland and natural landscape. Growth will be concentrated in Burrard Peninsula municipalities, the Coquitlam area and northern sections of Surrey and Delta. Increased population density in these areas will reduce pressures on the green zone, slow the spread of housing into the Fraser Valley and concentrate residential development close to metropolitan work opportunities. Such centres of high-density population favour pedestrian, cyclist and local transit, and can be linked more effectively and at less cost by rapid transit. They also reduce demand for highways to funnel commuters into the city from ever more distant bedroom suburbs.

This vision of "cities in a sea of green" provides a striking contrast to the current model in which suburban development sprawls out across the land from the metropolitan centre, destroying values of both city and nature. Connected by rapid transit corridors, separate and distinct communities could be located on the region's least sensitive terrain, leaving farmlands to produce food and allowing the Fraser River, tributary streams, estuary and wildlife habitats to flourish. Taxation policies could discourage land speculation while increasing affordability of housing in more densely populated areas; equitable farmland leasing arrangements and policies ensuring adequate farm income are other important strategies for preserving a viable green zone. Such cities enable their inhabitants to enjoy the economic benefits, the satisfactions and the delights of urban life while retaining a close relationship with nature. And—vital to success—there must be provision for effective public participation in the creation of this vision.

If urban development in the lower Fraser Basin is to reflect this decentralized model, each community must have a clearly defined edge at which the city ends and farmland or natural landscape begins. This is described as "urban containment," a policy so important that the B.C. Round Table on the Environment and the Economy describes it as "a key challenge in achieving sustainability in British Columbia." Urban containment is probably the best available tool for restricting the formless, outward suburban sprawl of the megalopolis, while fostering the creation of complete, livable communities. Urban planner Rod Clack suggests this could be accomplished through an "Urban Land Reserve," much like B.C.'s existing agricultural and forest land reserves. An urban land reserve would establish containment boundaries within which settlement could occur with minimal damage to the landscape and natural systems. As Clack points out, "The fundamental difference in this approach from what currently exists is that instead of urbanization being mainly developer driven, it would follow a plan and a pattern agreed upon as being in the public interest first and foremost." He notes how a century-old planning act in Great Britain enables that tiny island to accommodate 50 million people in a relatively green landscape.

Decentralized towns and cities with distinct boundaries would reverse the present trend in which we try desperately to protect islands of nature from the advancing sea of urban sprawl. Many natural systems can't survive in such isolation. The decentralized city model instead develops *urban* islands in a sea of natural landscape, preserving corridors of life between wild areas, providing the links that biodiversity studies are finding absolutely crucial for survival of species and the functioning of ecosystems. In the Fraser Valley, this model would add immeasurably to the quality of urban life, providing recreational, cultural and economic opportunities in an environment rich in wildlife and natural landscapes.

The Livable Region Strategy of the GVRD proposes some excellent policies, but incorporates two serious flaws. One is that municipalities are not obliged legally to follow it, and some, like Richmond, already are trying to circumvent it. Planner Alan Artibise of UBC says, "It's time for us to revisit regional government and to actually set up a structure that has some teeth."

The strategy's second serious flaw is its failure to address the implications of a continuing high rate of population growth. It extrapolates recent growth rates into the future, and without explaining how or why, adopts the resulting population explosion not only as inevitable but as a goal for the region. A Lower Mainland population of three million in 2021 becomes a target, requiring policies of economic growth and job creation to ensure its achievement.

A strategy explicitly rejecting any attempts to limit growth can be dangerous, says Rod Clack. The world doesn't end with the year selected as the planning horizon: 2021, in the case of the GVRD. A bigger problem will have been created for following years because the same growth rate will bring in even more people.

Acceptance of growth as inevitable and beyond control is convenient for governments and profitable for some corporations. The development industry maintains that it is anti-democratic to attempt in any way to stem rates of growth. But of course, growth *will* stop at some point. The only question is, *when*? The world is finite, and the Fraser Valley in particular is very limited in space and in biological resources to support life. Left to the market, growth will end when the region's natural amenities are gone, when resources are exhausted, when air, water and land can absorb no more waste, when most non-human species are eliminated and the Lower Mainland emulates Hong Kong or Los Angeles: an urban agglomeration interlaced with freeways all the way from the Strait of Georgia to Chilliwack.

When William Rees, head of the School of Community and Regional Planning at UBC, challenges a class of geographers, architects and economists to define "the city," they usually talk about buildings, parks, streets, boundaries, institutions, markets and other concepts normal to their disciplines. Rees pulls together all these interpretations of the city and says, "Let's enclose your city in a plastic bubble. We can call it a 'regional capsule.' What have you got now?"

It doesn't take students long to recognize that in defining their "city," they have enclosed a very incomplete and artificial system. To maintain life it requires air, water, food, fibre, minerals and energy from outside. "In ecological terms," says Rees, "the city is a node of pure consumption, an ecological black hole drawing on the material resources and productivity of a vast and scattered hinterland many times the size of the city itself."

Not a very flattering description of the city, the home of many of our proudest achievements. But obviously, no city could long subsist on the land it occupies. The amount of land, water and air within the boundaries of Greater Vancouver is a tiny fraction of what is required to support its population of 1.8 million people. Most of the city's biologically productive land has been paved and built upon, and if the atmosphere above it and the river running through it did not carry away wastes, citizens would quickly be poisoned by toxic air and water.

Unable to sustain itself on the resources within its borders, Vancouver clearly doesn't have sufficient "carrying capacity." This is the number of people for whom the resources and waste-absorbing capacity of an area can provide, without damaging the supporting ecosystems. The number may vary, depending on the culture and values of the people, and upon how efficiently they use their resources. So the next question Bill Rees asks his class is, "How large would you have to make it, this the regional capsule covering our city, before the city could in fact become sustainable? If we don't have sufficient carrying capacity ourselves, then we've got to get some from elsewhere. We can call that 'appropriated carrying capacity.'"

Rees and his UBC colleagues have calculated that to supply its needs for food, wood-fibre and energy, the lower Fraser Valley and estuary (including Greater Vancouver) requires the production of about 7.7 million hectares of land, an area almost twenty times larger than the valley's

400 000 hectares. They call this the region's "ecological footprint." As Greater Vancouver smothers the productive land that partly feeds it, its dependency on production by people beyond the valley increases. The city draws sustenance from around the world, sometimes outbidding local inhabitants in poorer regions or importing food from places like California, whose agricultural bounty has been achieved at enormous cost in decimated ecosystems and heavily subsidized water projects.

Vancouver also lives off the accumulations of the past, drawing down resources at the expense of future generations. Its economy has developed in part through exploitation of old-growth forests that will never be seen again, salmon runs and other fish of numbers and quality we can only imagine today, and farmland that sprouts fast-food outlets instead of real food. Beyond the lower Fraser Valley, the city has in a sense "appropriated" thousands of square kilometres of beautiful and productive valley lands in the Peace and Columbia River basins, drowned by giant reservoirs so that generators can feed hydroelectric power to Vancouver.

The ease with which a rich urban region like Greater Vancouver can import food, materials and energy from far away can have the effect, Rees suggests, of "physically and psychologically distancing urban populations from the ecosystems that sustain them." Losing sight of their ultimate dependency on the land, people may imagine that there are few limits to the expansion of their city. At the Westwater Research Centre, Michael Healy is convinced that as populations continue to grow everywhere and natural capital declines throughout the world, the people of the Fraser Basin will increasingly have to depend upon the ecological services of their own river and province. "We can't count on the U.S. doing it for us," he says. "We can't count on Mexico doing it, and we can't say the rainforests of the Amazon are going to save us because they aren't." So for those who live today on the banks of the Fraser, sustainability, not growth, must be the over-arching priority.

Ships moor at docks along the Fraser River and amid the towers of Burrard Inlet; they ride at anchor in English Bay. Their names and home ports reflect the seven seas; they carry resources from throughout the Fraser Basin to markets around the world, and return with finished products. Airplanes lift from Lulu Island bound for cities on every continent but Antarctica. Networks of communications, capital, technology and trade integrate the Fraser Basin into the world economy. Immigration and foreign travel, culture and politics forge links with peoples across the oceans.

Trade has been part of life in the Fraser Basin for thousands of years.

Exchange of goods along "grease trails" linking coastal Native communities to tribes of the Interior enhanced the lives of both groups. The purpose of most European exploration, including Simon Fraser's epic journey, was to establish trade in furs with aboriginal people—European hat fashions depended on beaver pelts from North America. Soon after the Hudson's Bay Company built Fort Langley in 1827, the company was shipping barrels of salted salmon to Hawaii and California. Well before 1900, canneries at the mouth of the Fraser were shipping hundreds of thousands of cases of canned salmon to Europe each year. Most timber cut in the Fraser Basin is exported.

Trade remains vital to the basin. Exports like wood products are fundamental to the economic wellbeing of the watershed, and imported goods, services and ideas enrich the lives of its people. But globalization of the economy and the rapid advancement of what is called "free trade" has turned trade into something entirely new, with profound implications for the future of the Fraser Basin. Essentially, the effect of free trade as embodied in the North American Free Trade Agreement and the World Trade Organization is to allow the free movement of capital by transnational corporations while severely restricting the power of local, provincial and federal governments to regulate trade for the benefit of the people they represent. As one trade expert put it, the intent of the NAFTA and the WTO is to "get governments out of the way."

With complete mobility of capital, transnational logging, agri-business, chemical, drug and other corporations roam the world looking for the cheapest labour, lowest taxes, slackest environmental regulations, least costly social support systems and most compliant governments. As they exhaust resources in successive locations, they must continually seek new investment opportunities. Economists Thomas Hutton and Craig Davis of UBC describe how corporate mergers and acquisitions associated with economic globalization have already reduced Vancouver's commercial independence, and "could significantly undermine future decision-making autonomy, influencing in turn investment and job generation in B.C."

From elimination of the cod off Newfoundland, to the decimation of the rainforests of Penang in Malaysia, to the disappearing old growth of the Fraser Basin, the global economy is wiping out the world's resources. There are some industries in the Fraser Basin, particularly those involving high technology and information systems, that may prosper in a free trade environment. But the sectors particularly threatened are those related to renewable resources and the biological sustainability of the region.

Sustainability in the Fraser Basin and around the world will be difficult to achieve and perhaps impossible unless new conditions regulating environmental and social issues are included in trade agreements. Yet better trade agreements won't happen without the introduction of democracy into trade matters; to date, all negotiations among governments have been closed to everyone except the transnational corporations that have dictated most of the terms. Economist Robert Costanza and his colleagues insist that trade agreements must include safeguards against "eco-dumping" of products created without adequate environmental care. They suggest fairness and sustainability may be achieved if social and environmental costs are added directly into trading operations, using tools such as ecological tariffs and green taxes. Other innovative proposals for financing public needs in the changing economy are evolving—the "Tobin tax" on international financial transactions, for instance, or the "bit tax" devised by Arthur Cordell and Ran Ide to adapt taxation to the global information economy.

Increased self-reliance in the Fraser Basin will reduce dependency on imports, the supply of which will inevitably become more precarious as global population increases and productivity of lands and oceans continues to decline. "If you trade, you do so in true ecological surpluses," says Bill Rees. "You don't export beyond the capacity of your region to produce, so you're not drawing down your capital stocks, your soil or your forest base. It's not a question of becoming self-sufficient, but it is a question of keeping options open, maintaining a multiplicity of skills within the community, a viable agriculture, a manufacturing base and so on. Recognizing that perhaps the world of the future won't be quite as reliable and as stable as the current economic development model assumes."

There are older and more profound relationships than trade linking the Fraser River to the wider world; the basin also echoes to faraway interactions of sun, wind and water. When warm water pushes north from an El Niño event off the coast of Peru, it may bring predators that decimate Fraser salmon stocks. Millions of birds link the river to Asia and South America when they sweep through the basin on annual migration. When salmon return to the Fraser after years of feeding and growing in distant reaches of the Pacific, they carry the bounty of the ocean far inland, up hundreds of kilometres of the Fraser and its tributaries, a supply of food for people and wildlife incomparably greater than the river alone could produce.

The great forces of nature that determine climates, cycles of water, carbon and nitrogen, ocean currents, migration of creatures of land, sea and air—these and a host of others, have always been considered beyond human influence. And until recently, pollution of air and water, excessive tree-cutting, poor agricultural practices and urban sprawl seemed problems limited to the region in which they occurred. Now, multiplied to many locations and growing rapidly in each, these regional impacts are combining to create phenomena that are global in scale. Linked to the world by powerful forces of nature and humanity, the Fraser Basin inevitably is swept by these storms of environmental, social and economic change. The watershed benefits from some global developments, is threatened by others and must share responsibility for them all. Most significant of global events caused by local activities multiplied over and over are the warming of Earth's climate, the so-called "greenhouse" effect, and depletion of the layer of ozone in the stratosphere that protects all planetary life from the sun's ultraviolet radiation.

Carbon dioxide is called a greenhouse gas because its presence in the earth's atmosphere traps energy normally radiated out into space, causing temperatures on earth to rise. Burning fossil fuels—coal, oil and gas—and burning tropical rainforests releases carbon dioxide into the earth's atmosphere. So does urbanization of forest and farmlands, replacement of forests by farms and grasslands by deserts, and industrial farm practices that release stored carbon from the soil. Rapid cutting of Fraser Basin forests adds to global greenhouse gases because living trees assimilate carbon dioxide and store it as carbon. The people of the Fraser Basin generate much more greenhouse gas than the average global citizen. Cars and other vehicles, electrical generating plants, heating systems and industrial activities in the lower Fraser Valley add millions of tonnes of carbon dioxide to the global atmosphere each year—about 20 tonnes of carbon per person, just about the highest rate in the world.

The Intergovernmental Panel on Climate Change, established by the United Nations in 1989 and representing 120 nations, predicts a doubling of carbon dioxide in the atmosphere over the next few decades. This is expected to raise global temperatures by an average of three degrees centigrade in the coming century—a full degree by 2025. In September 1995 the IPCC stated that the earth had entered a period of climatic instability likely to cause "widespread economic, social and environmental dislocation over the next century." Scientists expect more violent, variable and unpredictable weather, drought in some of the globe's most productive regions and excessive rain in others. And the debate over whether climate changes were due to natural or human causes is pretty much over. By the end of 1995 the IPCC could state that "the balance of evidence . . . suggests a discernible human influence on global climate."

The temperature of the Pacific Ocean along the coast of B.C. has been rising at a rate of one degree centigrade per century, while air temperatures in the province have been rising at a rate of one to two degrees per century. Temperatures in the Fraser Basin are expected to increase by from two degrees in summer at the mouth of the river to as much as five degrees in winter in the upper basin. While this might sound pretty good on a cold winter day, these increases in temperature over just 125 years are equal to an earlier, natural change that took 8,000 years. And that is exactly the trouble with the current global warming: it is happening so fast, much faster than the natural climatic shifts that have always occurred.

Climatic change of such speed may be too fast to permit adaptation by some ecosystems, and large numbers of animal and plant species will perish. In the Fraser Basin, as in other forested regions of Canada, global warming will increase the frequency and severity of forest fires. Research in B.C. shows that the combination of warmer temperatures and ozone depletion will lead to increased attacks by forest pests. Less moisture in areas that are already dry, along with increased ultraviolet radiation, will mean slower tree growth. And trees planted after logging may turn out to be the wrong species as climate warms—no small matter, considering that 300 million seedlings are planted in B.C. each year. Warmer seas and melting glacial ice will mean rising sea levels, with estimates ranging from 20 to 140 centimetres over the next century. The Fraser River estuary is particularly at risk; hundreds of thousands of people live below sea level in Richmond, Delta and Surrey, where dykes have been necessary to prevent the sea from inundating some of the basin's most productive land. Smog will worsen in the lower Fraser Valley during hotter, dryer summers.

Even marginally higher temperatures will have far-reaching consequences in the Fraser Basin—in the estuary, forests and fishery. Already, accumulations of snow in the mountains and flow of water in the Fraser River have been dropping since about 1976. Global warming means less water and warmer water in the river, intensifying trends already underway. Salmon are cold-water animals, and temperatures of many streams in the basin are already marginal for them; slightly warmer, and many salmon won't survive to spawn.

The thinning ozone layer is the other crucial global phenomenon that has accompanied postwar economic activity. Chlorofluorocarbons (CFCs) used in refrigeration and other industrial processes drift into the stratosphere and consume the ozone that normally screens the earth from the worst effects of ultraviolet rays. Increased ultraviolet radiation threatens people with skin cancer and attacks many biological processes. In the oceans, it diminishes the productivity of the plankton upon which most marine life, including salmon, depends; on land it slows plant growth and decreases crop yields. Ozone depletion and global warming often are synergistic in their effect—that is, together their impact is much greater than the sum of the two.

Wetlands in the Fraser Basin—fertile ecosystems like lakes, ponds, marshes and swamps—will be especially hard-hit by global warming and ozone depletion. The shallow edges are the most prolific part of a wetland and dry out first, seriously affecting the productivity of the entire area. Increased ultraviolet radiation is suspected of being a contributing factor in the worldwide crash in the number of frogs and other wetland amphibians. Global warming will increase demand for water; competition for it between urban dwellers and irrigated agriculture will leave less water for wetlands.

Upland habitat in the Fraser Basin will change with warmer temperatures, sometimes cutting off possibilities for wildlife migration. This is another reason for larger protected areas, connected by undisturbed wilderness corridors that provide creatures and plants of all kinds an opportunity to migrate towards conditions in which they have a chance to survive. The effect of climate change on birds is difficult to predict; it could be acceptable for some species, but injurious for others that are closely tied to their habitat.

Of course, warmer temperatures can have positive effects, too. Agrologist Bert Brink notes that in the Prince George region, for instance, potatoes are now regularly grown where they couldn't even be considered as a crop a few decades ago. Records show that temperatures at Prince George have been rising since 1943, particularly in the spring. Where soil quality allows it, warmer temperatures will enable agriculture to move farther north; new crops and higher yielding varieties may be possible in some regions. On the other hand, 26 per cent of farmers in the Fraser Basin irrigate, with most of that water coming from the Fraser River or its tributaries. Warmer temperatures and lower rainfall will mean more demand for irrigation water, but less will be available as stream levels drop. Water supplies for urban, industrial and irrigation uses throughout the basin will be less reliable.

Simply describing the causes of global warming suggests many of the steps necessary to slow its advance. And such measures deliver a very large bonus—they are the same steps needed to reduce stress on many other elements of the environment, and to improve quality of urban life and the economy. They involve better urban planning and public transportation facilities, more efficient use of energy and resources, preservation of greenspace, improved forestry and farming, and other measures—almost all of which will pay off handsomely even if global warming turns out to be less damaging than is now expected. The Fraser Basin would be a particularly big winner.

International agreements have been developed to control both global warming and ozone depletion. The Montréal Convention that developed targets for reduction in emissions of ozone-depleting gases is considered a success story, but progress towards control of global warming has been much slower. Oil and gas interests persuaded Prime Minister Jean Chrétien to back away from a carbon tax on fossil fuel, considered a key step in reducing carbon dioxide emissions. By July 1996, however, federal environment minister Sergio Marchi was saying, "The threat of climate change is real and present, and the cost in human discomfort and suffering is incalculable . . . there clearly is a clarion call for governments and politicians to take the next step." The United States announced that voluntary cuts had not worked and that binding targets would be set for cutting carbon dioxide emissions. British Columbia announced in 1995 the most stringent vehicle emission laws in Canada, and Ottawa agreed to similar federal standards in 1996.

The GVRD's document, *Creating Our Future*, begins with a vision:

> *Greater Vancouver can become the first urban region in the world to combine in one place the things to which humanity aspires on a global basis: a place where human activities enhance rather than degrade the natural environment, where the quality of the built environment approaches that of the natural setting, where the diversity of origins and religions is a source of social strength rather than strife, where people control the destiny of their community, and where the basics of food, clothing, shelter, security and useful activity are accessible to all.*

But others have a different vision for this great city at the mouth of the Fraser River. It is the stuff of daily headlines: promotion of rapid growth of Vancouver to "world city" status, a swollen metropolis of several millions whose electronic links with Tokyo, London, Hong Kong and New York take precedence over relationships with the rest of the Fraser Basin and the province. Turning away from the city's natural and cultural relationships within the basin in favour of what may amount to ephemeral and artificial connections with distant places holds ominous implications. For it is clear that the massive population at the mouth of the Fraser can only be sustained permanently if it is a full partner in the biological and economic health of the watershed.

Fortunately, identification with this "place" is particularly strong in British Columbians, even among recent arrivals. This can be the basis

of a society grounded here yet open to the wide world, closely connected with the land and its diverse communities while continuing to
develop a rich cultural life and a sound economy. Such a society will
recognize that it can ultimately count only on this place for food,
water, clean air and natural resources, along with the pleasure, satisfaction and wellbeing derived from a healthy environment.

Opportunities at the mouth of the Fraser River remain magnificent,
probably unsurpassed in the world. Vancouver can be the heart of a permanently sustainable community, offering a superb quality of life for its
people while sharing a healthy ecosphere with the region's panoply of
life. Perhaps, as the GVRD suggests, Vancouver *can* become another
Athens, but it will require a change in direction very soon. Perhaps such
changes will be made with greater wisdom if, as Robert Newbury suggests, we return in spirit to the Fraser's distant origins to recapture something of the lost innocence of the headwaters. We may find renewal in
landscapes where profound connections remain between water, land,
plants, animals and humans. We may find ways of re-establishing links
loosened and sometimes lost during the long descent of the river.
Returning to rediscover and understand these intimate relationships may
foster the creativity we will require if the Fraser River and all who
depend upon it are to survive and flourish.

CHAPTER 12

Flowing to the Future

The "realists" have had their time, and we see the fruits of their work.
It is time now for visionaries.

ADAPTED FROM DAVID W. ORR, *ECOLOGICAL LITERACY*

A s its brown plume spreads out across the Strait of Georgia in the
final act of a great drama, the Fraser River bears little resemblance
to its first trickle high in the Rocky Mountains. That small stream
was in fact just one of thousands of sources contributing to the river's
enormous flow; from tiny springs to spectacular lakes, the sources of
the Fraser comprise a total of unimaginable variety, beauty and power.

An exploration of the Fraser Basin is an exhilarating experience,
punctuated by optimism and depression. Throughout its 1370 dramatic
kilometres, the river is loved, feared, abused, nurtured, respected and
ignored. For those who know it best, the Fraser watershed is an awe-
inspiring presence, a rich source of life, a legacy to be protected. For
others, the basin is a treasure house to be looted, its assets transformed
to cash as quickly as possible.

In 1996 the Fraser River was named a British Columbia "Heritage
River."

In 1996 the Fraser River was named British Columbia's "most endangered river."

These two declarations provide a telling snapshot of the current state of
the Fraser Basin. The river has never been more appreciated, and its future
has never been more in jeopardy. The Fraser is not just a ribbon of water
flowing to the sea. It created most of the landscape through which it flows
and is central to life in the innumerable watersheds that combine to form
its basin. Descending through mountain valley, forest and desert, rocky
canyon and lush lowlands, the river grows to maturity and nourishes a

vast and magnificent landscape. It has witnessed an extraordinary human drama, from the aboriginal people who lived lightly on the land for millennia, to fur traders, gold seekers, ranchers, loggers, farmers and fishers who exploited its wealth of resources. They founded communities throughout the basin and a great city at the river's mouth. For most of its human history canoes travelled the turbulent waters of the Fraser; for half a century steamships churned its waters, and the valley of the Fraser River remains B.C.'s principal corridor for travel by land.

The extraordinary productivity of the aquatic ecosystems of the Fraser made its resources seem inexhaustible to the Europeans who arrived in the nineteenth century. But the river flows lower today because some of its tributaries have been diverted to generate hydro-electric power or irrigate crops. The water is warmer, and industrial and municipal pollution has compromised its quality. The vast runs of salmon that once thronged upriver have been decimated by a century of greed, poor management and carelessness. Wildlife populations are severely reduced due to a loss of habitat, and roads fragment much of what is left. Trees in the Fraser Basin have been logged at rates far above sustainable levels; centuries of forest growth are being rapidly cut and marketed by the transnational companies that control the industry. Near its mouth the river is dyked and constricted, no longer free to wander across the floodplains it created. Urbanization of the lower Fraser Valley and estuary has covered rich land with asphalt, and much of the remaining soil is of reduced fertility.

Forty-eight of Vancouver's fifty original streams were obliterated in the rush to build the city, and since 1967 more than 36 000 hectares of valley farmland have been converted to urban uses in the Greater Vancouver Regional District. More than 80 per cent of the productive salt marshlands in the river's estuary have been lost, primarily as a result of dyking. Some of those drained wetlands became fine farmland, much of which in turn disappeared under urban development. The Fraser River and the air above it are heavily laden with urban waste, and Vancouver exports sewage to the Strait of Georgia, solid waste to Cache Creek, and bad air to Abbotsford and Chilliwack.

There is a triple threat to the future of the Fraser Basin: excessive population growth in the Fraser Valley and estuary, rapid liquidation of the basin's natural capital, and waste production exceeding the absorptive capacity of water, land and air. Each new demand upon the Fraser adds stress that decreases the resilience of the whole system, making it less capable of coping with the next assault. For Michael Healy of the Westwater Research Centre, this means the entire Fraser Basin must be considered as one unit and we must "abandon our traditional project-by-project decision making. The ultimate consequence of that approach is the destruction of rivers by insignificant increments. The legacy of our incremental approach to water resources management is degraded rivers throughout the industrialized world."

The salmon symbolizes the unity of the Fraser Basin's vast landscape in one riverine ecosystem; it is central to the culture of the river and of British Columbia. More than anything else, the threat to Fraser River salmon has focused attention on the plight of the river. The robustness of its fish populations is the best indicator of a river's health and of the sustainability of its society and economy. A productive fishery reflects the quality of management of forestry and agriculture, of urban and industrial complexes—and provides a measure of the wisdom with which a river's resources are exploited.

And there's more. The salmon is, perhaps, the Fraser River's soul. When the salmon returns in millions from the depths of the Pacific to the Fraser each year, this great pulse of life is evidence of a natural continuity that offers a profound reassurance to the human psyche. When word went out that survival of Fraser River salmon was threatened in 1994, 1995 and 1996, there was consternation far beyond the fishing community. A Fraser River without salmon is unimaginable; it would not be the Fraser. A society that could destroy this magnificent creature, wiping out what is perhaps the greatest single natural source of high-quality food in the world, would bring shame on itself and earn the condemnation of succeeding generations. Without the salmon, a vast network of life would collapse—from eagles and grizzlies to trout and riparian vegetation. The continuity of many Native cultures is based on the salmon, and an industry worth more than a billion dollars a year would end.

In the absence of its "soul," the attitude towards the Fraser River by the people of the basin would be quite different. Without salmon, the Fraser would lose its living aura and become simply one more resource to be manipulated in accordance with whatever scheme seemed immediately profitable. Without salmon, there would be less incentive to enforce careful logging near streams and lakes, less impetus to reduce input of sediment and sewage. Dam builders and water exporters would parade their schemes for administering the Fraser's *coup de grace*. Without salmon, the Fraser River would no longer be a great living presence, and life throughout the basin would be diminished.

The Fraser Basin is still a highly productive natural system, due largely to its enormous flow, the wealth of resources in its watershed and its relatively small human population. But without significant change in patterns of exploitation, the power and productivity of the river may not be enough to protect it from the onslaught of a population expected to grow 50 per cent in the next twenty-five years. The boundaries of resilience in the Fraser Basin are much narrower than they once were, and the possibility grows that some of the river's natural systems may be driven into an irreversibly degraded state.

The Westwater Research Centre has undertaken a major study of sustainability in the lower Fraser River. Director Michael Healy explains that one important goal is early identification of potential problems. "How do we recognize when systems are beginning to show signs of distress so you can take remedial action before some catastrophe occurs?" asks Healy. Signals of danger ahead may come from change in population of a certain animal, bird or fish, or a shift in the temperature of the Fraser or a tributary, or a particular level of contamination in a water supply.

When resource economists Peter Pearse and Donald Tate consider the future of the Fraser Basin, their chief concern is not so much depletion of food and other materials provided by nature, but that "environmental deterioration threatens the productivity of natural systems, the quality of life, human health and perhaps survival . . . We have begun to threaten ecological life support systems . . . Sustainable development implies, if nothing else, avoiding the destruction of natural systems on which life on earth depends."

Ecological systems, in short, form the life-support system without which economic activity would be impossible. Healy says this means the maintenance or enhancement of ecosystems must take priority over economic expansion in the Fraser Basin. Ecologist Bill Rees puts it this way: "We may be fast approaching absolute limits to material economic growth. We no longer have the luxury of 'trading off' ecological damage for economic benefits if we hope to have a sustainable future." No prosperity is permanent when based on liquidation of old-growth forests, degradation of streams, soil, grasslands and diminution of the river's flow. This is a pattern of resource exploitation known as "overshoot," and is often followed by collapse of the resource and the economy dependent upon it.

The issue is sustainability, which in its simplest terms means that we should pass on to the next generation a stock of productive assets that is no less than that which we inherited. Unless we do, we are deliberately shifting to our children the problem of supporting greater numbers of people on fewer resources in a demeaned environment. This is a profoundly moral question. Law professor Edith Brown Weiss reminds us, "Every generation receives a natural legacy in trust from its ancestors and holds it in trust for its descendants." Former Toronto Mayor David

Crombie puts it more graphically: "We must leave at least as many choices to our children as we have—otherwise we are just scavengers." At Simon Fraser University, Chad Day sums up sustainability in two words: *preserving·options.*

There is no doubt that the natural capital of the Fraser Basin has been drawn down very rapidly during the last 100 years, and that in spite of recent initiatives, the resource base continues to decline. David Marshall of the Fraser River Basin Management Program sees reason for some optimism; he suggests that "while we are still slipping back from sustainability, we are slipping back at a slower rate than a few years ago." The FBMP has adopted the slogan "sustainability together," and defines sustainability as "managing the Fraser Basin in a way that considers the social, economic, and environmental implications of Basin activities in an attempt to meet the needs of today without compromising the needs of future generations."

For Rees, sustainability means more than simply trying to balance the social, economic and environmental aspects of the Fraser Basin. He writes, "nature imposes certain inviolable conditions on development . . . it is the productivity of the ecosphere that ultimately determines the potential level of economic activity." Logging, for example, has obviously exceeded these limits in the Fraser Basin, and Rees suggests that historic levels of profit from resource extraction may not be compatible with sustainable development. "Forestry and other resource corporations should be responsible for maintenance of the resource base before declaring dividends," he writes. This could mean higher prices—prices that reflect the real cost of maintaining and rehabilitating the ecosystems that produce the resources. Higher resource prices provide a boost towards sustainability, says World Bank economist Herman Daly, because they promote more efficient use of smaller quantities of the resource and encourage the production of value-added, finished products.

Sustainability, then, implies that there are limits to the extent to which we can degrade our natural environment without seriously compromising the future. People who live along the Fraser River want the basin to remain as productive, as beautiful and as fine a place to live for their children as it is for them. But often they can have little influence on the exploitation of basin resources, many of which are controlled by transnational corporations. In some corporate circles the idea of sustainability is considered dubious at best, and at worst as some sort of a plot against the existing economic system. Executives who rise or fall on the basis of quarterly financial statements and share values are unlikely to make long-term sustainability a priority. Decisions made in distant financial centres will not concern themselves with the permanence of

Fraser Basin forests, rivers or communities. Nor will trade rules enforced from Geneva bear much relationship to sustainable agriculture in the Fraser Valley or to the welfare of salmon runs.

Irving Fox, first director of the WRC, observes that "large corporate enterprises have the capability to exercise a degree of political influence that is incompatible with democratic decision-making." He would restrict tenure in Fraser Basin resources to organizations in which the majority of investors were located in the region, or at the very least within British Columbia. For Fox, sustainability includes a strong component of regional and community involvement in the management of resources, balanced with provincial and federal interests. But Fox insists that "you can't lose sight of the fact that unless you develop ways to have viable communities, with jobs and income for people, you're not going to get very far in maintaining the quality of the environment."

Elected governments are the obvious means of ensuring sustainability of resources and communities. Their work, however, is complicated by free trade agreements that are designed to minimize government control over corporate investment and operations. As the global economy evolves, environmental regulation by the Canadian government and several provinces is being severely cut back—evidence that the widely predicted "race to the bottom" in environmental protection under free trade is well under way. Sustainability of resources, ecosystems, communities and local economies must come first in any trading framework. In the NAFTA, an indication of concern for these issues was tacked on after the deal was signed, but so far has proven ineffective. The World Trade Organization deals only in corporate privilege.

Growth of the economy and population is the goal of much public policy in the Fraser Basin, since enlargement of the economic pie eases many difficulties faced by governments and provides opportunities for people. But growth is also the most important source of problems in the basin, whether related to pollution, traffic congestion, obliteration of farm and natural lands, excessive rates of resource exploitation or diminished viability of ecosystems. As economist Robert Costanza writes, "our economic system is operated as if it had a life independent of ecological system."

Part of the problem is the way we measure progress. The Gross Domestic Product indicates how much economic activity is occurring, but reveals little about quality of life. It values useful and harmful transactions equally, ignores resource depletion and environmental degradation, and says nothing about distribution of wealth within the population. In the Fraser Basin, the GDP will keep growing till the last tree is cut, the last fish caught and the last acre paved, without giving the slightest indication that something might be wrong. If sustainability is an essential part of social and economic progress, new ways of measuring the welfare of a society and its economy are needed; in the mid-1990s, several are being formulated and tested.

"For a statesman to try to maximize the GDP," says Garrett Hardin, "is about as sensible as for a composer of music to try to maximize the number of notes in a symphony." Maximum does not mean optimum, and beyond a certain point, the standard of living declines with economic and population growth. Peter Boothroyd of UBC's School of Community and Regional Planning suggests that a different kind of growth is appropriate: "growth in human activity directed to working with, rather than against, nature and the sun; growth in appropriate technology; growth in satisfaction from meaningful work, growth in community organization."

Fisheries biologist Thomas Northcote grew up on the banks of the Fraser River and has spent a lifetime studying its ecology. He is convinced that British Columbians have the means to protect and restore the health of the entire river ecosystem. But he's not sure they have the social and political will to do so. His anguish is palpable when he writes, "In the short run, without any change in our policies and practices of resource development we may continue to reap financial benefits, but at the cost of a rapid decline in our 'quality of living.' Surely and not so slowly, British Columbia will become Canada's California—economically, ecologically and perhaps even climatically! To those who knew it 'before,' the change will seem life threatening, if not unthinkable. To those who knew far worse, it will seem trivial, if not irrelevant."

The health of natural systems matters for reasons beyond physical survival or economic success. In *The End of Nature*, Bill McKibben eloquently describes how we are diminished as people when we realize that all existence is falling under human control, leaving nothing "out there" that functions without our manipulation. Perhaps there is more value than dollars can express in the knowledge that a great wild river continues to run free, full of salmon, where a grizzly bear fishes with mighty sweeps of a paw. In our crowded, over-used world, such phenomena are already rare and hence, for many people, vital. The natural world has "existence value," writes economist Michael Jacobs. "We want it to be there, in all its beauty and diversity, and its loss affects our well-being."

Hydrologist Robert Newbury ponders how people can best fit into a landscape in which water is the strongest element. He questions how far from "natural" humans can safely push the system. In other times and

places, cultures with different values related to nature and water with a
subtlety that contrasts remarkably to the brutality often displayed in
North America. One example is Moorish civilization in Spain before
1500, where scarce water in a hot, dry land was used with a sophistication owing as much to art as to technology. The Moors knew and celebrated the life that was most abundant at the water's edge. Vegetation,
insects and fish, birds and animals, and people too, thrive where land
meets water. Here we prefer to live, to work and to dream; here we have
been inspired to some of our finest art. And here we have inflicted the
most serious .damage to the life systems upon which we depend.
Wherever it occurs, by streams or lakes or oceans, the land–water margin
is particularly precious, deserving of the greatest possible care.

Concerns about the Fraser River don't have to translate into an
apocalyptic vision, and many recent developments provide reasons for
optimism. The Fraser's importance and the need to safeguard its qualities were recognized when it was named a B.C. Heritage River; it has
also been nominated as a Canadian Heritage River. One of the greatest
threats, the proposed Kemano Completion Project, was cancelled in
1995. New legislation bans large-scale interbasin transfer and export of
water from the province. Pollution from pulp mills along the river has
been greatly reduced, and new secondary sewage treatment facilities
have been constructed in the Lower Mainland. New regulations governing farm and industrial waste should reduce non-point pollution.
Many sensitive landscapes within the Fraser Basin are now permanently
protected by the B.C. government, though the work of creating parkland and conservation areas remains incomplete. The Forest Practices
Code should improve logging practices, particularly along the streams
of the basin, though after its first year in operation the effectiveness of
the code was not yet clear. The Forest Renewal Plan invests in better
future forests, watershed rehabilitation and stable communities.

In the Lower Mainland, the Livable Region Strategy provides a
vision for a more sustainable urban region, though enhanced regional
planning and a clear indication of the limits to urban growth are
required. Large new protected areas include Boundary Bay and other
locations important to fish and wildlife. New programs promote and
finance stream protection and rehabilitation in city landscapes and
farmlands, and many degraded streams are being renewed through local
volunteer efforts. The system of riverbank coding should reduce habitat
damage along the lower Fraser, though some authorities, even within
the DFO, are less than forceful in its application.

It became evident in the 1990s that salmon would not survive unless
B.C.'s fisheries were completely reorganized. Ideas are developing for

selective, terminal fisheries in which communities along the coast and within the Fraser watershed would have direct management involvement. In 1996 the B.C. government promised a Salmon Protection Act, "which will include banning dam construction on the Fraser River and its tributaries and lakes, protecting water flows needed by salmon, and prohibiting development along salmon streams."

Mark Angelo, chair of the B.C. Heritage Rivers Board, is encouraged that in the 1990s many more people are aware of the importance of the Fraser and understand the threats to the river and its resources. The board, a non-governmental body advising the B.C. cabinet, acts as an advocate for rivers in British Columbia. Its aims for the Fraser include a comprehensive watershed management plan. "I'd like to think that we could look towards transforming the Fraser from its endangered river status to a point where one day it may be viewed as a model of how such a large river system can be managed," says Angelo.

Anthony Dorcey, first chair of the Fraser Basin Management Board, considers increased involvement of local residents to be one of the most promising developments in the Fraser Basin. "I'm more optimistic than pessimistic by a substantial degree," says Dorcey, "because I see people changing their attitudes and changing what they're doing. We're going to have hard choices about how we change the way we do things, how do we back off, how do we rebuild? But the plus side is that the kind of development we've undertaken so far is much more reversible or less extensive than in many other parts of the world. That's the opportunity we've got."

The development of vigorous conservation organizations pushed the environmental agenda into the foreground in the 1990s—though this also incited the counter-formation of industry-sponsored groups pushing the corporate agenda. Solid new research material such as that compiled by the WRC and by DFO scientists provides information needed for better decision making about the future of the Fraser River. Informed people and organizations throughout the basin are making a difference, and Julia Gardner of the WRC is convinced they "have the potential to shift social priorities toward sustainability." (As anthropologist Margaret Mead once said, "Never doubt that a small group of thoughtful committed citizens can change the world; indeed, it is the only thing that ever has.") "If we really are going to build sustainability in the basin," says David Marshall of the FBMP, "it's got to be done creek by creek, stream by stream, watershed by watershed, or block by block, street by street, community by community. We require tools, opportunities and support from government, but change will happen through the individual at a community level."

The path towards sustainability in the Fraser Basin became clearer in the 1990s because of a remarkable series of events. The British Columbia Round Table on the Environment and the Economy suggested ways to approach sustainability in 1992 after holding open forums throughout the province. The Commission on Resources and Environment (CORE) developed in 1992 the first community-based, land-use planning techniques ever applied to the vast B.C. landscape. "Stakeholder involvement" and "consensus decision-making" were intended to be the operating norms. People representing many interests in a region worked intensively with government officials to come up with consensus on land-use plans for several parts of the Fraser Basin.

It wasn't easy. Progress was sometimes painfully slow and frustration flared. In some cases the process was a bitter disappointment, in others it worked very well. In the Kamloops region, most people seem to be pleased with the outcome, while in the Cariboo, conservationists say the giant international forest corporations are carrying on business as usual: there were indications by the summer of 1996 that logging operations were being concentrated in areas where the Cariboo-Chilcotin Land Use Plan called for low-intensity forestry.

Altogether, the outcome has been far from perfect, but CORE was an enormous step forward, with people of widely divergent interests beginning to understand each other for the first time. A key CORE document, *Strategy for Sustainability*, was particularly valuable, incorporating a Land Use Charter and Land Use Goals, and proposing a Sustainability Act to give all this the force of law. Such an act, says CORE's first commissioner, Stephen Owen, "will clearly announce to the world that British Columbia intends to be a leader on the path to a sustainable future." This is important legislation, and its enactment would play a useful role in safeguarding the future of the Fraser Basin.

The Fraser River Action Plan (FRAP) is a six-year federal government program initiated in 1991 by Environment Canada and the DFO. Its objective is to find ways of easing stress on the river caused by rapid growth of cities and their populations, large-scale industrial development and accelerated resource extraction. Scientists are studying the health of the river to develop base lines against which changes can be measured. Salmon studies are aimed at developing long-term plans for sustaining and rebuilding fish stocks in the Fraser. Under FRAP, partnerships of citizens, basin organizations and communities are being created to protect and rehabilitate fish and wildlife habitat; codes and guides are being developed that should reduce pollution, and they're backed by increased enforcement.

The Fraser Basin Management Program is the first attempt to

coordinate action towards sustainability across the entire Fraser Basin. In 1995 and 1996 the program issued "report cards" assessing progress towards this goal, and as it neared the end of its five-year mandate in 1996, the FBMP produced *BasinPlan: A Call to Action for Sustainability of the Fraser Basin*. The document suggests goals to be achieved and action programs to be undertaken by governments, industry, organizations and individuals in the pursuit of social, economic and environmental sustainability in the basin.

Yet after this remarkable progress in the first half of the 1990s, there is every indication that governments are losing interest in the mighty river and its future. Many sustainability initiatives are being terminated just as they are showing results. The B.C. Round Table on the Environment and the Economy is gone. The Commission on Resources and Environment was eliminated in 1995, and it remains to be seen if another agency will take up CORE's mandate to monitor and assess progress towards sustainability. The FBMP dies in May 1997 unless it receives a reprieve; FRAP funding runs out in 1997 and there is no indication of renewal. This is particularly serious because to make up for budget slashing in Ottawa, FRAP funds have been used to finance normal work in the basin by the DFO and Environment Canada. The capacity of these departments to continue work related to sustainability will largely collapse when FRAP funding ends in 1997. Many outstanding biologists, scientists and others with intimate knowledge of the Fraser will be discharged, and with them will go an enormous fund of knowledge. For several years now no new people have been hired to carry on this essential work, and few people will remain to enforce fishing regulations and habitat protection.

The federal government is drastically cutting biological and oceanographic research on the West Coast. In a particularly ironic twist, the West Vancouver DFO laboratory, which has contributed so much to understanding the salmon and its habitat, may be privatized and turned over to international corporations promoting fish farming, an industry considered by many to be a grave threat to the future of wild salmon in the Fraser River. Finance officials in Ottawa seem to have no interest in social, economic or environmental sustainability in the Fraser Basin; their political masters, however, owe the people of the basin an explanation for this betrayal of an important element of national interest. Single-minded emphasis on budget cuts may leave our children a deficit far more serious than the current monetary one.

It is not unusual to speak of "managing" the Fraser River. Since Francis Bacon introduced the concept 400 years ago, the management of nature on an ever larger scale has been considered a worthy human undertaking. Yet with the earth's natural systems in a downward spiral as humans take greater control of its functions, this approach is now widely disputed. One of the country's leading scientists and president of the Royal Society of Canada, Digby McLaren, warns that the idea of humans "managing the planet" is highly dangerous and responsible for many of the ecological and social problems we face. Others describe such human aspirations as the height of arrogance.

The consequences of human management of natural systems in the Fraser Basin are hardly encouraging. The catastrophic results of Alcan's management of the Nechako River, for instance; the looming "fall-down" in the Cariboo-Chilcotin forest industry after only three decades of forest management, and the Fraser River salmon crisis after a century of federal management of the fishery. Drawing on a lifetime studying aquatic systems, biologist Henry Regier writes, "We should not presume to think that we can manage large river ecosystems; we may be able only to manage human uses of these ecosystems." This is the key—it is we humans who need "managing," not ecosystems; they got along quite nicely without us for a very long time. Ecologist C.S. Holling and science historian Stephen Bocking suggest that we view humanity "as an integral part of a global ecosystem. Not a manager. Not even as steward. But in conscious partnership with all other life."

In spite of the abuse it has suffered, the Fraser Basin remains one of the most varied, beautiful and favoured landscapes on earth. Many of the great rivers of the world are sad remnants of their original grandeur. In the Fraser Basin there remains an opportunity to do much better. The people who live here must decide if they are willing to take responsibility for the future of this magnificent gift of nature, rejecting the domination of globalization and the tyranny of endless growth. They may choose instead a sustainable future for this great river, ensuring that the basin remains a permanent, productive home for its people. The Fraser River and its inhabitants can provide the world an example of what is possible, an image of hope.

As evidence of ecological and social stress mounts on planet Earth, what happens in the Fraser Basin will either add to the gathering crisis or contribute to its solution. The people of this mighty river still have a choice, and they know what to do. It is a rare opportunity. In much of the world, little choice remains.

Sources

INTRODUCTION

Boeckh, Ian et al. "Water Use in the Fraser Basin." In *Water in Sustainable Development: Exploring Our Common Future in the Fraser River Basin,* edited by Anthony H.J. Dorcey and Julian R. Griggs. Vancouver: Westwater Research Centre, UBC, 1991.

Boeckh, Ian et al. "Human Settlement and Development in the Fraser River Basin." In *Water in Sustainable Development.*

Boothroyd, Peter. "Distribution Principles for Compassionate Sustainable Development." In *Perspectives on Sustainable Development in Water Management: Towards Agreement in the Fraser Basin,* edited by Anthony H. J. Dorcey. Vancouver: Westwater Research Centre, UBC, 1991.

Daly, Herman E. "Sustainable Development: From Concept and Theory Towards Operational Principles." Quoted in W. Rees in "Conserving Natural Capital: The Key to Sustainable Landscapes." *International Journal of Canadian Studies,* (Fall 1991).

Dietrich, William. *Northwest Passage: The Great Columbia River.* New York: Simon & Schuster, 1995.

Dorcey, Anthony H. J. "Sustaining the Greater Fraser River Basin." In *Water in Sustainable Development.*

Ekins, Paul. *The Gaia Atlas of Green Economics.* New York: Anchor Books, 1992.

An Inventory of Undeveloped Watersheds in British Columbia. Victoria: Recreation Branch, B.C. Ministry of Forests, 1992.

Kew, Michael J. E., and Julian R. Griggs. "Native Indians of the Fraser Basin: Towards a Model of Sustainable Resource Use." In *Perspectives on Sustainable Development in Water Management.*

Northcote, Thomas G. and Michael D. Burwash. "Fish and Fish Habitats of the Fraser River Basin." In *Water in Sustainable Development.*

Rees, William E. "The Ecological Basis for Sustainable Development in the Fraser Basin." In *Perspectives on Sustainable Development in Water Management.*

State of the Environment Report for British Columbia. Victoria: B.C. Ministry of Environment, Lands and Parks, 1993.

Woodcock, George. *British Columbia: A History of the Province.* Vancouver: Douglas & McIntyre, 1990.

CHAPTER 1

Cheadle, Walter B. *Journal of a Trip Across Canada 1862–1863.* Edmonton: Hurtig Publishers, 1971.

DFO/MOEP Fish Habitat Inventory and Information Program, 1991. Stream Summary Catalogue. Subdistrict 29J, Clearwater. Vancouver: Department of Fisheries and Oceans.

Hutchison, Bruce. *The Fraser.* Toronto: Clarke, Irwin & Company Ltd., 1950.

Morice, A. G. *The History of the Northern Interior of British Columbia (1660 to 1880).* London: John Lane Publishers, 1906.

Northcote, T. G. and P. A. Larkin. "The Fraser River: A Major Salmonine Production System." In *Proceedings of the International Large River Symposium,* edited by D. P. Dodge. *Can. Spec. Publ. Fish. Aquat. Sci.,* 106 (1989).

Teit, James. *The Shuswap.* Edited by Franz Boas. New York: American Museum of Natural History, 1905.

Wade, M. S. *The Overlanders of '62.* Surrey, B.C.: Heritage House Publishing, 1931.

Watson, Lyall. *The Water Planet: A Celebration of the Wonder of Water.* New York: Crown Publishers Inc., 1988.

Wheeler, Marilyn J. (ed.). *The Robson Valley Story.* McBride, B.C.: The McBride Robson Valley Story Group, 1979.

Williams, M. B. *Jasper National Park.* Hamilton: H. R. Larson Publishing Company, 1949.

Zammuto, Rick. *Inventory and Management Plan, Robson Valley Wildlife Habitat Management Area "3155".* Unpublished report prepared for the Fish and Wildlife Branch, Northern Interior Region, B.C. Ministry of Environment, Lands and Parks, 1993.

CHAPTER 2

Chapman, John D. "The Evolution of British Columbia's Energy System and Implications for the Fraser Basin." In *Perspectives on Sustainable Development in Water Management.*

Foster, Bristol. "The Importance of British Columbia to Global Biodiversity." In *Our Living Legacy: Proceedings of a Symposium on Biological Diversity,* edited by M. A. Fenger et al. Victoria: Royal British Columbia Museum, 1993.

Hammond, Herb. *Seeing the Forest among the Trees: The Case for Wholistic Forest Use.* Vancouver: Polestar Press, 1991.

Harding, Lee E. "Threats to Diversity of Forest Ecosystems in British Columbia." In *Biodiversity in British Columbia,* edited by Lee E. Harding and Emily McCullum. Ottawa: Environment Canada, 1994.

Harding, Lee E., and Emily McCullum. "Overview of Ecosystem Diversity." In *Biodiversity in British Columbia.*

Hume, Stephen. "Habitat protection in fumbling hands." In the *Vancouver Sun,* October 5, 1996.

Hutchison, Bruce. *The Fraser.*

Lamb, W. Kaye (ed.). *The Journals and Letters of Sir Alexander Mackenzie.* London: Cambridge University Press, 1970.

Leopold, Aldo. *A Sand County Almanac.* New York: Oxford University Press, 1949.

Moore, R. Daniel. "Hydrology and Water Supply in the Fraser River Basin." In *Water in Sustainable Development.*

Newbury, Robert W., and Marc N. Gaboury. *Stream Analysis and Fish Habitat Design.* Gibsons, B.C.: Newbury Hydraulics Ltd., 1993.

Richardson, Boyce. *People of Terra Nullius.* Vancouver: Douglas & McIntyre, 1993.

Roberts, Jane. *The Codex Hammer of Leonardo da Vinci: The Waters, the Earth, the Universe.* Catalogue for a 1982 exhibit in the Palazzo Vecchio, Florence. Los Angeles: The Armand Hammer Foundation, 1981.

Roos, John F. *Restoring Fraser River Salmon.* Vancouver: The Pacific Salmon Commission, 1992.

Ryan, John. A report by *Northwest Environment Watch* (State of Washington). CBC Radio news, December 12, 1995.

Savard, Jean-Pierre L. "Birds of the Fraser Basin in Sustainable Development." In *Perspectives on Sustainable Development in Water Management.*

Wade, M. S. *The Overlanders of '62.*

Watson, Lyall. *The Water Planet.*

West, Willis J. *Stagecoach and Sternwheel Days in the Cariboo and Central B.C.* Surrey, B.C.: Heritage House Publishing, 1985.

Wheeler, Marilyn J. (ed). *The Robson Valley Story.*

CHAPTER 3

Boyanowsky, Ehor. "Water Wars: Public Responses to Environmental Threat." In *Water Export: Should Canada's Water Be for Sale?* Cambridge, Ont.: The Canadian Water Resources Association, 1992.

Burt, D. W., and J. H. Mundie. "Case Histories of Regulated Stream Flow and Its Effects on Salmonid Populations." *Can. Tech. Rep. Fish. Aquat. Sci.*, 1477 (1986).

Day, J. C., and Frank Quinn. *Water Diversion and Export: Learning from Canadian Experience.* Waterloo, Ont.: Department of Geography, University of Waterloo, 1992.

Fraser River Sockeye 1994: Problems and Discrepancies. Report of the Fraser River Sockeye Public Review Board, Hon. John A. Fraser, Chairman. Ottawa: Public Works and Government Services Canada, 1995.

Gomez-Amaral, J. C., and J. C. Day. "The Kemano Diversion: A Hindsight Assessment." In *Proceedings of the Symposium on Interbasin Transfer of Water: Impacts and Research Needs for Canada,* edited by W. Nicholaichuk and F. Quinn. Saskatoon: National Hydrology Research Centre and Canadian Water Resources Association, 1987.

Harrington, Robert F. "Thoughts on an Earth Ethic." In *Biodiversity in British Columbia.*

Henderson, Michael A. "Sustainable Development of the Pacific Salmon Resources in the Fraser River Basin." In *Perspectives on Sustainable Development in Water Management.*

Holling, C. S. *An Ecologist's View of the Malthusian Conflict.* A lecture presented at the Population-Environment-Development series of the Royal Swedish Academy of Sciences, Stockholm. 1993.

Holling, C. S. (ed.). *Adaptive Environmental Assessment and Management.* Laxenburg, Austria: International Institute for Applied Systems Analysis and John Wiley & Sons, 1978.

Hume, Mark. *The Run of the River.* Vancouver: New Star Books, 1992.

Kellerhalls, Rolf. "Morphologic Effects of Interbasin Diversions." In *Proceedings of the Symposium on Interbasin Transfer of Water.*

Lamb, W. Kaye (ed.). *The Letters and Journals of Simon Fraser 1806–1808.* Toronto: Macmillan, 1960.

Moss, Pat. Interview in *Trading Futures.* CBC Television documentary, produced by Michael Poole, 1993.

Northcote, Thomas G., and Burwash, Michael D. "Fish and Fish Habitats of the Fraser River Basin." In *Water in Sustainable Development.*

Overstall, Richard. Interview in *Trading Futures.*

Potential Effects of the Kemano Completion Project on Fraser River Sockeye and Pink Salmon. International Pacific Salmon Fisheries Commission, 1983.

Rankin, Murray. *Alcan's Kemano Project: Options and Recommendations.* A report commissioned by the Government of British Columbia, 1992.

Rees, William E., and Mathis Wackernagel. "Ecological Footprints and Appropriated Carrying Capacity: Measuring the Natural Capital Requirements of the Human Economy." In *Investing in Natural Capital: The Ecological Economics Approach to Sustainability,* edited by A. M. Jannson et al. Washington, D.C.: Island Press, 1994.

Richardson, Boyce. *People of Terra Nullius.*

Robertson, Mike. *The Story of the Surrender of the Cheslatta Reserves on April 21, 1952.* Burns Lake, B.C.: Cheslatta Carrier Nation, 1993.

Romain, Janet. Interview in *Trading Futures.*

Schmidt-Bleek, F., and H. Wohlmeyer. "Trade and the Environment: Report on a Study." In *Costly Tradeoffs: Reconciling Trade and the Environment,* Worldwatch Paper 113. Washington, D.C.: Worldwatch Institute, 1993.

Shirvell, Cole. Testimony at hearings of the B.C. Utilities Commission, May 30, 1994.

West, Willis J. *Stagecoach and Sternwheel Days in the Cariboo and Central B.C.*

CHAPTER 4

Cross-Country Checkup, CBC Radio, August 23, 1993.

Daly, Herman E. "Elements of Environmental Macroeconomics." In *Ecological Economics: The Science and Management of Sustainability,* edited by Robert Costanza. New York: Columbia University Press, 1991.

Downs, Art. *Wagon Road North.* Surrey, B.C.: Heritage House Publishing, 1960.

Durning, Allan. "Redesigning the Forest Economy." In *State of the World 1994.* New York: W. W. Norton & Company and Worldwatch Institute, 1994.

Goward, Trevor. 1995. *Macrolichens of the Oldgrowth Forests of the Robson Valley. Part 1: Goat River to Ptarmigan Creek.* Report prepared for the Robson Forest District, June 1995.

Haig-Brown, Roderick. *Measure of the Year.* Don Mills, Ont.: Wm. Collins Sons & Co., 1950.

Hammond, Herb. *Seeing the Forest among the Trees.*

Harding, Lee E. "Threats to Diversity of Forest Ecosystems in British Columbia." In *Biodiversity in British Columbia.*

Hutchison, Bruce. *The Fraser.*

Jobs, Trees & Us: The P.P.W.C.'s Forest Policy. Vancouver: The Pulp, Paper and Wood-workers of Canada, 1993.

Johnson, Byron. *Very Far West Indeed,* 1872. Quoted in Robin Skelton, *They Call It the Cariboo.* Victoria: Sono Nis Press, 1980.

Lamb, W. Kaye, (ed.). *The Journals and Letters of Sir Alexander Mackenzie.*

Lamb, W. Kaye, (ed.). *The Letters and Journals of Simon Fraser.*

Leopold, Aldo. *A Sand County Almanac.*

M'Gonigle, Michael, and Ben Parfitt. *Forestopia: A Practical Guide to the New Forest Economy.* Madeira Park, B.C.: Harbour Publishing, 1994.

Mahood, Ian, and Ken Drushka. *Three Men and a Forester.* Madeira Park, B.C.: Harbour Publishing, 1990.

Marchak, Patricia. *Green Gold: The Forest Industry in British Columbia.* Vancouver: University of British Columbia Press, 1983.

Marchak, Patricia. "A Global Context for British Columbia." In *Touch Wood.*

Maser, Chris. *The Redesigned Forest.* Toronto: Stoddart Publishing, 1990.

Meadows, Donella H., Dennis L. Meadows and Jorgen Randers. *Beyond the Limits: Confronting Global Collapse, Envisioning a Sustainable Future.* Toronto: McClelland & Stewart, 1992.

Outdoor Recreation Survey 1989/90: How British Columbians Use and Value Their Public Forest Lands for Recreation. Recreation Branch Technical Report 1, B.C. Ministry of Forests, 1991

Pielou, E. C. "A Clear Cut Decision." In *Nature Canada,* Spring (1996).

Roos, John F. *Restoring Fraser River Salmon.*

Schreier, H., S. J. Brown, and K. J. Hall. "The Land-Water Interface in the Fraser River Basin." In *Water in Sustainable Development.*

Sierra Legal Defence Fund. *Newsletter No. 13* (April 1996).

Skelton, Robin. *They Call It the Cariboo.* Victoria: Sono Nis Press, 1980.

Stangoe, Irene. *Cariboo-Chilcotin: Pioneer People and Places.* Surrey, B.C.: Heritage House Publishing, 1994.

State of the Fraser Basin: Assessing Progress Towards Sustainability. Vancouver: The Fraser Basin Management Board, June 1995.

The Future of Our Forests. A report to the Government of British Columbia by the B.C. Forest Resources Commission, 1991.

The State of Canada's Environment. Ottawa: Environment Canada, 1991.

Travers, O. R. "Forest Policy: Rhetoric and Reality." In *Touch Wood.*

"A Vision for the Future." A 1989 report of the Forest Planning Committee of the Science Council of B.C. Quoted in O. R. Travers, "Forest Policy: Rhetoric and Reality." In *Touch Wood: B.C. Forests at the Crossroads,* edited by Ken Drushka, Bob Nixon and Ray Travers. Madeira Park, B.C.: Harbour Publishing, 1993.

Williams, Ian. Quoted in the *Quesnel Cariboo Observer,* July 20, 1994.

CHAPTER 5

Chateaubriand, François R. de. Quoted in David W. Orr, *Ecological Literacy: Education and the Transition to a Postmodern World.* Albany, N.Y.: State University of New York Press, 1992.

Cherrington, John A. *The Fraser Valley: A History.* Madeira Park, B.C.: Harbour Publishing. 1992.

Clemson, Donovan. "Pioneer Fences." In *Pioneer Days in British Columbia*, Vol. 2., edited by Art Downs. Surrey, B.C.: Heritage House Publishing, 1975–1979.

Downs, Art. *Wagon Road North.*

Economic Benefits of British Columbia Parks. A report by Coopers & Lybrand Consulting for the B.C. Ministry of Environment, Lands and Parks. April, 1995.

Eliot, T. S. "The Dry Salvages." In *T. S. Eliot: The Complete Poems and Plays.* London: Faber and Faber, 1969.

Glavin, Terry. *Nemiah: The Unconquered Country.* Vancouver: New Star Books, 1992.

Hammond, Herb. *Seeing the Forest among the Trees.*

Hebda, Richard. "The Future of British Columbia's Flora." In *Biodiversity in British Columbia.*

Koster, Henry. "This Is a Brief History of the Empire Valley Ranch—How It Was Put Together." Unpublished manuscript, c. 1990.

Lamb, W. Kaye (ed.). *The Letters and Journals of Simon Fraser.*

Lee, Norman. *Klondike Cattle Drive.* Vancouver: Mitchell Press, 1960.

McLean, Alastair. "History of the Cattle Industry in British Columbia." In *Rangelands,* Vol. 4, No. 3 (June 1982).

Pitt, Michael, and Tracey D. Hooper. "Threats to Biodiversity of Grasslands in British Columbia." In *Biodiversity in British Columbia.*

Roos, John F. *Restoring Fraser River Salmon.*

Savard, Jean-Pierre L. "Birds of the Fraser Basin in Sustainable Development." In *Perspectives on Sustainable Development in Water Management.*

Shewchuk, Murphy. *Backroads Explorer: Thompson-Cariboo.* Vancouver: Maclean-Hunter, 1985.

Skelton, Robin. *They Call It the Cariboo.*

Slaymaker, Olav. "Implications of the Processes of Erosion and Sedimentation for Sustainable Development in the Fraser River Basin." In *Perspectives on Sustainable Development in Water Management.*

CHAPTER 6

Basque, Garnet. *Fraser Canyon and Bridge River Valley.* Langley, B.C.: Sunfire Publications, 1985.

CBC Radio news, March 15, 1995.

Dietrich, William. *Northwest Passage: The Great Columbia River.*

Edwards, Irene. *Short Portage to Lillooet.* Mission, B.C.: Cold Spring Books, 1977 (second revised printing, 1985).

Haig-Brown, Roderick. "The Fraser Watershed and the Moran Proposal." In *Nature Canada,* Vol. 1, No. 2 (April/June 1972).

Harding, Lee E. "Threats to Diversity of Forest Ecosystems in British Columbia." In *Biodiversity in British Columbia.*

Holling, C. S. (ed.). *Adaptive Environmental Assessment and Management.*

Krutilla, John V. *The Columbia River Treaty.* Baltimore: Johns Hopkins Press, 1976.

Lamb, W. Kaye (ed.). *The Letters and Journals of Simon Fraser.*

Lee, Kai N. "Deliberately Seeking Sustainability in the Columbia River Basin." In *Barriers and Bridges to the Renewal of Ecosystems and Institutions,* edited by L. H. Gunderson, C. S. Holling and S. S. Light. New York: Columbia University Press, 1995.

M'Gonigle, Michael, and Wendy Wickwire. *Stein: The Way of the River.* Vancouver: Talonbooks, 1988.

Moran Dam and the Fraser River Fishery. Canada: Department of the Environment (Fisheries Service) and the International Pacific Salmon Fisheries Commission, 1971.

Nisbet, Jack. *Sources of the River: Tracking David Thompson Across Western North America.* Seattle: Sasquatch Books, 1994.

Northcote, T. G., and P. A. Larkin. "The Fraser River: A Major Salmonine Production System." In *Proceedings of the International Large River Symposium.*

Obee, Bruce. "Hell-bent on the Fraser: Exploring the Middle Reaches of B.C.'s Mightiest River." In *Beautiful British Columbia.* Vol. 36, No. 1 (Spring 1994).

Quinn, Frank. "As Long as the Rivers Run: The Impacts of Corporate Water Development on Native Communities in Canada." In *The Canadian Journal of Native Studies,* Vol. 11, No. 1 (1991).

Roos, John F. *Restoring Fraser River Salmon.*

State of the Environment Report for British Columbia. Victoria: B.C. Ministry of Environment, Lands and Parks, and Environment Canada, 1993.

Thoreau, Henry David. An address to the Harvard graduating class, 1837. In *Familiar Letters of Henry David Thoreau,* edited by F. B. Sanborn. Boston and New York: Houghton Mifflin, 1894. Quoted in Wendell Berry, *What Are People For?* San Francisco: North Point Press, 1990.

Worster, Donald. *Rivers of Empire: Water, Aridity, and the Growth of the American West.* New York: Pantheon, 1985. Quoted in Kai N. Lee, "Deliberately Seeking Sustainability in the Columbia River Basin." In *Barriers and Bridges.*

CHAPTER 7

Boyanowsky, Ehor. "Water Wars: Public Responses to Environmental Threat." In *Water Export: Should Canada's Water Be for Sale?*

CBC Radio news, December 8, 1995.

Childerhose, R. J., and Marj Trim. *Pacific Salmon.* Vancouver: Douglas & McIntyre, 1979.

Coffey, J. et al *Shuswap History: The First 100 Years of Contact.* Kamloops, B.C.: Secwepemc Cultural Education Society, 1990

Dale, Norman G. "The Quest for Consensus on Sustainable Development in the Use and Management of Fraser River Salmon." In *Perspectives on Sustainable Development in Water Management.*

Fraser and Thompson River Canyons. Surrey, B.C.: Heritage House Publishing, 1986.

Haig-Brown, Alan. "The River Spirit." Foreword to *Adam's River* by Mark Hume. Vancouver: New Star Books, 1994.

Healy, Michael. "The Importance of Fresh Water Inflows to Coastal Ecosystems. In *Water Export: Should Canada's Water Be for Sale?*

Hume, Mark. *The Run of the River.*

Hutchison, Bruce. *The Fraser.*

Kew, Michael J.E., and Julian R. Griggs. "Native Indians of the Fraser Basin." In *Perspectives on Sustainable Development in Water Management.*

M'Gonigle, Michael, and Wendy Wickwire. *Stein: The Way of the River.*

Palmer, Tim. *The Snake River: Window to the West.* Washington, D.C.: Island Press, 1991.

Roos, John F. *Restoring Fraser River Salmon.*

Schreier, Hans, et al. "The Land-Water Interface in the Fraser River Basin." In *Water in Sustainable Development.*

Shewchuk, Murphy. *Backroads Explorer: Thompson-Cariboo.*

Teit, James. *The Shuswap.*

Thompson, Andrew R. "Aboriginal Rights and Sustainable Development in the Fraser-Thompson Corridor." In *Perspectives on Sustainable Development in Water Management.*

Wade, Mark S. *The Overlanders of '62.*

Wenger, Ferdi. "The Homesteaders." In *Pioneer Days in British Columbia,* Vol. 2.

Yarmie, Andrew H. "Smallpox and the British Columbia Indians, Epidemic of 1862." In *British Columbia Library Association Quarterly,* No. 31. Quoted in Michael M'Gonigle and Wendy Wickwire, *Stein: The Way of the River.*

CHAPTER 8

Berton, Pierre. *The Last Spike.* Toronto: McClelland and Stewart, 1971.

Childerhose, R. J., and Marj Trim. *Pacific Salmon.*

Creighton, Donald. *John A. Macdonald: The Old Chieftain.* Toronto: Macmillan, 1955.

Fraser River Sockeye 1994: Problems and Discrepancies. Report of the Fraser River Sockeye Public Review Board.

Glavin, Terry. *Dead Reckoning: Confronting the Crisis in Pacific Fisheries.* Vancouver: Douglas & McIntyre and the David Suzuki Foundation, 1996.

Harris, Cole. "The Lower Mainland, 1820–81" In *Vancouver and Its Region,* edited by Graeme Wynn and Timothy Oke. Vancouver: University of British Columbia Press, 1992.

Hume, Mark. *Adam's River: The Mystery of the Adams River Sockeye.* Vancouver: New Star Books, 1994.

Hutchinson, Bruce. *The Fraser.*

Hutchinson, Bruce. *The Struggle for the Border.* Toronto: Longman Canada, 1955.

Kew, Michael J. E., and Julian R. Griggs, "Native Indians of the Fraser Basin." In *Perspectives on Sustainable Development in Water Management.*

Lamb, W. Kaye (ed.). *The Letters and Journals of Simon Fraser.*

Lao Tsu. *Tao Te Ching.* Translation by Gia-Fu Feng and Jane English. Toronto: Random House, 1972.

M'Gonigle, Michael, and Wendy Wickwire. *Stein: The Way of the River.*

Meggs, Geoff. *Salmon: The Decline of the British Columbia Fishery.* Vancouver: Douglas & McIntyre, 1991.

Nowry, Laurence. *Man of Mana: Marius Barbeau.* Toronto: NC Press, 1995.

Public Archives of Canada, Department of Marine and Fisheries File 4572, A. W. R. Wilby to Agent, Marine and Fisheries, 29 Sept. 1913.

Regehr, T. D. *The Canadian Northern Railway.* Toronto: Macmillan, 1976.

Salute to the Sockeye. New Westminster, B.C.: International Pacific Salmon Fisheries Commission, 1974.

Slaymaker, Olav. "Implications of the Processes of Erosion and Sedimentation for Sustainable Development in the Fraser River Basin." In *Perspectives on Sustainable Development in Water Management.*

Teit, James Alexander. *The Thompson Indians of British Columbia.* New York: AMS Press, 1900.

Woodcock, George. *British Columbia: A History of the Province.*

CHAPTER 9

Birtwell, I. K. et al. "A Review of Fish Habitat Issues in the Fraser River System." *Water Poll. Research J. Canada,* Vol. 23, No. 1. (1988).

Boeckh, Ian et al. "Human Settlement and Development in the Fraser River Basin." In *Water in Sustainable Development.*

Butler, Robert W., and R. Wayne Campbell. *The Birds of the Fraser River Delta: Populations, Ecology, and International Significance.* Occasional Paper No. 65, Canadian Wildlife Service (1987).

CBC Radio news, September 5, 1995.

CBC Television news, B.C. Region. May 15, 1995.

Cherrington, John A. *The Fraser Valley.*

Childerhose, R. J., and Marj Trim. *Pacific Salmon.*

Country Life in British Columbia, January (1991).

Edwards, Irene. *Short Portage to Lillooet.*

Eisen, Jill (producer). "Biotechnology's Harvest." Broadcast on CBC Radio's *Ideas,* March 15 and 22, 1994.

Myers, Norman (ed.). *Gaia: An Atlas of Planet Management.* New York: Doubleday & Company, 1984.

Harris, Cole. "The Lower Mainland, 1820–81." In *Vancouver and Its Region.*

Hawken, Paul. *The Ecology of Commerce.* New York: HarperCollins, 1993.

Henderson, Michael A. "Sustainable Development of the Pacific Salmon Resources in the Fraser River Basin" In *Perspectives on Sustainable Development in Water Management.*

Holm, Wendy. "What Do These Farmers Want Anyway?" *Country Life in British Columbia,* September (1994).

Hutchison, Bruce. *The Fraser.*

Kennedy, Paul. *Preparing for the Twenty-First Century.* Toronto: HarperCollins, 1993.

Kew, Michael J. E., and Julian R. Griggs, "Native Indians of the Fraser Basin." In *Perspectives on Sustainable Development in Water Management.*

Meggs, Geoff. *Salmon.*

Milbrath, Lester. *Envisioning a Sustainable Society.* Albany, N.Y.: State University of New York Press, 1989.

North, Margaret. *Ecostudy of the Fraser Delta.* Unpublished manuscript, Dept. of Geography, University of British Columbia, 1970.

Northcote, T. G., and P. A. Larkin. "The Fraser River: A Major Salmonine Production System." In *Proceedings of the International Large River Symposium.*

Orr, David W. *Ecological Literacy.* Albany, N.Y.: State University of New York Press, 1992.

Ours to Preserve. The Boundary Bay Conservation Committee, 1992.

Rees, William E. "Why Preserve Agricultural Land?" A paper prepared for the B.C. Agricultural Land Commission, 1993.

Regier, Henry A. et al. "Rehabilitation of Degraded River Ecosystems." In *Proceedings of the International Large River Symposium.*

Rowe, J. Stan. "The Importance of Conserving Systems." In *Biodiversity in British Columbia.*

Rowe, J. Stan. *Home Place: Essays on Ecology.* Edmonton: NeWest Publishers Ltd., 1990.

Salatin, Joe. "Diversifying for Production and Profit." *Holistic Resource Management Quarterly,* Spring/April (1995).

Schreier, Hans et al. "The Land-Water Interface in the Fraser River Basin." In *Water in Sustainable Development.*

Schumacher, E. F. *Small is Beautiful.* New York: Harper & Row, 1973.

Stackhouse, John. "Severe Food Shortage Forecast." In the *Globe and Mail,* July 11, 1996.

The State of Canada's Environment. Ottawa: Government of Canada, 1991.

State of the Environment for the Lower Fraser River Basin, SOE Report No. 92-1. Ottawa: Environment Canada, and B.C. Ministry of Environment, Lands and Parks, 1992.

State of the Environment Report for British Columbia. Victoria: B.C. Ministry of Environment, Lands and Parks, and Environment Canada, 1993.

Stewart, Hilary. *Cedar.* Vancouver: Douglas & McIntyre, 1984.

Whose Common Future? Gabriola Island, B.C.: New Society Publishers, 1993.

Woodcock, George. *British Columbia: A History of the Province.*

CHAPTER 10

Berry, Wendell. *The Unsettling of America.* San Francisco: Sierra Club Books, 1977 (Sierra edition 1986).

Birtwell, I. K. et al. "A Review of Fish Habitat Issues in the Fraser River System."

Boyanowsky, Ehor. "To Save B.C.'s Salmon." In the *Globe and Mail,* May 30, 1996.

Butler, R. W. (ed.). *Abundance, Distribution and Conservation of Birds in the Vicinity of Boundary Bay, British Columbia.* Technical Report Series No. 155, Canadian Wildlife Service, Pacific and Yukon Region (1992).

Butler, Robert W., and R. Wayne Campbell. *The Birds of the Fraser River Delta.*

CBC Radio news, January 10, 1995.

CBC Radio news, July 17, 1996.

CBC Radio news, April 21, 1994.

Cherrington, John A. *The Fraser Valley.*

Childerhose, R. J., and Marj Trim. *Pacific Salmon.*

Clague, John J., and John L. Luternauer. "Where the River Meets the Sea: Studies of the Fraser Delta." In *Geos,* Vol. 11, No. 2 (Spring 1982).

Clarke, Richard E. *Point Roberts, USA: The History of a Canadian Enclave.* Bellingham, WA: Textype Publishing, 1980.

Cox, Kevin. "National Sea Has a Rare Catch: A Profit." In the *Globe and Mail,* May 11, 1995.

Dorcey, Anthony H. J. "Water in the Sustainable Development of the Fraser River Basin." In *Water in Sustainable Development.*

Ellis, David W. et al. *Net Loss: The Salmon Netcage Industry in British Columbia.* Vancouver: The David Suzuki Foundation, 1996.

Environmentally Important Sites in the Greater Vancouver Regional District. Vancouver: Federation of British Columbia Naturalists, 1992.

Fraser Basin Ecosystem Study, Annual Report 1993–1994. Vancouver: Westwater Research Centre, UBC.

Fraser River Sockeye 1994: Problems and Discrepancies. Report of the Fraser River Sockeye Public Review Board.

Georgia Basin Initiative: Creating a Sustainable Future. B.C. Round Table on the Environment and the Economy, May 1993.

Georgison, J. Paul, and J. C. Day. *Protecting Our Waters, or Protecting the System?*

Assessing Institutional Arrangements for Water Quality Management in British Colum-bia. Aquatic Resources Research Project Subcomponent VA. Burnaby: School of Resource and Environmental Management, SFU, 1993.

Glavin, Terry. *Dead Reckoning.*

Guerin, Glen. "Environmentalism as the New Colonialism? A Musqueam Perspec-tive." In *The New Catalyst,* (Spring 1994).

Hawken, Paul. *The Ecology of Commerce.*

Healy, Michael. "The Importance of Fresh Water Inflows to Coastal Ecosystems." In *Water Export: Should Canada's Water Be for Sale?*

Henderson, Michael A. "Sustainable Development of the Pacific Salmon Resources in the Fraser River Basin." In *Perspectives on Sustainable Development in Water Management.*

Hume, Mark. *Adam's River.*

Keeley, Martin. In the *Vancouver Sun,* April 25, 1996.

Kennedy, Des. "The Fraser Delta in Jeopardy." In *Canadian Geographic* (Aug./Sept. 1986).

Kennett, Kristal, and Michael W. McPhee. *The Fraser River Estuary: An Overview of Changing Conditions.* New Westminster, B.C.: Fraser River Estuary Management Program, 1988.

Kreutzwiser, R. et al. "Perceptions of Flood Hazard and Floodplain Development Regulations in Glen Williams, Ontario." In *Canadian Water Resources Journal,* Vol. 19, No. 2 (1994).

Lamb, W. Kaye (ed.). *The Letters and Journals of Simon Fraser.*

Langer, Otto E. *Application of the Concept of No Net Loss to the Management of Fish Habitats in the Fraser River Estuary.* Paper presented at the Eighth Annual Sub-merged Lands Management Conference, South Padre Island, Texas (Oct. 1989).

Linton, Jamie. "The Flood of '93: Mother Nature Fights Back." In *Canadian Water Watch.* Ottawa: The Rawson Academy of Aquatic Science (Sept./Oct. 1993).

Log Management in the Fraser River Estuary. New Westminster, B.C.: Fraser River Estuary Management Program, 1991.

McConnell, Hew D. "Planning for Metropolitan Liquid Waste Management in the GVRD: An Innovative Approach Towards Sustainable Development." In *Perspectives on Sustainable Development in Water Management.*

Meggs, Geoff. *Salmon.*

Meggs, Geoff, and Duncan Stacey. *Cork Lines and Canning Lines.* Vancouver: Dou-glas & McIntyre, 1992.

Moore, Jennie Lynn. *What's Stopping Sustainability? Examining the Barriers to Imple-mentation of "Clouds of Change."* Thesis submitted in partial fulfilment of the requirements for an M.A. in Planning, University of British Columbia, 1994.

North, Margaret. *Ecostudy of the Fraser Delta.*

Northcote, T. G., and P. A. Larkin. "The Fraser River: A Major Salmonine Pro-duction System." In *Proceedings of the International Large River Symposium.*

Ours to Preserve. Boundary Bay Conservation Committee.

Pinkerton, Evelyn, and Martin Weinstein. *Fisheries That Work: Sustainability through Community-Based Management.* Vancouver: The David Suzuki Foundation, 1995.

Savard, Jean-Pierre L. "Birds of the Fraser Basin in Sustainable Development." In *Perspectives on Sustainable Development in Water Management.*

Schreier, Hans et al. "The Land-Water Interface in the Fraser River Basin." In *Water in Sustainable Development.*

Slaymaker, O. et al. "The Primordial Environment." In *Vancouver and Its Region.*

Smith, Sandra E. "Floodplain Management in the Fraser Basin." In *Perspectives on Sustainable Development in Water Management.*

State of the Environment Report for British Columbia. Victoria: B.C. Ministry of Environment, Lands and Parks, and Environment Canada, 1993.

Stream Stewardship: A Guide for Planners and Developers. Ottawa: Department of Fisheries and Oceans, and B.C. Ministry of Environment, Lands and Parks, and Ministry of Municipal Affairs, 1996.

Surrey/North Delta Now. Pamphlet published by the Burns Bog Conservation Society, July 25, 1992.

The State of Canada's Environment. Ottawa: Government of Canada. 1991.

"The State of Food and Agriculture 1993." Food and Agriculture Organization, Rome. Quoted in Lester R. Brown and Hal Kane, *Full House.* New York: W. W. Norton and Worldwatch Institute, 1993.

Summary of the Task Force Review of the Fraser River Flood Control Program. Vancouver: Fraser Basin Management Program, May 1994.

Thompson, Richard. "Strait of Georgia." In *Oceanography of the British Columbia Coast. Can. Spec. Publ. Fish. Aquat. Sci.,* 56 (1981).

Walters, Carl. *Fish on the Line: The Future of Pacific Fisheries.* Vancouver: The David Suzuki Foundation, 1995.

White, Gilbert F. "Human Adjustment to Floods." In *Geography, Resources, and Environment: Selected Writings of Gilbert F. White,* edited by R.W. Kates and Ian Burton. Chicago: The University of Chicago Press, 1986.

CHAPTER II

Brown, Paul. *The Guardian,* London, reprinted in the *Vancouver Sun,* July 5, 1996.

Clack, Rod. *Victoria Times-Colonist,* January 16, 1995.

Costanza, Robert et al. "Sustainable Trade: A New Paradigm for World Welfare." In *Environment,* Vol. 37, No. 5 (June 1995).

Creating Our Future: Steps to a More Livable Region. Burnaby, B.C.: Greater Vancouver Regional District, 1993.

The Fraser River Action Plan. Progress Report, 1994–1995. Ottawa: Environment Canada, Fisheries and Oceans Canada.

Georgia Basin Initiative: Creating a Sustainable Future. B.C. Round Table on the Environment and the Economy, May 1993.

Globe and Mail, July 22, 1996.

Hammond, Herb. *Seeing the Forest among the Trees.*

Harding, Lee E., and Taylor, Eric. "Atmospheric Change in British Columbia." In *Biodiversity in British Columbia.*

Harding, Lee E. "Threats to Biodiversity in the Strait of Georgia." In *Biodiversity in British Columbia.*

Hebda, Richard. "The Future of British Columbia's Flora." In *Biodiversity in British Columbia.*

Harding, Lee E. "Threats to Diversity of Forest Ecosystems in British Columbia." In *Biodiversity in British Columbia.*

Hiss, Tony. *The Experience of Place.* New York: Alfred A. Knopf, 1990.

Holling, C. S. "The Resilience of Terrestrial Ecosystems: Local Surprise and Global Change." In *Sustainable Development of the Biosphere,* edited by W. Clark and R. Munn. Cambridge: Cambridge University Press, with the International Institute for Applied Systems Analysis, Laxenburg, Austria, 1986.

Holling, C. S. "What Barriers? What Bridges?" In *Barriers and Bridges.*

Hutton, Thomas A., and H. Craig Davis. "Prospects for Vancouver's Sustainable Development: An Economic Perspective." In *Perspectives on Sustainable Development in Water Management.*

Jacobs, Jane. *Cities and the Wealth of Nations.* Markham, Ont.: Penguin Books, 1984.

Livable Region Strategy: Proposals. Burnaby, B.C.: Greater Vancouver Regional District, 1993.

A Long-Range Transportation Plan for Greater Vancouver. GVRD and the Province of British Columbia: A Transport 2021 Report, September 1993.

Mathews, Jessica. "What's Still in Doubt about Global Warming." In the *Washington Post,* reprinted in the *Vancouver Sun,* December 29, 1995.

Meadows, Donella H., Dennis L. Meadows and Jorgen Randers. *Beyond the Limits.*

Myers, Norman (ed.). *Gaia: An Atlas of Planet Management.* Garden City, N.Y.: Anchor Press, 1984.

North, Robert N., and Walter G. Hardwick. "Vancouver Since the Second World War." In *Vancouver and Its Region.*

Orr, David W. *Ecological Literacy.*

Perkins, Ellie. "Building Communities to Limit Trade." In *Alternatives,* Vol. 22, No. 1 (Jan./Feb. 1996).

Perlman, Michael. "Animosity to Imagination Marks Early Response to Global Warming." In the *Los Angeles Times,* reprinted in the *Vancouver Sun,* January 6, 1996.

Rees, William E. "Ecological Footprints and Appropriated Carrying Capacity: What Urban Economics Leaves Out." In *Environment and Urbanization,* Vol. 4, No. 2 (October 1992).

Rees, William E. "Why Preserve Agricultural Land?"

Rees, William E., and Mark Roseland. "Sustainable Communities: Planning for the 21st Century." In *Plan Canada,* Vol. 31, No. 3 (May 1991).

Rees, William E., and Mathis Wackernagel. "Ecological Footprints and Appropriated Carrying Capacity: Measuring the Natural Capital Requirements of the Human Economy." In *Investing in Natural Capital.*

Sale, Kirkpatrick. *Dwellers in the Land: The Bioregional Vision.* Gabriola Island, B.C.: New Society Publishers, 1991.

Schoon, Nicholas. In *The Independent,* London, reprinted in the *Vancouver Sun,* December 28, 1995.

Schreier, Hans et al. "The Land-Water Interface in the Fraser River Basin." In *Water in Sustainable Development.*

The State of Canada's Environment. Ottawa: Environment Canada, 1991.

State of the Environment Report for British Columbia. Victoria: B.C. Ministry of Environment, Lands and Parks, and Environment Canada, 1993.

State of Sustainability: Urban Sustainability and Containment. B.C. Round Table on the Environment and the Economy, 1994.

Wackernagel, Mathis, and William Rees. *Our Ecological Footprint: Reducing Human Impact on the Earth.* Gabriola Island, B.C.: New Society Publishers, 1996.

Waldron, John. *The Fraser River Estuary: A Wildlife Site Under Threat.* A report for the Royal Society for the Protection of Birds, World Wildlife Fund, 1991.

Whose Common Future? Gabriola Island, B.C.: New Society Publishers, 1993.

Wilson, Edward O. *The Diversity of Life.* New York: W. W. Norton, 1992.

World's Leading Scientists Issue Urgent Warning to Humanity. Union of Concerned Scientists, Washington D.C., November 18, 1992.

Wynn, Graeme. "The Rise of Vancouver." In *Vancouver and Its Region.*

CHAPTER 12

Berg, Peter. "Growing a Life-Place Politics." In *Home! A Bioregional Reader.* Gabriola Island, B.C.: New Society Publishers, 1990.

Birtwell, I. K. et al. *A Review of Fish Habitat Issues in the Fraser River System.*

Boothroyd, Peter. "Distribution Principles for Compassionate Sustainable Development." In *Perspectives on Sustainable Development in Water Management.*

Costanza, Robert. "Assuring Sustainability of Ecological Economic Systems." In *Ecological Economics.*

Crombie, David. On *The Nature of Things,* CBC Television, August 17, 1995.

Daly, Herman E. "Elements of Environmental Macroeconomics." In *Ecological Economics.*

Fox, Irving K. "Institutional Design for the Management of the Natural Resources of the Fraser River Basin." In *Perspectives on Sustainable Development in Water Management.*

Gardner, Julia E. "Environmental Non-Government Organizations and Management of Water Resources in the Fraser River Basin." In *Water in Sustainable Development.*

Hardin, Garrett. "Paramount Positions in Ecological Economics." In *Ecological Economics.*

Healy, Michael C. Foreword to *Water in Sustainable Development.*

Holling, C. S. "An Ecologist's View of the Malthusian Conflict." In *Population, Economic Development and the Environment,* edited by K. Lindahl-Kiessling and H. Landberg. New York: Oxford University Press, 1994.

Holling, C. S., and Stephen Bocking. "Surprise and Opportunity." In *Planet Under Stress: The Challenge of Global Change,* edited by C. Mungall and D. J. McLaren. Don Mills, Ont.: Oxford University Press and Royal Society of Canada, 1990.

Jacobs, Michael. *The Green Economy: Environment, Sustainable Development and the Politics of the Future.* Vancouver: University of British Columbia Press, 1993.

McKibben, Bill. *The End of Nature.* New York: Anchor Books, 1989.

McLaren, D. J. *Newsletter of the Canadian Global Change Program,* 1 (1): 11–12. Quoted in *The State of Canada's Environment.* Ottawa: Environment Canada, 1991.

Meadows, Donella H., Dennis L. Meadows and Jorgen Randers. *Beyond the Limits.*

Northcote, Thomas G., and Burwash, Michael D. "Fish and Fish Habitats of the Fraser River Basin." In *Water in Sustainable Development.*

Orr, David W. *Ecological Literacy.*

Pearse, Peter H., and Tate, Donald M. "Economic Instruments for Sustainable Development of Water Resources." In *Perspectives on Sustainable Development in Water Management.*

Rees, William E. "The Ecological Basis for Sustainable Development in the Fraser Basin." In *Perspectives on Sustainable Development in Water Management.*

Rees, William E. "The Ecology of Sustainable Development." In *The Ecologist,* Vol. 20, No. 1 (Jan./Feb. 1990).

Regier, Henry A. et al. "Rehabilitation of Degraded River Ecosystems." In *Proceedings of the International Large River Symposium.*

State of the Fraser Basin: Assessing Progress Towards Sustainability. Vancouver: Fraser Basin Management Board.

Vitousek Peter M. et al. "Human Appropriation of the Products of Photosynthesis." In *Bioscience,* Vol. 34, No. 6 (1986).

Wackernagel, Mathis, and William Rees. *Our Ecological Footprint.*

Weiss, Edith Brown. "In Fairness to Future Generations." *Environment,* Vol. 32, No. 3 (April 1990).

Index